Fundamentals
of
California Litigation
for Paralegals

ASPEN PUBLISHERS

Fundamentals
of
California Litigation
for Paralegals

Third Edition

MARLENE A. MAEROWITZ
Attorney at Law
Phoenix, Arizona

Member, California and Arizona Bars

THOMAS A. MAUET
Professor of Law
University of Arizona

Wolters Kluwer
Law & Business

AUSTIN   BOSTON   CHICAGO   NEW YORK   THE NETHERLANDS

Aspen Publishers
Attn: Permissions Department
76 Ninth Avenue, 7th Floor
New York, NY 10011-5201

To contact Customer Care, e-mail customer.care@aspenpublishers.com, call 1-800-234-1660, fax 1-800-901-9075, or mail correspondence to:

Aspen Publishers
Attn: Order Department
PO Box 990
Frederick, MD 21705

Printed in the United States of America.

1 2 3 4 5 6 7 8 9 0

ISBN 978-0-7355-6388-9

Library of Congress Cataloging-in-Publication Data

Maerowitz, Marlene A.
    Fundamentals of California litigation for paralegals / Marlene A. Maerowitz, Thomas A. Mauet.—3rd ed.
        p. cm.
    Includes bibliographical references and index.
    ISBN 978-0-7355-6388-9
    1. Civil procedure—California.   2. Legal assistants—California—Handbooks, manuals, etc.   I. Mauet, Thomas A.   II. Title. III. Title: California litigation for paralegals.

KFC995.Z9M34 2008
347.73'5—dc22   2007014307

About Wolters Kluwer Law & Business

Wolters Kluwer Law & Business is a leading provider of research information and workflow solutions in key specialty areas. The strengths of the individual brands of Aspen Publishers, CCH, Kluwer Law International and Loislaw are aligned within Wolters Kluwer Law & Business to provide comprehensive, in-depth solutions and expert-authored content for the legal, professional and education markets.

CCH was founded in 1913 and has served more than four generations of business professionals and their clients. The CCH products in the Wolters Kluwer Law & Business group are highly regarded electronic and print resources for legal, securities, antitrust and trade regulation, government contracting, banking, pension, payroll, employment and labor, and healthcare reimbursement and compliance professionals.

Aspen Publishers is a leading information provider for attorneys, business professionals and law students. Written by preeminent authorities, Aspen products offer analytical and practical information in a range of specialty practice areas from securities law and intellectual property to mergers and acquisitions and pension/benefits. Aspen's trusted legal education resources provide professors and students with high-quality, up-to-date and effective resources for successful instruction and study in all areas of the law.

Kluwer Law International supplies the global business community with comprehensive English-language international legal information. Legal practitioners, corporate counsel and business executives around the world rely on the Kluwer Law International journals, loose-leafs, books and electronic products for authoritative information in many areas of international legal practice.

Loislaw is a premier provider of digitized legal content to small law firm practitioners of various specializations. Loislaw provides attorneys with the ability to quickly and efficiently find the necessary legal information they need, when and where they need it, by facilitating access to primary law as well as state-specific law, records, forms and treatises.

Wolters Kluwer Law & Business, a unit of Wolters Kluwer, is headquartered in New York and Riverwoods, Illinois. Wolters Kluwer is a leading multinational publisher and information services company.

To our students

Summary of Contents

Contents

CHAPTER 3   CASE EVALUATION AND STRATEGY   61

CHAPTER 4   PARTIES AND JURISDICTION   87

PART II   PRETRIAL LITIGATION   107

CHAPTER 5   PLEADINGS   109

CHAPTER 6 COMPLAINTS, ANSWERS, AND CROSS-CLAIMS   121

CHAPTER 7   SPECIAL PLEADINGS   **161**

CHAPTER 8   INTRODUCTION TO MOTIONS   175

CHAPTER 9   MOTIONS ATTACKING
THE PLEADINGS   193

CHAPTER 10 SUMMARY JUDGMENTS   **209**

CHAPTER 11 PROVISIONAL REMEDIES   **219**

CHAPTER 12 EVIDENCE   241

CHAPTER 13   INTRODUCTION TO DISCOVERY   265

CHAPTER 14   WRITTEN DISCOVERY   279

CHAPTER 15 DEPOSITIONS 335

PART III   SETTLEMENT, TRIAL, AND POST-TRIAL   357

CHAPTER 16   SETTLEMENTS   359

CHAPTER 17   TRIAL PREPARATION, TRIAL, AND APPEAL   373

CHAPTER 18   ENFORCEMENT OF JUDGMENTS   411

CHAPTER 19   ALTERNATIVE DISPUTE RESOLUTION   425

Preface

Approach

When I first started teaching litigation specialization for paralegal students at the University of West Los Angeles over 23 years ago, I struggled trying to find a textbook that was comprehensive enough to be useful for my students and, at the same time, conducive to learning. The result was always mixed. Either the text was too comprehensive and designed more for the practicing lawyer or it was not comprehensive enough, so that I found myself supplementing large portions of the materials. Finally, I had the good fortune of being teamed with Professor Thomas Mauet to write a litigation textbook designed specifically for paralegal students. Our efforts culminated in *Fundamentals of Litigation for Paralegals*, first published in 1991 and now in its fifth edition. However, while comprehensive, since the text concentrated on federal law and procedure, I still had to supplement the materials for my California students. Finally, in 2001, we were able to complete a text that I wish I had when I started teaching 23 years ago.

Our approach to this litigation textbook has been to include information on all areas of California civil litigation, even though due to time constraints not all areas are covered in a litigation course. The purpose for including this additional information is to allow you to use this book, not only as a text for learning but also as a reference book once you are in practice.

We have found that civil litigation can often be oversimplified, which hinders the learning and understanding process; on the other hand, although civil litigation is very rule oriented and can be complex, easy-to-follow steps can be given to help you learn the rules. Thus, we attempt to strike a balance between giving sufficient detail for you to learn and understand this area of law, while at the same time making the steps as easy as possible to follow. You will find that the text breaks down each civil procedure rule into easy-to-follow steps. Each step explains the process so that you are not just following the rules, but understanding them as well. We believe that as you progress through your litigation course and career, you will come to appreciate even more the detailed approach we have taken.

Organization

This book takes you through each stage of the litigation process from the initial fact-gathering stage through post-judgment proceedings. Because there are alternative ways to resolve disputes through either arbitration or mediation, the book also covers these topics. Each chapter is designed to give you a thorough understanding of the procedural rules governing the litigation process, as well as a system for transferring your knowledge of the procedural rules into the litigation skills necessary to draft litigation documents such as pleadings, discovery requests, and motions.

Always remember that behind every litigation case there are clients who are either suing or being sued and witnesses who have knowledge of the facts and events surrounding the dispute. Thus, important skills for collecting data, interviewing clients, and taking witness statements are discussed and demonstrated throughout the text. Checklists for locating witnesses, including Internet resource sites, are also provided.

Key Features

You will note that many of the legal terms that are central to the discussion in each chapter appear in bold type. Most of these boldfaced terms are defined in the margin of the book where they appear in the text and also in the Glossary at the end of the book. The Glossary also provides definitions of the other legal terms that are used in the text; should you encounter any legal term that is unfamiliar, you can refer to the Glossary for an explanation.

At the beginning of each chapter you will find two sections. The first section is an outline of the chapter. You may use this section to obtain a quick overview of the chapter and also to help you locate a particular area. The next section identifies the chapter's objectives. Keep these objectives in mind as you go through the chapter.

At the end of each chapter you also will find four important sections. The first section is the "Chapter Summary," which highlights the important concepts in each chapter. The summary, of course, should never be used as a substitute for reading the chapter. However, the summary is useful when you wish to review the content of each chapter. The "Key Terms" section acts as a checklist to ensure that you have identified and understood the legal terms that were defined and explained in the chapter. The third section at the end of each chapter is a series of questions. The "Review Questions" may be used as a study guide to further test your understanding of the main concepts discussed in each chapter. Since the Internet plays such a vital role in the litigation process today, a separate section has been added in this new edition. At the end of each chapter you will find an "Internet Resources" section that lists websites that can be used for downloading common forms or obtaining additional information to supplement the information in the chapter.

In addition to the review questions in this book, a workbook on disk is included with the text. The workbook is designed to give you an opportunity to work thoroughly with the rules and concepts discussed in the text and contains additional questions and assignments. Projects requiring computer usage and the Internet are included as optional assignments.

Acknowledgments

No textbook can be written without help and guidance from numerous individuals. A special thank you goes to Elizabeth Kenny who has worked with us for over 17 years since the first edition of *Fundamentals of Litigation for Paralegals*. Elizabeth continued to provide her guidance, suggestions, substantive comments, and support for this edition. Without her constantly keeping on top of us to meet deadlines, I am certain we would never be even close to on time. Candice Adams and Jason Thomas at Newgen–Austin oversaw the editing and proofing stages of the text, catching all those mistakes that we were so sure never existed. We are thankful to the individuals who have adopted this text for their classes and who provided invaluable suggestions that were incorporated into this edition. Finally, we gratefully acknowledge the permission of Aspen Publishers to reprint Exhibits 1.2 and 2.1.

Marlene Pontrelli Maerowitz

May 2007

Fundamentals
of
California Litigation
for Paralegals

PART I

Investigating and Planning the Litigation

CHAPTER **1**

Introduction to Litigation

CHAPTER OBJECTIVES

In this introductory chapter to litigation you will learn:

♦ What the differences are between civil litigation and other types of litigation
♦ Where to find the law applicable to litigation matters
♦ How the California court system is structured
♦ How a case moves through the process
♦ What types of remedies an aggrieved party may seek from the court
♦ What the paralegal's role is in the litigation process
♦ What ethical standards paralegals must follow

A. INTRODUCTION

You have just been called into the office of an attorney in the firm that recently hired you. The attorney tells you that a prospective client will be coming to the office shortly and has a "problem" that might lead to litigation—a problem that appears to be just right for you to assist with and help manage. With a smile the attorney hands you a note containing the prospective client's name and appointment time, and asks you to prepare for the client meeting. Apprehensively you walk out of the attorney's office, thinking: "What do I do now?"

What you do, when you do it, how you do it, and why you do it is what this book on litigation is all about. This first chapter provides an overview of the litigation process and your role in that process. Each step in the process will be discussed in detail in the following chapters.

B. THE LITIGATION PROCESS

Litigation
Resolution of disputes through the court system

Civil litigation
Resolution of disputes between private parties through the court system

Litigation is the resolution of disputes through the court system. This book is about the civil litigation process, as compared to criminal or administrative litigation. **Civil litigation** is the resolution of disputes between private parties through the court system.[1] Criminal litigation is not between private parties; rather, in criminal litigation the government prosecutes an action against individuals who have committed crimes against society. If the crime also results in damages to the victim's person or property, the victim may bring a civil action to obtain recovery for the damages. This civil action is separate from the criminal action.

1. An alternative to the use of courts, arbitration is becoming a popular method by which civil disputes are resolved. See Chapter 14.

Administrative litigation is the process by which administrative agencies resolve disputes that concern their administrative rules and regulations. For example, if an employee is injured on the job and a worker's compensation claim is filed, the worker's compensation agency will determine the claim and hear any appeal or dispute the employee has regarding the determination of the claim. In general, if an administrative remedy exists, the claimant must first exhaust the administrative remedies before proceeding with a court action.

Civil litigation permits parties to settle their disputes in an orderly and nonviolent manner. The entire litigation process is governed by formal rules that specify the procedures the parties must follow from commencement of the litigation until the litigation terminates. Accordingly, once a dispute is submitted to the courts for resolution, all parties to the litigation must carefully follow the court's procedural rules.

Each state has its own rules of procedure. A party filing an action in a state court must follow the procedural rules of that particular state court. Actions filed in federal court are governed by the Federal Rules of Civil Procedure. Always consult the appropriate rules of procedure before handling any litigation matter.

The rules discussed in this book are for the California state courts. However, in many respects, the Federal Rules of Civil Procedure are similar. Accordingly, once you have mastered the procedural requirements for California, you will be able to easily understand and apply the Federal rules if you have a litigation matter in federal court.

1. Sources of law

Where do you find the law applicable to the matter you are handling? There are three sources of law that you will need to consult for every litigation matter: statutes, court cases, and constitutions.

a. Statutes

Statutes are laws enacted by state or federal legislatures that govern substantive and legal rights and principles, as well as procedural rules. In some instances statutes are referred to as codes. For example, all laws enacted by Congress are found in the United States Code. The United States Code is divided into various Titles, which deal with specific subject matters such as agriculture, banking, copyrights, education, and so on.

In California there are a number of statutes and rules that govern the litigation process. The primary statutes and rules you will consult are the Code of Civil Procedure (the "CCP"), the Civil Code (the "CC"), and the

California Rules of Court. In addition, courts also have **local rules** that need to be followed. Local rules apply to each court within a particular county. For example, the superior courts within Los Angeles County will be governed by the Rules of Court for the Los Angeles Superior Court. The local rules govern everything from the type of paper on which a complaint might be filed to the dates on which motions may be heard. Judges often have rules for their individual court as well. Before the trial of any case it is important to check with each individual judge to determine whether the judge has special rules that need to be followed.

In addition to state and local statutes and rules that govern a litigation matter, individual municipalities, such as your town or city, may also enact their own laws, which apply only in their municipality. The municipal laws are often referred to as ordinances. These ordinances typically govern matters such as rent control, parking, and items of local interest. A municipality may not enact ordinances that conflict in any way with the law of the federal or state governments.

All of these statutes, codes, and ordinances help to determine the legal rights of parties and help to regulate the litigation process. Accordingly, they are all sources that must be referred to when handling any litigation matter.

b. Court cases

Court cases are decisions of the courts interpreting the law. Once a decision has been made, the court will generally write an opinion. Certain opinions that address a unique or important legal issue are published in bound volumes and are used by other litigants to determine how the law may be interpreted with respect to their particular dispute. Throughout the course of our nation's history, thousands of opinions have been published and relied on as precedents to decide new controversies as they arise.

Common law
Body of law
developed in England
from custom and
usage

Even prior to the published opinions of our courts, the early American colonists brought with them a body of law from England referred to as the **common law.** Common law developed in England from usage and custom, and was affirmed by the English judges and courts. Common law, to the extent it is not inconsistent with the constitutions or laws of the United States or of the individual states, is generally still applicable in the United States.

c. Constitutions

The federal **Constitution** is the highest law of the land. In addition to the United States Constitution, each of the 50 states has its own constitution. No rule of law enacted by a state may violate the state's constitution.

Moreover, no state constitution or state or federal law may violate the federal Constitution.

2. The court system

Litigation begins when the aggrieved party files a complaint in the appropriate court. The aggrieved party is called the **plaintiff.** The party whom the complaint is filed against is called the **defendant.** In the **complaint** the plaintiff must state the basis of the claim against the defendant so that the defendant will be apprised of the action giving rise to the claim. As discussed in section 4, the plaintiff must also request specific relief from the court. The complaint is served upon the defendant along with a **summons** commanding the defendant to appear before the court.

The complaint is always filed in the **trial court.** Under the California court system, the superior court is the trial court. The superior court hears unlimited general matters and also limited civil cases. Limited civil cases means that the court only has the power to hear and decide limited types of cases. When acting as a limited civil court, the court can only hear cases that are for a money judgment in the amount of $25,000 or less. Accordingly, the superior court of limited jurisdiction cannot hear cases involving divorce, title to real property, or probate. The type of limited cases are listed in CCP §86. A limited civil case may be brought in the **small claims division.** The small claims division hears matters involving less than $5,000 in dispute. The small claims division is often called the "people's court" because attorneys may not represent individual parties in a small claims matter. An unlimited jurisdiction case is everything else that is not limited; that is, all types of cases and matters seeking judgments greater than $25,000.

The federal court system also has trial courts. In the federal system this trial court is called the **United States District Court.** There are 90 district courts in the United States. Each state has at least one district court, and several states have two or more, depending on the state's population.

If a party loses in the trial court, that party has an automatic right to appeal to the next highest court. In California, the party appeals municipal court decisions to the appellate division of the Superior Court. Appeals from Superior Courts go to the **Courts of Appeal** for the appropriate district in which the lower court sits.

On appeal, the appellate court is limited to a review of the record of the court below. The court will not hear from any witnesses or take new evidence. The party appealing the decision of the trial court must demonstrate that there was an error in the court below that affected the outcome of the case. The appellate court will determine whether the law was incorrectly applied on the facts, or if the decision reached is not supported by the facts. Even though new evidence may not be

Complaint
Document filed by an aggrieved party to commence litigation

Summons
Notice accompanying the complaint that commands the defendant to appear and defend against the action within a certain period of time

presented to the court, all parties to the appeal will have an opportunity to submit a written brief on the issues before the appellate court. After the parties submit briefs, the court will hear oral argument. Oral argument is an opportunity for the lawyers to answer any questions the appellate judges may have and to more fully explain their clients' positions.

After oral argument, the court will render one of four decisions. The court will either **affirm, affirm with modification, reverse**, or **reverse and remand.** A decision is affirmed if the court rules the same way as the trial court. Sometimes the court will rule the same way, but modify some element of the decision below. For example, assume that a trial court rules in an action for unlawful detainer that the plaintiff is entitled to possession of property and back rent in the amount of $1,200. If the appellate court agrees that the plaintiff should be entitled to possession of the property, but believes the back rent owed is only $998, the appellate court will affirm the trial court's decision and modify the amount of back rent.

If the court disagrees with the trial court, the appellate court will reverse the decision. Sometimes, however, the appellate court is not certain, based on the record before it, whether it disagrees with the trial court. In this situation the court gives an opinion stating how it would rule assuming that certain facts are true. The appellate court will then reverse the decision and send it back (remand) to the trial court for a decision in accordance with the opinion expressed by the appellate court.

If a party loses in the appellate court, the losing party may petition the **Supreme Court** for review. The Supreme Court is the highest court in the California court system. If a case before the California Supreme Court involves a question of federal or constitutional law, the losing party may be able to petition the United States Supreme Court for review.

Appeal to the California Supreme Court is not automatic, but rather is discretionary with the Court. The losing party must petition the California Supreme Court to review the matter. If review is granted, the Court will affirm, affirm with modification, reverse, or reverse and remand the decision of the appellate court. If review is denied, the decision of the appellate court will become final.

An organizational chart for the California state court system is shown in Exhibit 1.1. The federal court system is shown in Exhibit 1.2. You will note that special courts such as bankruptcy courts and the Court of International Trade exist to hear specific cases in the federal court system.

3. Overview for litigation cases

Litigation consists of four basic stages: (1) information gathering, (2) pleading, (3) discovery and motions, and (4) trial and post-trial proceedings. Each of these stages is discussed in detail in subsequent

Exhibit 1.1. California State Court System

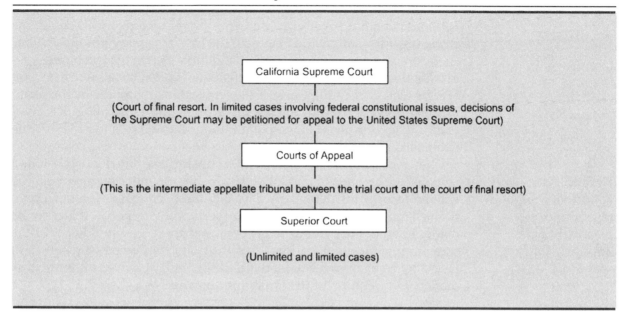

Exhibit 1.2. The Federal Court System

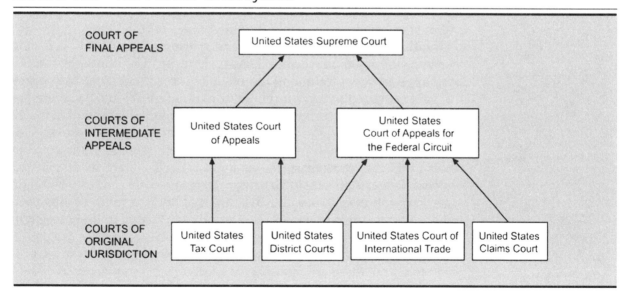

chapters. However, this section gives you a brief overview of the four stages and a sample path for a typical litigation case.

Prior to the filing of any lawsuit, you and the attorney will spend time gathering information and obtaining the facts necessary to support your client's case. This is the first stage of litigation. This stage will be engaged in by both sides since a potential defendant is often aware that a lawsuit may be filed against him. After sufficient facts are gathered by the plaintiff to support a lawsuit, the lawsuit will begin by the filing of a complaint. The complaint, along with the summons, is served on the defendant.

Default
Failure of a party to respond to the pleading of the opposing party

Upon receipt of the summons and complaint, the defendant must file a response, or else the defendant will be in **default** and a judgment may be entered against the defendant. This is the second stage. The defendant has several choices with respect to the type of response that may be made. First, if the defendant believes that there is some defect in the complaint, either a procedural rule that is not followed or insufficient facts alleged against the defendant, the defendant may file a **motion.** A motion is a request to the court for an order or ruling. The types of motions that may be filed by the defendant are discussed in Chapter 5. If the defendant does not file a motion or if the motion is denied by the court, the defendant will answer the complaint. The **answer** is the defendant's response to the specific allegations in the complaint and states any defenses the defendant may have. Once an answer is filed, the **pleading** stage—that is, formal written documents by the parties to either start litigation or respond to litigation—is complete.

The third stage is the **discovery and motion stage.** At this point the parties will conduct formal factual investigation through written responses and oral testimony received from the other side. The parties may also obtain discovery formally from other individuals who are not parties but who may be witnesses or in possession of information that is helpful to the case. During this stage there may also be a number of **pretrial motions.** These motions may include a request to the court to enter judgment without a trial if none of the facts are in dispute, or involve requests to obtain discovery from the other side if one side does not voluntarily provide the information. The bulk of litigation time is spent at this stage, and it is usually at this stage that cases will settle.

The final stage is the **trial and post-trial proceedings.** Both during trial and after trial, there are a number of different motions that either side can make. These motions include requests for judgments if one side has failed to prove its case, or requests to the court to enter a different judgment if the jury's verdict is not consistent with the evidence produced at trial. As discussed earlier, at this stage the losing party also has an automatic right to appeal the decision. An appellate court could reverse the judgment and require a new trial, which would start this stage over

Exhibit 1.3. Litigation Case Moves through the System

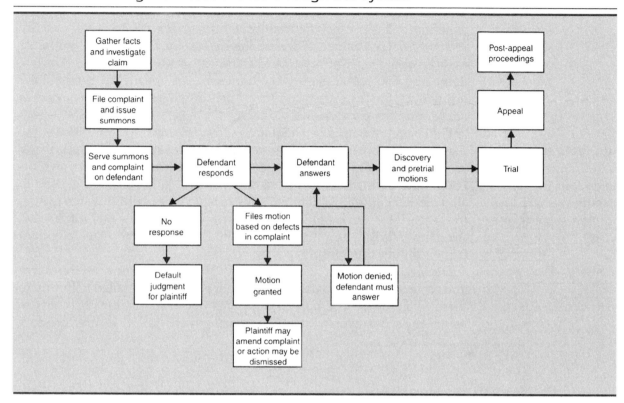

again. This explains why some cases go on for several years winding their way through the trial court, appellate courts, and back to the trial court again.

The chart in Exhibit 1.3 gives an example of how a litigation case may move through the several stages.

4. Remedies

When a party brings a civil action, the party must request some relief or remedy from the court. Remedies may be divided into two categories: legal and equitable.

The most common **legal remedy** is money **damages.** For example, if a party suffers a personal injury or is the victim of a breach of contract, the party will request to be compensated by payment from the defendant. Money damages are further divided into two main categories: compensatory and punitive.

Compensatory damages are all those damages that "compensate" the injured party, including damages that directly flow from the injury or

Damages
Monetary compensation requested by plaintiff from defendant

breach. Compensatory damages may be either general (i.e., compensation for pain and suffering) or specific (i.e., payment for medical expenses or loss of income from time missed at work).

In some types of action where the defendant's conduct is willful or malicious, the plaintiff may be entitled to **punitive damages.** Punitive damages, also called exemplary damages, are meant to "punish" the wrongdoer for his or her conduct. Such damages may be awarded in addition to the compensatory damages.

If the legal remedy is inadequate to compensate the plaintiff fully, the plaintiff may be able to obtain an **equitable remedy.** There are many kinds of equitable remedies. The two most commonly used in civil litigation are injunctions and declaratory relief. An **injunction** is used to stop certain conduct or actions. For example, if a plaintiff wants to stop the defendant from building a house that will impair the plaintiff's view, the plaintiff will seek an injunction from the court to stop the defendant from building the house.

Declaratory relief is used when a controversy arises over the rights and obligations of the parties and neither party has yet failed to live up to these obligations. The parties request a declaration from the court to settle the controversy so they may govern their future conduct accordingly.

Equitable remedy
Relief requested from defendant that is usually designed to prevent some future harm

C. THE PARALEGAL'S ROLE

Paralegals play a vital role in the efficient handling of litigation. Law firms are finding that paralegals can, and do, handle many tasks that were previously performed by attorneys. Use of paralegals not only frees the attorney to engage in other matters, but also helps reduce litigation expenses for the client.

As a paralegal you will find that, aside from appearing in court, representing witnesses at deposition, and giving legal advice, there is virtually nothing a lawyer can do that, as a litigation paralegal, you cannot do under the supervision of an attorney. Thus, you have the opportunity to play a significant role in analyzing, planning, and executing the lawsuit.

The following is just a sampling of the numerous tasks you may be called on to undertake in litigation:

1. Preparing for litigation
   - Interview the client
   - Gather background facts
   - Locate witnesses
   - Interview witnesses
   - Obtain medical records, tax records, educational records, etc.

   ◆ Research claims the client may have against other parties
   ◆ Draft demand letters
   ◆ Obtain and analyze documents from client

2. Conducting the litigation
   ◆ Draft pleadings
   ◆ Prepare summons
   ◆ Prepare pretrial motions
   ◆ Prepare discovery to propound upon the opposing parties
   ◆ Prepare responses to discovery propounded by the opposing parties
   ◆ Review and organize documents produced by opposing parties
   ◆ Arrange for the taking of depositions
   ◆ Prepare witnesses for deposition
   ◆ Prepare deposition summaries
   ◆ Take notes on testimony given at depositions
   ◆ Calendar due dates for filing briefs, motions, pretrial orders, etc.
   ◆ Prepare discovery plan

3. Trial preparation
   ◆ Prepare trial notebooks
   ◆ Organize exhibits
   ◆ Prepare witness files
   ◆ Prepare demonstrative exhibits
   ◆ Draft jury instructions
   ◆ Subpoena witnesses
   ◆ Draft trial brief
   ◆ Coordinate scheduling of trial witnesses
   ◆ Take notes at trial
   ◆ Assist attorney with exhibits at trial

4. Post-trial work
   ◆ Assist with any post-trial motions
   ◆ Prepare record for appeal
   ◆ Enforce judgment

5. Settlement
   ◆ Prepare settlement agreement
   ◆ Prepare releases
   ◆ Assist in closing file and obtaining necessary dismissals

Do not be alarmed by the breadth and complexity of these tasks. The purpose of this book and your litigation course is to familiarize and train you in each task so you perform your job competently and confidently.

D. ETHICAL CONSIDERATIONS

Ethical considerations underlie every aspect of the practice of law. Accordingly, while summarized here, throughout this text ethical considerations are identified and discussed.

The conduct of lawyers is governed by the rules of professional conduct enacted in their particular states. In 2000, the California state legislature enacted rules governing the regulation of the paralegal profession which became effective on January 1, 2004.[2] Under the rules, a "paralegal" means a person who is qualified "by education, training or work experience" who contracts with or is employed by an attorney, law firm, corporation, governmental agency or other entity, who performs substantial, specifically delegated legal work under the direction and supervision of an active member of the State Bar of California or an attorney practicing law in the California federal courts. Accordingly, a paralegal must work under supervision and not independently. In addition, unless you have met educational prerequisites, you may not call yourself a "paralegal." Also, under the rules, a paralegal may not provide legal advice or represent a client in court. However, a paralegal may represent clients before state or federal administrative agencies if permitted by statute, court rule, or administrative rule or regulation.

In addition to general continuing education requirements, one of the requirements of a paralegal is to certify completion every three years of a minimum of four hours of legal ethics mandatory continuing education. To fully understand the ethical role of a paralegal, it is first important to understand the nature of the attorney-client relationship.

The relationship between an attorney and client is one of trust. The client seeks the advice of an attorney to help counsel him with a potential legal problem. The situation is similar to advice you might seek from a doctor, counselor, or clergyperson. It is easy to understand in the context of these other professions. The trust that is necessary to establish a good early relationship then allows you to seek the consult of the professional. The same is true of an attorney. As an important part of the legal team, your trust is the same.

While it has always been important that paralegals keep client information confidential, the new rules specifically provide that a paralegal has a duty to maintain the confidentiality of client information. The

---

2. The rules are found in Business and Professions Code §6450 et seq.

communication between an attorney and client is **privileged.** This means that the attorney cannot reveal any information received by the client to anyone else. Thus, the privileged nature of a client's communications extends to paralegals as well. Accordingly, any information you receive in the course of your employment from the client or in connection with the client or the client's business must be kept confidential and not be disclosed to third parties. In addition, given the private nature of attorney-client communications, you must also be careful to avoid discussing a client's case in public places where eavesdroppers may be present.

Other ethical considerations paralegals should keep in mind are **conflicts of interest**, and communicating with adverse parties. A lawyer may never represent two or more parties who have adverse interests. Accordingly, as a paralegal charged with fact gathering, you should be cognizant of situations in which a conflict may arise. For example, your office may be representing two defendants who, at least initially, appear to have no conflict in their interests. Should a conflict develop, however, the lawyer has an ethical obligation to withdraw from representing one or both of the clients. Accordingly, immediately notify the attorney if you discover any facts in your investigation of a case indicating that a conflict may exist between two or more of your clients.

In addition, paralegals must avoid communicating directly with an adverse party who is represented by counsel. A party represented by counsel is entitled to be free of any direct contact with the opposing party's counsel or that counsel's employees. Even if the adverse party contacts you directly, you must refuse to speak with the client without the presence of the party's attorney. In essence, a party who is represented by counsel may not represent himself until he formally relieves that counsel from representation.

Finally, you are not authorized to practice law and therefore must never give anyone the impression that you are a lawyer. When speaking with a client, opposing counsel, or other parties, always identify yourself as a paralegal. Similarly, when writing any letter on behalf of the law firm, place a notation of "Legal Assistant" or "Paralegal" directly below your signature to avoid any misunderstandings as to your position with the law firm.[3]

These ethical considerations are by no means exclusive. You, of course, must be guided by a sense of moral integrity. If something doesn't seem right to you, it probably isn't. If you are unsure if something is ethically correct, check with the lawyer in charge or contact your local paralegal association for information.

Privileged
Rules providing that certain communications are inadmissible because the communications are deemed confidential

Conflict of interest
When two or more parties with adverse interests are represented by the same counsel

---

3. Pursuant to Business and Professions Code §6454, the terms "Legal Assistant" and "Paralegal" are synonymous.

CHAPTER SUMMARY

Civil litigation involves the resolution of disputes through the court system and starts with the plaintiff filing a complaint against the defendant in the trial court. In the complaint, the plaintiff will request either monetary or equitable relief (or both) from the court. The losing party in the trial court has an automatic right to appeal the decision to the next highest court.

As a paralegal, you will take on significant responsibility during all aspects of the litigation process from the initial fact gathering through trial preparation and post-trial proceedings. Throughout this entire process it is essential that your conduct conform to the following ethical guidelines discussed in this chapter:

- Keep all client communications confidential
- Avoid all conflicts of interest
- Do not communicate directly with an adverse party who is represented by counsel
- Always identify yourself as a paralegal

KEY TERMS

Affirm	Legal remedy
Affirm with modification	Litigation
Answer	Local rule
Civil litigation	Motion
Common law	Plaintiff
Compensatory damages	Pleading
Complaint	Pretrial motions
Conflict of interest	Privileged
Constitution	Punitive damages
Court cases	Reverse
Courts of Appeal	Reverse and remand
Damages	Statutes
Declaratory relief	Summons
Default	Trial and post-trial proceedings
Defendant	Trial court
Discovery and motion stage	United States District Court
Equitable remedy	United States Supreme Court
Injunction	

REVIEW QUESTIONS

1. What is civil litigation and how does it differ from other types of litigation?

2. How is the California court system structured?

3. What are the differences between equitable and legal remedies? Identify two types of equitable remedies.

4. Where do you find the sources of law applicable to litigation matters? Explain the differences between the various sources of law.

5. Once a litigation matter is appealed, what are the four types of decisions that an appellate court may make? Explain each type.

6. What are the four stages of the litigation process?

7. What is the role of a paralegal in the litigation process?

8. What ethical rules must be followed by paralegals? What are the goals of the ethical rules?

INTERNET RESOURCES

For additional information concerning the matters contained in this chapter, and for information helpful to you in your role as a paralegal, please see the following websites:

www.aapipara.org (American Alliance of Paralegals, Inc.)

www.caparalegal.org (California Alliance of Paralegal Associations)

www.lapa.org (Los Angeles Paralegal Association)

www.legalassistanttoday.com (*Legal Assistant Today*)

www.nala.org (National Association of Legal Assistants)

www.nals.org (NALS . . . The Association for Legal Professionals)

www.ocparalegal.org (Orange County Paralegal Association)

www.paralegalmanagement.org (International Paralegal Management Association)

www.paralegals.org (National Federation of Paralegal Associations)

www.sccparalegal.org (Santa Clara County Paralegal Association)

www.svpa.org (Sacramento Valley Paralegal Association)

www.sdparalegals.org (San Diego Paralegal Association)

www.sfpa.com (San Francisco Paralegal Association)

Informal Fact Gathering and Investigation

CHAPTER OBJECTIVES

This chapter introduces you to several important aspects of the preliminary gathering and investigation of facts to support your client's position. You will learn:

♦ How to structure a factual investigation
♦ Where to obtain the necessary facts to prove your client's position
♦ How to interview clients
♦ When and how to gather documents that may be used as evidence
♦ Where to locate witnesses
♦ How to use the Internet to gather facts

A. INTRODUCTION

Successful litigation starts with the proper gathering of information. Litigation outcomes are usually decided not by legal interpretations but according to which party's version of disputed events the **factfinder**—that is, the judge or the jury—accepts as true. Hence, much time is spent identifying and acquiring evidence that supports your party's contentions and that refutes the other side's contentions. The party who is more successful in doing this will have a better chance of convincing the factfinder that its version of the facts is what "really happened."

Your role as a paralegal is to assist the lawyer in identifying and gathering the evidence. Many times the paralegal is responsible for this initial fact gathering, a responsibility that is critical to the lawyer's determination of whether to proceed with the case and how to properly advise the client. If the lawyer decides to proceed, these initial facts are necessary to draft the complaint and make the required factual allegations.

This chapter provides a step-by-step approach for you to use when you are asked to gather the initial facts of a case. Each step will assist you in developing a complete and accurate account of the facts.

B. STRUCTURING FACT INVESTIGATIONS

Facts are the collective pieces of information explaining your client's version of what happened. For example, facts may consist of what people said, did, or heard regarding the particular incident. There are two ways of "getting the facts." You can obtain facts informally before filing suit and you can get them through formal discovery (as discussed in Chapter 13) after suit is filed. A common mistake inexperienced paralegals make is using the investigation, such as an initial client interview and the reviewing of an accident report, just to provide the lawyer with enough facts to decide whether to take the case, and using formal discovery methods as the principal fact-gathering method. This is a serious mistake. Consider the following advantages of informal discovery:

♦ First, information is power, and the party that has a better grasp of the favorable and unfavorable facts is in a stronger position to accurately evaluate the case.

♦ Second, information obtained early on, particularly from witnesses, is more likely to be accurate and complete.

♦ Third, information sought before the action is formalized is more likely to be obtained, since a lawsuit often makes people cautious or uncooperative.

♦ Fourth, information obtained before suit has been filed is less expensive to acquire. Formal discovery is the most expensive way to get information.

♦ Fifth, CCP §128.7(b) provides that by presenting to the court any pleading or similar paper, the attorney is certifying that, after "inquiry reasonable under the circumstances," the document is not being presented for an improper or frivolous purpose.

♦ Finally, you can get information informally without the opposing parties participating, or even being aware that you are conducting an investigation.

For all these reasons, then, you should use informal discovery as much as possible.

If your firm represents the defendant, you may also be involved in informal fact gathering and investigation before a complaint is filed. Many times the defendant is aware of a potential lawsuit as a result of oral or written communication received from the plaintiff or because of direct involvement in an accident or other incident. In these situations, it is likely the potential defendant will consult with an attorney prior to receiving the summons and complaint. Your fact gathering and investigation will be similar regardless of which party your firm represents.

1. What facts do I need to get?

Your job as a litigation paralegal is to obtain enough admissible evidence to prove your client's claims and to disprove the other side's claims. If you are representing the plaintiff, enough facts must be gathered to state in the complaint a **cause of action**, sometimes called a claim for relief. A cause of action is a theory of recovery that entitles the plaintiff to recover against the defendant. If you represent the defendant, you

Cause of action
Theory of recovery that entitles the plaintiff to recover against the defendant

will want to gather facts to support an affirmative defense. An **affirmative defense** is a defense pled by the defendant in the answer that, if proven, denies recovery to the plaintiff.

Identify in advance, with the assistance of the lawyer in charge, what you must prove or disprove. This is determined by the substantive law underlying the claims, relief, and defenses in the case. However, how do you research that law if you do not yet know what the pleadings will allege? What do you research first, the facts or the law?

There is no easy answer here. In litigation, the facts and law are intertwined. The investigation of one affects the investigation of the other. You will usually go back and forth periodically as the theory of the case develops.

Example

You have been asked to assist with what appears to be a routine personal injury case, involving an automobile accident between your client, George Andrews, and another driver, Mildred Jones. You conduct the initial interview with George, who appears to have a simple negligence case against the other driver—Ms. Jones clearly ran a stop sign. You do preliminary research on the negligence claim to see if the damages are sufficient to recommend litigation to the lawyer. You then continue your fact investigation and discover that Ms. Jones is uninsured. Since George may not be able to collect damages from an uninsured driver, you start wondering if there may be a claim against the municipality for not maintaining intersection markings and safe road conditions. Of course, you need to research the law here. If there is a legal theory supporting such a claim, you then need to go back and see if there are facts that support that theory. Back and forth you go between getting the facts and researching the law until you have identified those legal theories that have factual support.

2. How do I structure my fact investigation?

a. Use of a litigation chart

The easiest way to structure your investigation is to use a system of organizing the law and facts based on what the attorney will need to prove if the case goes to trial. In short, this is a good time to start a "litigation chart."[1] A litigation chart is simply a diagram that sets out what needs to be proven or disproven in a case and how to do it.

---

1. The litigation chart will become a "trial chart" if the case is ultimately tried.

The chart is not a formal court document but an aid to you and your attorney. The chart is a graphic way of identifying four major components of the litigation plan:

1. Elements of claims
2. Sources of proof
3. Informal fact investigation
4. Formal discovery

The litigation chart has two principal benefits. First, it helps you identify what needs to be proven or disproven so that you can focus your fact investigation on getting admissible evidence for each required element. Second, a litigation chart helps you pinpoint the strengths and weaknesses of your side's case as well as your opponent's. In most trials the side that wins is the one that convinces the factfinder to resolve disputed issues in its favor. The litigation chart will help identify those disputed matters for which additional admissible evidence must be developed to strengthen the client's version and to rebut the other party's version.

Jury instructions
Instructions that itemize the elements for various claims, relief, and defenses

b. How to structure a litigation chart

Start with the "elements" of each potential claim, relief, and defense in the case. In California, the Judicial Council of California posts on the World Wide Web pattern **jury instructions** for commonly tried claims, such as negligence, product liability, and contract claims, as well as common elements necessary to prove certain defenses. The instructions will list what elements must be proven for each claim, relief, or defense. You will find the elements necessary for each claim at www.courtinfo.ca.gov/reference/documents. After you find the applicable law and determine the specific elements, place these elements on your litigation chart. When you have done this, you will have completed the first step on your litigation chart.

Two of the more common causes of action that you will encounter are **negligence** and **breach of contract.** Certain elements are applicable to each of these causes of action. For example, to state a cause of action for negligence, the plaintiff must allege *each* of the following elements:

◆ A duty of care owed by one party to another
◆ A breach of that duty of care
◆ Causation (defendant's actions were the actual and proximate (probable) cause of plaintiff's injuries)
◆ Damages

Negligence
A cause of action in which the plaintiff must allege a duty of care by one party to another was breached and that was the cause of plaintiff's damages

Breach of contract
A cause of action in which the plaintiff alleges a contract breached by the defendant caused damages to the plaintiff. Also, the plaintiff must allege that he performed under the contract and therefore is excused from further performing

Once the plaintiff has proven each of these elements, the plaintiff will be entitled to relief against the defendant, unless the defendant can prove an affirmative defense.

To state a cause of action for breach of contract, the plaintiff must similarly allege a number of elements. These elements are:

- An executed contract
- Plaintiff's performance, or excuse for nonperformance
- Defendant's breach
- Plaintiff's damages

Again, only if all these elements are proven does the plaintiff have a cause of action against the defendant. The example that follows illustrates how each of these elements is placed on a litigation chart.

Example

You are assisting in the representation of Mary Garcia in a potential contract case. Mary had a contract with Wholesale Sporting Goods (WSG) to provide baseballs for the regional baseball league. She says she obtained baseballs from WSG and paid for them, but the balls were defective, missing stitching on one side. From the initial client interview, and from reviewing the documents and records Mary provided, the lawyer decides to bring a contract claim against WSG.

You set up the following chart to help keep track of the claims:

LITIGATION CHART
FOR MARY GARCIA'S CONTRACT CLAIM

Elements of Claims	Sources of Proof	Informal Fact Investigation	Formal Discovery
1. Contract			
(a) Contract executed			
(b) Mary Garcia's performance			
(c) Wholesale Sporting Goods' breach			
(d) Mary Garcia's damages			

This approach should be used for every other possible claim. For example, since the contract is for the sale of goods, a claim based on a breach of a warranty may be appropriate. If so, you should put the elements of this claim on your litigation chart. The defendant can use a similar litigation chart to place the elements that must be proven for each affirmative defense as well as the elements that the plaintiff must prove for each claim.

3. What are the likely sources of proof?

Facts come from five basic sources:

- The client
- Exhibits
- Witnesses
- Experts
- The opposing party

Of these categories, most can often be reached by informal investigations. The client, of course, must be interviewed. Whenever possible, obtain exhibits in the client's possession and other evidence such as physical objects, photographs, documents, and records in the possession of third parties. Witnesses can frequently be interviewed. You also may be asked to work with consulting experts who are hired to help analyze and prepare the case.

On the other hand, formal discovery, as discussed in Chapters 13 through 16, may sometimes be the only way to get essential information. For example, important witnesses may be uncooperative and need to be deposed. Exhibits in the possession of uncooperative third parties may need to be subpoenaed. Information from the opposing party can usually be obtained only through interrogatories, depositions, and other discovery methods. However, it is always worthwhile to try the informal approach first since it is quicker, less expensive, and may be more accurate and complete. The only exception concerns other parties: Ethics rules forbid lawyers to make direct contact with an opposing party who they know is represented by counsel. As previously discussed, paralegals are bound by the same ethical obligations. Accordingly, if a party is represented by a lawyer, you must deal with the other party's lawyer.

Regardless of the type of case, you must first identify the likely sources of proof, and then decide how that proof can be obtained. The second step on your developing litigation chart is to list the likely sources of proof and correlate them to the required elements of the claims.

Example

In Mary Garcia's case, determine the witnesses and exhibits that will provide the facts about the case. Mary is an obvious witness, and the contract for the sale of the baseballs is a central exhibit. Other than these obvious sources, where else can you go for proof? For example, what proof is there that Mary performed her obligations under the contract? Here again, Mary herself is a source of proof. In addition, Mary may have business records showing her performance. Wholesale Sporting Goods (WSG) may have written letters acknowledging Mary's performance. WSG may also have business records proving performance. There also may be nonparty witnesses, such as the secretary of the regional league, who have knowledge of Mary's performance. Because Mary needed to have the baseballs before opening day, she bought replacement balls from Balls R Us. Their records could help prove damages.

Put these sources on your developing litigation chart:

LITIGATION CHART
FOR MARY GARCIA'S CONTRACT CLAIM

Elements of Claims	Sources of Proof	Informal Fact Investigation	Formal Discovery
1. Contract			
(a) Contract executed	◆ Mary Garcia ◆ WSG ◆ Contract for sale of baseballs ◆ League secretary		
(b) Mary Garcia's performance	◆ Mary Garcia ◆ Garcia's records ◆ WSG's records		
(c) Wholesale Sporting Goods' breach	◆ Mary Garcia ◆ Garcia's correspondence ◆ WSG's correspondence ◆ Garcia's records ◆ WSG's records ◆ Experts to testify that lack of stitching constitutes a defective baseball		

LITIGATION CHART
FOR MARY GARCIA'S CONTRACT CLAIM (continued)

Elements of Claims	Sources of Proof	Informal Fact Investigation	Formal Discovery
(d) Mary Garcia's damages	◆ Mary Garcia ◆ Garcia's records ◆ Balls R Us ◆ Balls R Us' records ◆ Experts on measure of damages for defective baseballs		

The third step is to determine whether these sources of proof can be reached by informal fact investigation and, if so, what method is best suited to getting the necessary information. Witnesses can be interviewed; exhibits in the client's possession should be obtained and reviewed; exhibits possessed by third parties can frequently be obtained from friendly or neutral third parties simply by requesting them; experts can be interviewed, and you can sometimes obtain their reports. Once again, think expansively here, since obtaining information informally is quicker, less expensive, frequently more candid and accurate, and can be obtained without the opposing party participating or perhaps even being aware that you are investigating the case. Put the methods for obtaining the information on the litigation chart.

The last step is to decide what to use formal discovery methods for, and how and when to use them. These considerations are discussed in Chapters 3 and 13-15.

4. How much time should I spend?

The client's financial resources are an important consideration. The "value" of the case, the amount the client can reasonably expect in a jury verdict, is another. The amount of work the case requires for adequate preparation is a third consideration. Consequently, before spending numerous hours gathering facts and engaging in investigation, consult with the lawyer responsible for the matter to determine how much time you can devote to the case and whether the case can be adequately handled within that time.

5. What sources should I investigate?

There are four basic sources for informal investigations:

- The client
- Exhibits
- Witnesses
- Experts

Your litigation chart will provide the direction for your informal fact investigation. That investigation should focus on obtaining basic facts—favorable and unfavorable—about the case and identifying credible, admissible evidence for each claim you are considering.

Your fact investigation needs to be thorough enough to fill out your litigation chart, to the extent that you can do so through informal fact investigation. First, the client must be interviewed to learn everything she knows about the case. You will also need to interview her periodically as you gather additional information from other sources.

Second, you should try to obtain all key documents, records, and other exhibits. In a personal injury case, this includes the police accident reports, hospital and doctor's records, insurance claims records, and employment history. These can often be obtained informally either by the client signing a release so you can obtain the documents or by the client directly requesting the documents. In a contract case, the key documents include the contract, correspondence, invoices, shipping records, and related business records. Where physical evidence is important, it should be safeguarded or photographed before such evidence is altered or possibly lost.

Third, witnesses usually need to be identified, located, and interviewed, although what you do will depend on the particular case. In most cases, what witnesses say is critical. For example, in a personal injury case, where the plaintiff and defendant are likely to have contradictory versions of how the accident happened, the testimony of neutral witnesses will frequently control the liability issue. You need to identify, locate, and interview them whenever possible.

Finally, in some cases it may be necessary to consult appropriate experts early in the investigation. For example, in medical malpractice and products liability cases, plaintiff lawyers usually have the case reviewed by a physician and a technical expert before filing suit.

C. CLIENT INTERVIEWS

Client interviewing has two components: what information to get and how to get it. What to get will be determined by your litigation chart.

How to get it is based on interviewing techniques that must be fully understood in order to get vital information from the client.

As a paralegal your role is simply to obtain the facts. Remember your ethical obligations. You are not licensed to give legal advice and you cannot represent yourself as a lawyer. Some clients may never have consulted with a lawyer and may not realize that, as a paralegal, you cannot give them advice about the case or answer questions regarding the merits of their claim or defense. Accordingly, when you first speak with the client, identify yourself as a paralegal. Explain that you are gathering the facts for review by the lawyer who will ultimately make all decisions with respect to the case. By making such statements in the beginning, you avoid any undue embarrassment for you and the client.

1. Client attitudes and disclosure

A client comes to the law office to determine if there are legal issues related to his problems and, if so, how best to deal with them. The client is interviewed so legal issues can be identified and all relevant information can be obtained and analyzed. How do you get that information from the client?

There are several factors that can inhibit a client from full disclosure of information. First, a client being interviewed often feels that he is being judged. This causes the client to withhold or distort facts that may create negative impressions about himself or his case. Second, a client being interviewed often tries to satisfy what he feels are the interviewer's expectations. This may cause the client to tell the interviewer what he thinks will be a pleasing story, withholding negative and contradictory facts. Third, a client may have a variety of internal reasons—such as embarrassment, modesty, and fear—that, once again, prevent full disclosure of all information.

There are, however, positive factors that promote full disclosure. For example, a client is more likely to fully disclose if he feels the interviewer has a personal interest in him. A friendly, sympathetic interviewer is more likely to get all the facts from a client. Second, a client is more likely to fully disclose if he senses that the interviewer is identifying with him. The interviewer who lets the client know that she is familiar with and understands the client's situation is more likely to draw out all the facts. Finally, a client may enjoy feeling that he is doing the right thing. The interviewer who can instill in the client the feeling that full disclosure is the proper approach is more likely to achieve it.

You will obtain the fullest possible disclosure by stressing the positive psychological influences and by understanding and minimizing negative influences that inhibit disclosure. Paralegals who create a comfortable physical environment and show an understanding and appreciation of the client will be more successful in obtaining all the facts, both good and bad. This sensitivity will establish a positive context for client relations during the course of the litigation process.

2. Interview preparation

Interview preparation has several components. What kind of physical setting should you have? How will you record what the client says? What should the client do to prepare for the interview? What topics will you cover during the actual interview?

Many clients will be uncertain and insecure during the first interview. After all, it may be the first time they have ever been to a law office. A physical setting that is informal, friendly, and private will help make a client feel relaxed and comfortable. Your private office is a good place to conduct an interview; a small conference room is another.

Strive for informality. Sit in a place other than behind your desk, have coffee and soft drinks available. Avoid interruptions. Leave the telephone alone, and close the door to keep others out. Schedule the interview so that you will have enough time to accomplish what you have planned. An initial interview with a client can easily take one or two hours, but perhaps longer.

In addition to establishing rapport and gaining the client's trust, a principal function of a client interview is, again, to obtain information. This information needs to be recorded; there are two ways to do this. First, you can take notes yourself. This has the advantage of allowing for privacy, but has the disadvantage of interfering with your interview. Second, you can tape-record the interview with the client's permission. Here the advantage is completeness. However, you will still need to make a summary of the interview, and many clients are uncomfortable having their statements recorded.

The paramount consideration is creating an atmosphere where the client feels comfortable and tells everything she knows about the problems that brought her there. Remember, ethically, you have a duty to keep everything that the client tells you confidential. Explain to the client your ethical duty. The client should understand that even though you are not an attorney, everything the client says to you is protected from disclosure to anyone outside the law office.

How should the client prepare for the first interview? First, the client should be told to collect available paperwork, such as letters, documents, bills, and other records. Second, consider asking the client to write down a chronology of everything she remembers about the legal problems, particularly if they involve a recent event. The records and memo should be brought to the initial interview.

3. Initial client interview

The initial client interview should have several objectives. First, conduct yourself in a manner that establishes a good working relationship. When the client arrives at your office, don't make her wait. Greet her personally. Have the client make herself comfortable in your office or conference room, and spend a little time making small talk—about traffic or the weather, for instance. Offer coffee or a soft drink. Remember that you are a representative of your law firm and the client will make a judgment about the firm and its lawyers based on her impressions of you.

Example

Paralegal: Good afternoon, Ms. Garcia. I'm so glad you could meet with me today. Did you have any trouble finding the office?

Ms. Garcia: No, not at all. Your directions were very clear.

Paralegal: Before we go into the conference room, is there anything I can get for you? Water? Coffee?

Ms. Garcia: No. Nothing at this time. Thank you.

Second, spend a few minutes learning about the client's background. This shows the client that you see her as a human being and not as just another case. It also helps you evaluate the client as a witness and provides important biographical and financial information.

Example

Paralegal: I was very interested in learning that you worked with the regional baseball league. I go out and see their games on occasion. How long have you been involved with the league?

Ms. Garcia: Almost six years now. I became interested in working with the league when my oldest son started T-Ball. His T-Ball coach was playing at the time with the baseball league and he told me that the league needed an administrative director.

Paralegal: Sounds like a great position. Do you get to see many of the games?

Ms. Garcia: Oh, every chance I get. I have two other children, so we sometimes take the whole family out to watch the games.

Third, let the client know what is going to happen during the interview, what you need to accomplish, and the reasons for it. Explain that you need to get all the facts to provide the lawyer with an accurate description of the client's legal problems.

Example

Paralegal: Ms. Garcia, I want to take a few minutes to explain to you what is going to happen today. I would like to try and get a chronological overview from you of all the events that transpired between you and Wholesale Sporting Goods. I will be taking notes on what you tell me and will ask you questions to obtain more specific details concerning certain events. The facts that you tell me are important because after we are done, I will discuss the facts of your case with the lawyer in charge of this matter, Ms. Robbins, and give Ms. Robbins an accurate description of your legal problem. Do you have any questions?

Ms. Garcia: No.

Fourth, have the client identify the general nature of her problems. You will usually have a general idea—a "car accident," a "contract problem"—when the client makes the appointment. However, it is always useful to have the client initially tell her story in her own way, without interruptions, which allows you to size her up as a trial witness. You may also discover facts you might never otherwise have stumbled upon, and it allows the prospective client to get the matter off her chest in her own words. These considerations are well worth "wasting time" on, even if the client talks about seemingly irrelevant things. The usual way to get the client to tell the story her way is to ask open-ended, nonleading questions. For example, simply asking "I know you were in an accident. Why don't you tell me what happened in your own words?" will usually get the client started. While the client tells her story, listen not only to what she says but also note things she omits, things that would usually be mentioned. When the client is done, you can paraphrase what she has said. This serves as a check on accuracy and shows the client that you have been listening carefully.

Example

Paralegal: I know you have had a problem with some baseballs ordered from Wholesale Sporting Goods. Can you tell me what happened from the beginning?

Ms. Garcia: Yes. In my position as administrative director I am in charge of ordering supplies for all teams for the regional baseball league. Every year I need to order approximately fifteen hundred baseballs. So, I placed an order for the baseballs with Wholesale Sporting Goods, which is the first time I ever ordered anything from them. I signed a contract with them for the exact type of balls that I needed, and I paid for the balls. However, when the balls arrived, they were missing stitching on one side. I tried to obtain replacement balls from Wholesale Sporting Goods, but they could not guarantee that I would have the balls by opening day. I then went out and bought the balls from Balls R Us.

> *Paralegal:*   All right. Let me make sure I have the correct facts. You signed a contract with Wholesale Sporting Goods for fifteen hundred baseballs. However, when the balls arrived, they were defective because stitching was missing on one side. You tried to obtain new balls from Wholesale Sporting Goods, but they could not guarantee that you would have the new balls before opening day. You then purchased new balls from Balls R Us.
> *Ms. Garcia:*   That is correct.

Fifth, after the client has told her story, you need to get a detailed chronological history of the events and other background facts. It is often advantageous to make an outline or checklist so that you do not overlook important topics. (See the sample checklist in section 4.) Your litigation chart, setting out the elements of the claims you are considering, should provide a start. It is sometimes useful to look at books containing form interrogatories, which are written questions to the other side, for this type of case and witness.[2] These may help you develop ideas for the topics and necessary details as you go through the history of the case. However, don't use a checklist as a questionnaire because your interview will quickly lose the personal touch. The standard method is to use the chronological story-telling approach. Most people think chronologically, and that is usually the best way to elicit details. While your checklist should be tailored to fit the particular case involved, you will usually cover the same basic topics.

Example

> *Paralegal:*   I would like to go back and get a little bit more detail on certain facts that you told me. Can you go back to the beginning and tell me how you first came in contact with Wholesale Sporting Goods?
> *Ms. Garcia:*   I received a promotional flyer from them in the mail, and their prices seemed to be better than the company I had been using in the past.
> *Paralegal:*   What happened after that?
> *Ms. Garcia:*   I called them and spoke to a Mr. Tanner who was one of the sales representatives.
> *Paralegal:*   What did you discuss with Mr. Tanner?
> *Ms. Garcia:*   I told him how many baseballs I needed, and he told me he would work up the numbers and give me a call back with a price quote.

Sixth, you need to ask follow-up questions on potential problem areas. Here it is best to use specific, focused questions. A client naturally wants to impress the interviewer and convince him that the case is a good one, so she will often give only "her version" of what are disputed facts and

---

2. A detailed discussion of formal discovery methods such as interrogatories and depositions is contained in Chapters 13-15.

omit altogether the unfavorable ones. It is always better to get the bad news early. Remind the client that your job is to get all the facts, both good and bad. In addition, you have an ethical duty under the Code of Civil Procedure §128.7(b) to make a reasonable inquiry into all the facts and circumstances to ensure that the allegations have evidentiary support. Remind her that the opposing lawyers will discover the bad facts soon enough, so it is better to deal with them now.

Example

Paralegal: Part of my job here is to get all the facts, both the good and the bad. In litigation, the lawyer on the other side will discuss the bad facts, so it is best to get any facts that may be damaging to the case out in the open now so that we can be prepared to deal with those facts. Accordingly, there are a few areas I want to cover with you. If, while we are talking, you think of any facts that could possibly be damaging, please feel free to interrupt and tell me those facts. First, have you had any problem with defective balls from companies you have used in the past?

Ms. Garcia: No. In the six years I have been working for the league, we have never had this problem before.

Paralegal: Is there some reason, other than price, that you did not go back to using the company you had used in the past?

Ms. Garcia: Yes. I had initially tried to place an order for the baseballs with All-Star Supplies, which is the company we had used in the past. However, I really wanted to receive the balls for the preseason training, but they could only guarantee that we would receive them before opening day. I had quite a blowup with the sales representative over their inability to accommodate my request.

Where do you probe? Look for information that might adversely affect the client's credibility. Are there problems with the client's background? Is there a spotty work history? Are there prior convictions or other troubles with the law? Clients frequently omit negative facts in their background. Therefore, you should be asking what the client has left out of the story. For example, in an automobile accident case, has the client omitted the fact that he was given a traffic citation? Was driving with a suspended license? Was drinking? Had just left a bar before the accident happened? Or was using a car without permission?

A useful device in getting out these kinds of facts, without directly suggesting to the client that you don't believe his story, is to get the client to be a kind of devil's advocate. Ask him to state what he believes the other side is probably going to say to his lawyer about the event. This will frequently draw out the "other side's version" of the disputed facts. Keep in mind that under CCP §128.7 it is at your peril that you accept the client's version of the facts. (Under CCP §128.7(d) the court may impose sanctions against the attorney for violations.) The client needs to be pushed, probed, and even cross-examined to verify the facts he gives you.

The usual topics you will need to discuss with the client during the initial interview include the following: liability, damages, client background, parties, defenses and counterclaims, statutes of limitations, witnesses, records, physical evidence, other law firms, client goals, and next steps.

a. Liability

Facts bearing on the liability of all parties must be developed fully. Details are critical. Here a chronology of events usually works best. For example, in an automobile accident case, you will need to explore how the accident happened step by step. You need to get a detailed description of the scene of the collision. Diagrams and charts are very helpful. You will need to establish the location of each car involved before the collision occurred, at the point of impact, and after the accident. You need to get details on speed, distance, time, and relationship to road markings.

b. Damages

Damages information must be obtained for both the client and all other parties. The permissible damages for each possible claim should already be on your litigation chart. For example, in an automobile collision case, damages should include out-of-pocket expenses, lost income, future expenses, and future lost income, as well as intangible damages such as permanence of injury and pain and suffering. Find out if the client suffered an injury, the extent of it, how he was treated, how he felt then and feels now, and how the injury has affected his life. Find out if he had a preexisting condition that could affect damages. You should also explore insurance coverage for all parties, as well as collateral sources such as health insurance, employer benefits, and government entitlements (e.g., Social Security and Veterans Administration benefits). In contract and commercial cases, and cases in which equitable relief is sought, you need to determine if the injuries to the client can be measured in monetary terms.

As a paralegal working for the plaintiff's side, you must determine if the defendant has the ability to pay a judgment. Find out if the defendant has insurance, the amount of the policy's coverage, and if the policy covers the event or transaction. Determine the defendant's income sources and assets, particularly those that can easily be attached to collect a judgment.

c. Client background

The client's background is significant for several reasons. The client's personal background—education, employment, family history—is important for assessing the client's credibility as a trial witness. His financial background—income and assets—is important for assessing damages. Finally, the client's financial picture bears on a mundane but consequential question: Does he have the ability to pay the legal fees? You need to get this background information from the client early on, but be sure you let the client know why this personal information is important for the lawyer's evaluation of the case.

d. Parties

It is frequently difficult to ascertain which parties are involved in an event or transaction and, if businesses are involved, their proper legal identities. Often the client does not know and has given little thought to this aspect of the case. Now is the time to begin obtaining the facts that will help you identify the parties. For example, in an automobile accident case you will need to know not only who the other driver was, but also who owns the other vehicle and whether it is a business or rental vehicle, or was loaned or stolen. You will also need to know where the accident occurred and need to determine who owns, or is in control of, the accident location, since that entity may be responsible for designing, building, and maintaining the roadways.

From your fact investigation you will usually be able to identify the parties who should be named in the lawsuit. However, identifying parties is not the same thing as learning the proper technical identity of each party. For example, just because the truck that ran into the client had the name "Johnson Gas" on its side does not necessarily mean that the Johnson Gas Company is a properly named party. The potentially liable party may be a sole proprietorship or a corporation with a different name entirely. You need to find this out.

For individuals, learn their correct full names. For corporations, partnerships, unincorporated businesses, and other artificial entities, you must not only learn the proper names but also whether they are subsidiaries of other entities that should be brought in as parties. The secretary of state has a list of domestic and foreign corporations licensed to do business within the state. Such lists usually show the state of incorporation and principal place of business, and list who the resident agent is for service of process. If the party is an unincorporated business operating under a fictitious business name, you may be able to determine the true owners and properly named parties by consulting a fictitious business name index. In addition, don't forget to use the Internet for your searches. Information about a company, whether it is a corporation, a partnership, or some other legal entity, may often be found on a company's web page. (For a discussion about the Internet and locator services, see section E.2 of this chapter.)

e. Defenses and cross-claims

Plaintiffs and defendants alike must look closely at a frequently overlooked area: What do they have on us? And who else can be brought into the case? Cases are legion where a plaintiff has filed an action only to be hit with a much larger, previously dormant, **cross-claim.** Think expansively, particularly in the commercial area, since the parties usually will have had previous dealings that could raise cross-claims. During the interview, inquire about previous transactions between the parties and possible claims the other party may have against the client. Also inquire about facts that may give rise to defenses to the claims.

Cross-claim
A complaint brought by one codefendant against another codefendant

f. Statutes of limitation

All actions must be commenced within a certain time period or else are barred from being brought to court. This limitation is often referred to as a **statute of limitation.** The time period varies depending on the cause of action. For example, an action based on a claim of negligence must be brought within one year of the date of the incident. A claim based on a breach of a written contract must be brought within four years of the date of breach. CCP §312 et seq. prescribe the time periods in which actions must be commenced depending upon the type of claim.

Statutes of limitation have nothing to do with the substantive merits of the plaintiff's case. Rather, the concern is with the mere passage of time. Placing a limit on the time in which actions may be filed ensures that plaintiffs will not sit on their rights and allow a claim to become stale (resulting in loss of evidence or allowing memories of the witnesses to fade). Defendants are also protected since, after the time period has elapsed, they are assured that no future action will be taken against them.

When interviewing a client, always attempt to determine the exact date when the incident occurred that raises the various causes of action.

Sometimes a plaintiff may not consult an attorney until many months—or even years—after a claim arises. In this situation, knowing the exact date is essential in order to determine whether the applicable statute of limitations has run.

g. Witnesses

Question the client on all possible information sources, whether eye-witnesses, experts, or anyone else who could possibly have useful information. Get names or other facts that will help to identify and locate people with information. Think expansively here and do not be concerned with the admissibility of testimony at this point. Find out whom the client has already talked to about the case and what he has said.

h. Records

The client should bring to the interview all paperwork in his possession, such as accident reports, insurance claims, bills, checks, personal records, business records, and correspondence. If the client does not bring them, have him get them to you as soon as possible. You should keep these records; if the client needs them, make photocopies for him. A separate file labeled "client's original documents" should be set up so you do not misplace the records. Learn what other records may exist and who has them so that these can be obtained now, or later through discovery.

i. Physical evidence

Does the case involve objects such as vehicles, machinery, or consumer products? While most common in negligence and products liability cases, such evidence can exist in other cases as well. How to locate, obtain, and preserve physical evidence is discussed in section D on pages 43-44.

j. Other law firms

Clients often shop around for lawyers. While a client has a perfect right to talk to more than one law firm about taking a case, there are always clients who go from door to door until they find a law firm willing to take it. It is important to find out if the client has seen other law firms about the case. On the theory that law firms turn down cases because the cases lack merit, you should be appropriately cautious.

k. Client goals

What does the client really want? In some cases, such as personal injury, the answer is often simple. The plaintiff basically wants money damages, and the defendant wants to avoid paying them. But even then it is important to probe deeper. What does the client view as a favorable outcome? Does he want the case to go to trial, or is he willing to have it settled? Is he looking for vindication, revenge, or satisfaction not related to money damages? In other cases, such as contract and commercial disputes involving businesses, the answer may be difficult to discern. Money for damages is not always what the client wants or needs. The dispute may be with another business where the client has an ongoing relationship, and that relationship may be more important than the money damages. Perhaps relief, such as specific performance, is more important than money damages. Now is the time to find out what the client thinks he wants and whether the client's expectations are realistic or need to be modified.

l. Next steps

When you are concluding the interview, advise the client that you will relate the facts to the lawyer in charge, and either the lawyer or you will be in touch with the client shortly. Do not make any commitments about the case. It is the lawyer's ultimate decision to take the case or not.

Following the client interview, write a short memo to the lawyer in charge detailing the background facts. Also include an evaluation of the client and his story. It is easy to forget your specific impressions of a client, yet the client's credibility as a trial witness will often be critical to the success of the case. This is particularly important because the lawyer will need to evaluate the case without having met with the client.

4. Sample interview checklist

Interviewers often use a form or checklist to ensure that all the items identified in the preceding subsections are adequately covered. Your office may have a sample form or, after you have conducted several interviews, you may wish to develop your own form. If you do not have a sample form, the outline in this section may be used as a checklist when conducting the initial client interview.

Remember, however, that you should never let a checklist limit the questions you ask the client. Often, in the course of the interview, additional questions will come to mind, or other areas may be mentioned by the client. You should not hesitate to stray from your checklist to ask the additional questions or explore the other areas that may not be on the checklist.

☐ Background
  ☐ Name
  ☐ Address
  ☐ Telephone numbers: home, business
  ☐ Marital status, children
  ☐ Age
  ☐ Education (including name of institution, dates attended, degree obtained)
  ☐ Employment (starting with most recent and going backward)
  ☐ Military service
  ☐ Arrest record, if any
☐ Nature of claim
  ☐ Reasons for seeking legal advice
  ☐ Potential adverse parties
  ☐ Date of incident
  ☐ Chronology of events
  ☐ Submission of claims to insurance
  ☐ Statements made to anyone about incident (including claims adjuster, police)
☐ Damages
  ☐ Injuries sustained by client
  ☐ Injuries sustained by others
  ☐ Treatment for injuries (including dates of treatment)
  ☐ Doctors and hospitals administering treatment
  ☐ How injury has affected client's life
  ☐ Preexisting conditions
  ☐ Insurance for injuries
  ☐ Monetary loss to date
☐ Parties
  ☐ Names of potential parties
  ☐ Names of potential adverse parties
☐ Defenses and counterclaims
  ☐ Potential defenses
  ☐ Previous transactions between the parties
  ☐ Possible claims the adverse party may have against the plaintiff
☐ Statutes of limitation
  ☐ Date incident occurred
  ☐ Date client discovered that claim existed
  ☐ Why client has waited to consult a lawyer (if applicable)
☐ Witnesses
  ☐ Names of witnesses
  ☐ Description of witnesses whose names are unknown
  ☐ Addresses of known witnesses
  ☐ Any statements by witnesses to anyone

- ☐ Records
    - ☐ Identity of documents that exist
    - ☐ Was a police report made
- ☐ Physical evidence
    - ☐ List physical evidence (i.e., vehicles, machinery, consumer products)
    - ☐ Location of physical evidence
    - ☐ Condition of physical evidence
- ☐ Other law firms
    - ☐ Has client seen lawyers at other firms
    - ☐ If so, who and when
    - ☐ Why are other lawyers not representing the client
- ☐ Client goals
    - ☐ What does client want
    - ☐ What does client view as a favorable outcome

5. Follow-up client interviews

Many things should be covered during the initial interview of the client. Some cases are relatively simple, and interviewing a well-prepared client can take less than an hour. Many cases, however, will require more than one session to collect the basic information.

Follow-up interviews will also be periodically necessary during the litigation process. Whenever additional information is received, whether through informal fact investigation or during formal discovery, it should be reviewed with the client. The new information may differ from what the client has previously said. Obviously the contradictory information must be evaluated, discussed with the client, and dealt with. In some cases the client may admit that what he previously said was not entirely true and change his story. In others, he may deny the new information and stick to his version of the facts. Whatever the client's position, the new information, if it is at odds with the client's story, must be dealt with. Is it true? Is it more accurate? What does the new information do to the client's story? This is an ongoing process, but the key point to remember is that the client must be kept informed as the fact-gathering process progresses.

D. EXHIBITS ACQUISITION

Your interviews with the client should also identify future exhibits. **Exhibits** include the scene, physical evidence, documents, and records.

Exhibits
Tangible items of evidence presented at trial

In addition, interviews with witnesses and your review of exhibits when you get them, particularly documents and business records, may disclose additional exhibits.

You need to acquire these exhibits, get copies of them, or protect them from being lost or altered. The order in which you do things will depend on how important it is to obtain the particular exhibits. For example, physical evidence, such as the condition of a vehicle, machine, or consumer product, should be acquired quickly before it is repaired, altered, destroyed, or lost. Some records, such as a police accident report, are essential for you to begin your investigation.

The basic types of exhibits are the scene, physical evidence, and records.

1. Scene

If a lawsuit involves an event, such as an automobile accident, investigating the scene is vital. Whenever possible, visit the scene, even if someone else will do the technical investigation. The technical investigation should include taking photographs of all locations from a variety of perspectives and making all necessary measurements so that you can make scale diagrams. Photographs should be both in black and white and in color and will be enlarged for courtroom use. In courtrooms with the technology available digital photographs may be used and projected on a screen.

Numerous photographs should be taken from a variety of perspectives. For example, in an intersection collision case, you will normally want pictures of how the intersection looked to both drivers as they approached it. Accordingly, pictures should be taken in the road from the appropriate lane, with the camera held the same distance above the road as the driver's head. Several pictures should be taken, starting from perhaps 300 feet away, then moving to 150 feet, and so on. The photographs will show what each driver saw as he approached the intersection. In addition, photographs should be taken from where other eyewitnesses, such as other drivers and pedestrians, were when the crash occurred. Before you can determine what photographs you will need, you must review witness statements carefully to know where the witnesses were and what they saw and did. Finally, if there are nearby buildings, it's always useful to have overhead, bird's-eye-view pictures taken that will show lane markings, pedestrian walkways, traffic signs, and signals in the intersection.

Diagrams present a different problem. Since the person who took the measurements and made a scale diagram is often the only witness who can qualify the diagram for admission into evidence, it is better to have

Exhibit 2.1. Sample Diagram

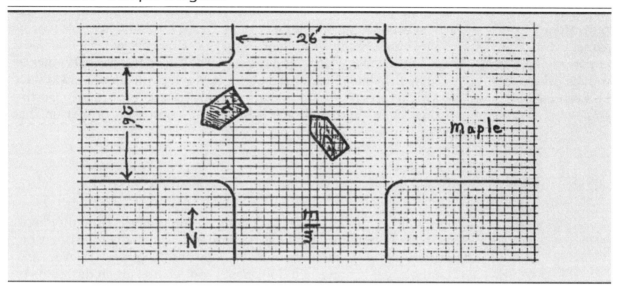

someone other than yourself do this so that you will not become an involuntary witness at trial. A sample diagram is shown in Exhibit 2.1.

2. Physical evidence

Physical evidence, such as vehicles, machinery, and consumer products, if not already in the possession of police, other investigative agencies, or the client, must be obtained and preserved for possible use at trial. This includes not only locating the evidence, but also keeping it in the same condition and establishing the **chain of custody**—that is, who has had custody of the evidence at all times. This is particularly important if the evidence will be tested by experts before trial. When you cannot take or move evidence for safekeeping, take a thorough series of photographs and sufficient measurements so that you can make accurate diagrams and models for trial.

Physical evidence Tangible personal property that may be used as trial exhibits

Evidence is frequently in the possession of a **third party**—that is, someone who is not a party to the lawsuit. Examples of such third parties are police departments and repair shops. If the evidence does not belong to your client, the third parties are probably under no legal obligation to preserve the evidence for you. However, most will be cooperative when they learn that what they have is important evidence. They will usually keep the evidence in an unaltered condition until you have an opportunity to photograph and measure it. You should check if someone else, such as an investigator from the police department or insurance company, has already taken these steps. Finally, a third party will

Subpoena
Court order
compelling a
nonparty to appear or
produce documents
or other tangible
items

sometimes agree to preserve evidence until you can serve the third party with a **subpoena**—that is, a written court order compelling the third party to produce the evidence.

Many times, of course, a client seeks legal assistance when it is already too late to take these steps, and the evidence is lost. If the client comes to your law firm shortly after the event, however, you should always act quickly to preserve the evidence. Many cases, particularly in the personal injury and products liability areas, are won or lost on this type of evidence.

3. Records

You should obtain all available documents and records from the client. Obtain everything the client has because once suit is filed the opposing party will be able to discover from the client anything that is relevant and not privileged. If important documents and records are in the hands of third persons, see if those persons will voluntarily turn them over or provide copies. Public records are usually available on request. A public record is one made by public officers in the course of performing their duties. Documents such as police reports, accident investigations, and personnel records of city and state employees may be obtained by simply making a proper request to the appropriate public agency.

Pursuant to Evidence Code §1158, persons have a statutory right to obtain their own medical records upon demand. A written demand on behalf of the client, coupled with his written authorization, will suffice.

The sample letter and authorization shown in Exhibits 2.2 and 2.3, respectively, may be sent to obtain the client's medical records. The letter and authorization may be revised to send to any other type of agency that possesses records of the client.

Records are, of course, available by subpoena after suit is filed, but it is better to get them as soon as possible because the records may be essential to evaluate the case before suit is filed. For example, in a personal injury case you will need to review police accident reports, doctors' reports, hospital reports, employment records, and perhaps others.[3] In a contract action you will need to get the contract itself as well as records that relate to the performance and nonperformance of the parties, such as orders, shipping documents, invoices, and payment records.

If you can get these kinds of records from third parties, maintain them properly. Keep the records you receive together and in order, and do not mark them. Keep a record of how, from whom, and when you got them.

---

3. Since some records, such as hospital reports, will be technical, get a good dictionary or encyclopedia to help you understand them.

Exhibit 2.2. Sample Letter

[Name of Doctor]   [Date]
[Address]

Re: John J. Smith

Dear Sir/Madam:

Our office represents John J. Smith for personal injuries sustained in an automobile accident on April 21, 2006. Mr. Smith advises that you treated him for the injuries on April 22, 2006. Accordingly, please provide us with copies of his medical records, including any notes, laboratory reports, and fee statements. Enclosed is an authorization from Mr. Smith requesting a release of records to our custody.

We will, of course, pay your copying costs. Alternatively, if you prefer, we will arrange for a copying service to come directly to your office. Please call me immediately in the event you would like us to provide the copy service.

In order for us to complete our investigation of this matter in a timely manner, please provide us with the records on or before [insert date approximately ten days after the date of the letter].

Thank you for your assistance.

Sincerely,

_____
Jane J. Jones
Paralegal [or Legal Assistant]

Make additional copies that you can mark up and use during client and witness interviews. The sample chart that follows shows this system for maintaining the records.

E. WITNESS INTERVIEWS

After you have interviewed the client and obtained the available exhibits, the next stage of your informal fact investigation is interviewing

Exhibit 2.3. Sample Authorization

AUTHORIZATION FOR RELEASE OF MEDICAL RECORDS

To: [Name of Doctor]   [Date]

You are hereby authorized to release a complete copy of my medical records, including all notes, laboratory reports, and fee statements, to my attorneys Mack, Meyer and Miller or their representatives. This authorization is effective immediately and remains in effect until such time as you receive written notice of my revocation of this authorization.

John J. Smith

witnesses. Here, a great deal of flexibility is possible, and it is critical to plan ahead.

1. Whom and when to interview

The more you know, the more accurately you can assess the strengths and weaknesses of the client's case. It makes sense, then, to interview every witness, favorable, neutral, and unfavorable, to find out what each knows. The benefits of interviewing everyone, however, are always tempered by economic realities. There are few cases in which you can interview everyone regardless of expense. Always check with the lawyer to determine the extent of the interviewing that you should do.

After consulting with the lawyer in charge, make a list of all known witnesses who must be interviewed and a list of other witnesses who may not be known but an attempt will be made to identify and interview. For example, bystanders may not be known, but you may be able to identify them by canvassing homes or stores near the accident scene. These bystanders may be able to corroborate the client's version of the accident.

When you have the list of witnesses you need to interview, you must decide the order in which to interview them. Here again, flexibility is required. It is frequently better to interview favorable and neutral witnesses first, before you interview the unfavorable ones, since you will have better success in pinpointing the differences in their stories. Identifying and interviewing the favorable and neutral witnesses first will give you the basis for your side's version of any disputed events and will help you identify the areas of disagreement

SAMPLE CHART

Document	Date Received	How Obtained	From Whom
Contract	8/2/06	Client	
Shipping order	10/23/06	Document request	Defendant
Invoice	10/23/06	Document request	Defendant
Letter by defendant to former employee	11/15/06	Deposition subpoena	Jim Johnson, former employee

when you interview the unfavorable witnesses. These areas can then be explored in detail. Frequently, however, you won't know for sure if a witness will be favorable.

On the other hand, there are advantages in interviewing unfavorable witnesses early, before their attitudes and recall have solidified. For example, in an accident case you learn that a witness will be unfavorable based on quotations from that witness in a police accident report. It may be useful to interview that witness quickly. She may change her mind, or tell you that she "didn't really see it happen," or "isn't sure" about important facts. You may minimize the impact of the witness through an early interview.

2. Locating witnesses

Paralegals are capable of locating many witnesses. The client frequently knows the important ones. Records, such as business records and accident reports, will usually identify others. When their names are known, it is surprising how many witnesses can be located using the telephone or by checking basic, available sources. The telephone book, neighbors at a previous address, workers at a former job, friends, and relatives are all good sources when trying to locate a known witness. Often a witness has merely changed a telephone number, moved to a different apartment, or changed jobs, and tracking her down is relatively simple. If these leads do not work, the following checklist of sources can be used to locate the witness. This checklist may also be used for ascertaining information about witnesses.

☐ Post office
☐ Voter registration
☐ Motor vehicle departments
☐ Utility companies
☐ The Veterans Administration
☐ Social Security office
☐ Unemployment agencies
☐ Welfare agencies
☐ County Assessor's office
☐ Board of Education
☐ License bureaus
☐ Army/Air Force register
☐ Credit associations
☐ *Who's Who in America*
☐ Real estate and rental agencies

The Internet is also an easy way to find people. The **Internet** links computers and databases of information from all over the world and is sometimes referred to as the World Wide Web. By searching these worldwide databases you can locate not only information, but also people and businesses. Some websites will even give you the location of residences and businesses on a map. A search using the search engine "Google" will be especially useful for finding an uncommon name.

Although there are many websites that will search for individuals for a fee, there are also several good sites that can be used for free. A list of sites to use to start locating telephone numbers and potential addresses is included in the Internet Resources section at the end of this chapter. A word of warning: Websites on the Internet sometimes change. If this happens, you will generally get a message advising of the new website.

If the witness is important to the case and cannot be located through these types of leads, it may be necessary to hire an experienced investigator.

3. Purposes of the interview

There are several goals you should try to accomplish during a witness interview and they differ slightly from a client interview. These goals usually should be pursued in the following order:

1. Learn what the witness knows and doesn't know.
2. Get specific, admissible facts.

3. Get admissions.
4. Get information that might be used to discredit the witness.
5. Get leads to other witnesses and information.
6. Record interview or get written statement.

First begin by learning everything the witness knows and does not know that is relevant to the case. Elicit what the witness knows by using open-ended questions. These can be followed later with specific, focused questions; however, you want details of the critical events and transactions only, not everything the witness knows may be relevant. When learning what the witness knows, make sure you pinpoint the admissible facts based on firsthand knowledge.[4] With witnesses who have unfavorable information, you should try to limit the damage by limiting the witness' testimony. Find out what the witness does not know, is not sure of, is only guessing about, or has only secondhand information about.

Second, pin the witness down. This means going beyond generalizations and getting to specific, admissible facts. For example, "driving fast" must be changed to an approximation of speed in miles per hour. "He looked drunk" should be pursued to get the details underlying the conclusion, such as "staggering, glassy eyed, and smelling of alcohol." Getting only generalizations and conclusions makes it easy for a witness to change his testimony later.

Third, get admissions. With unfavorable witnesses, having the witness admit that he "isn't sure," "didn't really see it," "was only guessing," or "was told" all serve to prevent the witness from changing or expanding his testimony at trial.

Fourth, get information that might be used to discredit the witness so the witness will not be believed at trial. This is known as **impeachment.** If an unfavorable witness says something that later may be useful to impeach him, pin him down. For example, if an unfavorable witness to an accident says he was 200 feet away when it happened, make sure you commit him to that fact. Use "200 feet" in other questions to recommit him to that fact, since at trial he may claim that the distance was shorter.

Fifth, get leads to other witnesses and information. It is surprising how often a witness will name other witnesses or divulge information not previously mentioned in any report. For example, asking a witness if anyone else was present at an accident scene will sometimes get a response like: "Sure, Ellen, my supervisor, was standing right next to me and saw the whole thing." Finally, try to record the interview or get some type of written statement. How to do this is discussed in section 6.

---

4. As discussed in later chapters, certain facts are not admissible if they are based on speculation or hearsay.

4. Arranging the interview

Often the most difficult part of witness interviews is getting witnesses to agree to be interviewed in the first place. With favorable witnesses this is not usually a problem, and selecting a convenient time and place for the interview is a routine matter. Unfavorable witnesses, however, are frequently reluctant. Here you can take either of two approaches: attempt to arrange an interview or attempt a surprise interview. A reluctant witness may agree to be interviewed at a convenient time and place, where privacy is assured, if the interview won't take too long.

If a witness will not agree to an arranged interview, the only alternative is the unannounced interview. Frequently, a witness who doesn't want to be bothered will nevertheless agree to talk when an investigator "pops into" the witness' office or "stops by" the house. Again, it may help to reassure the witness that the questions won't take long and may eliminate the need for further involvement. However, a witness has a perfect right to refuse to be interviewed, and you cannot harass or badger the witness hoping to change his mind. The only alternative is to depose the witness later.

5. Structuring the interview

How do you go about structuring a witness interview? First, review the case file, which should contain client interviews, exhibits such as police reports, perhaps other witness interviews, and the developing litigation chart. Second, get copies of any diagrams, photographs, and records you may use during the interview. Third, decide if and how you will record the interview. Finally, prepare an outline for the interview. A frequently followed order for witness interviews is the following:

1. Witness background
2. Story in witness' own words
3. Detailed chronological story
4. Questions focused on the theory of the case

First, witness background is important for assessing witness credibility and determining if there is any bias, interest, or other facts that affect credibility. Most witnesses don't mind talking about their work, family, and home. Asking these background questions usually puts witnesses at ease. Some witnesses, however, may resent what they consider to be intrusions into their private lives. In such cases, you may want to slip the background information into the interview or simply touch on it at the end.

Example

> *Paralegal:*   I understand, Ms. Kramer, that you are the secretary for the regional baseball league. Can you tell me a little about your work?
>
> *Ms. Kramer:*   I do all the typing and act as an administrative assistant for the four staff members we have at the league.
>
> *Paralegal:*   How long have you been working for the league?
>
> *Ms. Kramer:*   Two years. Prior to that I was working as a secretary for an advertising account executive.
>
> *Paralegal:*   How long have you been a secretary?
>
> *Ms. Kramer:*   Almost fourteen years.

Second, let the witness tell her story in her own words, even at the price of hearing irrelevant facts. It gives you a good picture of the kind of witness she will be at trial, and you may discover important facts that would never have come to light.

Example

> *Paralegal:*   As you know, we are handling the matter involving the delivery of approximately fifteen hundred baseballs ordered by Mary Garcia from Wholesale Sporting Goods. I would like for you to tell me as much as you can about what you know about the events surrounding the ordering and delivery of the baseballs.

Third, go over the story in chronological order and in detail. Get specifics on what the witness saw, heard, and did at all important times, and what she saw others do and say. Find out what exhibits the witness knows of, and other witnesses she is aware of. Find out what the witness personally knows of the facts, as opposed to the witness' opinions or speculation about the facts or what the witness was told by others. Find out to whom the witness has talked.

Example

> *Paralegal:*   I would like to go back to the beginning where you indicated that the first time you heard of Wholesale Sporting Goods is when Mr. Tanner from Wholesale Sporting Goods called for Ms. Garcia. Did you hear any part of the conversation Mr. Tanner had with Ms. Garcia?
>
> *Ms. Kramer:*   I heard part of what Ms. Garcia was saying to Mr. Tanner because after I transferred the call to her, I went into her office to deliver the mail. I heard her say that if he could beat the price she was presently paying, he would have our account.

Finally, ask focused questions based on the theory of the case. For example, if the witness gives information that contradicts the client's version of the events, see how you can minimize its effect. If the witness is "not sure," "guessing," "didn't see it myself," or says other things that lessen the damage, make sure you note it. In addition, see if the witness can corroborate something useful to your client's side. Witnesses are rarely completely unfavorable; a little searching will often turn up something positive.

Example

Paralegal: Do you know when Ms. Garcia sent payment to Wholesale Sporting Goods for the baseballs?

Ms. Kramer: Not exactly. I do recall filling out a check requisition for Ms. Garcia for payment of the baseballs soon after she received the contract.

Paralegal: Do you recall if this was before or after the baseballs had been delivered?

Ms. Kramer: Oh, it was definitely before.

6. Recording the interview

Regardless of the witness, you should make a record of the interview. There are several possibilities:

- ◆ Obtain a written, signed statement
- ◆ Use a court reporter
- ◆ Make a tape recording, with the witness' consent
- ◆ Take notes during the interview
- ◆ Make notes after the interview

The approach you use depends on what will best serve your interests and what the witness will permit. If you expect the witness to give favorable information and be cooperative, a short, written, and signed statement is often best. After interviewing the witness, simply type a summary of her story and ask her to sign it. Another method is to send the witness a confirming letter summarizing what she said, and ask the witness to sign and return a copy acknowledging its accuracy. This will lock a favorable witness into her basic story, and there is no damage if the opposing side obtains the statement during discovery.[5]

---

5. While witness statements are usually not discoverable, under CCP §2018 even trial preparation materials are not absolutely protected from discovery. Upon a showing that denial of discovery will unduly prejudice the party seeking discovery, such materials are discoverable, except that an attorney's "impressions, conclusions, opinions, or legal research or legal theories" are always protected from disclosure.

With unfavorable witnesses, it is often advantageous to get a detailed statement. This improves your chances of getting contradictions, admissions, and impeachment that may be valuable at trial. Using a court reporter or a tape recorder is probably the most reliable method. Get the witness' permission if you plan to tape-record, since surreptitious recordings are illegal in some jurisdictions. Avoid later criticism that the recording does not include everything the witness said by being mindful of when conversation is off-the-record.

What is best, and what a witness is willing to do, are two different things. Many witnesses are reluctant to talk, and they are usually under no legal obligation to talk to anyone unless compelled by legal process. Of those willing to talk, many are understandably reluctant to give a signed statement or to have their statements recorded or reduced to a writing. Hence, your priority should be to get the witness to tell what she knows so you will learn what her trial testimony is likely to be and get leads on other witnesses and evidence. Only then should you try to get the most reliable type of statement the witness agrees to give. In short, it is usually better to conduct an interview without any recording than to have no interview at all. You can always dictate immediately afterward what the witness has said.

7. Interviewing techniques

Every witness is influenced by both positive and negative factors that affect the witness' willingness to be interviewed and disclose what he knows. These factors impact both friendly and hostile witnesses. Hostile witnesses may be unwilling to talk at all; friendly witnesses, although willing to talk, are influenced by factors that inhibit or promote full disclosure. An interviewer, therefore, should understand these factors and use them to accomplish her primary purpose of finding out what the witness knows.

Negative factors inhibit witness disclosure. Some witnesses feel that they are being judged by the interviewer. Others tell the interviewer what she apparently wants to hear. Still others become inhibited by emotions such as fear or embarrassment. The interviewer must learn to recognize situations in which these factors exist and use interviewing techniques that reduce their effect.

Positive factors promote disclosure. Witnesses usually respond favorably when the interviewer shows a personal interest in them. Witnesses like to feel that they are doing the decent thing by talking to the interviewer. They tend to identify with the side that values their testimony. Witnesses enjoy feeling important, and may be more likely to help if they feel that the information they can provide will help resolve a dispute fairly. Positive reinforcement is a strong motivator.

Getting witnesses to disclose fully and accurately is best achieved by minimizing the negative factors and reinforcing the positive ones. Accordingly, pick a convenient time and place for the interview. When scheduling the interview, remind the witness that it's always better to talk when events are fresh in mind. Remind him that it is natural to want to help others, and that his disclosing information will help ensure a just and accurate result. Use open-ended, direct examination questions to get the witness talking, to obtain the basic story, and to pursue leads. For example, to find out what the witness knows about the incident you might ask "Describe how fast you believe the defendant was traveling just prior to the accident" or "Tell me what you saw." But use narrow or closed cross-examination questions to pin the witness down and develop potential impeachment. These questions focus on specific, isolated facts and guide the witness to specific information. For example, to pin a witness down, ask him "You're sure the car was going 40 miles per hour?" and "She couldn't have been going faster than that, could she?" The content of questions can also effectively influence responses. Let the witness know your attitude on the matter being discussed, since he has a psychological interest in satisfying his listener's expectations. For example, telling a witness that you feel badly about your side's client having been cheated by the defendant may get a more sympathetic story from the witness. Second, word choices can influence responses. For example, it is well known that using "how fast" rather than "how slow" will increase estimations of speed. Third, leading questions are more likely to get the kind of answer you want. For example, asking a witness "That car was going faster than the speed limit, wasn't it?" is more likely to elicit a "yes" response. Fourth, knowing what other people have said or what other evidence has already been shown can influence witnesses because witnesses prefer consistency and dislike conflict. For example, telling a witness that another eyewitness has stated that the car was speeding will often influence the witness.

8. Evaluating witnesses

Following a witness interview, write a short memo evaluating the witness and her information. It is easy to forget your impressions of the witness, yet witness credibility is frequently the critical component in case evaluation. The memo is especially important if more than one lawyer will work on the file. The memo should evaluate the witness' credibility and effectiveness as a trial witness, note the witness' attitude toward the case, and summarize where the witness' anticipated testimony will help and hurt the case.[6]

F. EXPERT REVIEWS

Wrongful death, medical malpractice, product liability, major negligence, and commercial cases almost always use expert witnesses at trial. The plaintiff's case will probably require expert testimony to establish a prima facie case on liability and causation and to make out a solid case on damages.

In a **prima facie case** the plaintiff can prove each of the elements of the claim as indicated on the litigation chart. The defense case will probably have opposing experts. A case investigation is often incomplete until the case file is reviewed by appropriate experts.

The lawyer may need two experts: one to review the file and consult with to develop facts and theories for trial, the other to be a trial witness. Of course, one expert can and often does perform both roles.

If the lawyer requests that the file be reviewed by an expert, you may be asked to provide the necessary documents to the expert for review. Do not send out a file for expert review until you have collected the reports and records the expert will need. Make sure the written materials you send her give a complete and neutral picture of the case, but do not give the expert privileged materials. Keep in mind that an expert who becomes the testifying expert at trial can often be deposed and forced during cross-examination to produce all materials she received for her review. Factual materials that are given to the expert may not be protected by the work product privilege; therefore, do not give an expert any materials that contain the lawyer's mental impressions and thought processes.

In addition, rather than have the expert review the file generally, you may want to direct the expert to specific areas where there are potential problems. This is best done in conversations with the expert, after you have sent her the necessary materials. For example, in a medical malpractice case you might tell the expert that the potential case theory of liability is that the anesthetic was improperly administered, and ask the expert if the standard of reasonable care was breached. A focused review is usually more productive.

Hiring an expert consultant does not prevent the lawyer from using her as an expert at trial. That decision will have to be made at the discovery stage. CCP §2034 provides a method whereby parties may

> **Prima facie case**
> A case in which each element in the plaintiff's claim can be proven

---

6. Under CCP §2018, materials prepared by a lawyer, or under a lawyer's directions, are considered the lawyer's work product. Thus, a memo should be absolutely privileged as an attorney's work product and, therefore, not discoverable by the opposing party.

require, after the initial trial date has been set, the exchange of expert trial witnesses.

As a paralegal, you may be asked to assist the lawyer in selecting an expert. Because an expert is so important, and because a consulting expert may later be the testifying expert at trial, you must be careful in selecting one. Perhaps the best way to select an expert is simply to ask litigators you know to recommend one who is knowledgeable in the subject area of your case, is willing to work with and educate you, and will be an effective trial witness. If this fails, or you need an expert in a specialized area, some lawyers' groups, such as the American Trial Lawyers Association, maintain expert directories, and law libraries sometimes have directories for various specialties.[7]

G. COMPUTERIZED FACT GATHERING

In our fast-moving computer age, the use of the Internet has become a significant way to gather information in litigation matters. Whether you want to conduct basic legal research on a specific topic or find out more information about an area, product, or even a company that is involved in the litigation, you will likely find it by surfing the Internet.

To access the World Wide Web on the Internet, you must have the necessary equipment. Virtually every law firm has computers set up for Internet access that you may use to assist you in gathering information. In addition, you can obtain access through a computer at your local library.

There are numerous legal sites available to assist you with your research and fact gathering. The California state bar site, the state, as well as many counties, have sites that allow you to access recorded documents such as trust deeds and property liens. In addition, the legal sites at the end of this chapter are good places to start your research.

Do not overlook the value of gathering facts through use of the Internet. To see how valuable such a search can be, let's go back to our interview with Ms. Garcia and the shipment of defective baseballs. Using the Internet, it may be possible for us to locate background information on Wholesale Sporting Goods, such as how large a company they are, when they first started in business, and any consumer representations that they make through promotional materials placed on the Internet.

---

7. See, e.g., H. Philo et al., Lawyer's Desk Reference (8th ed. 1993), which lists experts by category. TASA, the Technical Advisory Service for Attorneys, is an organization that refers experts in numerous fields. Many legal newspapers and journals also contain listings and information about experts. Local universities are also a good source.

In addition, by searching the Internet you can quickly become an expert on baseballs. By searching the Internet using the query "baseball and supplies" you will find literally hundreds of sites regarding different types of baseballs and prices. This information can be valuable to you in learning something about the business, as well as in comparing the terms that were offered to the client by Wholesale Sporting Goods and what other companies could realistically offer.

CHAPTER SUMMARY

This chapter has discussed the paralegal's role in conducting an informal fact investigation, the importance of informal fact gathering, and ways in which you may structure your investigation. Facts necessary to the investigation may be informally obtained from the client, exhibits, witnesses, experts who are consulted about the client's case, and through surfing the Internet. This informal fact gathering is usually more effective and less expensive than waiting until after a lawsuit is filed to undertake discovery.

The client and all available witnesses must be interviewed as part of the initial fact gathering. This chapter described the steps in conducting a good client interview, as well as various interviewing techniques, and provided a checklist for locating witnesses.

Equally important to the initial fact gathering is the acquisition of physical evidence, including records. Much of the evidence will be in the client's possession. However, when this is not so, you may be able to obtain third party evidence voluntarily and without a subpoena. Any records you receive should be placed on a Record of Documents chart, such as the one provided in this chapter.

KEY TERMS

Affirmative defense	Internet
Breach of contract	Jury instructions
Cause of action	Negligence
Chain of custody	Physical evidence
Cross-claim	Prima facie case
Exhibits	Statute of limitations
Factfinder	Subpoena
Impeachment	Third party

REVIEW QUESTIONS

1. What is the difference between a cause of action and an affirmative defense?

2. How should you structure your fact investigation?

3. Identify at least five sources for locating the whereabouts of a witness.

4. What information should you attempt to obtain from the client during an initial interview? Why is this information important?

5. What goals should be accomplished during a witness interview? What are the question-asking techniques you can use to accomplish these goals? Give an example of each.

6. What are the differences between a breach of contract and a negligence cause of action?

7. What is a statute of limitations? What is the statute of limitations for negligence actions in California?

8. What documents should you attempt to obtain before a lawsuit is filed during the informal fact-gathering stage? What sources are available to you to locate these documents?

9. How can you use the Internet to help you in your informal fact gathering and investigation?

INTERNET RESOURCES

Websites useful for locating people:

www.yahoo.com/search/people (a good place to start locating telephone numbers and postal addresses; if you have the city, state, and zip code, you can type in an address and pinpoint a location on the map by using Yahoo's map website (www.maps.yahoo.com)

www.iaf.net (Internet address finder)

www.whowhere.com

www.bigfoot.com (this site will give you a choice of a directory assistance search for individuals or a yellow page search for businesses)

Websites useful for research and fact gathering:

www.calbar.org (provides links to a number of California legal sites)

www.law.cornell.edu (provides links to court decisions, U.S. Code, and some state statutes and constitutions)

www.law.emory.edu (provides links to court decisions, federal agencies, U.S. Code, as well as several legal-related databases)

www.law.indiana.edu (provides links to court decisions and legal-related databases)

www.law.villanova.edu (provides links to court decisions, U.S. Code, and some state statutes and constitutions)

www.kentlaw.edu (law-related discussion groups)

There are also a number of websites for specific resources that can be helpful depending on your topic and needs:

www.access.gpo.gov (Federal Register from 1994 to the present)

www.municode.com (municipal ordinances from a number of jurisdictions)

www.usdoj.gov (Department of Justice)

www.uspto.gov (Patent and Trademark Office)

www.ftc.gov (Federal Trade Commission)

The following list of sites can be used to conduct searched using key words or terms:

www.google.com

www.lycos.com

www.yahoo.com

www.ask.com

CHAPTER 3

Case Evaluation and Strategy

CHAPTER OBJECTIVES

Once the preliminary factual and legal investigations are complete, attention turns to planning the litigation. In this chapter you will discover:

♦ How to establish the terms of the attorney-client agreement
♦ How a lawyer's fee is charged
♦ What steps to take in planning the litigation
♦ How to develop a litigation strategy
♦ What prefiling requirements should be considered

A. INTRODUCTION

Case evaluation requires that you gather enough facts and sufficiently consider the legal issues to assist the lawyer in deciding whether to take the case. If the lawyer decides to take the case, the evaluation requires a realistic, cost-effective litigation plan. This chapter gives you an overview of how the terms of the attorney-client relationship are established once the lawyer decides to take the case. This overview will familiarize you with the process the lawyer must go through and will enable you to assist the lawyer with that process.

In addition, once a decision has been made to take the case, you will need to assist the lawyer in developing a litigation strategy and in completing prefiling requirements. This chapter provides guidelines for preparing a litigation plan and a checklist for prefiling requirements.

B. ESTABLISHING THE TERMS OF THE ATTORNEY-CLIENT AGREEMENT

Once the lawyer decides to take the case, the terms of the attorney-client relationship should be formally established in a written agreement. There are three reasons for this. First, any contractual relationship is best established in writing. Second, the agreement will prove the existence of an attorney-client relationship for purposes of asserting the attorney-client privilege. Third, the agreement will establish the work to be done, what will not be done, and the basis for compensation, all of which must be understood to ensure a good working relationship between lawyer and client.

Unless the client is sophisticated and has experience working with lawyers, the client will have little understanding of the legal work involved in litigation and the various fee arrangements that can be made.

It is in everyone's best interests that the client be educated on these matters. The lawyer will discuss with the client how fees are set and what costs can be expected.

In California where the lawyer expects the fees and cost to be $1,000 or more, the fee agreement must be in writing. It is most common to use either a written contract or a letter to the client, a copy of which the client signs and returns. Regardless of which method is used, it should cover all aspects of the relationship in detail. Unfortunately, disputes between lawyers and clients are common, but they can usually be avoided by making sure that the agreement is drafted in clear and simple English, covers all likely issues, and specifies what is not covered. The lawyer is held responsible for any ambiguities and omissions in attorney-client agreements, so it is in a lawyer's best interest to draft an agreement that leaves no room for misunderstanding. The State Bar has sample fee agreements for a small fee, which can be obtained by calling the State Bar Fee Arbitration Department. If a sample form is not used the agreement should cover the following basic subjects.

1. Work covered

The agreement should specify what work will be performed and what will not. For example, the agreement might be to prosecute a negligence claim arising from a car accident on a certain date and time. If the lawyer will not handle any appeal, or if there will be an additional charge for any appeal, the agreement should specify this. If the lawyer will not handle a workers' compensation claim, insurance claim, or other related matters, the agreement should say so. In general, it is important to guard against a client thinking that the lawyer will do more than the lawyer has agreed to do. Spelling out what is not covered should prevent this from happening.

2. Lawyer's fee

A lawyer's fee is the compensation the lawyer will receive for professional services rendered on behalf of the client. The amount of the lawyer's fee, the way it will be determined, and when it will be paid must be spelled out. The total fee must be reasonable in light of the work to be done, the difficulty of the work, the amount of time it will involve, and the customary range of fees for similar work in that locality.

The agreement should specify how the fee will be determined. Three approaches are commonly employed: an **hourly rate** (common

Fixed flat fee
Lawyer receives a predetermined fee regardless of how much work is done on the client's behalf

Retainer fee
Amount the client pays to the lawyer at commencement of the representation; fee is credited against fees and costs incurred by client

in corporate, commercial, and insurance defense cases), a **fixed flat fee** (common in criminal defense cases and in family law), and the **contingency fee** (common in plaintiff's personal injury cases). Obviously, the agreement can specify any number of combinations or modifications of these basic approaches, unless the fee is regulated or set by statute. For example, agreements frequently specify a minimum **retainer fee,** paid up front, that is credited against an hourly billing rate. A retainer is simply a cash payment of a sum of money to a lawyer before work begins on the client's case.

When the fee is based on an hourly rate, the client must understand that what is being paid for is the lawyer's expertise and time. Hence, any time expended on a client's case will be billed to the client, regardless of whether the time is spent on court appearances, conferences, research, drafting documents, or making telephone calls.

A lawyer has an ethical duty to make the fee reasonable. This may mean that the lawyer must discount the fee, even in a contingent fee situation, to make sure it is reasonable before submitting it to the client. California Business and Profession's Code Section 6000 et seq. regulates and limits attorney's fees. Accordingly, make sure the fee agreement complies with the applicable code section.

An **attorney's lien** is a claim by the lawyer on any judgment or recovery obtained by the client and can usually be imposed to ensure payment of the lawyer's fee. This is frequently done in contingent fee situations.

3. Retainers

In some situations the lawyer may require a retainer to ensure payment of the fee and reimbursement of other costs that the lawyer advances. A common arrangement is to insist on a retainer and then periodically deduct fees and costs as they are incurred. Regardless of the precise agreement, the agreement must specify the amount of the retainer, when it must be remitted, and what fees and costs will be deducted from it.

Whenever a lawyer receives advanced funds from a client, the funds must be put in a separate client trust account. Under no circumstances can any client's funds be commingled with the lawyer's funds.[1] Funds from all of a lawyer's clients can be held in one trust account; however, a separate ledger must be kept for each client showing receipts and disbursements. The Interest on Lawyer's Trust Accounts (IOLTA) system in California requires holding client funds in interest-bearing accounts.

---

1. See Model Code of Professional Responsibility, Ride 9-102; Model Rules of Professional Conduct, Rule 1.15.

E. PERSONAL JURISDICTION

In addition to subject matter jurisdiction, the court also must have personal jurisdiction over the defendant. **Personal jurisdiction** refers to the power of a court to bring a party before it. A judgment is not enforceable against a party unless that party can lawfully be brought into court and has received notice of the lawsuit. Thus, constitutional concepts of due process underlie this requirement. Code of Civil Procedure §410.10 provides that a California court "may exercise jurisdiction on any basis not inconsistent with the Constitution of this state or of the United States." Thus, California may exercise personal jurisdiction to the full extent allowed by the federal Constitution. There is a great deal of overlap between federal and state law in this area. This is sometimes referred to as the "long-arm" of the law. The law reaches out across state boundaries to bring an out-of-state defendant before courts in California.

Personal jurisdiction
The power of a court to bring a party before it and to make a decision binding on such a person

1. Types of jurisdiction

Jurisdiction of a court over the defendant can be in personam, in rem, or quasi in rem. **In personam jurisdiction** refers to the court's power to personally bind the parties to the court's judgment. This jurisdiction can be either general or specific. If a court has general jurisdiction over a defendant, the defendant can be sued on any matter. It is not necessary that the cause of action be specifically based on the contacts that the defendant has with California. For example, if the defendant lives, works, or goes to school in California, he will be able to be sued in all California courts because the defendant has sufficient contacts with the state to give the state personal jurisdiction over him. These contacts are considered general enough to give the California courts the power to hear any claims against the defendant. If the jurisdiction is specific, it means that the defendant's contacts with the state of California are limited in nature and are not sufficient and pervasive enough to be sued on all matters in California. Rather, the complaint must arise out of the specific contacts that the defendant has in California. For example, if the defendant lives in Arizona, but came to California and was involved in an automobile accident in California, then a court would have specific in personam jurisdiction over the defendant in any action involving the automobile accident. However, if the same defendant entered into a contract with a plaintiff in Arizona and then the plaintiff moved to California, the court would not be able to compel the Arizona defendant to come to California to defend the breach of contract action.

An **in rem** action is one that involves property (the **res**) located within the state in which the court sits and in which the parties have their dispute. Jurisdiction over the party exists by virtue of the party's ownership of the property. With in rem jurisdiction, the court decides rights in the property, and that determination is then binding on any party claiming an interest in the property. For example, assume that the plaintiff and defendant jointly owned a piece of vacant property in California. If a dispute later arises between the plaintiff and defendant over ownership of the property, the plaintiff brings the action in state court to determine title to the property, even if the defendant no longer lives in California.

Finally, **quasi in rem** is a type of jurisdiction that allows a plaintiff to use a defendant's property to satisfy a claim as long as the property is in the state. Thus, even if the defendant is not in the state and there is no in personam jurisdiction over the defendant, jurisdiction can still be obtained over the property. Only the property, however, may be used to satisfy the claim. For example, assume that the defendant does not live in California, but has a horse that he has boarded in California. If the defendant breaches his contract with the owner of the boarding facility and fails to pay for the boarding fees, the court could order that the horse be sold and the proceeds paid to the plaintiff to satisfy the plaintiff's claim against the defendant. This is because the court is said to have jurisdiction over the defendant's property (the horse) because the property is in the state. If the property is not sufficient to satisfy the claim, the plaintiff may not try to enforce the balance of the claim or subsequent judgment against the defendant since the court does not have in personam jurisdiction against the defendant.

Issues surrounding personal jurisdiction involve two separate questions:

1. Can the defendant constitutionally be subject to the court's jurisdiction?
2. Was service of process on the defendant proper?

The first question involves the due process limitations on personal jurisdiction, and the second involves the service-of-process requirements.

2. Due process requirements

Due process
A constitutional
doctrine requiring
fairness in judicial
proceedings

Due process is a constitutional doctrine requiring fairness in judicial proceedings. Due process issues do not arise for plaintiffs, since by initiating suit a plaintiff is considered to have voluntarily submitted to the court's jurisdiction for all purposes, including being required to respond to counterclaims and other claims brought in that action. When a defendant is a resident of the **forum state**—that is, the state in which the action is brought—due process problems do not arise. Since the defendant is a resident of the state, it is fair to require the defendant to defend against an action brought in the state.

When a nonresident defendant, however, is sued in the forum state and does not consent to the jurisdiction of the court, due process problems may prevent that defendant from being required to defend there. Determining what the due process limitations are is a difficult question that the Supreme Court has considered several times.

The leading constitutional cases include International Shoe Co. v. State of Washington, 326 U.S. 310 (1945), and World-Wide Volkswagen Corp. v. Woodson, 444 U.S. 286 (1980). Other significant Supreme Court cases are Burger King Corp. v. Rudzewicz, 471 U.S. 462 (1985), and Asahi Metal Industry Co. v. Superior Court, 480 U.S. 102 (1987). For California cases see Von's Cos., Inc. v. Seabest Foods, Inc. 14 Cal. 4th 434, 444 (1996).

In *International Shoe* the Court addressed the question of what activities by a corporation within a particular state will subject it to suit within that state consistent with due process concepts. It held that where a corporation's "minimum contacts" in the forum state were such that being forced to defend a suit in that state would not offend "traditional notions of fair play and substantial justice," jurisdiction was proper. 326 U.S. at 316, quoting Milliken v. Meyer, 311 U.S. 457, 463 (1940). The **minimum contacts** standard requires that there be sufficient activities of the defendant in the forum state to subject the defendant to the jurisdiction of the court. Many subsequent decisions, of course, expounded on what are sufficient minimum contacts to satisfy due process.

One of these, *World-Wide Volkswagen*, appeared to narrow the scope of such contacts. There the Court rejected the argument that an out-of-state seller should be subjected to suit in another state simply because it was foreseeable that the vehicle sold might be involved in a collision in another state. Instead, the Court stressed that minimum contacts protect a defendant from being sued in a remote or inconvenient forum, and that foreseeability does not by itself create such contacts as would satisfy due process requirements. Requiring a defendant to defend in the forum state, the Court held, must be fair and not impose unreasonable burdens on the defendant.[2] In order to understand the minimum contacts required for personal jurisdiction, consider the following examples:

♦ Simply posting information on a website, even though the defendant knew that it would harm the movie industry in California, is not sufficient contact to invoke personal jurisdiction. Pavlovic v. Copy Control Assoc., 127 Cal. Rptr. 2d 329 (2002).

2. In *Asahi Metal*, 480 U.S. 102 (1987), a closely divided Court held that merely placing a product into the stream of commerce is not an act that will subject a party to the forum state's jurisdiction, even if the party was aware that the stream of commerce would sweep the product into the forum state. Minimum contacts requires some action purposely directed toward the forum state. The case has not been followed by all courts.

♦ California resident could sue Nebraska defendant in California for the wrongful death in connection with an accident that occurred in Nevada because the defendant engaged in shipping and hauling by trucks that had made frequent visits to California. Cornelius v. Chaney, 16 Cal. 3d 143 (1976).

♦ California may exercise jurisdiction over fast food restaurant franchisees who failed to properly cook hamburger patties in Washington causing outbreak of E. coli in California where there was evidence of sufficient business being conducted in California by mail, telephone, meetings, and training sessions in California of employees. Von's Companies Inc. v. Seabest Foods, Inc., 14 Cal. 4th 434 (1996).

♦ Publisher who distributed magazines in another state can be brought to defend action for damages arising from an allegedly defamatory story. Keeton v. Hustler Magazine, 465 U.S. 770 (1984).

♦ California does not have jurisdiction over divorced father who acquiesces to daughter living with mother in California. Kulko v. Superior Court, 438 U.S. 908 (1978).

The minimum-contacts analysis applies with equal force to in rem and quasi in rem actions.[3] Because of this, distinctions such as in rem or quasi in rem have no direct bearing on the due process question of a defendant's amenability to suit in a particular forum. However, the distinctions are still important for determining the enforceability of judgments.

3. Service-of-process requirements

Service of process refers to the actual delivery of the legal document (usually the initial summons and complaint) to the defendant. It is important to keep in mind that jurisdiction over the party is different from, and independent of, the adequacy of service of process. If a party is not properly served in a manner prescribed by the Code of Civil Procedure, any service on that party will have no effect unless the party waives objections to the service.

Service must be properly made because due process considerations require that service be made in a manner that will reasonably put defendants on notice that they have been sued. Service of process under the Code of Civil Procedure is discussed in Chapter 5, section C. In general,

---

3. The Supreme Court so held in Schaffer v. Heitner, 433 U.S. 186 (1977), deciding that a defendant's ownership of personal property by itself did not establish such contacts as would create proper personal jurisdiction over the defendant where the claims were not related to the property.

however, the Code recognizes four ways service may be made upon a defendant.

♦ First, service may be made by personally delivering the document to the defendant. This is obviously the best method of service for due process purposes because such service ensures that the defendant has received notice and thus has an opportunity to be heard.

♦ Second, service may be made by leaving the legal document with an adult at either the residence or place of business of the individual or entity, and thereafter mailing a copy of the document to the address where the document was left. This method, although not as reliable as the personal delivery to the defendant, seeks to provide a reasonable substitute for personal delivery in the event the defendant cannot be located for personal service.

♦ A third method is by notice and acknowledgment of receipt. This method allows the plaintiff to send the defendant the summons and complaint in the mail along with a form notice and acknowledgment of receipt. Service is deemed complete when the defendant signs and returns the acknowledgment of receipt. While this method ensures that the defendant has received the document, there is very little compelling the defendant to voluntarily acknowledge receipt of the documents. Hence, you cannot count on the defendant returning the acknowledgment of receipt, and you may have to complete service of process by another method.

♦ A final method is service of process by publication. This method is usually a last alternative, reserved for when notice cannot be given to the defendant by any other method. Pursuant to CCP §415.50, the plaintiff must receive an order from the court before the plaintiff may serve a complaint by publication. If publication is allowed, then notice of the summons and complaint will be published in a newspaper of general circulation.

F. FEDERAL VERSUS STATE COURT

If your side has the choice of filing a complaint in either federal or state court because both courts have jurisdiction, a decision must be made before the complaint is filed as to which court you would like to commence the litigation in. Although the lawyer will be responsible for making the ultimate decision, the paralegal should be aware of certain considerations that go into the decision process.

The decision about which court to file in includes considerations concerning the time of claim, the time it takes to get to trial, the ability of one judge to hear the entire case, and the potential jury pool. The lawyer will also give substantial consideration to which law the federal court may apply. Although a federal court sitting in a diversity case must apply the substantive law of the state in which it sits, there may be differences in the way the federal court judges interpret the laws of the particular state.

In addition, consideration should be given to the differences in the federal and state rules of procedure and evidence. Many times, the procedural and evidentiary rules in federal court are more stringent than in state court. All of these considerations must be examined carefully before making a choice between federal and state court.

G. VENUE

Venue
The geographic district where a lawsuit may properly be heard

A lawsuit must be filed in a proper place. Where a lawsuit can be filed is governed by **venue** statutes. Such statutes determine the geographic districts where the case can properly be heard.

Since venue provisions are designed in part to protect a defendant from being forced to litigate in an "unfair" forum, it follows that a defendant can waive the benefits of the venue rules. Hence, a defendant must raise improper venue in a timely manner by filing an appropriate responsive pleading or by filing a motion for an order transferring the action to the proper court; otherwise, any of the defendant's objections will be deemed waived.

1. Determining venue

Before filing a lawsuit, the plaintiff must determine which county is the proper venue for the action. Under CCP §395, proper venue is in the county in which the defendants, or some of them, reside at the start of the action. If the action is for injury to person or personal property, or for death due to a wrongful act or negligence, the proper venue is either where the defendants, or some of them reside, or in the county where the injury or death occurs.

There are numerous special venue provisions that need to be consulted before filing a lawsuit. These provisions are found at CCP §392 et seq. For example, under §394 an action against a county or city may be tried in such county or city unless the action is brought by a city or county, in which case it must be brought in a county or city not party to the action. Under §395.5 actions against corporations may be brought (i) where the contract is made or is to be performed, (ii) where the obligation or liability arises or the breach occurs, or (iii) in the county where the principal place of business of the corporation is located.

Consequently, you must always check whether a special venue statute exists that overrides the general provisions of §395.

If basing venue on the "residence" of a defendant, the resident of any one of the defendants is sufficient. If there are three defendants, two that reside in Los Angeles County and one that resides in Alameda County, venue would be proper in either Los Angeles County or Alameda County.

The venue provisions control where a plaintiff files the initial complaint against the original defendants. They do not apply to cross-claims since these are seen as ancillary to the initial suit and raise no additional venue issues.

2. Change of venue

A change of venue may be raised by the defendant in a motion to transfer to the proper venue, before the defendant files any other type of responsive pleading. Alternatively, the defendant may raise the change of venue in the answer, or other responsive pleadings as discussed in Chapter 5. If a defendant does not raise the objection, the object to improper venue will usually be considered waived.

Under §397, the court may on motion change the place of a trial in five instances: (i) when the court designated in the complaint is not the proper court; (ii) where there is reason to believe an impartial trial cannot be had; (iii) when "the convenience of witnesses and the ends of justice would be promoted"; (iv) where there is no judge of the court qualified to act; and (v) when the "ends of justice would be promoted" by changing marriage dissolution proceedings to the respondent's county of residence. This section recognizes that a plaintiff frequently has venue choices and that the plaintiff's choice, while proper, may not be the most convenient forum for the case when seen as a whole.

H. CHOICE OF COURT BASED ON CHOICE OF LAW

After completing your jurisdictional analysis, you may find that there are courts in several different states that have jurisdiction over the defendant. If you determine that more than one court has jurisdiction over the defendant, how do you decide in which court the complaint should be filed? This question involves both practical and legal considerations. On the practical side, convenience and cost to the plaintiff, the plaintiff's lawyer, and the witnesses will frequently dominate the decision. If practicing in California, and the plaintiff resides in California, then a California state court often will be the choice if it is available. However, before jumping to any immediate conclusions,

Choice-of-law decisions
Determining in which court a complaint should be filed

consideration should be given to whether there is jurisdiction over the defendant, and whether the plaintiff's principal witnesses are in another state. In addition, **choice-of-law decisions** may be critical because applicable substantive law may differ for such matters as statutes of limitation, elements of claims, and allowable damages, and the lawyer will want to choose the jurisdiction with the laws most favorable to your client.

For example, suppose an Arizona driver is injured by a California driver in an automobile accident in Nevada. Certainly it would appear that the plaintiff has, at a minimum, a choice between filing in California (the defendant's residence) or Nevada (where the claim arose). When deciding in which state to file the action, the plaintiff should consider the law of the forum state. If California and Nevada tort law differ, the plaintiff will obviously want to pick the more advantageous forum.

Furthermore, the subpoena power of a district is generally limited to its geographical boundaries; thus, if uncooperative witnesses are out of state, you and the lawyer may need to choose another available forum to reach these witnesses. Finally, factors such as the choice of judges, the desirability of prospective jury pools, and length of time until trial should all be considered.

CHAPTER SUMMARY

This chapter has considered a number of important legal issues that you must investigate before a lawsuit is filed. The first is to decide who may, or must, be a party to the litigation and what claims may, or must, be brought in the litigation. You must also consider whether the court has jurisdiction over the subject matter of the controversy. Because a court has power to hear only those cases that are properly before it, a determination of the type of case and the amount of relief sought must be made prior to the filing of a complaint. In some instances, even if a case is properly filed in state court, the defendant may have a right to remove the case to federal court.

In addition to subject matter jurisdiction, the court must also have personal jurisdiction. Personal jurisdiction is the power of the court to bring a party before it. Personal jurisdiction must meet due process and service-of-process requirements.

Often your side will have the choice of filing in either federal or state court. Certain matters must be considered in choosing the court. These considerations include how long it takes to get to trial, the benefit of the case being assigned to one judge, the jury pool, and the differences in the procedural and substantive law that may apply in the case.

Finally, once a determination is made in which court to file the lawsuit, consideration must be given to choosing the proper venue. Venue can be changed by the defendant only if the venue chosen by the plaintiff is improper or there is another appropriate ground to base a motion to transfer.

KEY TERMS

Assignment

Choice-of-law decisions

Corporation

Diversity jurisdiction

Due process

Forum state

Guardian ad litem

Improper venue

Inconvenient venue

In personam jurisdiction

In rem jurisdiction

Intervention

Joinder of claims

Joinder of parties

Long-arm statutes

Minimum contacts

Parties to an action

Partnership

Permissive joinder

Personal jurisdiction

Principal place of business

Quasi in rem jurisdiction

Real party in interest

Removal

Res

Service of process

Sole proprietorship

Subject matter jurisdiction

Unincorporated association

Venue

REVIEW QUESTIONS

1. Why is it necessary to name the real party in interest in a lawsuit?

2. Under what circumstances should a party be joined in an action?

3. What are the two tests for determining whether a party may be joined in a lawsuit?

4. Why would a defendant want to remove an action from state court to federal court? What is the procedure the defendant must follow in order to remove an action filed in state court?

5. Why can subject matter jurisdiction never be waived by the defendant?

6. Explain the difference between in personam, in rem, and quasi in rem jurisdiction and give an example of each.

7. What are the different ways in which a defendant may be served with process?

INTERNET RESOURCES

The following sources are useful in further examining the concepts discussed in this chapter:

www.law.cornell.edu (access to federal rules)

www.lawschoolhelp.com (general basic information)

www.leginfo.ca.gov/calaw.html (database for searching California Code of Civil Procedure and case law)

www.west.net/~smith/jurisdiction.htm (overview of subject matter and personal jurisdiction)

PART

Pretrial Litigation

CHAPTER **5**

Pleadings

A. Introduction
B. General Pleading Requirements

CHAPTER OBJECTIVES

Pleadings refer to all documents filed by the plaintiff to initiate a lawsuit and all documents filed by the defendant in response to the lawsuit. In this chapter you will learn:

♦ What the general requirements are for all pleadings
♦ How to draft a statement of fact for complaints
♦ What needs to be contained in the caption of a complaint
♦ How pleadings must be signed
♦ What format requirements must be met
♦ What rules apply to service and filing of pleadings

Pleadings
Formal written documents by the parties to the litigation to either start or respond to the litigation

A. INTRODUCTION

Pleadings are defined in CCP §420 as the formal allegations by the parties of their respective claims and defenses for judgment by the court. Pleadings are used by the plaintiff to start the litigation and by the defendant to respond to the litigation.

The pleading rules are principally contained in the CCP. However, the California Rules of Court as well as local rules also contain pleading rules. Local rules generally do not affect the substance of pleadings, but ordinarily control mechanics such as the number of copies filed, size of paper, format, and bindings. Accordingly, while this text discusses the rules applicable to all California courts as contained in the CCP and California Rules of Court, you should always check the local rules to determine if there are any special rules that apply to your particular case.

Good pleadings practice is a combination of two things: a solid litigation plan and technically precise drafting. The litigation plan, which you have already developed, will control the claims and remedies (if a plaintiff) or the defenses and cross-claims (if a defendant). The drafting of pleadings then becomes the primary concern, since pleadings that are technically precise will avoid attacks by motions and eliminate the need to file amended pleadings to cure defects that should have been avoided in the first place.

B. GENERAL PLEADING REQUIREMENTS

The CCP has made simplicity and limited purpose the touchstones of the pleadings stage of the litigation process. Under CCP §422.10 the only basic pleadings allowed in civil actions are complaints, demurrers, answers, and cross-complaints.

1. Statement of fact requirements for claims

California is a fact pleading state. This means that the complaint, or cross-complaint, must contain a statement of the facts constituting the **cause of action** in ordinary and precise language.[1] A cause of action is the basis for the relief that the plaintiff seeks such as breach of contract, negligence, or fraud. The Judicial Council of California has developed a number of forms that may be used to ensure that you have satisfied the necessary pleading requirements. A list of the approved pleading forms are found in division III of the Appendix to the California Rules of Court, and also on the California Courts website at www.courtinfo.ca.gov. Some forms are mandatory and are identified by an asterisk on the list of forms. Other forms are permissible but not mandatory. For simple breach of contract cases, the easiest approach is to use the approved form to ensure you have covered all the required allegations.

Cause of action
Basis for relief the plaintiff seeks

In addition to stating the facts for each cause of action, CCP §425.10 requires that each complaint or cross-complaint also contain a demand for judgment for relief. If the plaintiff or cross-defendant seeks money as a form of relief, then the amount of money sought must be stated, unless the action is brought in superior court and seeks actual or punitive damages for personal injury or wrongful death. In these latter cases, the amount is not stated.

2. Content requirements

Content requirements are set forth in CCP §§422.30 and 422.40. There are several requirements that must be followed for every pleading.

a. Caption

Every pleading must have a caption containing three elements:

♦ The name of the court and county where filed
♦ The title of the action
♦ Names of all parties

---

1. This differs from federal rules which require only "notice" pleading. Under notice pleading the only requirement is that the pleading contain enough information to fairly notify the opposing party of the basis of the claim.

i. Name of Court

The name of the court must include the county, and in limited municipal civil cases, the fact that the case is a limited civil case. For example, the name of the court in the Superior Court for Los Angeles county may look like this:

Superior Court of California
For the County of Los Angeles

ii. Title of the Action

The title of the action identifies the parties to the action. The complaint must list all the parties to the action. Subsequent pleadings need only list the first plaintiff and first defendant, with an appropriate reference to additional parties such as "et al."

Make sure that your caption correctly states the proper name and legal description of each party. Under CCP §367 every action must be brought in the name of the real party in interest. Pursuant to CCP §369 some parties may sue as representatives of other parties, such as the personal representative of a probate matter or a trustee of a trust. Remember also that corporations may sue or be sued, as well as partnerships and unincorporated associations. Examples of common designations include the following:

- John Smith
- Sharon Jones, as guardian of the Estate of Robert Jones, a minor
- Robert Smith, as conservator of the Estate of Ellen Smith, an incompetent
- Frank Watson, as executor of the Estate of James Morley, deceased
- R. J. Smith Company, a corporation
- Johnson Hospital, a not-for-profit corporation
- Robert Smith, d/b/a Smith Cleaners
- Barnett and Lynch, a partnership
- Western Ranches Association, an unincorporated association

Where a party is being sued both individually and in a representative capacity, it should be spelled out.

- John Smith, individually and as administrator of the Estate of Franklin Smith, deceased

A sample caption is shown in Exhibit 5.1.

Exhibit 5.1. Sample Caption

SUPERIOR COURT OF CALIFORNIA
FOR THE COUNTY OF LOS ANGELES

JOHN SMITH, an individual

Plaintiff

v.

RANDOLPH CONSTRUCTION
COMPANY, a Delaware Corporation,
and DOES 1 through 10 inclusive.

Defendants

Case No. C-23444

COMPLAINT FOR BREACH
OF CONTRACT

Sometimes it is impossible to identify a proper party by name before filing. In these circumstances you can designate a party as "John Doe, the true name being presently unknown," and the identity of the party can be pursued through formal discovery. This sometimes happens when a plaintiff has been able to identify some but not all liable parties. It is a good idea to always name some defendants as "Doe" defendants in case you discover the names of additional parties after the **statute of limitations** has run. (See Chapter 7 for a detailed discussion.)

Statute of limitations
The time limit required by the plaintiff to bring a complaint against the defendant

b. Designation

Each pleading should be labeled to show what type it is, such as a complaint, cross-complaint, or answer. Where multiple parties are involved, it is useful to show against whom the pleading is directed. Sample designations are shown in Exhibit 5.2.

Exhibit 5.2. Sample Designation

COMPLAINT FOR (Identify the causes of action)

DEFENDANT BAKER'S ANSWER TO COMPLAINT

CROSS-COMPLAINT AGAINST JONES CONSTRUCTION COMPANY

c. Signing pleadings

Every pleading or other court paper must be signed by the party or one of the party's lawyers. *See* CCP §446. The signing is by an individual, not a law firm, although in practice the lawyer's firm is frequently shown immediately above the signature.

In California, unless specifically required by statute for the particular cause of action, pleadings do not need to be "verified." A verified pleading is one signed by the party and declared, under penalty of perjury that the statements are true or that the party believes in the truth of the statements. However, if a party chooses to file a verified complaint, then the answer must be verified. A sample **verification** is shown at Exhibit 5.3.

3. Format requirements

The format of papers presented for filing with the court is stated in Rule 2.101 of the California Rules of Court. In general, all papers must be typewritten on 8½ by 11 inch opaque paper in type no smaller than 12 point. Only one side of the paper may be used and lines must be one and one-half spaced or double spaced and numbered consecutively. Descriptions of real property, footnotes, and quotations may be single-spaced. Recycled paper is required for all original papers filed with the court and all copies of papers "whether filed with the court or served on other parties."

Rule 2.111 proscribes the format of the first page. The name, address, telephone number, fax number, e-mail address if provided, and state bar number of the attorney for the party must appear on the left-hand side commencing with line one. The right-hand side between lines one and seven are to be left blank for the clerk's file stamp. Commencing with line eight, the title of the court shall be listed. Below the title of the case, the names of the parties are on the left-hand side and on the right-hand side the number of the case. Immediately below the number of the case is

Exhibit 5.3. Sample Verification

VERIFICATION

I am the plaintiff in this proceeding and have read this Complaint. I declare under penalty of perjury under the laws of the State of California that this Complaint is true and correct.

Dated: ___March 30, 2006___   _____

John W. Smith

the type of action. If the case is a limited civil case, this designation must also appear in the caption. A sample of the format for the first page of a complaint is shown in Exhibit 5.4.

In addition, under CRC 2.110, for all papers filed in court, there must be a footer in the bottom margin below each page number, with the title of the paper in at least 10-point type.

Example

10. Plaintiff's Opposition to Motion to Dismiss

4. Service and filing

Pleadings and other court papers must be served on all parties in one of the permitted ways. How to serve pleadings is discussed in Chapter 6. Generally, service of any complaint or summons must be made on the party in accordance with the provisions of CCP §415.10 et seq. When a party is represented by a lawyer, service of pleadings other than a complaint should be made on the party's lawyer. This is customarily done either by personal delivery or mail, although delivery includes leaving the pleading or other court paper at the lawyer's office with the person in charge. If a party is not represented by a lawyer, the party himself must be served, and the permitted methods essentially parallel those for lawyers.

Unless otherwise ordered, all pleadings and other court papers that are actually served on parties must be filed with the court clerk either before service or within a reasonable time after service. The usual practice is to have the original and appropriate number of copies of the pleading or other court paper taken to the clerk of the court for filing and have another copy stamped "filed" and dated for your law firm's files. This is usually done the same day papers are being served on the lawyers for the other parties. For service of the summons and complaint, a proof that the summons was served on a person must be made on a form adopted by the Judicial Council. For other pleadings, the usual practice is to have the proof of service attached to the end of the pleading that shows when and how service was made and includes the signature of the attorney or the signature of a member of the attorney's staff. A sample proof of service is shown in Exhibit 6.2.

5. Civil cover sheet

A civil cover sheet must be filed when the first pleading is filed. A copy of the mandatory cover sheet is shown in Exhibit 5.4. Failure to file the

Exhibit 5.4. Mandatory Civil Cover Sheet

CM-010

ATTORNEY OR PARTY WITHOUT ATTORNEY *(Name, State Bar number, and address):*	FOR COURT USE ONLY

TELEPHONE NO.:   FAX NO.:

ATTORNEY FOR *(Name)*:

SUPERIOR COURT OF CALIFORNIA, COUNTY OF
  STREET ADDRESS:
  MAILING ADDRESS:
  CITY AND ZIP CODE:
  BRANCH NAME:

CASE NAME:

CIVIL CASE COVER SHEET	**Complex Case Designation**	CASE NUMBER:
☐ **Unlimited** (Amount demanded exceeds $25,000) ☐ **Limited** (Amount demanded is $25,000 or less)	☐ **Counter** ☐ **Joinder** Filed with first appearance by defendant (Cal. Rules of Court, rule 3.402)	JUDGE: DEPT:

Items 1–5 below must be completed (see instructions on page 2).

1. Check **one** box below for the case type that best describes this case:

Auto Tort
☐ Auto (22)
☐ Uninsured motorist (46)

Other PI/PD/WD (Personal Injury/Property Damage/Wrongful Death) Tort
☐ Asbestos (04)
☐ Product liability (24)
☐ Medical malpractice (45)
☐ Other PI/PD/WD (23)

Non-PI/PD/WD (Other) Tort
☐ Business tort/unfair business practice (07)
☐ Civil rights (08)
☐ Defamation (13)
☐ Fraud (16)
☐ Intellectual property (19)
☐ Professional negligence (25)
☐ Other non-PI/PD/WD tort (35)

Employment
☐ Wrongful termination (36)
☐ Other employment (15)

Contract
☐ Breach of contract/warranty (06)
☐ Collections (09)
☐ Insurance coverage (18)
☐ Other contract (37)

Real Property
☐ Eminent domain/Inverse condemnation (14)
☐ Wrongful eviction (33)
☐ Other real property (26)

Unlawful Detainer
☐ Commercial (31)
☐ Residential (32)
☐ Drugs (38)

Judicial Review
☐ Asset forfeiture (05)
☐ Petition re: arbitration award (11)
☐ Writ of mandate (02)
☐ Other judicial review (39)

Provisionally Complex Civil Litigation (Cal. Rules of Court, rules 3.400–3.403)
☐ Antitrust/Trade regulation (03)
☐ Construction defect (10)
☐ Mass tort (40)
☐ Securities litigation (28)
☐ Environmental/Toxic tort (30)
☐ Insurance coverage claims arising from the above listed provisionally complex case types (41)

Enforcement of Judgment
☐ Enforcement of judgment (20)

Miscellaneous Civil Complaint
☐ RICO (27)
☐ Other complaint *(not specified above)* (42)

Miscellaneous Civil Petition
☐ Partnership and corporate governance (21)
☐ Other petition *(not specified above)* (43)

2. This case ☐ is ☐ is not complex under rule 3.400 of the California Rules of Court. If the case is complex, mark the factors requiring exceptional judicial management:
  a. ☐ Large number of separately represented parties
  b. ☐ Extensive motion practice raising difficult or novel issues that will be time-consuming to resolve
  c. ☐ Substantial amount of documentary evidence
  d. ☐ Large number of witnesses
  e. ☐ Coordination with related actions pending in one or more courts in other counties, states, or countries, or in a federal court
  f. ☐ Substantial postjudgment judicial supervision

3. Type of remedies sought *(check all that apply):*
  a. ☐ monetary b. ☐ nonmonetary; declaratory or injunctive relief c. ☐ punitive

4. Number of causes of action *(specify):*

5. This case ☐ is ☐ is not a class action suit.

6. If there are any known related cases, file and serve a notice of related case. *(You may use form CM-015.)*

Date:

_____
(TYPE OR PRINT NAME)

_____
(SIGNATURE OF PARTY OR ATTORNEY FOR PARTY)

NOTICE
- Plaintiff must file this cover sheet with the first paper filed in the action or proceeding (except small claims cases or cases filed under the Probate Code, Family Code, or Welfare and Institutions Code). (Cal. Rules of Court, rule 3.220.) Failure to file may result in sanctions.
- File this cover sheet in addition to any cover sheet required by local court rule.
- If this case is complex under rule 3.400 et seq. of the California Rules of Court, you must serve a copy of this cover sheet on **all** other parties to the action or proceeding.
- Unless this is a complex case, this cover sheet will be used for statistical purposes only.

Page 1 of 2

| Form Adopted for Mandatory Use
 Judicial Council of California
 CM-010 [Rev. January 1, 2007] | **CIVIL CASE COVER SHEET** | American LegalNet, Inc.
 www.FormsWorkflow.com | Cal. Rules of Court, rules 3.220, 3.400–3.403;
 Standards of Judicial Administration, § 19 <br> www.courtinfo.ca.gov |

Exhibit 5.4. Continued

INSTRUCTIONS ON HOW TO COMPLETE THE COVER SHEET
CM-010

To Plaintiffs and Others Filing First Papers

If you are filing a first paper (for example, a complaint) in a civil case, you **must** complete and file, along with your first paper, the *Civil Case Cover Sheet* contained on page 1. This information will be used to compile statistics about the types and numbers of cases filed. You must complete items 1 through 5 on the sheet. In item 1, you must check **one** box for the case type that best describes the case. If the case fits both a general and a more specific type of case listed in item 1, check the more specific one. If the case has multiple causes of action, check the box that best indicates the **primary** cause of action. To assist you in completing the sheet, examples of the cases that belong under each case type in item 1 are provided below. A cover sheet must be filed only with your initial paper. You do not need to submit a cover sheet with amended papers. Failure to file a cover sheet with the first paper filed in a civil case may subject a party, its counsel, or both to sanctions under rules 2.30 and 3.220 of the California Rules of Court.

To Parties in Complex Cases

In complex cases only, parties must also use the *Civil Case Cover Sheet* to designate whether the case is complex. If a plaintiff believes the case is complex under rule 3.400 of the California Rules of Court, this must be indicated by completing the appropriate boxes in items 1 and 2. If a plaintiff designates a case as complex, the cover sheet must be served with the complaint on all parties to the action. A defendant may file and serve no later than the time of its first appearance a joinder in the plaintiff's designation, a counter-designation that the case is not complex, or, if the plaintiff has made no designation, a designation that the case is complex.

CASE TYPES AND EXAMPLES

Auto Tort
Auto (22)–Personal Injury/Property Damage/Wrongful Death
Uninsured Motorist (46) *(if the case involves an uninsured motorist claim subject to arbitration, check this item instead of Auto)*

Other PI/PD/WD (Personal Injury/Property Damage/Wrongful Death) Tort
Asbestos (04)
  Asbestos Property Damage
  Asbestos Personal Injury/Wrongful Death
Product Liability *(not asbestos or toxic/environmental)* (24)
Medical Malpractice (45)
  Medical Malpractice–Physicians & Surgeons
  Other Professional Health Care Malpractice
Other PI/PD/WD (23)
  Premises Liability (e.g., slip and fall)
  Intentional Bodily Injury/PD/WD (e.g., assault, vandalism)
  Intentional Infliction of Emotional Distress
  Negligent Infliction of Emotional Distress
  Other PI/PD/WD

Non-PI/PD/WD (Other) Tort
Business Tort/Unfair Business Practice (07)
Civil Rights (e.g., discrimination, false arrest) *(not civil harassment)* (08)
Defamation (e.g., slander, libel) (13)
Fraud (16)
Intellectual Property (19)
Professional Negligence (25)
  Legal Malpractice
  Other Professional Malpractice *(not medical or legal)*
Other Non-PI/PD/WD Tort (35)

Employment
Wrongful Termination (36)
Other Employment (15)

Contract
Breach of Contract/Warranty (06)
  Breach of Rental/Lease Contract *(not unlawful detainer or wrongful eviction)*
  Contract/Warranty Breach–Seller Plaintiff *(not fraud or negligence)*
  Negligent Breach of Contract/Warranty
  Other Breach of Contract/Warranty
Collections (e.g., money owed, open book accounts) (09)
  Collection Case–Seller Plaintiff
  Other Promissory Note/Collections Case
Insurance Coverage *(not provisionally complex)* (18)
  Auto Subrogation
  Other Coverage
Other Contract (37)
  Contractual Fraud
  Other Contract Dispute

Real Property
Eminent Domain/Inverse Condemnation (14)
Wrongful Eviction (33)
Other Real Property (e.g., quiet title) (26)
  Writ of Possession of Real Property
  Mortgage Foreclosure
  Quiet Title
  Other Real Property *(not eminent domain, landlord/tenant, or foreclosure)*

Unlawful Detainer
Commercial (31)
Residential (32)
Drugs (38) *(if the case involves illegal drugs, check this item; otherwise, report as Commercial or Residential)*

Judicial Review
Asset Forfeiture (05)
Petition Re: Arbitration Award (11)
Writ of Mandate (02)
  Writ–Administrative Mandamus
  Writ–Mandamus on Limited Court Case Matter
  Writ–Other Limited Court Case Review
Other Judicial Review (39)
  Review of Health Officer Order
  Notice of Appeal–Labor Commissioner Appeals

Provisionally Complex Civil Litigation (Cal. Rules of Court Rules 3.400–3.403)
Antitrust/Trade Regulation (03)
Construction Defect (10)
Claims Involving Mass Tort (40)
Securities Litigation (28)
Environmental/Toxic Tort (30)
Insurance Coverage Claims *(arising from provisionally complex case type listed above)* (41)

Enforcement of Judgment
Enforcement of Judgment (20)
  Abstract of Judgment (Out of County)
  Confession of Judgment *(non-domestic relations)*
  Sister State Judgment
  Administrative Agency Award *(not unpaid taxes)*
  Petition/Certification of Entry of Judgment on Unpaid Taxes
  Other Enforcement of Judgment Case

Miscellaneous Civil Complaint
RICO (27)
Other Complaint *(not specified above)* (42)
  Declaratory Relief Only
  Injunctive Relief Only *(non-harassment)*
  Mechanics Lien
  Other Commercial Complaint Case *(non-tort/non-complex)*
  Other Civil Complaint *(non-tort/non-complex)*

Miscellaneous Civil Petition
Partnership and Corporate Governance (21)
Other Petition *(not specified above)* (43)
  Civil Harassment
  Workplace Violence
  Elder/Dependent Adult Abuse
  Election Contest
  Petition for Name Change
  Petition for Relief from Late Claim
  Other Civil Petition

cover sheet can result in sanctions. The sheet must also be served on all other parties. The cover sheet identifies the type of case and whether it is limited ($25,000 or less) or unlimited (over $25,000). The court uses the information contained in the cover sheet to gather statistics about the type and number of cases filed.

CHAPTER SUMMARY

Good pleadings require a solid litigation plan and technically precise drafting. Since California is a fact pleading state, the complaint must state specific facts to give rise to a cause of action against the defendant. A cause of action is the basis for the relief that the plaintiff seeks, such as breach of contract, negligence, and fraud. As a result of your fact investigation, you should be able to state the facts in each cause of action. The pleadings must also provide a statement of the relief requested. Precise drafting includes knowing the notice requirements for claims and the format requirements.

The complaint requires that you name the proper parties as defendants. It is a good idea to always name a number of fictitious defendants as "Doe" defendants. In this way, in the event that additional parties are discovered to be responsible for the damages of the plaintiff or that the wrong name was used in the pleading, the proper defendant can be substituted for one of the fictitious Doe defendants. In addition, all pleadings must be properly served and must be filed with the court either before service or shortly after the time of service. This ensures that the court is aware of the pleadings and responses, and can ensure that the case is progressing.

KEY TERMS

Cause of action
Civil cover sheet
Doe defendants
Fact pleading

Pleadings
Statute of limitations
Verification

REVIEW QUESTIONS

1. What pleading is used to commence a lawsuit?

2. What is meant by the term "fact pleading"?

3. What three elements must be included in the caption of a complaint?

4. Who can sign a pleading?

5. What is a verified pleading?

6. What are the possible consequences for failing to file the civil cover sheet?

INTERNET RESOURCES

www.calbar.org
www.courtinfo.ca.gov/cgi-bin/forms.cgi
www.lalaw.lib.ca.us

CHAPTER **6**

Complaints, Answers, and Cross-Claims

CHAPTER OBJECTIVES

The complaint is the document filed by the plaintiff to initiate a lawsuit. In this chapter you will learn:

- ◆ How to draft a complaint
- ◆ How to identify parties in the complaint
- ◆ What format to use for stating a cause of action
- ◆ When to use the official form complaints
- ◆ What the methods are for service of a summons and complaint
- ◆ What pleadings the defendant may file in response to the complaint
- ◆ How to draft an answer to a complaint

A. INTRODUCTION

Complaint
The document filed by the aggrieved party to commence litigation

The **complaint** is the plaintiff's initial pleading, which, when filed, starts the litigation. Prior to serving the complaint, the plaintiff will have the court issue a summons commanding the defendant to appear. The summons and complaint must be properly served upon each defendant, and proof of service filed with the court. After service of the summons and complaint on the defendant, the defendant will generally file an answer stating whether the defendant agrees with or denies the statements of facts stated by the plaintiff and alleging a number of defenses. If the defendant also has a claim against the plaintiff or any of the other defendants, the defendant may state that claim in a cross-claim. The rules discussed in this section are the rules for complaints filed in the superior court. However, the rules for complaints filed in federal court are substantially similar.

B. COMPLAINTS

The complaint has specific requirements that must be followed in order to bring the allegations against the defendant before the court. Some requirements relate to the format of the complaint. For example, the complaint must be on 8½ by 11 recycled white pleading paper. Pleading paper means that there will be numbers along the left side so that the court and other parties may easily refer to each line of the pleading. The rules for the type of paper to use, along with the spacing and type requirements, are found in Rule 2.100 of the California Rules of Court.

The body of the complaint contains three parts; a statement identifying the parties to the action, one or more causes of action, and the request for relief. A sample complaint appears in Exhibit 6.1 and in the Litigation File at the end of this book. In this section you will learn the requirements necessary for drafting the complaint.

Exhibit 6.1. Sample Complaint

Tamara Sellers, Esq.
State Bar No. 997788
789 E. Larchmont Lane
Encino, CA 91356
(818) 777-8888

SUPERIOR COURT OF CALIFORNIA
FOR THE COUNTY OF LOS ANGELES

JOHN SMITH, an individual) Plaintiff) v.) RANDOLPH CONSTRUCTION) COMPANY, a Delaware Corporation,) and DOES 1 through 10 inclusive.) Defendants)	Case No. C-23444 COMPLAINT FOR BREACH OF CONTRACT

Plaintiff John Smith alleges as follows:

FIRST CAUSE OF ACTION

1. Plaintiff John Smith ("Smith") is, and at all time relevant hereto was, a resident of the State of California, County of Los Angeles.

2. Defendant Randolph Construction Company ("Randolph") is, and at all time relevant hereto was, a Delaware Corporation licensed to do business and doing business in the State of California, County of Los Angeles.

3. Smith does not know the names or capacities of defendants sued herein as DOES 1 through 10, inclusive, and therefore sues them by these fictitious names. Smith will amend this Complaint to allege the true names and capacities of Does 1 through 10 when the same is ascertained.

4. . . .

1. Identification of the parties

The first several paragraphs of the complaint generally allege the identity of the parties to the action, and an allegation concerning the Doe defendants. Thus, while it is not necessary to affirmatively allege proper venue, except in actions on certain consumer obligations, the allegation of the identity of the parties and place of resident is an easy way to demonstrate to the court that the complaint has been filed in the proper venue.

Example

1. Defendant John Roberts is, and at all times material hereto was, a natural person residing in Los Angeles County, California.

2. Defendant XYZ Corporation is a Delaware corporation, with its principal place of business in Orange County, California.

3. The identity of Defendants identified as Does 1 through 10, inclusive, are unknown to the Plaintiff at this time. Plaintiff will seek leave to amend this Complaint and insert the true names of Does 1 through 10 when their identity becomes known to Plaintiff.

2. Cause of action

Complaints are broken up into the various causes of action that a plaintiff is asserting against the defendant. The cause of action will contain all the factual allegations against the defendant and must contain the proper legal elements to prove a cause of action. These elements were discussed in Chapter 2.

a. Format

Each cause of action must be separately stated and numbered.[1] For example, if a plaintiff has two causes of action against a defendant, one for breach of contract and one for negligence, the cause of action will be identified and numbered. In addition, if a particular cause of action is against less than all the defendants, then the names of the defendants that must respond to each cause of action should also be identified. The following is an example.

1. Rule 2.100 of the California Rules of Court refers to separately stated cause of action or count. Cause of action and count are used interchangeably. However, the more common practice is to refer to the allegations as separate causes of action rather than counts.

Example

FIRST CAUSE OF ACTION FOR BREACH OF CONTRACT

(Against Defendants Jones, Roberts, and Does 1 through 5)

SECOND CAUSE OF ACTION FOR IMPLIED WARRANTY

(Against Defendants Jones and Doe 1 only)

In addition, each statement of fact under the cause of action must be numbered using Arabic, not Roman, numerals. The numbers should run sequentially rather than starting the numbers over for each cause of action. If subparagraphs are used, the subparagraphs should be indented and use lower case letters rather than numbers.

Example

FIRST CAUSE OF ACTION FOR BREACH OF CONTRACT

(Against Defendants Jones, Roberts, and Does 1 through 5)

1. . . .
2. . . .
3. . . .
4. . . .

SECOND CAUSE OF ACTION FOR IMPLIED WARRANTY

(Against Defendants Jones and Doe 1 only)

5. . . .
6. . . .
7. . . .

b. Pleading statement of facts

Once you have determined the essential legal elements of a cause of action, you must state the elements by turning the elements into a statement of facts as the facts apply to your case. Remember Mary Garcia from our example in Chapter 2? Mary had a contract with Wholesale Sporting Goods ("WSG") to provide baseballs for the regional baseball league. Mary obtained the baseballs, but it turned out that the baseballs were missing stitching on one side and were therefore defective. Your research discovered that the legal elements to state a cause of action for breach of contract required (i) a contract; (ii) Mary's performance; (iii) WSG's breach; and (iv) Mary's damages. Your factual investigation will give you the facts that you need for your statement of facts.

Example

1. On January 8, 2008, Plaintiff entered into a written contract with Defendant for the purchase of 1,000 baseballs. A true and correct copy of the written contract is attached hereto as Exhibit A and incorporated herein by reference.

2. On February 1, 2008, Plaintiff paid for the baseballs in the amount of $10,000.

3. On March 1, 2008, Defendant delivered the baseballs to Plaintiff at which time the Plaintiff discovered that the baseballs were missing stitching and could not be used in regulation play.

4. Plaintiff made demand upon the Defendant for a refund of the money paid but Defendant has refused. Plaintiff has therefore been damaged in the amount of $10,000.

In this example, you can see how each of the legal elements are changed into factual statements that can be alleged in the Complaint. If Mary had a second cause of action against WSG, for perhaps negligence in providing a defective product, then a second cause of action could be stated going through each of the necessary legal elements and stating a concise statement of facts for each element.

Pleading the necessary facts for each element is essential. If you fail to plead the necessary facts for each cause of action, the complaint may be subject to a **demurrer.** A demurrer is a type of motion filed by the defendant to challenge the sufficiency of the complaint. Under CCP §430.10 a demurrer may be based on a claim that the complaint does not "state facts sufficient to state a cause of action." Demurrers as a response to the Complaint will be explained more fully in Chapter 9.

Demurrer
Motion that challenges the legal sufficiency of the complaint

Good sources for finding the essential elements of a cause of action are treatises that provide a summary of California law such as *Witkin's Summary of the Law.* Witkins is a multivolume treatise that provides summaries of statutes and cases on virtually all substantive areas of California law. In addition, you can use the form jury instructions as discussed in Chapter 2 to ascertain the elements of a cause of action.

c. Use plain English

In recent years the trend in legal drafting has been away from legalese in favor of plain English. The same approach should be applied when drafting pleadings. Commonly used words, short sentences of simple construction, active verbs, and a preference for nouns and verbs over adjectives and adverbs create clear, forceful language. This benefits everyone in litigation—parties, lawyers, judge, and jury.

The preference for using simple English also should apply to naming parties. Use names rather than the pleading's designations (e.g., plaintiff, defendant) or other legal designations (e.g., trustee, drawer, or obligor). If there are multiple parties, using names keeps things clearer. A common practice is to set out the full name of each party the first time it is used, then show in parentheses how you will refer to that party from then on:

◆ Defendant William B. Smith (hereafter "Smith") . . .
◆ The International Business Machines Corporation ("IBM") . . .

d. Use exhibits

Exhibits may be attached to pleadings. This is most commonly done in contract cases, where the contract that forms the basis for the claim is attached to the complaint. When attached to the pleading, the exhibit becomes an integral part of it. This is usually a more efficient way of stating a claim than setting out the exhibit's contents in the body of the complaint. The following example shows how to incorporate attached exhibits into the complaint.

Example

1. Plaintiff Jones and defendant Smith entered into a contract on June 1, 2009. A true and correct copy of this contract is attached as Exhibit A and incorporated herein by reference.

Even if the exhibit is attached to the pleading, language from the exhibit can still be quoted in the complaint.

e. Official form complaints

As discussed earlier, the Judicial Council of California has developed a number of form complaints that may be used for a variety of causes of action including breach of contract and tort actions. In using a form complaint, the general allegations identifying the parties and place of residence will be stated and you will merely have to check the appropriate boxes. However, most of the more common causes of action will need to be attached to the complaint in order for the form complaint to withstand a demurrer. The Judicial Council has developed a number of form causes of action that may be attached to a form complaint. In addition, the clerk's office for the Superior Court also has a number of standard complaint forms available. Exhibit 6.2 contains a sample form complaint based on contract, and Exhibit 6.3 contains the attachment for a cause of action based on breach of the contract. Exhibit 6.4 provides a sample for complaint for personal injury actions.

3. Prayer for relief

Prayer for relief
A section at the end of a complaint specifying the relief requested by the plaintiff

Default judgment
Judgment entered against a defendant who fails to appear and defend against the lawsuit after having been given proper notice of the lawsuit

Code of Civil Procedure §425.10(b) requires that a complaint contain a "demand for judgment for the relief to which the pleader claims to be entitled." Relief in the alternative or of several different types may be demanded. This is called the **prayer for relief.** The code makes no distinction between legal and equitable relief.

Care in pleading relief is important for two reasons. First, since the nature of the remedy sought is often controlling on the question of the right to a jury trial, the demand for relief should be drafted to ensure the right to a jury trial, or to avoid it, as the case may be. Second, where a defendant fails to respond to the complaint and a **default judgment** is requested, the method under which default can be obtained is affected by the type of relief sought, and the relief granted is limited to that requested in the pleadings. Since default is always a possibility, you should always draft the prayer carefully.

The prayer for relief appears at the end of the body of the complaint. It specifies, with sufficient detail, the types of relief sought including legal and equitable remedies, interest, costs, attorney's fees, and any special damages. Where several specific types of relief are sought, it is best to itemize and number them. An example of a prayer for relief is shown in Exhibit 6.5.

Exhibit 6.2. Form Complaint in Contract

PLD-C-001

ATTORNEY OR PARTY WITHOUT ATTORNEY *(Name, State Bar number, and address):*	*FOR COURT USE ONLY*

TELEPHONE NO.:   FAX NO. *(Optional)*:
E-MAIL ADDRESS *(Optional)*:
ATTORNEY FOR *(Name)*:

SUPERIOR COURT OF CALIFORNIA, COUNTY OF
STREET ADDRESS:
MAILING ADDRESS:
CITY AND ZIP CODE:
BRANCH NAME:

PLAINTIFF:

DEFENDANT:

☐ DOES 1 TO _____

CONTRACT
☐ COMPLAINT   ☐ AMENDED COMPLAINT *(Number)*:

☐ CROSS-COMPLAINT   ☐ AMENDED CROSS-COMPLAINT *(Number)*:

Jurisdiction *(check all that apply):*
☐ **ACTION IS A LIMITED CIVIL CASE**
    Amount demanded ☐ **does not exceed $10,000**
                        ☐ **exceeds $10,000 but does not exceed $25,000**
☐ **ACTION IS AN UNLIMITED CIVIL CASE (exceeds $25,000)**
☐ **ACTION IS RECLASSIFIED by this amended complaint or cross-complaint**
        ☐ **from limited to unlimited**
        ☐ **from unlimited to limited**

CASE NUMBER:

1. **Plaintiff*** *(name or names):*

   alleges causes of action against **defendant*** *(name or names):*

2. This pleading, including attachments and exhibits, consists of the following number of pages:
3. a. Each plaintiff named above is a competent adult
      ☐ **except** plaintiff *(name):*
         (1) ☐ a corporation qualified to do business in California
         (2) ☐ an unincorporated entity *(describe):*
         (3) ☐ other *(specify):*

   b. ☐ Plaintiff *(name):*
      a. ☐ has complied with the fictitious business name laws and is doing business under the fictitious name *(specify):*

      b. ☐ has complied with all licensing requirements as a licensed *(specify):*
   c. ☐ Information about additional plaintiffs who are not competent adults is shown in Attachment 3c.
4. a. Each defendant named above is a natural person
      ☐ **except** defendant *(name):*   ☐ **except** defendant *(name):*
         (1) ☐ a business organization, form unknown   (1) ☐ a business organization, form unknown
         (2) ☐ a corporation   (2) ☐ a corporation
         (3) ☐ an unincorporated entity *(describe):*   (3) ☐ an unincorporated entity *(describe):*

         (4) ☐ a public entity *(describe):*   (4) ☐ a public entity *(describe):*

         (5) ☐ other *(specify):*   (5) ☐ other *(specify):*

* If this form is used as a cross-complaint, plaintiff means cross-complainant and defendant means cross-defendant.   **Page 1 of 2**

Form Approved for Optional Use
Judicial Council of California   **COMPLAINT—Contract**   Code of Civil Procedure, § 425.12
PLD-C-001 [Rev. January 1, 2007]

American LegalNet, Inc.
www.FormsWorkflow.com

Exhibit 6.2. Continued

	PLD-C-001
SHORT TITLE:	CASE NUMBER:

4. *(Continued)*

    b. The true names of defendants sued as Does are unknown to plaintiff.

        (1) ☐ Doe defendants *(specify Doe numbers):* _____ were the agents or employees of the named defendants and acted within the scope of that agency or employment.

        (2) ☐ Doe defendants *(specify Doe numbers):* _____ are persons whose capacities are unknown to plaintiff.

    c. ☐ Information about additional defendants who are not natural persons is contained in Attachment 4c.

    d. ☐ Defendants who are joined under Code of Civil Procedure section 382 are *(names):*

5. ☐ Plaintiff is required to comply with a claims statute, **and**

    a. ☐ has complied with applicable claims statutes, *or*

    b. ☐ is excused from complying because *(specify):*

6. ☐ This action is subject to ☐ Civil Code section 1812.10 ☐ Civil Code section 2984.4.

7. This court is the proper court because

    a. ☐ a defendant entered into the contract here.

    b. ☐ a defendant lived here when the contract was entered into.

    c. ☐ a defendant lives here now.

    d. ☐ the contract was to be performed here.

    e. ☐ a defendant is a corporation or unincorporated association and its principal place of business is here.

    f. ☐ real property that is the subject of this action is located here.

    g. ☐ other *(specify):*

8. The following causes of action are attached and the statements above apply to each *(each complaint must have one or more causes of action attached):*

    ☐ Breach of Contract

    ☐ Common Counts

    ☐ Other *(specify):*

9. ☐ Other allegations:

10. **Plaintiff prays** for judgment for costs of suit; for such relief as is fair, just, and equitable; and for

    a. ☐ damages of: $

    b. ☐ interest on the damages

        (1) ☐ according to proof

        (2) ☐ at the rate of *(specify):* percent per year from *(date):*

    c. ☐ attorney's fees

        (1) ☐ of: $

        (2) ☐ according to proof.

    d. ☐ other *(specify):*

11. ☐ The paragraphs of this pleading alleged on information and belief are as follows *(specify paragraph numbers):*

Date:

▶

_____   _____

           (TYPE OR PRINT NAME)   (SIGNATURE OF PLAINTIFF OR ATTORNEY)

(If you wish to verify this pleading, affix a verification.)

Exhibit 6.3. Breach of Contract Cause of Action

PLD-C-001(1)

SHORT TITLE:	CASE NUMBER:

CAUSE OF ACTION—Breach of Contract

_____
(number)

ATTACHMENT TO ☐ Complaint ☐ Cross - Complaint

(Use a separate cause of action form for each cause of action.)

BC-1. Plaintiff *(name):*

alleges that on or about *(date):*
a ☐ written ☐ oral ☐ other *(specify):*
agreement was made between *(name parties to agreement):*

☐ A copy of the agreement is attached as Exhibit A, or
☐ The essential terms of the agreement ☐ are stated in Attachment BC-1 ☐ are as follows *(specify):*

BC-2. On or about *(dates):*
defendant breached the agreement by ☐ the acts specified in Attachment BC-2 ☐ the following acts
(specify):

BC-3. Plaintiff has performed all obligations to defendant except those obligations plaintiff was prevented or
excused from performing.

BC-4. Plaintiff suffered damages legally (proximately) caused by defendant's breach of the agreement
☐ as stated in Attachment BC-4 ☐ as follows *(specify):*

BC-5. ☐ Plaintiff is entitled to attorney fees by an agreement or a statute
☐ of $
☐ according to proof.

BC-6. ☐ Other:

Page _____

Page 1 of 1

Form Approved for Optional Use
Judicial Council of California
PLD-C-001(1) [Rev. January 1, 2007]   **CAUSE OF ACTION—Breach of Contract**   Code of Civil Procedure, § 425.12
www.courtinfo.ca.gov

Exhibit 6.4. Form Complaint for Personal Injury

PLD-PI-001

ATTORNEY OR PARTY WITHOUT ATTORNEY *(Name, State Bar number, and address):*	FOR COURT USE ONLY
TELEPHONE NO: FAX NO. *(Optional):* E-MAIL ADDRESS *(Optional):* ATTORNEY FOR *(Name):*	

SUPERIOR COURT OF CALIFORNIA, COUNTY OF
STREET ADDRESS:
MAILING ADDRESS:
CITY AND ZIP CODE:
BRANCH NAME:

PLAINTIFF:

DEFENDANT:

☐ DOES 1 TO _____

COMPLAINT—Personal Injury, Property Damage, Wrongful Death
☐ **AMENDED** *(Number):*
Type *(check all that apply):*
☐ **MOTOR VEHICLE**   ☐ **OTHER** *(specify):*
     ☐ **Property Damage**   ☐ **Wrongful Death**
     ☐ **Personal Injury**   ☐ **Other Damages** *(specify):*

Jurisdiction *(check all that apply):*
☐ **ACTION IS A LIMITED CIVIL CASE**
  Amount demanded ☐ **does not exceed $10,000**
                ☐ **exceeds $10,000, but does not exceed $25,000**
☐ **ACTION IS AN UNLIMITED CIVIL CASE (exceeds $25,000)**
☐ **ACTION IS RECLASSIFIED by this amended complaint**
     ☐ **from limited to unlimited**
     ☐ **from unlimited to limited**

CASE NUMBER:

1. **Plaintiff** *(name or names):*

   alleges causes of action against **defendant** *(name or names):*

2. This pleading, including attachments and exhibits, consists of the following number of pages:

3. Each plaintiff named above is a competent adult
  a. ☐ **except plaintiff** *(name):*
     (1) ☐ a corporation qualified to do business in California
     (2) ☐ an unincorporated entity *(describe):*
     (3) ☐ a public entity *(describe):*
     (4) ☐ a minor ☐ an adult
        (a) ☐ for whom a guardian or conservator of the estate or a guardian ad litem has been appointed
        (b) ☐ other *(specify):*
     (5) ☐ other *(specify):*
  b. ☐ **except plaintiff** *(name):*
     (1) ☐ a corporation qualified to do business in California
     (2) ☐ an unincorporated entity *(describe):*
     (3) ☐ a public entity *(describe):*
     (4) ☐ a minor ☐ an adult
        (a) ☐ for whom a guardian or conservator of the estate or a guardian ad litem has been appointed
        (b) ☐ other *(specify):*
     (5) ☐ other *(specify):*

   ☐ Information about additional plaintiffs who are not competent adults is shown in Attachment 3.

Page 1 of 3

Form Approved for Optional Use Judicial Council of California PLD-PI-001 [Rev. January 1, 2007]	**COMPLAINT—Personal Injury, Property Damage, Wrongful Death**	Code of Civil Procedure, § 425.12 www.courtinfo.ca.gov American LegalNet, Inc. www.FormsWorkflow.com

Exhibit 6.4. Continued

PLD-PI-001

SHORT TITLE:	CASE NUMBER:

4. ☐ Plaintiff *(name)*:

is doing business under the fictitious name *(specify)*:

and has complied with the fictitious business name laws.

5. Each defendant named above is a natural person
   a. ☐ **except** defendant *(name)*:
      (1) ☐ a business organization, form unknown
      (2) ☐ a corporation
      (3) ☐ an unincorporated entity *(describe)*:

      (4) ☐ a public entity *(describe)*:

      (5) ☐ other *(specify)*:

   c. ☐ **except** defendant *(name)*:
      (1) ☐ a business organization, form unknown
      (2) ☐ a corporation
      (3) ☐ an unincorporated entity *(describe)*:

      (4) ☐ a public entity *(describe)*:

      (5) ☐ other *(specify)*:

   b. ☐ **except** defendant *(name)*:
      (1) ☐ a business organization, form unknown
      (2) ☐ a corporation
      (3) ☐ an unincorporated entity *(describe)*:

      (4) ☐ a public entity *(describe)*:

      (5) ☐ other *(specify)*:

   d. ☐ **except** defendant *(name)*:
      (1) ☐ a business organization, form unknown
      (2) ☐ a corporation
      (3) ☐ an unincorporated entity *(describe)*:

      (4) ☐ a public entity *(describe)*:

      (5) ☐ other *(specify)*:

   ☐ Information about additional defendants who are not natural persons is contained in Attachment 5.

6. The true names of defendants sued as Does are unknown to plaintiff.
   a. ☐ Doe defendants *(specify Doe numbers)*: _____ were the agents or employees of other named defendants and acted within the scope of that agency or employment.
   b. ☐ Doe defendants *(specify Doe numbers)*: _____ are persons whose capacities are unknown to plaintiff.

7. ☐ Defendants who are joined under Code of Civil Procedure section 382 are *(names)*:

8. This court is the proper court because
   a. ☐ at least one defendant now resides in its jurisdictional area.
   b. ☐ the principal place of business of a defendant corporation or unincorporated association is in its jurisdictional area.
   c. ☐ injury to person or damage to personal property occurred in its jurisdictional area.
   d. ☐ other *(specify)*:

9. ☐ Plaintiff is required to comply with a claims statute, **and**
   a. ☐ has complied with applicable claims statutes, **or**
   b. ☐ is excused from complying because *(specify)*:

PLD-PI-001 [Rev. January 1, 2007]	**COMPLAINT—Personal Injury, Property Damage, Wrongful Death**	Page 2 of 3

Exhibit 6.4. Continued

PLD-PI-001

SHORT TITLE:	CASE NUMBER:

10. The following causes of action are attached and the statements above apply to each *(each complaint must have one or more causes of action attached)*:
   a. ☐ Motor Vehicle
   b. ☐ General Negligence
   c. ☐ Intentional Tort
   d. ☐ Products Liability
   e. ☐ Premises Liability
   f. ☐ Other *(specify)*:

11. Plaintiff has suffered
   a. ☐ wage loss
   b. ☐ loss of use of property
   c. ☐ hospital and medical expenses
   d. ☐ general damage
   e. ☐ property damage
   f. ☐ loss of earning capacity
   g. ☐ other damage *(specify)*:

12. ☐ The damages claimed for wrongful death and the relationships of plaintiff to the deceased are
   a. ☐ listed in Attachment 12.
   b. ☐ as follows:

13. The relief sought in this complaint is within the jurisdiction of this court.

14. **Plaintiff prays** for judgment for costs of suit; for such relief as is fair, just, and equitable; and for
   a. (1) ☐ compensatory damages
      (2) ☐ punitive damages
   The amount of damages is *(in cases for personal injury or wrongful death, you must check (1))*:
   (1) ☐ according to proof
   (2) ☐ in the amount of: $

15. ☐ The paragraphs of this complaint alleged on information and belief are as follows *(specify paragraph numbers)*:

Date:

▶

_____
(TYPE OR PRINT NAME)

_____
(SIGNATURE OF PLAINTIFF OR ATTORNEY)

Exhibit 6.5. Prayer for Relief

> WHEREFORE, plaintiff demands judgment against defendant for the sum of $25,000, with interest and costs.
>
> WHEREFORE, plaintiff demands a preliminary and permanent injunction, an accounting for all damages, and interest and costs.
>
> WHEREFORE, plaintiff demands:
> 1. That defendant pay damages in the sum of $22,000;
> 2. That defendant be specifically ordered to perform his obligations under the contract;
> 3. That defendant pay interest, costs, and reasonable attorney's fees incurred by plaintiff.

C. FILING AND SERVICE OF SUMMONS

An action is commenced when the complaint is filed and the **summons** issued by the clerk of the court. A summons is the notice to the defendant that commands the defendant appear and defend against the action within a certain period of time or else judgment may be entered against the defendant. Code of Civil Procedure §412.20 provides a number of requirements for the content of the summons. However, use of the official form summons satisfies all the requirements. A copy of the official form summons is shown in Exhibit 6.6.

Summons
Notice accompanying the complaint that commands the defendant appear and defend against the action within a certain period of time

1. Issuing the summons

When the complaint is filed and all fees have been paid, the clerk will issue the summons. In practice, the summons form, which is available from the clerk's office, is usually filled out in advance and taken to the clerk's office when the complaint is filed. The clerk then "issues" the summons by signing and stamping it with the court seal, the date, and the case file number. Make sure that you have enough copies of the complaint and summons for the clerk's administrative needs, for service on each defendant, and for your law firm's files.

2. Persons who may serve the summons

Under CCP §414.10, the complaint and summons can be served by any person who is not a party and is at least 18 years old. Service by the certain peace officers, such as the sheriff or marshal, is allowed, but not

Exhibit 6.6.   Official Form Summons

SUM-100

SUMMONS
(CITACION JUDICIAL)

	FOR COURT USE ONLY *(SOLO PARA USO DE LA CORTE)*

NOTICE TO DEFENDANT:
(AVISO AL DEMANDADO):

YOU ARE BEING SUED BY PLAINTIFF:
(LO ESTÁ DEMANDANDO EL DEMANDANTE):

> You have 30 CALENDAR DAYS after this summons and legal papers are served on you to file a written response at this court and have a copy served on the plaintiff.   A letter or phone call will not protect you. Your written response must be in proper legal form if you want the court to hear your case. There may be a court form that you can use for your response. You can find these court forms and more information at the California Courts Online Self-Help Center (www.courtinfo.ca.gov/selfhelp), your county law library, or the courthouse nearest you. If you cannot pay the filing fee, ask the court clerk for a fee waiver form. If you do not file your response on time, you may lose the case by default, and your wages, money, and property may be taken without further warning from the court.
>
> There are other legal requirements. You may want to call an attorney right away. If you do not know an attorney, you may want to call an attorney referral service. If you cannot afford an attorney, you may be eligible for free legal services from a nonprofit legal services program. You can locate these nonprofit groups at the California Legal Services Web site (www.lawhelpcalifornia.org), the California Courts Online Self-Help Center (www.courtinfo.ca.gov/selfhelp), or by contacting your local court or county bar association.
>
> *Tiene 30 DÍAS DE CALENDARIO después de que le entreguen esta citación y papeles legales para presentar una respuesta por escrito en esta corte y hacer que se entregue una copia al demandante. Una carta o una llamada telefónica no lo protegen. Su respuesta por escrito tiene que estar en formato legal correcto si desea que procesen su caso en la corte. Es posible que haya un formulario que usted pueda usar para su respuesta. Puede encontrar estos formularios de la corte y más información en el Centro de Ayuda de las Cortes de California (www.courtinfo.ca.gov/selfhelp/espanol/), en la biblioteca de leyes de su condado o en la corte que le quede más cerca. Si no puede pagar la cuota de presentación, pida al secretario de la corte que le dé un formulario de exención de pago de cuotas. Si no presenta su respuesta a tiempo, puede perder el caso por incumplimiento y la corte le podrá quitar su sueldo, dinero y bienes sin más advertencia.*
>
> *Hay otros requisitos legales. Es recomendable que llame a un abogado inmediatamente. Si no conoce a un abogado, puede llamar a un servicio de remisión a abogados. Si no puede pagar a un abogado, es posible que cumpla con los requisitos para obtener servicios legales gratuitos de un programa de servicios legales sin fines de lucro. Puede encontrar estos grupos sin fines de lucro en el sitio web de California Legal Services, (www.lawhelpcalifornia.org), en el Centro de Ayuda de las Cortes de California, (www.courtinfo.ca.gov/selfhelp/espanol/) o poniéndose en contacto con la corte o el colegio de abogados locales.*

The name and address of the court is: *(El nombre y dirección de la corte es):*	**CASE NUMBER:** *(Número del Caso):*

The name, address, and telephone number of plaintiff's attorney, or plaintiff without an attorney, is:
(El nombre, la dirección y el número de teléfono del abogado del demandante, o del demandante que no tiene abogado, es):

DATE: *(Fecha)*	Clerk, by _____ , Deputy *(Secretario)* *(Adjunto)*

(For proof of service of this summons, use Proof of Service of Summons (form POS-010).)
(Para prueba de entrega de esta citatión use el formulario Proof of Service of Summons, (POS-010)).

[SEAL]

NOTICE TO THE PERSON SERVED: You are served
1. ☐ as an individual defendant.
2. ☐ as the person sued under the fictitious name of *(specify):*

3. ☐ on behalf of *(specify):*

    under: ☐ CCP 416.10 (corporation)   ☐ CCP 416.60 (minor)
           ☐ CCP 416.20 (defunct corporation) ☐ CCP 416.70 (conservatee)
           ☐ CCP 416.40 (association or partnership) ☐ CCP 416.90 (authorized person)
           ☐ other *(specify):*
4. ☐ by personal delivery on *(date):*

Page 1 of 1

Form Adopted for Mandatory Use Judicial Council of California SUM-100 [Rev. January 1, 2004]	**SUMMONS**	Code of Civil Procedure §§ 412.20, 465 American LegalNet, Inc. www.USCourtForms.com

required. It is not necessary to have the complaint and summons served by a professional process server.

3. Methods of service

Service of summons may be made depending on the entity being served.

a. Individuals

An individual can be served a summons in several ways. First, service can be made by personally giving the individual a copy of the complaint and summons. Second, it can be made by leaving a copy of the complaint and summons "at such person's dwelling house, usual place of abode, usual place of business, or usual mailing address" other than a post office address, with a person at least 18 years of age. Third, service can be made on an agent authorized by law to receive service on his behalf. Fourth, service can be made by mail, together with two copies of the notice and acknowledgment of receipt. Exhibit 6.7 is a sample of the notice of acknowledgment and receipt. Fifth, where the individual is out of state, service may be made by first class mail, return receipt requested. Finally, if the court so orders, service may be by publication in a newspaper of general circulation. However, this method is generally only used if no other method of service is available.

The preferred method of serving the summons is by personal service. Pursuant to CCP §415.10, service under this method is deemed complete upon the delivery. Service by leaving a copy with another person and thereafter mailing a copy, is not deemed complete until the tenth day after the mailing. In the case of notice of acknowledgment, when and if the defendant executes the acknowledgment of receipt and returns it to the plaintiff.

b. Minors, wards, and conservatees

Service on minors, wards, and conservatees is made by serving the parents, in the case of minors, or in the case of all three, on the guardian, conservator, or other appointed fiduciary.

c. Corporations, partnerships, and associations

Service on domestic and foreign corporations, partnerships, and unincorporated associations that can be sued in their own name can be made in several ways. First, service can be made by personal delivery to an officer, manager, or general agent. Second, service can be made to an agent authorized to receive service of process; the list of domestic and

Exhibit 6.7.   Acknowledgment and Receipt

982(a)(4)

NAME AND ADDRESS OF **SENDER**:	TELEPHONE NO.:	For Court Use Only:

Insert name of court, judicial district or branch court, if any, and Post Office and Street Address:

PLAINTIFF:

DEFENDANT:

NOTICE AND ACKNOWLEDGMENT OF RECEIPT	Case Number:

TO: . . . .
(Insert name of individual being served)

This summons and other document(s) indicated below are being served pursuant to Section 415.30 of the California Code of Civil Procedure. Your failure to complete this form and return it to me within 20 days may subject you (or the party on whose behalf you are being served) to liability for the payment of any expenses incurred in serving a summons on you in any other manner permitted by law.

If you are being served on behalf of a corporation, unincorporated association (including a partnership), or other entity, this form must be signed by you in the name of such entity or by a person authorized to receive service of process on behalf of such entity. In all other cases, this form must be signed by you personally or by a person authorized by you to acknowledge receipt of summons. Section 415.30 provides that this summons and other document(s) are deemed served on the date you sign the Acknowledgment of Receipt below, if you return this form to me.

Dated: . . . .   _____
(Signature of sender)

ACKNOWLEDGMENT OF RECEIPT

This acknowledges receipt of: (To be completed by sender before mailing)
1. ☐ A copy of the summons and of the complaint.
2. ☐ A copy of the summons and of the Petition (Marriage) and:
   ☐ Blank Confidential Counseling Statement (Marriage)
   ☐ Order to Show Cause (Marriage)
   ☐ Blank Responsive Declaration
   ☐ Blank Financial Declaration
   ☐ Other: (Specify)

(To be completed by recipient)

Date of receipt: . . . .   _____
(Signature of person acknowledging receipt, with title if
acknowledgment is made on behalf of another person)

Date this form is signed: . . . .   _____
(Type or print your name and name of entity, if any,
on whose behalf this form is signed)

Form Adopted by the Judicial Council of California Revised Effective January 1, 1975 [982(a)(4)] Mandatory Form	**NOTICE AND ACKNOWLEDGMENT OF RECEIPT**	CCP 415.30, 417.10; Cal. Rules of Court, Rule 1216

American LegalNet, Inc.
www.USCourtForms.com

foreign corporations, compiled by the California secretary of state shows the authorized agent for process. Third, when the corporation is out of state, service can be made the same as with an individual, by first class mail, return receipt requested. Again, however, service by personal delivery is preferable.

d. Officers and agencies of the state and municipal government organizations

Code of Civil Procedure §416.50 details the requirements for service on public entities. The summons may be served by delivering a copy to the "clerk, secretary, president, presiding officer, or other head of its governing body."

In addition, before filing a complaint against a public entity, claim statutes must be followed. Government Code §910 et seq. provides a detailed set of rules to follow in presenting claims and time limits. Before serving the lawsuits, ensure that all claims procedures have been followed.

4. Timeliness of service

Under CCP §583.210, dismissal of the complaint is mandatory if the defendant has not been served with the summons and complaint within three years after the complaint has been filed. Under CCP §583.420(a)(1), dismissal is discretionary with the court if the defendant has not been served within two years. These time periods are substantially longer than for complaints filed in federal courts. In federal court cases, the summons and complaint must be served within 120 days after the complaint has been filed.

Be aware, fast track rules, where individual courts accelerate the time requirements are in effect in virtually every county in California. Some judges will threaten to dismiss a case if it is not served within 60 days after filing. In some courts, such as Marin County, local fast-track rules require the plaintiff to appear in court 75 days after the summons is issued to explain why the defendant has not yet been served. Always check your local court rules to ensure timelines of service.

5. Proof of service

Code of Civil Procedure §417.10 requires that the person serving process establish **proof of service.** Proof must be in affidavit form. In practice, the proof of service affidavit is usually found on the summons form. The person serving the summons and complaint should fill in the proof of service affidavit and return it to you for filing with the court. An example is shown in Exhibit 6.8.

Exhibit 6.8.   Proof of Service Affidavit

POS-010

ATTORNEY OR PARTY WITHOUT ATTORNEY *(Name, State Bar number, and address):*	*FOR COURT USE ONLY*
TELEPHONE NO.: FAX NO. *(Optional):*	
E–MAIL ADDRESS *(Optional):*	
ATTORNEY FOR *(Name):*	

SUPERIOR COURT OF CALIFORNIA, COUNTY OF
STREET ADDRESS:
MAILING ADDRESS:
CITY AND ZIP CODE:
BRANCH NAME:

PLAINTIFF/PETITIONER:	CASE NUMBER:
DEFENDANT/RESPONDENT:	
PROOF OF SERVICE OF SUMMONS	Ref. No. or File No.:

(Separate proof of service is required for each party served.)

1.   At the time of service I was at least 18 years of age and not a party to this action.

2.   I served copies of:

   a. ☐   summons

   b. ☐   complaint

   c. ☐   Alternative Dispute Resolution (ADR) package

   d. ☐   Civil Case Cover Sheet *(served in complex cases only)*

   e. ☐   cross-complaint

   f. ☐   other *(specify documents):*

3.   a. Party served *(specify name of party as shown on documents served):*

   b. ☐   Person (other than the party in item 3a) served on behalf of an entity or as an authorized agent (and not a person under item 5b on whom substituted service was made) *(specify name and relationship to the party named in item 3a):*

4.   Address where the party was served:

5.   I served the party *(check proper box)*

   a. ☐   **by personal service.** I personally delivered the documents listed in item 2 to the party or person authorized to receive service of process for the party (1) on *(date):*   (2) at *(time):*

   b. ☐   **by substituted service.** On *(date):*   at *(time):*   I left the documents listed in item 2 with or in the presence of *(name and title or relationship to person indicated in item 3):*

     (1) ☐   **(business)** a person at least 18 years of age apparently in charge at the office or usual place of business of the person to be served. I informed him or her of the general nature of the papers.

     (2) ☐   **(home)** a competent member of the household (at least 18 years of age) at the dwelling house or usual place of abode of the party. I informed him or her of the general nature of the papers.

     (3) ☐   **(physical address unknown)** a person at least 18 years of age apparently in charge at the usual mailing address of the person to be served, other than a United States Postal Service post office box. I informed him or her of the general nature of the papers.

     (4) ☐   I thereafter mailed (by first-class, postage prepaid) copies of the documents to the person to be served at the place where the copies were left (Code Civ. Proc., § 415.20). I mailed the documents on *(date):*   from *(city):*   or ☐   a declaration of mailing is attached.

     (5) ☐   I attach a **declaration of diligence** stating actions taken first to attempt personal service.

Page 1 of 2

Form Adopted for Mandatory Use Judicial Council of California POS-010 [Rev. January 1, 2007]	**PROOF OF SERVICE OF SUMMONS**	Code of Civil Procedure, § 417.10 American LegalNet, Inc. www.FormsWorkflow.com

Exhibit 6.8. Continued

PLAINTIFF/PETITIONER:	CASE NUMBER:
DEFENDANT/RESPONDENT:	

5. c. ☐ **by mail and acknowledgment of receipt of service.** I mailed the documents listed in item 2 to the party, to the address shown in item 4, by first-class mail, postage prepaid,

    (1) on *(date):*   (2) from *(city):*

    (3) ☐ with two copies of the *Notice and Acknowledgment of Receipt* and a postage-paid return envelope addressed to me. *(Attach completed* Notice and Acknowledgement of Receipt.*)* (Code Civ. Proc., § 415.30.)

    (4) ☐ to an address outside California with return receipt requested. (Code Civ. Proc., § 415.40.)

  d. ☐ **by other means** *(specify means of service and authorizing code section):*

    ☐ Additional page describing service is attached.

6. The "Notice to the Person Served" (on the summons) was completed as follows:
  a. ☐ as an individual defendant.
  b. ☐ as the person sued under the fictitious name of *(specify):*
  c. ☐ as occupant.
  d. ☐ On behalf of *(specify):*
    under the following Code of Civil Procedure section:

    ☐ 416.10 (corporation)   ☐ 415.95 (business organization, form unknown)
    ☐ 416.20 (defunct corporation)   ☐ 416.60 (minor)
    ☐ 416.30 (joint stock company/association)   ☐ 416.70 (ward or conservatee)
    ☐ 416.40 (association or partnership)   ☐ 416.90 (authorized person)
    ☐ 416.50 (public entity)   ☐ 415.46 (occupant)
        ☐ other:

7. **Person who served papers**
  a. Name:
  b. Address:
  c. Telephone number:
  d. **The fee** for service was: $
  e. I am:
    (1) ☐ not a registered California process server.
    (2) ☐ exempt from registration under Business and Professions Code section 22350(b).
    (3) ☐ a registered California process server:
      (i) ☐ owner ☐ employee ☐ independent contractor.
      (ii) Registration No.:
      (iii) County:

8. ☐ **I declare** under penalty of perjury under the laws of the State of California that the foregoing is true and correct.

    or

9. ☐ **I am a California sheriff or marshal and** I certify that the foregoing is true and correct.

Date:

▶

_____   _____
(NAME OF PERSON WHO SERVED PAPERS/SHERIFF OR MARSHAL)   (SIGNATURE)

POS-010 [Rev. January 1, 2007]   **PROOF OF SERVICE OF SUMMONS**   Page 2 of 2

6. Service by mail

Sometimes you will know the lawyer who will represent the defendant in the lawsuit. You or the lawyer in charge may have already had contact with the defendant's lawyer before filing suit, or you may know the lawyer who regularly handles the defendant's legal matters. In such instances, a good practice is for you or the lawyer to call the defendant's lawyer and let her know that your client is about to file suit. Ask her if she will accept service of process and acknowledge receipt on behalf of the defendant. See CCP §415.30. If so, simply deliver or mail the complaint to her.

   If you think the defendant will try to avoid service of process or contest the validity of service, serve the defendant formally. Otherwise, informal service can be a convenient approach; it is frequently used in commercial litigation with corporate parties.

D. ANSWERS

When the plaintiff's complaint has been served, every defendant must respond, either by filing one of the types of motions that extends a defendant's time to answer (discussed in Chapter 9) or by filing an **answer** to the complaint. The answer admits or denies the various allegations in the complaint and usually asserts a number of defenses. An example appears in the Litigation File at the end of the book.

1. Timing

As a general rule, under CCP §412.20(a)(3) the defendant must serve an answer within 30 days of service of the complaint and summons.

2. General requirements

As with complaints, there are several rules that regulate the form and content of the answer. Rule 2.100 of the CRC provides for the general form of the papers that are presented for filing. Local rules, however, should also be consulted. In general, the answer must either admit or deny the allegations, or state that the defendant is without sufficient knowledge or information to form a belief as to their truth. The defendant should go through each allegation of the complaint and plead a response. Since a complaint must be answered, failing to answer will constitute an admission of all facts alleged in the complaint; this does not apply, however, to the prayer for relief.

To parallel the complaint, the answer should be organized in paragraphs and by causes of action, with the defenses to each cause of action identified at the end of the response to allegations. When there is only one defendant, the answer is simply titled "<u>ANSWER</u>." If there are multiple defendants, however, the title should specify the party answering, for example, "<u>ANSWER OF DEFENDANT ACME TOOL CORPORATION</u>."

The answer, therefore, may have three parts:

♦ Responses of the complaint's allegations
♦ Affirmative defenses
♦ Defendant's prayer for relief.

A well-drafted answer will set out each part clearly.

3. Specific denials

There are two types of answers to a complaint, a general denial and a specific denial. If the answer is a specific denial, it may either admit or deny the allegations, or state that the party is without sufficient knowledge or information to form a belief as to their truth.

If the response is "no knowledge or belief," this must be based on good faith. Such a response should not be available on matters that are common knowledge or that can easily be learned by the defendant. For example, if the complaint alleges that the defendant corporation had "gross receipts during 2008 in the amount of $6,450,000," the defendant's lawyer cannot answer "no knowledge or belief" since the lawyer can easily find out if the allegation is true or not.

The answer may admit only part of an allegation and deny the remainder or may admit having no knowledge or information as to the remainder, whichever the case may be. Each paragraph of the complaint must be responded to individually unless the defendant can, in good faith, collectively deny every allegation of the complaint. Sample responses are shown in Exhibits 6.9 and 6.10.

Within these guidelines there is considerable drafting flexibility. The trend is toward brevity and conciseness. The standard approach is to simply have causes of action and numbered paragraphs corresponding to the causes of action and paragraphs of the complaint. However, it is just as effective to set out admissions, denials, and no-knowledge-or-information responses collectively when the situation is appropriate. If the complaint incorporates several paragraphs in the first count, the

Exhibit 6.9. *Sample Answer*

[Caption]

ANSWER

Defendant Jones answers the complaint as follows:
1. Defendant admits the allegations in paragraph 1 of the complaint.
2. Defendant admits the allegations in paragraph 2.
3. Defendant denies each and every allegation in paragraph 3 of the complaint.
4. Defendant denies each and every allegation in paragraph 4 of the complaint.
5. Defendant is without knowledge or information sufficient to form a belief as to the truth of the allegations in paragraph 5 of the complaint, and therefore denies each and every allegation contained therein.

Exhibit 6.10. *Sample Response*

1. Defendant admits he is a citizen of the State of California, but denies the remaining allegations in paragraph 1 of the complaint.
2. With respect to paragraph 2 of the complaint, defendant admits he entered into a written contract with plaintiff on June 1, 2005, but denies that the contract was modified under an agreement on August 1, 2005, or on any other date.
3. Defendant denies he owned and operated a business known as Jones Excavating in 2005 or any other year. Defendant does not have sufficient knowledge or information to form a belief as to the truth of the other allegations in paragraph 3, and therefore denies each and every remaining allegation contained therein.

Exhibit 6.11. Sample Cause of Action

<u>First Cause of Action</u>

1. Defendant admits the allegations of paragraphs 1, 2, 3, 4, 5, and 6 of the complaint.

2. Defendant denies the allegations of paragraphs 8, 9, and 10 of the complaint.

3. Defendant is without knowledge or information sufficient to form a belief as to the truth of the allegations in paragraph 7 of the complaint and therefore denies each and every allegation contained therein.

<u>Second Cause of Action</u>

1. Defendant incorporates her answers to paragraphs 1-3 of Count I as if fully set forth.

2. Defendant denies all other allegations of the complaint not specifically admitted.

answer can do the same. A response following this format is shown in Exhibit 6.11. Denying all allegations not specifically admitted is a safe practice, since this prevents a typographical error in the answer from prejudicing the client. The California Judicial Council has adopted optional use form answers that can be used in certain cases. The form answer contains the format for admitting and denying allegations and already includes a number of defenses. A copy of the form for an answer is shown in Exhibit 6.12.

When there are multiple defendants, not every allegation in the complaint must be responded to since not every cause of action, or every paragraph in a cause of action, will contain an allegation directed at the defendant your law office is representing. Where the lawyer represents one defendant in a case that has multiple defendants, and some causes of action or paragraphs do not apply to that defendant, the usual practice is to point this out in the answer. This avoids the possibility of "silence" in the answer being interpreted as an admission. Paragraphs like those in the following two examples can be incorporated into your answer to point out claims that do not apply to your client.

Exhibit 6.12. Form Answer

PLD-PI-003

ATTORNEY OR PARTY WITHOUT ATTORNEY *(NAME AND ADDRESS)*: TELEPHONE NO.:	FOR COURT USE ONLY

ATTORNEY FOR *(NAME)*:

Insert name of court, judicial district or branch court, if any, and post office and street address:

PLAINTIFF:

DEFENDANT:

ANSWER—Personal Injury, Property Damage, Wrongful Death
   ☐ **COMPLAINT OF (name):**
   ☐ **CROSS-COMPLAINT OF** *(name):*

CASE NUMBER:

1. This pleading, including attachments and exhibits, consists of the following number of pages: _____

DEFENDANT OR CROSS-DEFENDANT *(name)*:

2. ☐ Generally **denies** each allegation of the unverified complaint or cross-complaint.

3 a. ☐ DENIES each allegation of the following numbered paragraphs:

  b. ☐ ADMITS each allegation of the following numbered paragraphs:

  c. ☐ DENIES, ON INFORMATION AND BELIEF, each allegation of the following numbered paragraphs:

  d. ☐ DENIES, BECAUSE OF LACK OF SUFFICIENT INFORMATION OR BELIEF TO ANSWER, each allegation of the following numbered paragraphs:

  e. ☐ ADMITS the following allegations and generally denies all other allegations:

Page 1 of 2

Form Approved for Optional Use Judicial Council of California PLD-PI-003 [Rev. January 1, 2007]	**ANSWER—Personal Injury, Property Damage, Wrongful Death**	Code of Civil Procedure, § 425.12 *www.courtinfo.ca.gov*

American LegalNet, Inc.
www.FormsWorkflow.com

Exhibit 6.12. Continued

SHORT TITLE:	CASE NUMBER:

ANSWER—Personal Injury, Property Damage, Wrongful Death

f. ☐ DENIES the following allegations and admits all other allegations:

g. ☐ Other *(specify)*:

AFFIRMATIVELY ALLEGES AS A DEFENSE

4. ☐ The comparative fault of plaintiff or cross-complainant *(name)*:
    as follows:

5. ☐ The expiration of the Statute of Limitations as follows:

6. ☐ Other *(specify)*:

7. DEFENDANT OR CROSS - DEFENDANT PRAYS
    For costs of suit and that plaintiff or cross-complainant take nothing.
    ☐ Other *(specify)*:

_____   _____
        (Type or print name)   (Signature of party or attorney)

Example

<u>Second Cause of Action</u>
The allegations in this cause of action are not directed to this defendant and accordingly no response by this defendant is made to the cause of action. In the event it is ever determined that this cause of action is directed to this defendant, this defendant reserves his right to respond to this cause of action.

Example

12.   The allegations in paragraph 12 of plaintiff's complaint are not directed toward this defendant, so this defendant makes no answer to the allegations.

---

4. General denials

In some cases, a defendant may generally deny all allegations of a complaint. The Judicial Council has developed a General Denial form. A copy of the General Denial form is shown in Exhibit 6.13. A general denial may be used in a limited civil case and if the Complaint is not verified by the plaintiff. Otherwise, a defendant must use a specific denial format. In some cases, you may wish to use a specific denial format even if the complaint is not verified because a general denial "only puts in issue the material allegations of the complaint." CCP §431.30(d). Material allegations are any allegations that are essential to the claim or defense. Thus, the allegation that the defendant ran a red light which caused the accident is a material allegation, since that alleged fact goes to help prove the defendant was negligent. The allegation that the defendant was driving a blue car at the time of the accident is an immaterial allegation.

5. Affirmative defenses

Affirmative defense
Defense pled by the defendant in the answer that, if proven, denies recovery to the plaintiff

An **affirmative defense** is an allegation by the defendant that raises new matters or defects in the plaintiff's case not otherwise in issue by defendant's denial of an allegation in the complaint. Even if plaintiff proves the allegations of her complaint, an affirmative defense entitles the defendant to have judgment in his favor. The defenses must be stated separately and must indicate the cause of action which they intend to answer. CCP §431.30(g). The CCP provides some of the

Exhibit 6.13. General Denial Form

PLD-050

| ATTORNEY OR PARTY WITHOUT ATTORNEY *(Name, State Bar number, and address):* | TELEPHONE NO. | FOR COURT USE ONLY |

ATTORNEY FOR *(Name):*

NAME OF COURT:
STREET ADDRESS:
MAILING ADDRESS:
CITY AND ZIP CODE:
BRANCH NAME:

PLAINTIFF:

DEFENDANT:

GENERAL DENIAL

CASE NUMBER:

You MUST use this form for your general denial if the amount asked for in the complaint or the value of the property involved is $1000 or less.

You MAY use this form if:

1. The complaint is not verified, OR

2. The complaint is verified, and the action is subject to the economic litigation procedures of the municipal and justice courts, EXCEPT

You MAY NOT use this form if the complaint is verified and involves a claim for more than $1000 that has been assigned to a third party for collection.

(See Code of Civil Procedure sections 90–100, 431.30, and 431.40).

---

1. DEFENDANT (name):
   generally denies each and every allegation of plaintiff's complaint.

2. ☐ DEFENDANT states the following FACTS as separate affirmative defenses to plaintiff's complaint *(attach additional pages if necessary):*

Date:

▶

....
(TYPE OR PRINT NAME)   (SIGNATURE OF DEFENDANT OR ATTORNEY)

If you have a claim for damages or other relief against the plaintiff, the law may require you to state your claim in a special pleading called a cross-complaint or you may lose your claim. (See Code of Civil Procedure sections 426.10–426.40.)

The original of this General Denial must be filed with the clerk of this court with proof that a copy was served on each plaintiff's attorney and on each plaintiff not represented by an attorney. *(See the other side for a proof of service.)*

Page 1 of 2

Form Adopted for Mandatory Use
Judicial Council of California
PLD-050 [Rev. January 1, 2007]

GENERAL DENIAL

Code Civ. Procedure, §§ 431.30, 431.40
www.courtinfo.ca.gov

American LegalNet, Inc.
www.FormsWorkflow.com

Exhibit 6.13. Continued

PLD-050

PLAINTIFF *(name)*:	CASE NUMBER:
DEFENDANT *(name)*:	

PROOF OF SERVICE
☐ **Personal Service**   ☐ **Mail**

> A General Denial may be served by anyone at least 18 years of age EXCEPT you or any other party to this legal action. Service is made in one of the following ways:
> (1) Personally delivering a copy to the attorney for the other party or, if no attorney, to the other party.
> **OR**
> (2) Mailing a copy, postage prepaid, to the last known address of the attorney for the other party or, if no attorney, to the other party.
> Be sure whoever serves the General Denial fills out and signs a proof of service. File the proof of service with the court as soon as the General Denial is served.

1. At the time of service I was at least 18 years of age and **not a party to this legal action.**

2. I served a copy of the General Denial as follows *(check either a or b)*:

    a. ☐ **Personal service.** I personally delivered the General Denial as follows:
        (1) Name of person served:
        (2) Address where served:

        (3) Date served:
        (4) Time served:

    b. ☐ **Mail.** I deposited the General Denial in the United States mail, in a sealed envelope with postage fully prepaid. The envelope was addressed and mailed as follows:
        (1) Name of person served:
        (2) Address:

        (3) Date of mailing:
        (4) Place of mailing *(city and state)*:
        (5) I am a resident of or employed in the county where the General Denial was mailed.

    c. My residence or business address is *(specify)*:

    d. My phone number is *(specify)*:

I declare under penalty of perjury under the laws of the State of California that the foregoing is true and correct.

Date:

▶

....
(TYPE OR PRINT NAME OF PERSON WHO SERVED THE GENERAL DENIAL)   (SIGNATURE OF PERSON WHO SERVED THE GENERAL DENIAL)

PLD-050 [Rev. January 1, 2007]

GENERAL DENIAL
(Proof of Service)

Page 2 of 2

grounds upon which a denial can be made. In addition, by researching the substantive law for the causes of action alleged by the plaintiff you will find a number of other defenses that may be alleged by the defendant.[2] Some defenses may be raised by a demurrer (a motion filed by the defendant before an answer is filed that challenges the sufficiency of the pleadings) or in the answer. CCP §430.10 lists the grounds which may be raised by an answer or demurrer. These grounds challenge the sufficiency of the pleading which must be overcome by the plaintiff before the defendant is required to answer. These defenses include:

- The court has no subject matter jurisdiction
- The plaintiff does not have legal capacity to sue
- There is another action pending between the same parties on the same causes of action
- There is a defect or misjoinder of parties
- The pleading does not state facts sufficient to constitute a cause of action
- The pleading is uncertain
- In a cause of action for contract it cannot be ascertained whether the contract is oral, written, or implied

An affirmative defense based upon one of these causes of action may look like this:

Example

FIRST AFFIRMATIVE DEFENSE TO ALL CAUSES OF ACTION

The complaint fails to state a claim against the defendant on which relief can be granted.

SECOND AFFIRMATIVE DEFENSE TO THE SECOND CAUSE OF ACTION

The second cause of action alleges breach of contract yet it cannot be ascertained whether the contract is oral, written, or implied.

---

2. As a practical matter, many paralegals and practitioners use sources such as Witkins Summary of the Law and California BAJI (Book of Approved Jury Instructions) to ascertain a number of affirmative defenses that may be made.

Other common affirmative defenses include the following:

Contract Actions:

- ◆ The statute of limitations has run (two years for oral contract, and four years for written)
- ◆ Statute of Frauds (certain contracts must be in writing to be enforceable)
- ◆ Mistake (either by one party or both)
- ◆ Satisfaction (obligation has been paid)
- ◆ Failure of performance (plaintiff has failed to perform their part of the contract)
- ◆ Waiver (plaintiff has waived the right to require performance by defendant)
- ◆ Duress (the defendant was under duress in signing the contract)
- ◆ Fraud (plaintiff fraudulently induced the defendant to enter into the contract)

Negligence Actions:

- ◆ Statute of limitations (one year for personal injury)
- ◆ Comparative fault (plaintiff was also negligent)
- ◆ Assumption of Risk (plaintiff was aware of risk and knowingly assumed the risk)

As you can see there are a number of affirmative defenses that can be alleged depending on the type of cases and facts available. Just as plaintiffs must do factual investigation to determine the causes of action that exist, defendants also will have to conduct a factual investigation to determine what defenses may be alleged.

Example

FIRST AFFIRMATIVE DEFENSE TO SECOND CAUSE OF ACTION

Plaintiff's cause of action set out in the complaint did not occur within two years before commencement of this action and is thus barred by the applicable statute of limitations.

SECOND AFFIRMATIVE DEFENSE TO THIRD CAUSE OF ACTION

Plaintiff's cause of action is barred by the doctrine of waiver since plaintiff agreed not to require further performance by the defendant.

6. Prayer for relief

After the affirmative defenses are stated, the defendant will list his prayer for relief. However, unlike the plaintiff, the defendant cannot, in the answer, ask for an affirmative relief. Affirmative relief is what the party is entitled to from the defendant, such as money, specific performance, etc. However, it is common practice for the defendant to include a prayer at the end of the answer as well. An example is as follows:

Example

WHEREFORE the defendant prays that the court dismiss the action, that the plaintiff receive nothing and that defendant be awarded his cost of suit and attorneys fees and such other relief as the court may deem just and proper.

Although a prevailing party in any action is entitled to their costs of suit (such as filing fees and certain other fees provided by statute) the prevailing party is only entitled to attorney's fees if allowed by statute or if provided in a written contract between the parties. Accordingly, you would only request attorney's fees if you had grounds to do so. Costs and attorney's fees are not considered "affirmative relief" and may be requested in the defendant's prayer for relief.

7. Practice approach

Drafting answers to complaints involves two basic considerations. First, you and the lawyer should respond to every allegation in every paragraph of every cause of action of the complaint, since any allegation not responded to is deemed admitted. A safe practice is to deny, at the end of every count, all allegations not specifically admitted or otherwise answered. Where the allegations are admitted in part and denied in part, make sure that the answer clearly states the facts being admitted and clearly denies all remaining allegations. Clear, simple language is critical here.

Second, set out all the affirmative defenses that you and the lawyer can raise in good faith. There is no penalty for raising inconsistent or alternative defenses. If you are in doubt whether a defense is considered an affirmative defense, the safer course is to raise it in the answer. The real danger is that you fail to raise a defense resulting in it being waived. If you and the lawyer need additional time to study potential defenses, it is better to move for additional time to respond than to serve a hastily considered answer.

Remember also, that if a complaint is verified, the defendant must also verify his answer.

E. CROSS-CLAIMS

In addition to the answer, a defendant can also file a **cross-complaint.** There are three types of cross-complaints. The first is a pleading brought against a plaintiff within the time the defendant has to answer. If the defendant requests affirmative relief from the plaintiff, the defendant must seek such relief by way of a cross-complaint. For example, in an automobile accident where both parties are alleging the other party is at fault, whichever party files first would file the initial complaint against the defendant. However, the defendant may file a cross-complaint to also seek relief against the plaintiff.

The second type of cross-complaint is one the defendant files against a co-defendant. For example, suppose the defendant believes that the true party at fault is one of the other defendants. The defendant could file the cross-complaint against the other defendant seeking affirmative relief from that defendant.

The third type of cross-complaint is where the defendant files against a party that is not currently a defendant in the lawsuit. The defendant's cross-complaint has the effect of bringing the other party into the lawsuit.

In federal court, each of the three types of cross-complaints has a different name. The complaint back against the defendant is called a "counterclaim," the complaint against a co-defendant is called a "cross-complaint," and the complaint against an outside party is called a "third-party complaint." However, in California, all three types are called the same thing.

The cross-complaint is functionally identical to a complaint. The analytical approach and the pleading strategy for the cross-complaint are the same as for a complaint. The plaintiff, co-defendant, or third party must respond to the cross-complaint, either with an appropriate motion, such as a demurrer, or by answer within the usual time limits. Cross-complaints are either compulsory or permissive, and substantially different rules apply to each. A form cross-complaint is shown in Exhibit 6.14.

1. Compulsory cross-complaints

Compulsory cross-complaints governed by CCP §426.10 et seq., are claims that a defendant is required to bring against the plaintiff. The purpose of the compulsory cross-complaint rule is clear: If the court

Exhibit 6.14. Cross-Complaint

PLD-PI-002

ATTORNEY OR PARTY WITHOUT ATTORNEY *(Name, state bar number, and address):*	FOR COURT USE ONLY

TELEPHONE NO: FAX NO. *(Optional):*

E-MAIL ADDRESS *(Optional):*

ATTORNEY FOR *(Name):*

NAME OF COURT:

STREET ADDRESS:

MAILING ADDRESS:

CITY AND ZIP CODE:

BRANCH NAME:

SHORT TITLE:

CROSS-COMPLAINANT:

CROSS-DEFENDANT:

☐ DOES 1 TO _____

CROSS-COMPLAINT—Personal Injury, Property Damage, Wrongful Death
    ☐ **AMENDED** *(Number):*

Causes of Action *(check all that apply):*
☐ **Apportionment of Fault**   ☐ **Declaratory Relief**
☐ **Indemnification**   ☐ **Other** *(specify):*

Jurisdiction *(check all that apply):*
☐ **ACTION IS A LIMITED CIVIL CASE ($25,000 or less)**
☐ **ACTION IS AN UNLIMITED CIVIL CASE (exceeds $25,000)**
   It ☐ **is** ☐ **is not reclassified as unlimited by this cross-complaint**

CASE NUMBER:

1. CROSS-COMPLAINANT *(name):*

   alleges causes of action against CROSS-DEFENDANT *(name):*

2. This pleading, including exhibits and attachments, consists of the following number of pages: _____

3. Each cross-complainant named above is a competent adult
   a. ☐ **except** cross-complainant *(name):*
       (1) ☐ a corporation qualified to do business in California
       (2) ☐ an unincorporated entity *(describe):*
       (3) ☐ a public entity *(describe):*
       (4) ☐ a minor ☐ an adult
          (a) ☐ for whom a guardian or conservator of the estate or a guardian ad litem has been appointed
          (b) ☐ other *(specify):*
       (5) ☐ other *(specify):*

   ☐ Information about additional cross-complainants who are not competent adults is contained in
   Cross-Complaint—Attachment 3.

Page 1 of 3

Form Approved for Optional Use Judicial Council of California PLD-PI-002 [Rev. January 1, 2007]	**CROSS-COMPLAINT—Personal Injury,** **Property Damage, Wrongful Death**	Code of Civil Procedure, § 425.12 American LegalNet, Inc. www.Forms*Workflow*.com

Exhibit 6.14. Continued

PLD-PI-002

SHORT TITLE:	CASE NUMBER:

4. Each cross-defendant named above is a natural person

   a. ☐ **except** cross-defendant *(name)*:   b. ☐ **except** cross-defendant *(name)*:

     (1) ☐ a business organization, form unknown   (1) ☐ a business organization, form unknown

     (2) ☐ a corporation   (2) ☐ a corporation

     (3) ☐ an unincorporated entity *(describe)*:   (3) ☐ an unincorporated entity *(describe)*:

     (4) ☐ a public entity *(describe)*:   (4) ☐ a public entity *(describe)*:

     (5) ☐ other *(specify)*:   (5) ☐ other *(specify)*:

   ☐ Information about additional cross-defendants who are not natural persons is contained in Cross-Complaint—Attachment 4.

5. The true names and capacities of cross-defendants sued as Does are unknown to cross-complainant.

6. ☐ Cross-complainant is required to comply with a claims statute, **and**

   a. ☐ has complied with applicable claims statutes, **or**

   b. ☐ is excused from complying because *(specify)*:

7. ☐ _____   **Cause of Action—Indemnification**
      (NUMBER)

   a. Cross-defendants were the agents, employees, co-venturers, partners, or in some manner agents or principals, or both, for each other and were acting within the course and scope of their agency or employment.

   b. The principal action alleges, among other things, conduct entitling plaintiff to compensatory damages against me. I contend that I am not liable for events and occurrences described in plaintiff's complaint.

   c. If I am found in some manner responsible to plaintiff or to anyone else as a result of the incidents and occurrences described in plaintiff's complaint, my liability would be based solely upon a derivative form of liability not resulting from my conduct, but only from an obligation imposed upon me by law; therefore, I would be entitled to complete indemnity from each cross-defendant.

8. ☐ _____   **Cause of Action—Apportionment of Fault**
      (NUMBER)

   a. Each cross-defendant was responsible, in whole or in part, for the injuries, if any, suffered by plaintiff.

   b. If I am judged liable to plaintiff, each cross-defendant should be required: (1) to pay a share of plaintiffs judgment which is in proportion to the comparative negligence of that cross-defendant in causing plaintiff's damages; and (2) to reimburse me for any payments I make to plaintiff in excess of my proportional share of all cross-defendants' negligence.

PLD-PI-002 [Rev. January 1, 2007]   **CROSS-COMPLAINT—Personal Injury,**   Page 2 of 3
                      Property Damage, Wrongful Death

Exhibit 6.14.   Continued

SHORT TITLE:		PLD-PI-002
		CASE NUMBER:

9. ☐ _____ **Cause of Action—Declaratory Relief**
      (NUMBER)

   An actual controversy exists between the parties concerning their respective rights and duties because cross-complainant contends and cross-defendant disputes ☐ as specified in Cross-Complaint—Attachment 9
   ☐ as follows:

10. ☐ _____ **Cause of Action—*(specify)*:**
       (NUMBER)

11. ☐ The following additional causes of action are attached and the statements below apply to each *(in each of the attachments, "plaintiff" means "cross-complainant" and "defendant" means "cross-defendant")*:
   a. ☐ Motor Vehicle
   b. ☐ General Negligence
   c. ☐ Intentional Tort
   d. ☐ Products Liability
   e. ☐ Premises Liability
   f. ☐ Other *(specify)*:

12. **CROSS-COMPLAINANT PRAYS** for judgment for costs of suit; for such relief as is fair, just, and equitable; and for
   a. ☐ total and complete indemnity for any judgments rendered against me.
   b. ☐ judgment in a proportionate share from each cross-defendant.
   c. ☐ a judicial determination that cross-defendants were the legal cause of any injuries and damages sustained by plaintiff and that cross-defendants indemnify me, either completely or partially, for any sums of money which may be recovered against me by plaintiff.
   d. ☐ compensatory damages
      (1) ☐ (unlimited civil cases) according to proof.
      (2) ☐ (limited civil cases) in the amount of: $
   e. ☐ other *(specify)*:

13. ☐ The paragraphs of this cross-complaint alleged on information and belief are as follows *(specify paragraph numbers)*:

Date:

_____   ▶   _____
(TYPE OR PRINT NAME)   (SIGNATURE OF CROSS-COMPLAINANT OR ATTORNEY)

PLD-PI-002 [Rev. January 1, 2007]	**CROSS-COMPLAINT—Personal Injury, Property Damage, Wrongful Death**	Page 3 of 3

already has jurisdiction over the plaintiff, the defendant, and the subject matter of the lawsuit, it makes sense to hear and adjudicate, at one time, all claims related to the occurrence or transaction involved.

A claim is compulsory if the claim arises out of the same transaction or occurrence on which the complaint is based. If the defendant fails to file a cross-complaint in such instances, the defendant will have waived her right to relief based on any claim that should have been asserted. However, this rule does not apply if

1. The court cannot obtain jurisdiction over any necessary additional parties;
2. The court does not have personal jurisdiction over the defendant;
3. The defendant did not file an answer to the complaint; or
4. The cross-complaint is the subject of a pending action.

The court continues to have jurisdiction over the cross-complaint even if the plaintiff voluntarily dismisses the complaint. However, if the complaint is dismissed for jurisdictional defects, the counterclaim will be dismissed unless it as an independent jurisdictional basis.

The principal difficulty with compulsory cross-complaints is determining if the defendant's claim involves the same transaction or occurrence that gave rise to the plaintiff's claim. While this is often easy to determine in tort claims, such as an automobile accident, it is a more difficult question in the corporate and commercial areas where numerous lengthy transactions are often involved. Courts have devised several approaches for determining whether the "same transaction or occurrence" is involved. These include deciding whether the legal or factual issues are the same, whether the trial would involve the same proof, and whether the complaint and cross-complaint are logically related.

2. Permissive cross-complaints

Permissive cross-complaints, governed by CCP §428.10(a), are claims that a defendant may bring, but is not required to bring, against a plaintiff in the pending lawsuit. Across-complaint is permissive if it does not arise out of the transaction or occurrence on which the plaintiff's complaint is based. Thus, the cross-complaint can be about any matter. The purpose is to allow the plaintiff and defendant to resolve all differences that they have against one another, rather than filing separate lawsuits. However, if the filing of the cross-complaint on unrelated matters makes the lawsuit too confusing, the trial judge may sever the action and have separate trials on the complaint and cross-complaint.

3. Limitations on cross-complaints against third parties

Pursuant to CCP §428.10(a), in the event that a defendant wishes to file a cross-complaint against a third party, he may do so only if:

(a) the cause of action to be asserted arises out of the same transaction, occurrence, or series of transactions or occurrences; or

(b) the cross-complaint asserts a claim or interest in the property or controversy which is the subject matter of the main action.

These limitations are necessary so that a defendant is not tempted to bring in unrelated claims and causes of action which might only confuse the main issues which are the subject of the plaintiff's complaint.

4. Practice approach

When doing your factual investigation on behalf of a client-defendant, be sure to explore all claims that the defendant may have against the plaintiff. These claims, if related to the subject matter of the action, may have to be brought as a cross-complaint. Otherwise, the defendant may lose her right to bring the action at a later time. Even if the subject matter of the claim is unrelated, it still may be more advantageous to bring all the claims in one action. Therefore, always consider whether there are grounds for a cross-complaint.

CHAPTER SUMMARY

The complaint is the initial pleading filed by the plaintiff to commence the litigation. The body of the complaint contains three parts: a statement identifying the parties, one or more causes of action, and the request for relief. Each cause of action will state the essential legal elements in the form of a statement of the facts as applied to the case. In some cases, it may be possible to use a Judicial Council of California form complaint. The form complaint will state all the necessary general allegations.

After the complaint has been prepared, it will need to be filed with the court, and the summons and complaint will be served upon all the defendants. Proof of service will then be filed with the court.

The defendant has a number of options when responding to a complaint. The defendant may answer the complaint and allege a number of affirmative defenses. In addition, the defendant may file a responsive motion that attacks the pleadings such as a demurrer or motion to strike. If a defendant does not file an answer or an appropriate motion, the plaintiff may take a default judgment against the defendant.

The defendant also may assert claims against the plaintiff, or against a codefendant, or against a new party, these claims are filed in a cross-complaint. Each of these claims appears in the same format as a complaint.

KEY TERMS

Affirmative defense

Answer

Complaint

Compulsory cross-complaint

Cross-complaint

Default judgment

Prayer for relief

Proof of service

Reasonable inquiry

Summons

REVIEW QUESTIONS

1. What pleading is used to commence a lawsuit?

2. What is meant by the term "fact pleading"?

3. What qualifications does an individual need to serve a summons and complaint?

4. How can a corporation that has its offices out of state be served?

5. Explain the different ways that a summons may be served on individuals.

6. What is an affirmative defense? Why is it important for the defendant to include affirmative defenses in the answer?

7. What is the proof of service?

INTERNET RESOURCES

www.courtinfo.ca.gov/cgi-bin/forms.cgi (Judicial Council forms)

www.courtinfo.ca.gov/jury/civiljuryinstructions (jury instructions)

www.ss.ca.gov (California secretary of state website to locate agents for service of process on corporations)

CHAPTER 7

Special Pleadings

A. Introduction
B. Interpleader
C. Intervention
D. Class Actions
E. Amendments of Pleadings
   and Supplemental Pleadings

CHAPTER OBJECTIVES

In some instances special pleadings are required to protect a non-party's interest in the subject matter of the litigation or to ensure that the rights of a large group of individuals are protected. In addition, after the initial pleadings are filed, it often becomes necessary to file an amendment to the pleadings or supplement the pleadings with additional information. In this chapter you will learn:

◆ What the procedures are for a third-party stakeholder to deposit funds with the court
◆ How a third party can intervene in an action
◆ When a class action lawsuit is possible
◆ What the requirements are for bringing a class action lawsuit
◆ How to amend a pleading once it is filed with the court
◆ When a supplemental pleading is appropriate

A. INTRODUCTION

In Chapters 5 and 6 you learned about the general requirements for all pleadings and the initial pleadings filed by plaintiffs and defendants. However, there are some instances where special pleadings by nonparties may be necessary. One of these circumstances is when a nonparty holds funds for the benefit of another party or parties. A second situation is when a nonparty has an interest in the litigation and wants to join in the action.

There are also situations where a large class of people may have an interest in an action, but because the class number is so large it is more practical to join all the parties together in one action rather than have each individual litigate separate claims. Special pleading rules need to be examined in these cases.

Finally, what happens if you file an initial pleading and then discover that you need to amend or correct something previously stated in the pleading or you discover additional information that you need to add to the pleading? In these cases, special rules to amend the pleading or supplement the pleading must be followed. Each of these rules is discussed and explained in this chapter.

Interpleader
Procedure under which a party subjected to double liability may deposit into court a fund or property

B. INTERPLEADER

Interpleader is the procedure under which a party, called a "stakeholder," who is or may be subjected to double liability can resolve these claims. Double liability occurs when two or more claimants are

There are two types of interpleader actions. Both are governed by CCP §386.

1. Interpleader when defendant is named as a party

CCP §386(b) provides that a defendant, in a cause of action based upon contract or for specific property, may, anytime before he files an answer, apply to the court for an order to deposit the money or property with the court and thereafter discharge him from any further liability. For example, this may be appropriate in a case where an escrow is holding funds that have been deposited by joint parties. If one party thereafter sues another party claiming entitlement to the funds in the escrow, it will be necessary to name the escrow company as a party to the lawsuit. However, since the escrow company does not claim any interest in the money, it would be beneficial for the escrow company to simply deposit the money with the court and allow the action to continue between the two interested parties.

2. Where multiple claims are alleged

Pursuant to CCP §386(b) where a party is likely to be subject to multiple claims which potentially can create liabilities, the stakeholder may take the initiative and file an interpleader action naming the parties who claim a right in the property or money as defendants. Thus, in our escrow example above, if two or more parties made a demand upon the escrow company for payment of the money, it would not be wise for the escrow company to make the determination as to who is entitled to the money. Rather, the escrow company could file a lawsuit, name both parties as defendants, and force the defendants to obtain a court order as to who is entitled to the funds. In this way, the escrow company avoids being liable to one party for giving the money to the other. The escrow company could still deposit the funds in court, and essentially withdraw from further proceedings in the lawsuit while the two defendants continue the litigation.

3. Practice approach

An interpleader complaint should have all the components of an ordinary complaint: a cause of action for interpleader stating the conflicting claims and a prayer for relief. The prayer for relief should ask for all relief that is appropriate, including a determination of the amount of liability, if any; a determination of which claimants are entitled to the fund or property and in what amounts; an injunction against any claimants pursuing other actions in state or federal courts based on this claim; and fees and costs, including attorney's fees where permitted. An example of an interpleader complaint is shown in Exhibit 7.1.

C. INTERVENTION

Intervention, governed by CCP §387, is the procedure by which a non-party having an interest in a pending action can protect its rights by becoming an additional party and presenting a claim or defense. There are two types of intervention allowed: intervention of right and permissive intervention.

1. Intervention of right

Intervention of right
The ability of a person to become a party to the lawsuit when such a person has an interest in the outcome of the lawsuit

CCP §387(b) governs **intervention of right.** The Code provides two ways in which a person has an absolute right to intervene. The first is when a provision of the law confers such right. For example, there are a number of statutory provisions that give a party the right to intervene into a pending action, such as those claiming an interest in property that is subject to condemnation (CCP §1250.230).

In addition, a party has a right to intervene in an action if they claim an interest in the property or transaction which is the subject matter of the action, and their interests cannot be protected without being permitted to join in the action. Thus, keep these three points in mind in determining whether intervention is proper:

1. The intervenor must claim "an interest relating to the property or transaction which is the subject of the action" pending.

What if a sufficient "interest" requires you to analyze the intervenor's claimed interest, the relief sought, and the nature of the claims and defenses asserted in the pending action?

2. The intervenor must be "so situated that the disposition of the action may, as a practical matter, impair or impede his ability to protect that interest."

Exhibit 7.1. Interpleader Complaint

Whole Life Insurance Co., a corporation	
Plaintiff	Case No. C-13454
v.	
Thomas Smith, James Smith and DOES 1 through 10 inclusive.	COMPLAINT FOR INTERPLEADER
Defendants	

Plaintiff Whole Life Insurance, Co. complains of defendants Thomas Smith, James Smith and Does 1 through 10 as follows:

1. Plaintiff is a California Corporation, doing business in the State of California.

2. Thomas Smith and James Smith are, and at all times relevant herein were, individuals residing in California.

3. On June 1, 2007, Plaintiff issued a life insurance policy on the life of Franklin Smith. A true and correct copy of the policy is attached hereto as Exhibit A and incorporated herein by this reference.

4. . . .

5. . . .

6. By reason of defendants' conflicting claims, plaintiff cannot determine with certainty which defendant, if either, is entitled to any proceeds of the policy, or if either is entitled, in what amount.

7. Plaintiff has deposited the face amount of the policy, $80,000, with the clerk of the court.

WHEREFORE, plaintiff requests that the court enter a judgment finding that:

(1) Neither defendant is entitled to recover any money from the policy.

(2) Each defendant is permanently enjoyed from pursuing any other actions or claims on this policy.

Exhibit 7.1. Continued

> (3) If the court finds the policy in force at the time of Franklin Smith's death, that the defendants be required to interplead and settle their claims on the policy between themselves, and that plaintiff be discharged from any liability except to any person in such amount has the court adjudges plaintiff is liable.
>
> (4) Plaintiff is entitled to recover its costs, including reasonable attorney's fees to the extent permitted by law.

The critical term "as a practical matter" was included to make clear that this determination should include any substantial functional difficulties that might adversely affect the intervenor's interests.

3. The intervenor must not be "adequately represented by existing parties."

This requires a comparison of the interests of the existing parties with the claimed interests of the intervenor to determine how closely they are related. If the intervenor's interests are essentially identical to those of an existing party, so that the existing party will necessarily assert the same positions as the intervenor would, intervention should be denied.

2. Permissive intervention

CCP §387(a) permits three grounds for **permissive intervention.** If a person claims (1) "an interest in the matter in litigation" or (2) "in the success of either of the parties" or (3) "an interest adverse to both," the person may make an application for intervention. The request to intervene is left to the court's discretion, and the court may deny it when the intervenor's request would delay or prejudice the rights of the pending parties or inject unimportant issues into the case.

If a court denies intervention, there are no adverse legal consequences because **res judicata**—a legal doctrine that provides that a judgment, once final, is binding on the parties—will not apply to the unsuccessful intervenor. The common situation in which intervention is permitted is when the intervenor has a claim against the defendant that is factually and legally similar to the plaintiff's pending claim against the defendant.

3. Timing

A prospective intervenor must move to intervene in a timely fashion, regardless of whether the intervention sought is of right or is permissive.

CCP §387(a) requires a "timely application," but where intervention of right is requested, it will ordinarily be permitted regardless of when the application is made because the intervenor's right might otherwise be adversely affected. Despite this, it is possible to seek intervention of right so late in the pending action that it is considered untimely and is therefore denied.

When permissive intervention is sought, the court will consider whether the intervention will delay or prejudice the determination of the rights of the original parties. This requires analyzing the relief the intervenor wants, whether the intervenor will be an active or passive party, and particularly the stage that the pending action is in. Intervention obviously will be more favorably viewed when sought early in the pleading stage than if substantial discovery already has been taken.

4. Practice approach

A party seeking intervention should file a motion for leave to intervene. The motion should follow the general rules for all motions discussed in Chapter 6. However, in addition to the motion, the intervenor must attach an appropriate pleading in the event the motion is allowed. The pleading will be captioned "Complaint in Intervention." The motion, which must be served on all existing parties, should state the reason why intervention is appropriate under the circumstances. A motion to intervene is shown in Exhibit 7.2.

If the motion to intervene is granted, the intervenor becomes a party and has the rights of any party. The intervenor usually cannot contest past orders, but can cross-claim, present any appropriate motions, and fully participate in discovery. Note, however, that the court has power to limit intervention to certain matters if permissive intervention has been granted.

D. CLASS ACTIONS

The topic of **class actions**—a lawsuit brought by individuals representing a large group of identifiable members—by itself can fill volumes, and literature on the subject in treatises, cases, and journals is extensive. It is a complicated area, one in which inexperienced litigators and paralegals should tread cautiously, if at all. Hence, this section is limited to a brief overview of the class-action requirements and the initial considerations and steps in such suits. One's principal concern should be determining whether a case can be pursued as a class action. If so, assistance from someone with more experience in this area should be sought.

Exhibit 7.2. Motion to Intervene

Whole Life Insurance Co., a corporation	
Plaintiff	Case No. C-13454
v.	NOTICE OF MOTION AND MOTION TO FILE A COMPLAINT IN INTERVENTION
Thomas Smith, James Smith and DOES 1 through 10 inclusive.	
Defendants	

PLEASE TAKE NOTICE THAT on June 14, 2007, at 1:30 P.M. or as soon thereafter as the matter may be heard in Courtroom No. 215 of the California Superior Court located at 111 N. Hill Street, Jacob Franklin will move to file a complaint in intervention into this action on the grounds that he is an interested party and has a right to the insurance proceeds which are the subject of this action. A copy of the proposed complaint in intervention is attached hereto as Exhibit A.

In addition to the general rules discussed below, be sure to check your local rules of court. For example, Los Angeles County has specific class action rules governing the procedure that must be followed. However, other courts often look to the Los Angeles County rules for guidance in this area.

1. General class requirements

CCP §382 allows for one or more to sue or defend for the benefit of all "when the question is of common or general interest, of many persons, or when the parties are numerous, and it is impractical to bring them all before the court. . . ."

The Code itself does not define what a class is or how its members should be determined. Impracticability depends on the type of claims asserted and the persons asserting those claims. Because of this, the numbers necessary for a class action are quite flexible, and the ultimate decision whether a class action is the preferred method of dealing with a claim is left to the discretion of the trial court. While it is usually clear that hundreds of potential plaintiffs or defendants make the action suitable for class-action treatment and that fewer than 30 ordinarily is not enough, the case law on class numbers in the middle range—perhaps 30 to 50 members—shows no obvious pattern. Some of such classes have been held to be of an appropriate number, others not. The outcome is as dependent on other considerations as it is on the number of class members.

The representatives who "sue or defend for the benefit of all" must be actual members of the class. In addition, the claims or defenses of the class must be reviewed, and there must be enough representative parties to ensure that each claim or defense is represented fairly. This obviously requires that lawyers and paralegals closely analyze the facts before selecting actual parties and initiating suit.

2. General facts requirements

While California does not specify the precise requirements for the class, many of the rules that have developed through case law are derived from federal law. Rule 23(b) of the Federal Rules of Civil Procedure sets out three fact situations in which a class action is appropriate.

1. It is appropriate when separate actions would "create a risk of inconsistent or varying adjudications" that would "establish incompatible standards of conduct" for the party opposing the class, or when separate adjudications as a practical matter would determine the interests of the others in the class who are not parties to that adjudication.

The former is commonly relied on in actions against municipal entities to declare actions invalid, such as expenditures and bond issues. The latter is frequently relied on in shareholder actions against corporations, such as to compel declaration of a dividend.

2. A class action is appropriate when the party opposing the class has "acted or refused to act on grounds generally applicable to the class."

Many of the cases brought on this basis are civil rights actions in which a party is asking for injunctive or other equitable relief under Title VII of the 1964 Civil Rights Act. Some are employment discrimination cases.

3. A class action is appropriate when "questions of law or fact common to the members of the class predominate over any questions affecting only individual members" and a class action is the best method for handling the entire controversy.

This has become the most common basis for class actions, and one that is frequently relied on in antitrust and securities fraud cases. However, a class action under this Rule—Rule 24(b)(3)—is rarely permitted in mass tort cases, such as airline crashes, because the plaintiffs' claims are usually seen as too diverse to justify class-action treatment.

3. Procedure

A class-action lawsuit is started the same as other lawsuits, by the filing of a complaint by the representative party against the defendant. The complaint however must indicate on the first page "CLASS ACTION." After the class-action complaint is filed, the court will hold a hearing on whether the class action should be permitted to proceed. The hearing will be held by either the plaintiff bringing a motion to certify the class as a class action, or by the defendant opposing certification of the class.

The court will determine whether the class-action requirements have been met, and make a determination of what issues can be tried as a class action, and a determination of what the class or classes will be.

If a class is certified, court must direct what notice is the best and most practicable under the circumstances. This notice will likely include individual notice to all members who can be identified through reasonable effort. Aside from related concerns such as the actual technical requirements for notice, the ability to opt out of being a class member, and res judicata issues, the immediate concern is a practical one. Notice can be an expensive undertaking, sometimes prohibitively so. For class members whose identity can be ascertained with reasonable effort, notice by first-class mail is usually required; for unknown class members, some form of notice by publication is required. Since each side must bear its costs of litigation, the expense of actually notifying the individual class members can effectively prevent a claim from being pursued as a class action.

E. AMENDMENTS OF PLEADINGS AND SUPPLEMENTAL PLEADINGS

The principal concepts behind the pleading requirements are that pleadings should accurately notify the parties of the claims involved and that enough flexibility should be permitted so that substantial justice is achieved in every case. CCP §§472 and 473, the amendments rules, reflect these concerns. Amended pleadings should be freely allowed when fairness requires it—that is, whenever an amendment would create a more accurate or complete pleading and the opposing parties will not be substantially prejudiced. This Rule applies to all pleadings—complaints, answers, and cross-claims.

1. Amendments by right

Pursuant to CCP §472, any party has a right to amend a pleading once, at any time before a responsive pleading is made. If no responsive pleading is permitted, such as with an answer, an amendment by right can be made within ten days after service. A motion that attacks a pleading, such as a demurrer or motion to strike as discussed in Chapter 7, is not considered a responsive pleading. Even if such a motion is filed by a defendant, the plaintiff could file an amendment before the hearing on the motion. If an amendment is by right, it is simply served on the other parties; no court action is needed.

2. Amendments by leave of court

CCP §473 permits amendments by leave of court. The Code expressly provides that amendments may be allowed when the court determines that such amendments are in the "furtherance of justice." Courts have been fairly indulgent in permitting amendments, and grounds such as oversight, error, or delay by themselves are generally held insufficient to deny leave to amend.

Courts may exercise their discretion and deny leave to amend when, in addition to delay or neglect, there is some actual prejudice to the opposing party. In other situations, the court may grant leave to amend while restricting it to particular matters so that prejudice to an opposing party is minimized. Obviously, the amending party should seek leave to amend as early in the litigation process as possible to minimize prejudice. A motion during the pleading stage will, in all likelihood, be granted. One made after discovery is underway, however, may well encounter difficulties.

3. Statutes of limitation and "relation back"

An important concern in amending pleadings is if the statute of limitations applies to amended pleadings. This question exists only if the amended pleading is filed after the applicable statute of limitations has run on a particular claim. If the statute of limitations has not run, there is no concern since the pleading can be timely filed. When the statute has run, the issue of whether the statute will bar the amended pleading depends on whether the concept of "relation back" will apply. **Relation back** is a legal doctrine that permits an amended pleading to be deemed filed at the time the original pleading was filed. In other words, the amended pleading "relates back" to the initial pleading.

Relation back
Doctrine that permits an amended pleading to be deemed filed at time of original pleading

There are two principal types of amendments—changing facts and legal theories and changing parties—that must be considered separately in determining if the relation-back doctrine applies.

a. Changing facts and theories

California case law provides that if the amended pleading's claims or defenses arise from the same general conduct, transaction, or occurrence set forth in the original pleading, the amendment will relate back to the date the original pleading was filed so that the statute of limitations will not operate as a bar. When the amended pleading alleges an entirely new claim, the concept of relation back will not apply. Whether the claims or defenses in the amended pleading arise from the same general conduct, transaction, or occurrence set forth in the original pleading is an imprecise standard, but courts have been reasonably lenient in permitting amendments, particularly when only a change in legal theory is involved.

b. Changing parties

The more difficult situation concerns changing parties with an amended pleading. In order for the relation back doctrine to apply, the original complaint must name "Doe" defendants and identify a valid cause of action against the Doe defendant. In this way, when the plaintiff amends the Complaint, the plaintiff is really just changing the name of the defendant from the fictitious "Doe" to the defendant's actual name. If an adequate "Doe" allegation is not stated in the original complaint, the adding of a new party will not relate back.

4. Supplemental pleadings

Under CCP §464 a party may move to file a supplemental pleading alleging facts material to the case that have occurred since the time the original pleading was served. Permitting the motion is discretionary with the court, which can impose any reasonable terms to protect the other parties.

Since a supplemental pleading by definition raises new matters that have arisen since the original pleading, statute of limitations and relation-back issues will rarely be involved.

5. Practice approach

A motion of leave to amend, like any other motion, must meet the general motion requirements which will be discussed in Chapter 8. However, generally, the motion must state with particularity the grounds for the motion and the relief sought. Timely notice must be sent to other parties. The better practice is to attach the amended pleading as an exhibit to the motion. In addition, it is both more convenient and a safer practice to have a complete amended pleading, rather than incorporate by reference parts of the original pleading. It is simply easier to deal with a complete pleading, and responses will likely be more accurate.

If the motion is allowed, or the amended pleading is of right, a party that is required to respond to the amended pleading must do so in the same time frame as the original pleading.

CHAPTER SUMMARY

If a nonparty can possibly be subject to double liability because two or more parties are making a claim to the same fund or property, the nonparty stakeholder may want to file an interpleader. This allows the nonparty to deposit the funds or property with the court and relieve himself from double liability. The interpleader complaint will have the same components as a regular complaint.

In cases where a nonparty has an interest in the litigation, the nonparty may be able to file a complaint in intervention and join in the lawsuit. In some cases, this ability to join in is only permissive. It will be up to the discretion of the court to determine if the nonparty may join. Other times, however, the right to join is automatic. This happens when either the law confers the absolute right to join in such as when a person's interest in property is at issue or when the nonparty's interest cannot be protected unless she is allowed to join.

If there are issues in the lawsuit that are common or of general interest to many people, a class action may be appropriate. In such cases, a representative of the class will sue or defend on behalf of all the other parties.

In the event a party wishes to change or correct a pleading, the pleading may, under most circumstances, be amended or supplemented. However, if a responsive pleading already has been filed, the party wishing to amend may have to seek leave of court.

KEY TERMS

Class action
Interpleader
Intervention of right

Relation back
Res judicata

REVIEW QUESTIONS

1. In what situations would an interpleader procedure be used?

2. When does a party have an automatic right to amend a pleading?

3. Under what circumstances does a nonparty have an absolute right to intervene?

4. When would a class action lawsuit be appropriate?

INTERNET RESOURCES

www.calbar.org
www.courtinfo.ca.gov/cgi-bin/forms.cgi
www.lalaw.lib.ca.us
www.uscourts.gov

CHAPTER **8**

Introduction to Motions

CHAPTER OBJECTIVES

This chapter covers the law relating to motions that may be made by the parties after a complaint is filed and before trial begins. The chapter includes:

- ◆ What the general requirements are for all motions
- ◆ How to obtain an extension of time and continuances
- ◆ When to serve motions
- ◆ When there must be a substitution of parties
- ◆ Why a case may be removed to federal court

A. INTRODUCTION

Motions are a significant part of the litigation process. They are used to regulate the routine "housekeeping" matters in litigation, such as the rescheduling of discovery, hearings, and other deadlines. Motions are also used to reach dispositive results, such as motions to dismiss or motions for summary judgment. Every litigated matter will involve motions, so knowing how to present appropriate, well-drafted motions is an essential skill for every litigation paralegal.

A **motion** is simply an application to a court for an order. Presenting an effective motion, however, involves both technical requirements, such as format and service rules, and substantive requirements, which control how the body of a motion should be organized and constructed so that the motion will be persuasive to the judge.

This chapter discusses the technical requirements as well as the law relating to the filing of motions. In addition, there are a number of motions that routinely come up in cases, such as requests for extensions of time and substitution of parties. The rules relating to these motions are also discussed in this chapter. Specific motions are discussed in subsequent chapters.

B. GENERAL REQUIREMENTS FOR MOTIONS

The Code of Civil Procedure and California Rules of Court govern how motions are made. However, local rules must always be checked because they often detail matters such as special requirements and specific court days when motions may be heard. While motions may present numerous matters and seek a wide variety of relief, their basic requirements are generally the same.

1. Form

A motion must generally include three basic items:

- A written notice of motion
- A memorandum of points and authorities identifying the law supporting the motion
- Proof of service

Within these broad requirements a great deal of flexibility is allowed, and how a particular motion is structured is controlled primarily by tactical considerations.

The format requirements for motions are identical to those for pleadings. A motion must have a caption showing the name of the court, the names of the parties to the action, and a designation of the motion involved. Where there are multiple parties, the name of the first party on each side, with an "et al." designation, is sufficient.

Pursuant to Rule 3.1110(b) of the CRC, immediately below the case number the first page of each paper filed must state:

- Date, time, and location, if ascertainable, of any scheduled hearing and the nature of the hearing judge, if ascertainable
- Nature of any attached document other than an exhibit
- Date of filing of the action
- Trial date if set

Every motion must be signed by a lawyer representing the moving party. The motion must show the lawyer's name and address, and will customarily include a telephone number. Effective January 1, 2007, the Judicial Council has preempted all local rules relating to the form and format of papers to be filed in the trial courts. "No trial court, or any division or branch of a trial court, may enact or enforce any local rule concerning the form or format of papers." Rule 2.100(a) of the CRC. The format of the first page of a motion is shown in Exhibit 8.1.

2. Notice of motion

Rule 3.1110 of the CRC governs the formatting and filing of motions. That Rule provides that a notice of motion must state, in the first paragraph, the type of order requested as well as the "grounds for issuance of an order." The opening paragraph will also indicate where and when the motion will be heard. A notice of motion is shown in Exhibit 8.2. How far in advance you must serve the motion on the other party, prior to the

Exhibit 8.1. Sample Motion

Tamara Sellers, Esq.
State Bar No. 997788
789 E. Larchmont Lane
Encino, CA 91356
(818) 777-8888

SUPERIOR COURT OF CALIFORNIA
FOR THE COUNTY OF LOS ANGELES

JOHN SMITH, an individual

Plaintiff

v.

RANDOLPH CONSTRUCTION
COMPANY, a Delaware Corporation,
and DOES 1 through 10 inclusive.

Defendants

Case No. C-23444

NOTICE OF MOTION AND
MOTION TO STRIKE

Date: August 2, 2005
Time: 9:00 A.M.
Place: Department A
Trial Date: None Set

Exhibit 8.2. Notice of Motion

TO THE PLAINTIFF AND HIS ATTORNEY OF RECORD:

PLEASE TAKE NOTICE THAT on August 2, 2005 at 9:00 A.M., or as soon thereafter as the matter be heard in Department A of the above entitled court located at 111 N. Hill Street, the Defendant Randolph Construction Company will move the Court for an order _____ on the grounds that _____. This motion will be based on this notice of motion and motion, the accompany memorandum of points and authorities, the pleadings and papers on file herein, and on such additional argument and evidence as may be presented at the hearing on the motion.

hearing, will depend on the type of motion. As a general rule, CCP §1005 provides that a motion must be served and filed at least twenty-one days in advance of the hearing. If the motion is served by mail, the period must be increased by at least five calendar days. If the notice is served by overnight delivery or facsimile transmission, the time is increased by two calendar days. Always check the time period for the particular motion you are serving because some time periods may be changed. For example, a motion for summary judgment, discussed in Chapter 10, requires that the motion be filed at least seventy-five days in advance.

For the convenience of the court and other parties, it is good practice to give more notice when possible than the minimum required under the circumstances. It is also good practice to call the lawyers for the other parties to select a mutually agreeable hearing date, if possible, before sending out the written notices. This gives the court time to read the motion, avoids disputes over whether notice was adequate, minimizes continuances, and fosters a good working relationship with the lawyers for the other parties in the case.

A motion can be served in any of the ways set out in CCP §§1010-1013. The standard methods are to mail the motion and notice of motion to a lawyer for each party or have the motion and notice delivered to them or someone at their offices. Following service, the originals of the notice and motion should be filed with the clerk of the court along with a proof of service. Filing must occur "within a reasonable time" after service, but obviously must be done before the date set for the hearing. The usual procedure is to file the originals immediately after service. Be sure you get a copy of the motion, notice, and proof of service stamped "filed" and dated by the clerk to keep in the client's files maintained by your firm.

How do you select the day for the hearing on the motion? Check with the clerk of the court to determine on what days the court hears motions, since practices vary widely. Some judges hold daily court calls; others hear motions only on designated days. Find out what the judge's practice is so that the date you select will be one on which the motion can be heard. Next, check with the lawyer in your office who will argue the motion so that the date is cleared on her calendar. Finally, check with the clerk the day before the hearing to make sure the case will actually appear on the next day's motion calendar and to find out what time the lawyer should be in the courtroom. Many judges arrange their court calendars to hear uncontested and routine cases first and contested matters afterward.

3. Content of the motion

CRC Rule 3.1112 identifies what papers must be filed in support of a motion. The papers must include at least the following: (1) the motion itself; (2) a notice of hearing; and (3) a memorandum of points and authorities. A **memorandum of points and authorities** is a document

Memorandum of points and authorities
Document setting forth facts and legal authorities to support a motion

setting forth the background facts and legal authorities to support the motion. In addition, depending on the type of motion that is filed a declaration or affidavit with any necessary exhibits and supporting documents should also be attached. In this way a judge can scan the motion quickly, then review the more detailed supporting materials.

Rule 3.1113(d) of the CRC governs the length of the memorandum. With the exception of summary judgment or summary adjudication motions, no supporting or opposing memorandum shall exceed fifteen pages. Any reply memorandum must not exceed ten pages. The page limit does not include exhibits, declarations, table of contents, table of authorities, or proof of service.

The detail necessary to support the motion must be examined in light of such factors as the relative seriousness and complexity of the motion and local practice. For example, a motion to reset a hearing date because the lawyer will be on trial in another case should be brief. The motion need only point out when the hearing is presently scheduled, state where and when the conflicting trial is scheduled, and how long the case will take to try, and then suggest a new date for the hearing. In this situation the judge will want brevity, and the factual representations by counsel in the motion and supporting declaration should be enough.

At the other extreme, a motion for summary judgment usually must be a thorough presentation of both law and facts. The supporting memorandum of points and authorities will thoroughly discuss applicable law and existing facts. In addition, it should contain excerpts from the pleadings and discovery, exhibits such as documents and records, and witness statements in declaration or affidavit form. The motion and accompanying materials should be a self-contained package having everything the judge will need to decide the motion.

In short, drafting a motion requires a flexible approach. The relative complexity of the motion, local custom in presenting motions, and even the preferences of the judge all come into play. Motions that are specifically tailored to these considerations—that is, motions that do not mechanically follow a set blueprint—have a much better chance of succeeding.[1]

4. Proof of service

Proof of service is merely a certificate, issued by a lawyer or a nonlawyer, that states that service on the other parties has been made in a proper way. The proof of service will identify the date, method, and person making the service. The certificate of service is usually attached to the end of the motion. A sample certificate is shown in Exhibit 8.3.

---

1. The motion should be drafted with precision the first time, since unlike pleadings, no rule expressly allows amendments of motions. In practice, however, amendments of motions are sometimes permitted.

Exhibit 8.3. Certificate of Service

POS-020

ATTORNEY OR PARTY WITHOUT ATTORNEY *(Name, State Bar number, and address):*

FOR COURT USE ONLY

TELEPHONE NO.:
E-MAIL ADDRESS *(Optional):*   FAX NO. *(Optional):*
ATTORNEY FOR *(Name):*

SUPERIOR COURT OF CALIFORNIA, COUNTY OF
STREET ADDRESS:
MAILING ADDRESS:
CITY AND ZIP CODE:
BRANCH NAME:

PETITIONER/PLAINTIFF:

RESPONDENT/DEFENDANT:

PROOF OF PERSONAL SERVICE—CIVIL

CASE NUMBER:

(Do not use this Proof of Service to show service of a Summons and Complaint.)

1. I am over 18 years of age and **not a party to this action**.
2. I served the following **documents** *(specify):*

   ☐ The documents are listed in the *Attachment to Proof of Personal Service—Civil (Documents Served)* (form POS-020(D)).
3. I personally served the following **persons** at the address, date, and time stated:
   a. Name:
   b. Address:
   c. Date:
   d. Time:

   ☐ The persons are listed in the *Attachment to Proof of Personal Service—Civil (Persons Served)* (form POS-020(P)).
4. I am
   a. ☐ not a registered California process server.   c. ☐ an employee or independent contractor of a
   b. ☐ a registered California process server.   registered California process server.
                                                          d. ☐ exempt from registration under Business & Professions
                                                                Code section 22350(b).

5. My name, address, telephone number, and, if applicable, county of registration and number are *(specify):*

6. ☐ I declare under penalty of perjury under the laws of the State of California that the foregoing is true and correct.
7. ☐ I am a California sheriff or marshal and certify that the foregoing is true and correct.

Date:

▶

_____   _____
(TYPE OR PRINT NAME OF PERSON WHO SERVED THE PAPERS)   (SIGNATURE OF PERSON WHO SERVED THE PAPERS)

Form Approved for Optional Use
Judicial Council of California
POS-020 [New January 1, 2005]   **PROOF OF PERSONAL SERVICE—CIVIL**   Code of Civil Procedure, § 1011
www.courtinfo.ca.gov

American LegalNet, Inc.
www.USCourtForms.com

Exhibit 8.3. Continued

INFORMATION SHEET FOR PROOF OF PERSONAL SERVICE—CIVIL
(This information sheet is not a part of the Proof of Service form and does not need to be copied, served, or filed.)

NOTE: This form should **not** be used for proof of service of a summons and complaint. For that purpose, use *Proof of Service of Summons* (form POS-010).

Use these instructions to complete the *Proof of Personal Service* (form POS-020).

A person at least 18 years of age or older must serve the documents. There are two main ways to serve documents: (1) by personal delivery and (2) by mail. Certain documents must be personally served. You must determine whether personal service is required for a document.

The person who personally served the documents must complete a proof of service form for the documents served. **You cannot serve documents if you are a party to the action.**

INSTRUCTIONS FOR THE PERSON WHO SERVED THE DOCUMENTS

The proof of service should be printed or typed. If you have Internet access, fillable versions of the form are available at *www.courtinfo.ca.gov/forms.*

Complete the top section of the proof of service form as follows:

First box, left side: In this box print the name, address, and phone number of the person *for* whom you served the documents.

Second box, left side: Print the name of the county in which the legal action is filed and the court's address in this box. The address for the court should be the same as on the documents that you served.

Third box, left side: Print the names of the Petitioner/Plaintiff and Respondent/Defendant in this box. Use the same names as are listed on the documents that you served.

First box, top of form, right side: Leave this box blank for the court's use.

Second box, right side: Print the case number in this box. The number should be the same as the case number on the documents that you served.

Complete all applicable items on the form:

1. You are stating that you are over the age of 18 and that you are not a party to this action.

2. List the name of each document that you delivered to the person. If you need more space, check the box in item 2, complete the *Attachment to Proof of Personal Service–Civil (Documents Served)* (form POS-020(D)), and attach it to form POS-020.

3. Provide the name of each person served, the address where you served the documents, and the date and time of service. If you served more than one person, check the box in item 3, complete the *Attachment to Proof of Personal Service–Civil (Persons Served)* (form POS-020(P)), and attach it to form POS-020.

4. Check the box that applies to you. If you are a private person serving the documents for a party, check box "a."

5. Print your name, address, and telephone number. If applicable, include the county in which you are registered as a process server and your registration number.

6. You must check this box if you are not a California sheriff or marshal. You are stating under penalty of perjury that the information you have provided is true and correct.

7. Do not check this box unless you are a California sheriff or marshal.

At the bottom, fill in the date on which you signed the form, print your name, and sign the form at the arrow. By signing, you are stating under penalty of perjury that all the information that you have provided on form POS-020 is true and correct.

POS-020 [New January 1, 2005]

PROOF OF PERSONAL SERVICE—CIVIL

5. Responses to motions

Once served with a motion, the responding party has two choices: The responding party can either oppose or not oppose the motion. If the respondent is not going to oppose the motion, then a party should give notice that they will not appear. The court will then rule on the motion as if the party had appeared.

Another approach is to agree to a **consent order**, in which both parties draft an agreed-upon order that disposes of the motion. While this does not guarantee that the judge will sign it, in practice the judge usually will.

On the other hand, if you are asked to oppose the motion, serve and file the response at least ten calendar days in advance of the hearing (CCP §1005). The response should set out in the form of a memorandum of points and authorities the reasons for the opposition and include case law and other authority that the judge should consider. It is good practice to follow the points in the order raised in the moving papers so it is easier for the court to follow the argument. Draft the opposition early to allow the responsible attorney sufficient time to review it before the filing deadline.

After the response is filed, the moving party may file a **reply** at least five calendar days before the hearing. The reply is the moving party's response to any issues raised in the opposition and should also include a memorandum of points and authorities.

Reply
Response to opposition to a motion

6. Hearing and argument

Although a paralegal is not permitted to argue motions in court, you nonetheless should be familiar with the hearing process. This familiarity will give you a better understanding of motion practice.

At the hearing the judge will usually dispense with all routine and uncontested matters first. These matters can be handled quickly and dispensing with them ensures that attorneys need not wait while more lengthy matters are heard. If the matter is contested, the clerk will call the case. The usual practice is for the lawyers to approach the bench when their case is called and state who they are and which party they represent. Sometimes the judge will make a **tentative ruling**, in which case the party the tentative ruling is against will have the opportunity to speak first in an effort to persuade the judge to change the ruling. If no tentative ruling is given and the motion is a routine one, the judge will usually let the lawyers make brief comments, and then the judge will make a decision from the bench and immediately enter an appropriate order. If a significant motion is involved, the judge will probably permit lengthier arguments and take the case

Tentative ruling
A ruling by the judge based on the written beliefs submitted by the parties and before oral argument is heard

Under submission
Refers to the judge
delaying decision on
a motion until the
judge has an
opportunity for
further consideration

under submission, meaning that the judge will research and consider the issues further before deciding the motion.

With respect to oral argument, each judge's practice is different. Some judges disfavor oral argument and dispense with it altogether for routine motions or, for other motions, give the lawyers very little time to argue. Other judges use oral argument principally as an opportunity to ask the lawyers questions about the law or facts. In this situation all points must be made in the written motion. At the other extreme are judges who at best scan written motions and rely heavily if not exclusively on oral argument in deciding whether to grant a motion. Most lawyers' preparation for oral argument depends a great deal on knowing what the judge wants to hear.

If the judge's practice is to allow substantial oral argument, the lawyer needs to decide what will persuade the judge to rule favorably. Sometimes the weight of prevailing law will be persuasive, at other times the facts of the case. Whatever it is, judges do not want the lawyers to repeat the contents of the motion unless the judge specifically requests that the judge's memory needs to be refreshed.

7. Order

Regardless of when the motion is decided, the court will enter an order. In federal court, routine motions are usually decided by a **minute order**, which is merely a form on which the clerk makes an entry reflecting the ruling. The minute order is then signed by the judge or stamped with the judge's signature, and a copy is mailed to the lawyers. If the motion is important, the judge may prepare a written opinion and order explaining the reasons for the ruling. Or, the judge may ask that the prevailing party prepare an order for the judge's signature. If this is done, the proposed order is served on the opposing party and the judge will wait a few days before signing the proposed order to allow the opposing party to object to the form of the order.

C. EXTENSIONS OF TIME AND CONTINUANCES

The kinds of motions that can be presented to the court are limited only by the movant's imagination. Practically, however, the routine housekeeping motions invariably deal with time and date modifications. These are the motions for extensions of time, continuances, and new hearing and trial dates. Before seeking an extension of time or continuance in court, always check with opposing counsel first. Oftentimes the parties will stipulate to the extension or continuance without the need to go to court.

Section 1054 of the Code of Civil Procedure governs extensions of time. If a motion to extend time is made the court may grant the motion for "good cause." However, such extension shall not exceed 30 days unless the adverse party consents.

What constitutes "good cause" is in the court's discretion and must be evaluated in the context of the pending case. Courts have generally been realistic and accommodating in permitting extensions of time when the applicable period has not yet run. Usually any reason other than one involving bad faith and actual prejudice to an opponent will result in the court's granting a reasonable extension of time.

In addition, in all cases where the court is empowered to grant an extension, the parties may agree in writing to an extension of time. In such cases, the court must give the extension of time.

Motions for extension of time may be made for such matters as extending the time to file an answer, or otherwise plead in a case, or service of notices of motion. Some time periods for post-trial matters usually cannot be enlarged. These include a motion for new trial and service of notices of appeal.

Continuances are similar to motions for extension, and usually occur when the party has a hearing or other matter already scheduled and simply wants the court to continue the hearing date. If all the parties agree to a continuance, the court will generally honor such agreement. You should always check the court's local rules to determine the procedure for requesting continuances for that particular court. Some of the rules are very specific, such as requiring the moving party to notify the court clerk so many days in advance of the need for a continuance.

Any motions for change of time or continuance should be made and decided within the applicable time period. In the motion, give the court solid reasons why an extension is necessary, and ask only for such additional time as is reasonably needed. Above all, avoid missing a deadline. Some time periods cannot be enlarged; others can only be enlarged after expiration upon a showing of excusable neglect. The best way to avoid having these disasters arise in the first place is by creating, maintaining, and following a reliable docket control system, which will remind you and the lawyer of all significant dates for each case you are handling. These vary from simple calendars to sophisticated computer systems, but are critical for every litigation paralegal.

Routine motions for extensions of time or continuances should be structured simply. The pertinent information that forms the basis for the motion can ordinarily be put in the body of the motion. A sample motion for an extension is shown in Exhibit 8.4.

When the facts supporting the motion are based on the lawyer's knowledge or information, or on that of a third party, a declaration signed under penalty of perjury must be filed in support of the facts.

Exhibit 8.4. Motion of Extension

[Caption]

<u>MOTION FOR ADDITIONAL TIME TO ANSWER OR RESPOND</u>

Defendant Robert Johnson moves this court for an order granting defendant an additional ten days to answer or respond to plaintiff's complaint. In support of his motion defendant states:

1. Defendant was served with the summons and complaint on June 1, 2007. Under the rules defendant's answer is due on or before June 21, 2007.

2. Defendant's attorney received the complaint on June 13, 2007.

3. Plaintiff's complaint has five counts and is based on an alleged series of contracts with the defendant.

4. To answer the complaint, defendant's attorney will have to evaluate numerous business records, which the defendant is presently locating, and review them with defendant.

5. Defendant's attorney believes he can prepare and serve an answer or otherwise respond if an additional ten days to answer or respond is granted.

WHEREFORE, defendant requests that this court enter an order extending defendant's time to answer or respond to July 1, 2007.

_____

Attorney for Defendant

D. SUBSTITUTION OF PARTIES

While an action is pending, occurrences may take place that will require that a named party be replaced by another. Such a substitution of parties can be required when a party dies, becomes incompetent, or loses all legal interest in the action. A public official named as a party can die, resign, or be voted out of office. In these situations the action is allowed to go forward by or against the party's representative. CCP §375 governs disability of a party, and CCP §377.11 governs matters in case of death of a party.

The usual procedure is to make a motion for substitution of parties, state the reason for the substitution in the body of the motion, and attach any necessary documents as exhibits. For example, if a party dies and will be substituted by the administrator of the estate, attach a copy of the death certificate and the probate court order appointing the administrator of the estate.

E. REMOVAL

Removal, as discussed in Chapter 4, is the procedure in which the defendant may transfer a case already filed in state court to the federal court for the same district in which the state action is pending. The right of a defendant to remove a case from state to federal court is a statutory right governed by 28 U.S.C. §§1441-1452. The following sections discuss the practical steps for filing a notice for removal.

Removal
Procedure to transfer action from state court to federal court

1. Should you remove?

Removal is nothing more than a change from a state to a federal forum. Consequently, there is no point in removing unless the defendant will benefit from the change. The potential advantages include a quicker trial date since federal courts frequently have less of a backlog than state courts. Many federal districts, however, make diversity cases the lowest priority on the trial calendar. Another potential advantage is the procedural differences that may exist between the state and federal courts. For example, the pleading possibilities may be greater and the discovery rights broader in federal court. Also, the Federal Rules of Evidence may be more relaxed on admissibility issues than the state evidence rules. Removing to federal court is also a way of getting the case away from an unfavorable judge. Also, federal jury panels are usually from a larger geographical pool and may have different characteristics than a state jury panel. Finally, changing to federal court may result in different substantive law being applied in diversity cases. These types of strategic possibilities must be carefully evaluated before proceeding further.

2. What are the procedural requirements for removal?

If the lawyer decides that removal is the proper course, make sure that you follow the procedures set out in 28 U.S.C. §§1446-1450, since case law requires that the procedures be closely followed. There are several basic steps that are requirements of the removal process.

a. Timing

The notice for removal must, under §1446(b), be filed in the federal district court in the division in which the state action is pending within 30 days after the defendant receives notice of the plaintiff's initial pleading. Accordingly, defendants must act quickly in removing a case.

b. Notice of removal

A verified petition for removal is no longer required under the Federal Rules. Instead a party must simply give notice of the removal. A sample notice is shown in Exhibit 8.5.

Exhibit 8.5. Notice of Removal

[Federal court caption]

Mary Jones,

                 Plaintiff-respondent   No. _____

       v.

John Smith,   NOTICE OF REMOVAL

                 Defendant-petitioner

To: The United States District Court for the District of Arizona:

Defendant John Smith hereby removes the above captioned case from the Superior Court of San Diego County, California, to the United States District Court for the Southern District of California. In support of this removal defendant states:

    1. Plaintiff Mary Jones commenced this action against defendant John Smith in the Superior Court of San Diego County under the caption of "Mary Jones, Plaintiff v. John Smith, Defendant," Case No. C-002344, by serving a copy of the complaint and summons on defendant on June 1, 2005.

    2. A copy of the complaint and summons is attached to this petition. No other pleadings or other proceedings have been filed or taken to date.

    3. This action is a civil action and is one over which this court has original jurisdiction under 28 U.S.C. §1331 [and/or §1332, etc.] and is an action that can be removed on the petition of defendant to this District Court pursuant to 28 U.S.C. §1441.

    4. [If federal question:] This court has original jurisdiction over this action because it appears from plaintiff's complaint that this is a civil action that arises under the _____ Act, _____ U.S.C. §____, [or Constitution or treaty] because plaintiff claims that . . . .

Exhibit 8.5. Continued

> 5. [If diversity:] This court has original jurisdiction over this action because it appears from plaintiff's complaint that this is a civil action, and:
>
> (a) Plaintiff, both when this action was commenced and now, was and is a citizen of the State of California.
>
> (b) Defendant, both when this action was commenced and now, was and is a citizen of the State of Nevada. Defendant was not, when this action was commenced, nor is he now, a citizen of the State of Arizona.
>
> (c) The amount in controversy, exclusive of interest and costs, exceeds $75,000.
>
> _____
> Attorney for Defendant
>
> [Verification]

c. Filing a notice in state court

A notice of removal should be filed with the clerk of the state court. This act terminates the jurisdiction of the state court. Notice must also be given to all the adverse parties.

d. Further proceedings

Once the notice is filed, removal is complete. There is no order required to effect removal. The district court retains jurisdiction unless and until the case is remanded, and can proceed as with any other case.

The usual status of affairs after a case has been removed is that the defendant who has been served has not yet responded to the complaint, and other defendants have not been served. The served defendant must, under Rule 81(c) of the Federal Rules of Civil Procedure, answer or otherwise plead within 20 days of receipt of the initial pleading or summons, or within 5 days of filing the removal petition, whichever is longer. The answer or other response must comply with the federal pleading rules. If plaintiff has not served all defendants before the removal petition is filed, service must be made in compliance with Rule 4 of the Federal Rules of Civil Procedure. In short, all action taken after removal must be taken under the Federal Rules.

CHAPTER SUMMARY

This chapter has provided an overview of the general law and procedures relating to motions. All motions must be in writing and contain a caption, a statement of the grounds for the motion, the relief or order requested, and the signature of the lawyer representing the moving party. Beyond these general requirements, specific requirements must also be met depending on the type of motion. For example, the usual procedure is to draft a concise statement setting forth the matter and relief requested and to support it with a memorandum of points and authorities. Local rules must be consulted for the time and day the court hears law and motion matters.

After the motion, opposition, and any reply papers are filed, the court may hear oral argument. Sometimes the judge issues a tentative ruling in advance of the oral argument. After the oral argument, the judge may issue a ruling from the bench or else take the matter under submission. Once a ruling is made, the clerk will enter the ruling in a minute order. A formal order also may be prepared by either the judge or the lawyer for the party in whose favor the judge ruled.

KEY TERMS

Consent order

Memorandum of points and authorities

Minute order

Motion

Notice of motion

Proof of service

Removal

Substitution of parties

Tentative ruling

Under submission

REVIEW QUESTIONS

1. What are the three basic items all motions must include?

2. What are the page limitations for memorandum of points and authorities?

3. What must the respondent do to oppose a motion?

4. What is a "minute order"?

5. Under what circumstances might a court deny a motion to extend time?

6. What is the procedure for substituting parties during the course of a pending lawsuit?

7. What document must the defendant file if the defendant wants to remove an action to federal court?

8. How many days does the defendant have to remove an action to federal court after the defendant receives notice of the plaintiff's state court complaint?

INTERNET RESOURCES

www.calawnet.com (links to California forms, codes, and jury instructions)

www.lawsource.com/also

www.netlawlibraries.com (links to California Rules of Court)

www.washlaw.edu (links to state and federal laws and forms)

CHAPTER **9**

Motions Attacking the Pleadings

CHAPTER OBJECTIVES

This chapter discusses the types of motions that a party can make after the pleadings are complete, in particular those motions that a defendant can use to attack the complaint. In this chapter you will learn:

♦ How to draft a demurrer
♦ When to file a motion to strike
♦ When to use a motion for judgment on the pleadings
♦ How to obtain a dismissal of a lawsuit
♦ How to cure a default judgment
♦ When consolidation and separation of trials may occur

A. INTRODUCTION

In Chapter 8 you learned the general requirements for all motions. However, there are certain motions that have special requirements. Two of the major motions, a demurrer and a motion to strike, may be brought before an answer is filed to attack the complaint filed by the plaintiff. This chapter discusses how to make these motions and the appropriate responses to the motions.

Other motions that may arise during this stage are dismissals and defaults. Voluntary dismissals can be done either by simply giving notice or by stipulation. However, involuntary dismissals require a motion as discussed in this chapter.

Motions for default judgment can be taken against a defendant that does not respond to a complaint. If a default judgment is entered, under certain circumstances a defendant may make a motion to vacate the default.

While this chapter discusses some of the motions that may arise during the course of a lawsuit, there are many other motions that you may need to address at different stages of the lawsuit. In Chapter 10 you will learn about summary judgments and how to obtain a judgment without trial.

B. DEMURRERS

A **demurrer** is a type of motion that may be used to attack the pleadings before an answer is filed. If the defendant believes that the Complaint, on its face, shows that the plaintiff is not entitled to the relief requested, the defendant may file a demurrer. A demurrer must be filed within the time period the defendant has to answer the complaint. The filing of the demurrer extends the time for the defendant to answer the complaint, until there has been a ruling by the court on the demurrer. If the demurrer is sustained, the plaintiff will need to amend the complaint to correct the defect raised by the demurrer, or risk that the complaint will be dismissed. If the demurrer is overruled, the defendant will have ten days after the ruling on the demurrer to answer the complaint.

Pursuant to CCP §430.10, there are several grounds that may be raised by a demurrer. These grounds are as follows:

♦ The court lacks subject matter jurisdiction;
♦ The person who filed the pleading does not have the legal capacity to sue;
♦ There is another action pending between the same parties on the same causes of action;
♦ There is a defect or misjoinder of parties;
♦ The complaint, or cross-complaint, fails to state facts sufficient to state a cause of action;
♦ The pleading is uncertain (ambiguous, unintelligible);
♦ In contract actions, it cannot be determined that the contract is oral, written, or implied;
♦ Certificate by the attorney of review and consultant in certain malpractice actions.

Rule 3.1320 of the California Rules of Court (CRC) provides that each ground of demurrer must be in a separate paragraph and must state whether it applies to the entire complaint, cross-complaint, or answer, or to specified causes of action or defenses. These same grounds may be raised as affirmative defenses in the answer as well. However, sometimes for strategic reasons it is better to raise the objections by demurrer and force the plaintiff to amend the complaint early on in the pleading stage.

Demurrers are sometimes referred to as either a **general** demurrer or a **specific** demurrer. A general demurrer is one that is based on either a failure to state a cause of action or lack of subject matter jurisdiction. All other grounds are special demurrers. The only time you need to know the difference is if you are filing in municipal court. Pursuant to CCP §92(c), special demurrers are not allowed in municipal court.

A demurrer will follow the same format as discussed for filing motions generally in Chapter 8. However, in addition to the notice of motion (called a notice of hearing on demurrer), you will also file a document entitled "Demurrer to Complaint." The demurrer may be made to one or more causes of action, and the grounds for the demurrer should be clearly stated. An example is shown in Exhibit 9.1. Even if the demurrer is to only one of several causes of action, the defendant does not need to answer the remaining causes of action until there is a ruling on the demurrer.

Exhibit 9.1. Demurrer

PLEASE TAKE NOTICE THAT on October 24, 2006, at 9:00 A.M. or as soon thereafter as the matter may be heard in Department E of the above-entitled Court, located at 6230 Sylmar Avenue, Van Nuys, California, defendant Walter Mabry will present his demurrer to the first and third causes of action of the Plaintiff's Complaint. Pursuant to Code of Civil Procedure Section 430.10(e), defendant demurs generally to the first cause of action on the ground, more fully set forth in the accompany memorandum of points and authorities, that it does not state facts sufficient to state a cause of action against defendant. In addition, defendant specifically demurs to the third cause of action on the ground that it is ambiguous, confused, and uncertain.

The court will set the hearing on the demurrer not more than 35 days following the filing of the demurrer or on the first date available to the court thereafter. If another date is needed, then the court may, for good cause, hold the hearing earlier or later as specified in the notice prescribed by the court.

While generally a demurrer is filed to attack the sufficiency of a complaint, it is also possible to demurrer to an answer. Pursuant to CCP 430.20, a party against whom an answer has been filed may object by demurrer as to the answer on the following grounds:

(a) The answer does not state facts sufficient to constitute a defense.
(b) The answer is uncertain. As used in this subdivision, "uncertain" includes ambiguous and unintelligible.
(c) Where the answer pleads a contract, it cannot be ascertained from the answer whether the contract is written or oral.

A demurrer to an answer must be filed within 10 days after service of the answer.

C. MOTIONS TO STRIKE

Motions to strike
A type of motion that attacks a defect in the complaint

Motions to strike are governed by CCP §§435, 436, and 437. If a defect exists in the complaint that is not subject to one of the grounds for a demurrer, it may be possible to attack the complaint by filing a motion to strike. A motion to strike may be used to attack an entire cause of action, or even individual allegations within a cause of action. Similar to a demurrer, the filing of a motion to strike must be made within the time limit for filing an answer. A timely filed motion to strike will extend the time that the defendant has to answer the complaint until a ruling on the motion. Accordingly, the plaintiff may not take the defendant's default while a motion to strike is pending, even if the motion to strike does not address the entire complaint.

There are two grounds for filing a motion to strike pursuant to strike. First, a motion to strike may be filed to strike any "irrelevant, false or improper matter inserted in any pleading." CCP §436(a). Secondly, a motion to strike may be filed to strike any pleading or part of a pleading that is "not drawn or filed in conformity with the laws of this state, a court rule or order of court." An example of "irrelevant, false or improper matter" may include allegations that are not material to the cause of action or the relief requested. For example, in an action for breach of contract, it may be wholly irrelevant to allege other business dealings between the parties that have no bearing on the current contract between the parties. Similarly, allegations that are mere legal conclusions, such as an allegation that the defendant "acted illegally" is irrelevant and may be stricken if there are not facts also stated to support such conclusion.

A complaint that is "not drawn in conformity with the laws of this state" might include where the complaint does not contain a required verification, or where the complaint is filed by a nonlawyer representing another party.

The notice of motion must include the items to be stricken, if the motion is not addressed to the entire complaint. Each of the grounds and portions to be stricken should be numbered consecutively. A sample of a motion to strike is shown in Exhibit 9.2. In addition to the notice of motion, you must also include a memorandum of points and authorities as discussed in Chapter 8.

D. JUDGMENT ON THE PLEADINGS

Motions for **judgment on the pleadings** are governed by CCP §438. After the pleadings are closed, but sufficiently before trial so that trial will not be delayed, any party can move for judgment on the pleadings. The motion determines if, based on the allegations in the pleadings, the moving party is entitled to judgment. For purposes of the motion, the movant's well-pleaded allegations that have been denied are deemed false, while the opponent's allegations are deemed true. In short, the pleadings are viewed in the light most favorable to the opponent. It is only when the undisputed facts as pled show that the movant is entitled to judgment that the motion should be granted. If a party presents matters outside the pleadings and the court decides to receive them, the

Exhibit 9.2. Motion to Strike

PLEASE TAKE NOTICE THAT on April 11, 2006, at 1:30 P.M., or as soon thereafter as the matter may be heard in Department 6 of the above-entitled Court, located at 700 Civic Center Drive West, Santa Ana, California, defendant Beverly Ward will move the Court for an order striking the following portions of the Complaint:

1. "For no valid reason other than to increase Defendant's profits at Plaintiff's expense." (Para. 9)
2. Plaintiff alleges that Defendant was acting maliciously, with malice, without good cause, and solely with the intent to injure the Plaintiff.

This motion to strike will be made on the grounds that the above allegations are improper and irrelevant to the purported causes of action in which they are alleged.

motion is treated as one for summary judgment, discussed in the next chapter, and not as a judgment on the pleadings.

There is only one ground upon which plaintiff may make a motion for judgment on the pleadings, and that is if the plaintiff can show that the complaint, on its face, states facts sufficient to state a cause of action, and the defendant's answer does not state facts sufficient to state a defense. The defendant may make a motion for judgment on the pleadings on two grounds. First, that the court has not subject matter jurisdiction, or second, that the complaint does not state facts sufficient to constitute a cause of action.

As a general rule, motions to amend pleadings should be freely given "in the furtherance of justice." CCP §473. Therefore, if it appears likely that a motion for judgment on the pleadings will be granted, the plaintiff should move for leave to amend if the defect can be cured. Under these circumstances the motion for leave to amend should be attached to the proposed amended pleading. When the motion to amend is made before substantial discovery has been conducted, it should ordinarily be granted, despite the fact that a motion for judgment on the pleadings is pending.

The motion for judgment on the pleadings is closely related to the demurrer discussed above. Of the several grounds for a demurrer, the most commonly asserted one is failure to state facts sufficient to state a cause of action. A demurrer is made, however, after the defendant has received the plaintiff's complaint and before answering. If the demurrer is granted, the plaintiff will usually be given leave to file an amended complaint; usually the plaintiff can cure the defect. The litigation then continues.

By contrast, a motion for judgment on the pleadings is made after the pleadings are closed and it has become evident that there is a legal bar, such as an applicable statute of limitations, that will prevent plaintiff from recovering anything. For this reason, a motion for judgment on the pleadings should not be made unless it is clear from the facts in the pleadings, in light of applicable substantive law, that plaintiff cannot recover on his complaint. Such motions are made infrequently.

E. DISMISSALS AND DEFAULTS

There are two types of dismissals, voluntary and involuntary. Dismissals may be of a complaint or cross-complaint, and may be of the entire action, or only part of the action.

1. Voluntary dismissals

There are two ways to obtain a **voluntary dismissal.** First, under CCP §581(b)(1), a plaintiff has an absolute right to dismiss a complaint any time before the commencement of trial. Subject to certain exceptions, no court order is required. The plaintiff will simply file with the clerk of the court a request for dismissal on the form provided by the judicial council (see Exhibit 9.3). The clerk has no discretion, and must accept the request for dismissal.[1] The dismissal is **without prejudice**—meaning the claim can be refiled later—unless otherwise stated.

Second, a plaintiff may dismiss the action, or any cause of action or party to the action, once the trial starts. However, in such cases, the dismissal will be **with prejudice**, unless all the parties agree to the dismissal. With prejudice means that the plaintiff is barred from ever refiling the same claim again.

In all other circumstances, plaintiff may obtain a voluntary dismissal only by court order. The court has power to impose terms and conditions that are appropriate under the circumstances, which may include the payment of costs, expenses, and attorney's fees to the defendant. Under ordinary circumstances the motion should be granted, unless the defendant can show that some actual legal prejudice would result from a second lawsuit. A sample notice of dismissal is set forth in Exhibit 9.4.

Voluntary dismissal
A withdrawal of a claim by the party originally asserting the claim

Without prejudice
Once dismissed, the claim may be filed again

With prejudice
Once dismissed, the claim may not be refiled

---

1. There are a few exceptions to the absolute right to dismiss. For example, if a cross-complaint has been filed by the defendant, the plaintiff must obtain the consent of the defendant prior to dismissing the complaint. CCP §581(h).

Exhibit 9.3. Request for Dismissal

CIV-110

ATTORNEY OR PARTY WITHOUT ATTORNEY *(Name and Address):*	TELEPHONE NO.:	*FOR COURT USE ONLY*

ATTORNEY FOR *(Name):*

Insert name of court and name of judicial district and branch court, it any.

PLAINTIFF/PETITIONER:

DEFENDANT/ RESPONDENT:

REQUEST FOR DISMISSAL
☐ **Personal Injury, Property Damage, or Wrongful Death**
    ☐ **Motor Vehicle** ☐ **Other**
☐ **Family Law**
☐ **Eminent Domain**
☐ **Other** *(specify)* :

CASE NUMBER:

- A conformed copy will not be returned by the clerk unless a method of return is provided with the document. -

1. TO THE CLERK: Please **dismiss** this action as follows:
  a. (1) ☐ With prejudice (2) ☐ Without prejudice
  b. (1) ☐ Complaint (2) ☐ Petition
    (3) ☐ Cross-complaint filed by *(name):*   on *(date):*
    (4) ☐ Cross-complaint filed by *(name):*   on *(date):*
    (5) ☐ Entire action of all parties and all causes of action
    (6) ☐ Other *(specify):**

Date:

▶

(TYPE OR PRINT NAME OF ☐ ATTORNEY ☐ PARTY WITHOUT ATTORNEY)   (SIGNATURE)

*If dismissal requested is of specified parties only of specified causes of action only, or of specified cross-complaints only, so state and identify the parties, causes of action, or cross-complaints to be dismissed.

Attorney or party without attorney for:
☐ Plaintiff/Petitioner   ☐ Defendant/Respondent
☐ Cross - complainant

2. **TO THE CLERK:** Consent to the above dismissal is hereby given.**
  Date:

▶

(TYPE OR PRINT NAME OF ☐ ATTORNEY ☐ PARTY WITHOUT ATTORNEY)   (SIGNATURE)

** If a cross-complaint-or Response (Family Law) seeking affirmative relief -is on file, the attorney for cross-complainant (respondent) must sign this consent if required by Code of Civil Procedure section 581 (i) or (j).

Attorney or party without attorney for:
☐ Plaintiff/Petitioner   ☐ Defendant/Respondent
☐ Cross - complainant

(To be completed by clerk)
3. ☐ Dismissal entered as requested on *(date):*
4. ☐ Dismissal entered on *(date):*   as to only *(name):*
5. ☐ Dismissal **not entered** as requested for the following reasons *(specify):*

6. ☐ a. Attorney or party without attorney notified on *(date):*
    b. Attorney or party without attorney not notified. Filing party failed to provide
    ☐ a copy to conformed ☐ means to return conformed copy

Date: Clerk, by _____ , Deputy

Page 1 of 1

Form Adopted for Mandatory use
Judicial Council of California
CIV-110 [Rev. January 1, 2007]

REQUEST FOR DISMISSAL

Code of Civil Procedure, § 581 et seq.;
Cal. Rules of Court, rule 3.1390
www.courtinfo.ca.gov

American LegalNet, Inc.
www.FormsWorkflow.com

Exhibit 9.4. Notice of Dismissal

CIV-120

ATTORNEY OR PARTY WITHOUT ATTORNEY *(Name and Address)*:

TELEPHONE NO.:

FOR COURT USE ONLY

ATTORNEY FOR *(Name)*:

Insert name of court and name of judicial district and branch court, if any:

PLAINTIFF/PETITIONER:

DEFENDANT/RESPONDENT:

NOTICE OF ENTRY OF DISMISSAL AND PROOF OF SERVICE
- ☐ **Personal Injury, Property Damage, or Wrongful Death**
  - ☐ **Motor Vehicle** ☐ **Other**
- ☐ **Family Law**
- ☐ **Eminent Domain**
- ☐ **Other** *(specify)*:

CASE NUMBER:

TO ATTORNEYS AND PARTIES WITHOUT ATTORNEYS: A dismissal was entered in this action by the clerk as shown on the Request for Dismissal. *(Attach a copy completed by the clerk.)*

Date:

▶

....

(TYPE OR PRINT NAME OF ☐ ATTORNEY ☐ PARTY WITHOUT ATTORNEY)

(SIGNATURE)

PROOF OF SERVICE

1. I am over the age of 18 and not a party to this cause. I am a resident of or employed in the county where the mailing occurred. My residence or business address is:

2. ☐ I served a copy of the Notice of Entry of Dismissal and Request for Dismissal by mailing them, in a sealed envelope with postage fully prepaid, as follows:
   a. ☐ I deposited the envelope with the United States Postal Service.
   b. ☐ I placed the envelope for collection and processing for mailing following this business's ordinary practice with which I am readily familiar. On the same day correspondence is placed for collection and mailing, it is deposited in the ordinary course of business with the United States Postal Service.
   c. Date of deposit:
   d. Place of deposit *(city and state)*:
   e. Addressed as follows *(name and address)*:

3. ☐ I served a copy of the Notice of Entry of Dismissal and Request for Dismissal by personally delivering copies to the person served as shown below:
   Name: Date: Time: Address:

4. I declare under penalty of perjury under the laws of the State of California that the foregoing is true and correct.
   Date:

▶

....

(TYPE OR PRINT NAME)

(SIGNATURE OF DECLARANT)

Page 1 of 1

Form Adopted for Mandatory Use
Judicial Council of California
CIV-120 [Rev. January 1, 2007]

**NOTICE OF ENTRY OF DISMISSAL
AND PROOF OF SERVICE**

Code of Civil Procedure, § 581 et seq.;
Cal. Rules of Court, rule 3.1390
www.courtinfo.ca.gov

American LegalNet, Inc.
www.Forms*Workflow*.com

2. Involuntary dismissals

Involuntary dismissals
Method of terminating a claim when the plaintiff or other claimant has been guilty of misconduct or inaction

Involuntary dismissal provides a method for terminating a claim when the plaintiff or other claimant has been guilty of misconduct. CCP §§583.110-583.360 govern involuntary dismissals. There are several grounds upon which a defendant can obtain an involuntary dismissal of the plaintiff's complaint.

First, dismissal is mandatory if the plaintiff has failed to serve and return the summons and complaint within three years after the summons has been issued. In this way, the plaintiff cannot simply toll any statute of limitations by filing the complaint, and thereafter not serving the defendant for several years. If the plaintiff has failed to serve the summons and complaint within two years, dismissal is discretionary. The defendant may obtain the dismissal by filing a motion to dismiss.

Second, a plaintiff's failure to prosecute a claim can result in dismissal. This depends on the nature of the case, but includes a plaintiff's lack of diligence in litigating, such as failing to respond to motions or to appear at hearings, and other repeated dilatory behavior. Involuntary dismissal is a drastic remedy and will normally not be imposed unless other remedies are inadequate. Difficult cases often involve situations in which the plaintiff's inaction is a result of his attorney's misconduct, but the plaintiff may have a valid claim. In these situations the court will usually do something short of involuntary dismissal.

Third, the court can involuntarily dismiss when the plaintiff fails to comply with rules of procedure or with court orders. As a consequence of the plaintiff's failure to comply, as in situations such as failing to respond to the discovery requests, the court may, as the ultimate sanction, dismiss plaintiff's complaint.

3. Defaults

Default
A failure of a party to respond to the pleading of the opposing party

Closely related to dismissals are **defaults.** The plaintiff may obtain a default judgment against a party that fails to plead or take any steps to defend against the pending action. The usual situation involves a defaulting defendant.

If a defendant has not responded within the time required to answer, the plaintiff may ask that the clerk enter a default against the defendant. The plaintiff does this by filing a Request to Enter Default. A sample is in Exhibit 9.5. The next step is to move for default judgment. If the claim is for a specific sum or a sum that can be computed to a specific amount, a default judgment can be entered by the clerk of the court. The judgment can be for no more than the amount requested in the complaint.

Exhibit 9.5. Request to Enter Default

982(a)(6)

ATTORNEY OR PARTY WITHOUT ATTORNEY *(Name, state bar number, and address)*	FOR COURT USE ONLY
TELEPHONE NO. FAX NO. ATTORNEY FOR *(Name)*	

Insert name of court and name of judicial district and branch court, if any:

PLAINTIFF:

DEFENDANT:

REQUEST FOR ☐ **ENTRY OF DEFAULT** ☐ **CLERK'S JUDGMENT** (Application) ☐ **COURT JUDGMENT**	CASE NUMBER

1. TO THE CLERK: On the complaint or cross-complaint filed
   a   on *(date)*:
   b   by *(name)*:
   c   ☐   Enter default of defendant *(names)*:

   d   ☐   I request a court judgment under Code of Civil Procedure sections 585(b), (c), 989, etc., against defendant *(names)*.

   (Testimony required. Apply to the clerk for a hearing date, unless the court will enter a judgment on an affidavit under Code of Civil Procedure section 585(d).)

   e   ☐   Enter clerk's judgment
       (1)☐   for restitution of the premises only and issue a writ of execution on the judgment. Code of Civil Procedure section 1174(c) does not apply. (Code Civ. Proc., § 1169.)
         ☐   Include in the judgment all tenants, subtenants, named claimants, and other occupants of the premises. The *Prejudgment Claim of Right to Possession* was served in compliance with Code of Civil Procedure section 415.46.
       (2)☐   under Code of Civil Procedure section 585(a). *(Complete the declaration under Code Civ. Proc., § 585.5 on the reverse (item 5).)*
       (3)☐   for default previously entered on *(date)*:

2. **Judgment to be entered**

	Amount	Credits acknowledged	Balance
a. Demand of complaint	$	$	$
b. Statement of damages *			
(1) Special	$	$	$
(2) General	$	$	$
c. Interest	$	$	$
d. Costs *(see reverse)*	$	$	$
e. Attorney fees	$	$	$
f. **TOTALS**	$	$	$

   g. **Daily damages** were demanded in complaint at the rate of: $ per day beginning *(date)*:
   (* *Personal injury or wrongful death actions: Code Civ. Proc., § 425.11)*

3. ☐   *(Check if filed in an unlawful detainer case)* **LEGAL DOCUMENT ASSISTANT OR UNLAWFUL DETAINER ASSISTANT** information is on the reverse *(complete item 4)*.

Date:

                             ▶

_____   _____
(TYPE OR PRINT NAME)   (SIGNATURE OF PLAINTIFF OR ATTORNEY FOR PLAINTIFF)

FOR COURT USE ONLY	(1)☐ Default entered as requested on *(date)*: (2)☐ Default NOT entered as requested *(state reason)*: Clerk, by _____ , Deputy

Page 1 of 2

Form Adopted for Mandatory Use
 Judicial Council of California
 982(a)(6) [Rev. July 1, 2003]

REQUEST FOR ENTRY OF DEFAULT
 (Application to Enter Default)

Code of Civil Procedure,
 §§ 585-587, 1169 <br> www.courtinfo.ca.gov

 American LegalNet, Inc.
 www.USCourtForms.com

Exhibit 9.5. Continued.

SHORT TITLE:	CASE NUMBER

4. **LEGAL DOCUMENT ASSISTANT OR UNLAWFUL DETAINER ASSISTANT (Bus. & Prof. Code, § 6400 et seq.)** A legal **document assistant or unlawful detainer assistant** ☐ did ☐ **did not** for compensation give advice or assistance with this form. *(If declarant has received any help or advice for pay from a legal document assistant or unlawful detainer assistant, state).*

   a. Assistant's name: b. Telephone No:

   c. Street address, city, and ZIP:

   d. County of registration:

   e. Registration No.:   e. Expires on *(date)*

5. ☐ **DECLARATION UNDER CODE OF CIVIL PROCEDURE SECTION 585.5** *(Required for entry of default under Code Civ. Proc., § 585(a))* This action

   a. ☐ is ☐ is not on a contract or installment sale for goods or services subject to Civ. Code. § 1801 et seq. (Unruh Act).

   b. ☐ is ☐ is not on a conditional sales contract subject to Civ. Code, § 2981 et seq. (Rees-Levering Motor Vehicle Sales and Finance Act).

   c. ☐ is ☐ is not on an obligation for goods, services, loans, or extensions of credit subject to Code Civ. Proc., § 395(b).

6. **DECLARATION OF MAILING (Code Civ. Proc., § 587)** A copy of this *Request for Entry of Default* was

   a. ☐ **not mailed** to the following defendants whose addresses are **unknown** to plaintiff or plaintiff's attorney *(names)*:

   b. ☐ **mailed** first-class, postage prepaid, in a sealed envelope addressed to each defendant's attorney of record or, if none, to each defendant's last known address as follows:

      (1) Mailed on *(date)*:   (2) To *(specify names and addresses shown on the envelopes)*:

I declare under penalty of perjury under the laws of the State of California that the foregoing items 4, 5, and 6 are true and correct.
Date:

▶

(TYPE OR PRINT NAME)	(SIGNATURE OF DECLARANT)

7. **MEMORANDUM OF COSTS** *(Required if judgment requested)* **Costs and disbursements** are as follows (Code Civ. Proc. § 1033.5):

   a. Clerk's filing fees .... $

   b. Process server's fees .... $

   c. Other *(specify)*: .... $

   d. .... $

   e. **TOTAL** .... $_____

   f. ☐ Costs and disbursements are waived

   g. I am the attorney, agent, or party who claims these costs. To the best of my knowledge and belief this memorandum of costs is correct and these costs were necessarily incurred in this case.

I declare under penalty of perjury under the laws of the State of California that the foregoing is true and correct.
Date:

▶

(TYPE OR PRINT NAME)	(SIGNATURE OF DECLARANT)

8. ☐ **DECLARATION OF NONMILITARY STATUS** *(Required for a judgment)* No defendant named in item 1c of the application is in the military service so as to be entitled to the benefits of the Soldiers' and Sailors' Civil Relief Act of 1940 (50 U.S.C. Appen. § 501 et seq.).

I declare under penalty of perjury under the laws of the State of California that the foregoing is true and correct.
Date:

▶

(TYPE OR PRINT NAME)	(SIGNATURE OF DECLARANT)

982(a)(6) [Rev. July 1, 2003]

REQUEST FOR ENTRY OF DEFAULT
(Application to Enter Default)

Page 2 of 2

American LegalNet, Inc.
www.USCourtForms.com

In all other cases, the plaintiff must **"prove up"** the default. The plaintiff does this by making a motion for default judgment to be heard by the Court. The plaintiff must file a notice of motion, motion and supporting affidavits, or declarations to show the amount of the judgment the plaintiff is entitled to receive. (An example of a motion for default is shown in Exhibit 9.6.)

At the hearing on the motion, the plaintiff must be prepared to show that service on the defaulting party was proper, that the allegations of the complaint are true, and what the proper damages are. While judges vary on the formality of the prove-up hearing, all supporting documentation should be available at the hearing and any witnesses that may be necessary to prove the case should be on hand. For example, in an action on a contract, proper service can be shown with the proof of service in the court file. If necessary, the person who served the complaint and

Exhibit 9.6. Motion for Default

[Caption]

<u>MOTION FOR DEFAULT</u>

Plaintiff Joan Franklin moves for an order finding defendant Thomas Johnson in default, finding that the defendant owes plaintiff the sum of $24,246.80 plus costs, and for judgment against defendant in that amount. In support of her motion plaintiff states:

1. On March 1, 2004, defendant Thomas Johnson was personally served with the summons and the complaint, as shown by the affidavit of service on the summons.

2. Defendant has failed to answer the complaint, has failed to make an appearance, or in any way respond or defend, although over 90 days have passed since service upon him.

3. Defendant has not responded to three letters sent to him by plaintiff's attorneys. Copies of these letters are attached as Exhibits A, B, and C.

4. Plaintiff is prepared to testify to her reasonable damages, which total $24,246.80.

WHEREFORE, plaintiff requests that the court find defendant Thomas Johnson in default, hold a hearing to determine the exact amount due plaintiff, and enter judgment for plaintiff and against defendant in that amount.

_____
Attorney for Plaintiff

summons may testify. The existence and execution of the contract may be proven by calling a witness who was present at its execution.

Another witness, along with exhibits, can prove performance by the plaintiff, typically payment of the contract price. Other witnesses and records can show nonperformance by the defendant and the extent of the plaintiff's damages. Although the court may not require them, or permit witnesses to summarize what they know in a narrative fashion, it is always safer to have all the witnesses available and prepared to testify as if the proceeding were a trial.

A defaulting party can only have the default judgment set aside for specific reasons. The specific reasons depend on when the defaulting party brings the motion to set aside the default. Under CCP §473, if the defaulting party makes a motion to set aside the default within 6 months of the Clerk's entry of default, the default can be set aside for "mistake, inadvertence, surprise, or excusable neglect." If the six months has expired, but is less than two years, the defendant must show either "extrinsic fraud or mistake" or "lack of actual notice." *See* CCP §473.5. After two years, fraud and mistake are the only grounds.

To avoid having a default judgment set aside, take the following steps. First, serve the defendant by the most direct of the permitted service methods. Second, wait an appropriate period of time, at least 60 to 90 days, before seeking a default. Third, during this time send the defendant periodic letters asking for a response and spelling out the consequences of a default. Finally, send the defendant a notice of motion for the default motion, even though this is required only if the defendant has previously appeared in the case.

Taking these steps now will support the motion itself and will make it less likely that the defaulted defendant will succeed in having the default judgment set aside later. The defendant will usually try to vacate the judgment only after steps have been taken to execute the judgment against the defendant's property, such as garnishing a savings account, and the matter suddenly has become "serious."

F. CONSOLIDATION AND SEPARATE TRIALS

Upon motion of the parties or the court's own motion, the court may consolidate separate cases for trial or have parts of a single case tried separately.

1. Consolidations

Consolidation has several elements. First, actions can be consolidated only when all actions are pending before the court. This means that the cases have all been filed and are presently pending in the same court.

Second, the actions must have common questions of law or fact. Typical are personal injury actions by several plaintiffs arising out of a single accident. Third, the court may decide to consolidate only certain issues for hearing or trial, such as the liability issues. This is a discretionary matter for the court and is usually decided after discovery has been completed and the cases are scheduled on the trial calendar.

2. Separate trials

The court may also bifurcate issues or parties in order to have separate trials. This is permitted where separation will create convenience, avoid prejudice, or permit a case to be tried more efficiently and economically. The typical situation involves unrelated permissive cross-complaints or third parties where it makes sense to try unrelated claims later or spin off third parties to keep the trials simpler. This decision is also usually made only when discovery is complete and the case is on the trial calendar.

CHAPTER SUMMARY

This chapter has described the common motions you may be asked to draft after the pleading stage is complete. Based solely on the allegations of the pleadings, a demurrer may be appropriate. If the complaint contains information that is not relevant, or there is a defect in the complaint, a motion to strike may be made. When one party is entitled to judgment based solely on the pleadings, then the appropriate motion to make is a motion for judgment on the pleadings.

A lawsuit also may be terminated by either a voluntary or involuntary dismissal. If the dismissal is voluntary, notice of the dismissal must be sent to all parties, although no court order is required. If all parties agree on the dismissal, the parties may simply file a stipulation with the court.

A lawsuit also may terminate because a defendant has failed to timely respond to the complaint. If the claim is for a specific sum, the plaintiff may be able to have the default judgment entered by the clerk of the court. In all other instances, the plaintiff should make a motion for a default judgment to be entered.

KEY TERMS

Consolidation
Default
Demurrer
Involuntary dismissal
Judgment on the pleadings

Motion to strike
Prove up
Voluntary dismissal
With prejudice
Without prejudice

REVIEW QUESTIONS

1. Identify the grounds for a demurrer.

2. When would you use a motion to strike?

3. What is a motion for judgment on the pleadings?

4. What are the two ways a party may obtain a voluntary dismissal of an action?

5. Identify at least three grounds for an involuntary dismissal of an action.

INTERNET RESOURCES

www.chesslaw.com
www.courtinfo.ca.gov/rules/index
www.findlaw.com
www.ilrg.com/forms/index
www.lawguru.com
www.leginfo.ca.gov

Summary Judgments

CHAPTER OBJECTIVES

This chapter discusses motions for summary judgment and summary adjudication. In this chapter you will learn:

♦ When a motion for summary judgment is appropriate
♦ What must be included in a motion for summary judgment
♦ What response the opponent should make to a summary judgment motion
♦ When to seek a summary adjudication
♦ How to oppose a motion for summary judgment
♦ What must be included in a separate statement

A. INTRODUCTION

In Chapters 8 and 9 you learned about the basic format requirements and the types of motions that attack the pleadings in this case. In this chapter you will learn how to attack a case or defense based on the merits, without the necessity of going to trial. A motion for summary judgment allows you to obtain a judgment and end the lawsuit as if there had been a trial.

Motions for summary judgment are generally done after all the pleadings have been completed and substantial discovery has taken place. You will support your motion for summary judgment with evidence that you have collected during the informal and formal fact-gathering stages. Specific motion rules apply and you must be careful to follow the rules for summary judgment and calendar all time requirements so that you do not miss the opportunity to bring a summary judgment prior to trial.

B. SUMMARY JUDGMENT

Summary judgment
A judgment rendered by a court before trial

Summary judgment, a judgment rendered by the court before trial, is governed by CCP §437(c) in California Courts and Rule 56 of the Federal Rules of Civil Procedure in Federal Court.[1] It is designed to be an efficient method of deciding a case and may be made when there are no genuine disputes over any material facts, and the only issues are questions of law. A motion for summary judgment can be made on

---

1. The procedure discussed here is substantially the same for state and federal courts. However, if filing a motion for summary judgment in federal court, you should refer to the federal rules.

any claim—complaint, cross-complaint—or on a separate complaint for declaratory judgment. **Summary adjudication** may be brought on one or more causes of action within a case, one or more affirmative defenses, one or more claims for damages, or one or more issues of duty. The purpose of a summary adjudication is to obtain a decision on at least a partial portion of the case, even if there are trial issues of fact on other portions.[2]

1. When made

A party must wait for 60 days after appearance of the other party before moving for summary judgment, unless an earlier time is mandated by the court. The purpose is to give the parties an opportunity to investigate, through discovery methods, the other side's case.

Although the hold period at the beginning of the case is only 60 days, summary judgments early in the litigation process, have little chance of success since motions are usually supported by answers to discovery requests, such as interrogatories and requests for admissions, the motion is usually made after substantial discovery has been conducted. In this way, the important facts have become known, and it becomes increasingly apparent that there are no serious disputes over the essential facts.

2. Standards and matters considered

A moving party is entitled to summary judgment only if there is no genuine issue as to any material fact and the moving party is entitled to a judgment as a matter of law. The motion merely asks the court to decide if there are any material facts in issue and whether the substantive law entitles the moving party to judgment. It is not the court's function here to determine what facts are true. In deciding if material facts are in dispute, however, the court can consider the pleadings, discovery, and witness affidavits.

What facts are material is determined by the claim involved and the allegations in the pleadings. The court will review the movant's motion and supporting matters and determine if any material facts remain disputed. The court will resolve any doubts against the moving party. Keep in mind, however, that the formal pleadings do not dictate the court's decision. If the pleadings show a dispute, but the discovery and affidavits show that no dispute over any material fact exists, the motion should be granted.

---

2. In federal court, summary adjudication is referred to as partial summary judgment.

If the motion fails to demonstrate that summary judgment should be granted, the opponent theoretically needs to do nothing. As a matter of practice, of course, the opposing party always responds to the motion with a memorandum and, if possible, affidavits showing why the motion should not be granted. However, if the motion with accompanying materials shows that the motion should be granted, the opponent ordinarily must, if able to, present a response and opposing affidavit to show that disputes over material issues still remain. If the court then finds that disputed issues remain, the motion will be denied.

3. Hearing, order, and appealability

At the hearing on the motion for summary judgment, the judge will usually allow oral argument, and then ordinarily will take the case under advisement and enter a written order at a later time. The order will set out whether the motion is granted or, if summary adjudication is requested, on what causes of action the motion is granted or denied. It will also set out the findings and reasoning that are the basis of the order.

Appealability of the order depends on whether the order disposes of all or only part of the case. When an order granting the motion disposes of the entire case, the order is final and appealable. Where the order grants only summary adjudication, either for some but not all parties or for some but not all of the causes of action, the order may be appealable, depending on whether the court makes it an appealable one.

When the motion is denied, the usual reason is that material facts are still in dispute. An order denying summary judgment on that basis is not final and cannot be appealed.

4. Practice approach

A motion for summary judgment is most frequently successful in simple cases where the "facts" cannot be disputed, such as actions on contracts and notes where the signatures are conceded to be either genuine or fraudulent. The motion is unlikely to be granted in cases where a mental state or a witness' credibility is critical.

Motions for summary adjudication should be considered in more complex cases when at least one cause of action or party can possibly be disposed of. This may streamline the case and make the remaining causes of action easier to try.

If you are asked to draft a motion for summary judgment, keep several points in mind. First, draft the motion sufficiently in advance of the hearing date to allow time to serve and file the motion. Motions for summary judgment must be served at least 75 days before the hearing, increased to 80 days if mailed to a party in California. The opposing party must file and serve the opposition papers at least 14 days in advance. Any reply to the opposition filed by the moving party must be filed and served at least 5 days before the hearing.

Second, the moving and responding papers have several requirements that differ from the general motion practice discussed in Chapter 8.

a. Notice

There should be a notice of motion that specifies the time, date, and place of hearing, as well as the relief requested, grounds for the motion, and evidence relied upon. *See* CCP §1010. An example of notice of motion for summary judgment is shown in Exhibit 10.1.

b. Motion

The motion must be supported by the facts showing why the party is entitled to summary judgment. In Chapter 11 you will learn the rules of

Exhibit 10.1. Motion for Summary Judgment

TO ALL PARTIES AND TO THEIR ATTORNEYS OF RECORD:

PLEASE TAKE NOTICE THAT on August 28, 2006, at 9:00 A.M., or as soon thereafter as the matter may be heard, in Department 83 of the above-entitled Court, located at 111 N. Hill Street, Los Angeles, California, defendant Beverly Hughes will move this Court for an Order entitled summary judgment in favor of defendant and against plaintiff on the Complaint on the grounds that there are no trial issues of material fact and judgment should be entered in favor of defendant and against plaintiff as a matter of law.

This motion is based upon this notice of motion, the accompanying memorandum of points and authorities, the separate statement of undisputed facts required by Code of Civil Procedure Section 437c(b) and filed concurrently herewith, the Declaration of Beverly Hughes, the record of this action and such additional argument and evidence as may be presented at the hearing of this motion.

Dated: July ___, 2006 _____

Signature

evidence that govern whether the facts you have discovered in the case are admissible in court. However, in general, to support your motion for summary judgment you will gather facts from declarations of your client and witnesses, admissions made by the other party in answers to interrogatories or at depositions, documents produced by the other party, and matters to which the court is required to take judicial notice.

These facts will be woven into a statement of facts that you will put at the beginning of your motion. In addition, it is important to submit these facts to the court in the form of admissible evidence. You can do this by attaching to the motion copies of the declarations and documents properly authenticated. *See* Chapter 11 for rules governing how to authenticate.

In addition, you will also include a supporting memorandum of points and authorities that give the legal reasons, supported by cases as to why your client is entitled to summary judgment.

c. Separate statement

Unlike other motions, a motion for summary judgment or summary adjudication, must also contain a "Separate Statement of Undisputed Facts." The separate statement must be separately bound and filed, rather than included as an attachment to the motion for summary judgment. The separate statement lists, in numbered paragraphs, all of the facts that are not in dispute. After each fact, the moving party must list the evidence submitted in the motion that demonstrates the fact is not in dispute. In essence, think of it as a mini-trial. For example, if one fact that a plaintiff would have to prove in a breach of contract action is that the parties entered into the contract, the first fact would be to prove the existence of the contract. After that fact, the party would list the evidence that proves the fact. Example:

1. The parties entered into a written contract on July 1, 2008. (Defendant's Answer admitting paragraph 3 of the Complaint which attached a true and correct copy of the July 1, 2008 Contract.)

The moving party would continue in this way for all of the facts necessary to prove the cause of action. A sample Separate Statement is shown in Exhibit 10.2.

Witness affidavits must be carefully prepared for the motion. **Affidavits** are sworn statements by witnesses, and their contents should be drafted so that the facts asserted will be admissible at trial. In California state courts, rather than file affidavits, which require that they be witnessed and signed by a notary public, a party may use **Declarations** instead. Declarations are statements by witnesses made

Declaration
Refers to statements by witnesses made under penalty of perjury

Exhibit 10.2. Separate Statement

Plaintiff Kelly James submits the following separate statement of undisputed material facts and reference to supporting evidence pursuant to California Code of Civil Procedure Section 437c(b). These material facts include every essential element to entitle defendant to summary judgment as a matter of law:

1. The parties entered into a written contract on July 1, 2004. (Defendant's Answer admitting paragraph 3 of the Complaint which attached a true and correct copy of the July 1, 2004 Contract.)
2. On September 3, 2004 Plaintiff delivered the goods required by the contract to the Defendant, and invoiced the Defendant the sums then due. (Declaration of Plaintiff Kelly James, paragraph 3.)
3. Defendant failed to pay the sums due to the Plaintiff. (Declaration of Plaintiff Kelly James, paragraph 4.)
4. Plaintiff made demand for payment or the return of goods, however, to this date Defendant has refused to either pay or return the goods. (Declaration of Plaintiff Kelly James, paragraph 5.)

under penalty of perjury. No notary attestation is required. Under either affidavits or declarations, the witness must be shown to be competent and to have first-hand knowledge of the facts. The facts asserted must comply with all other evidence rules. The testimony of each witness is usually set out in statement form, although in some situations a question-and-answer format may be appropriate. The statement is then sworn to before a notary public showing that the witness has personal knowledge of the facts and that they are true. The notary's attestation and seal should be on the affidavit. A sample declaration, which is commonly used in California, is shown in Exhibit 10.3.

5. Opponent's responses

What should the opponent of a motion for summary judgment do? CCP §473c(b) expressly states that an opposition shall consist of, where appropriate, "affidavits, declarations, admissions, answers to interrogatories, depositions, and matters of which judicial notice shall or may be taken." Accordingly, the adverse party should present an opposing memorandum with supporting declarations to demonstrate that issues of material fact remain. The supporting declarations will usually present testimony that contradicts the movant's declarations on some material facts, thus creating an issue of witness credibility. Credibility issues that

Exhibit 10.3. *Sample Declaration*

<u>DECLARATION OF KELLY JAMES</u>

I, Kelly James, declare as follows:

1. I am the Vice-President of Baker Corporation, the Plaintiff in this action. I make this Declaration in support of Baker Corporation's Motion for Summary Judgment in this action. If called as a witness in this matter, I am competent to testify, of my own personal knowledge, as to all facts set forth in this Declaration.
2. On July 1, 2004 Baker Corporation entered into a written contract with the Defendant. A true and correct copy of this contract is attached hereto as Exhibit A.
3. On September 3, 2004 Plaintiff delivered the goods required by the contract to the Defendant, and invoiced the Defendant the sums then due.
4. Defendant failed to pay the sums due to the Plaintiff.
5. Plaintiff made demand for payment or the return of goods, however, to this date Defendant has refused to either pay or return the goods.

---

exist concerning material facts can only be decided by a trial, so the motion should be denied. If the movant's witness declarations contain information that the witness would not be able to testify to because of evidentiary objections or because the affidavit is improperly sworn to or notarized, these defects should be raised in the opposing memorandum, and a separate motion to strike those portions of the witness statement should be filed along with the opposing papers.

The opposition papers must also include a separate statement of disputed facts which responds to each of the material facts contained in the moving party's separate statement. The opposing separate statement should follow in numerical order all of the statements made in the moving party's papers, and state whether the opposing party agrees or disagrees. If the opposing party disagrees, the opposing party should reference the evidence in the opposing papers which demonstrates there is a dispute. For example, assume that in the contract example above, the opposing party disputes that the July 1, 2008 contract is the contract between the parties because the parties subsequently entered into an amended contract. The opposing party may respond as follows:

1. Disputed. (Defendant's Declaration, paragraph 4, attached to the Opposition to Motion for Summary Judgment.)

The important point to remember in opposing a motion for summary judgment is that you must be able to show that genuine issues of material fact exist. As long as you can prove that a dispute over the facts exists, the motion for summary judgment must be denied.

CHAPTER SUMMARY

This chapter described the method to use if a motion must discuss facts beyond the mere allegations in the pleadings. The appropriate motion is for summary judgment. A motion for summary judgment is an efficient way to dispose of a lawsuit prior to trial when there are no material issues in dispute. Either side can bring a motion for summary judgment. If the motion is brought on fewer than all causes of action, a motion may be made for summary adjudication.

KEY TERMS

Affidavit

Declaration

Summary adjudication

Summary judgment

REVIEW QUESTIONS

1. Under what circumstances is a moving party entitled to summary judgment?

2. What are the differences between summary judgment and summary adjudication?

3. What is the purpose of a declaration?

4. What does the responding party need to do to object to a motion for summary judgment?

5. How far in advance of trial must a motion for summary judgment be filed?

INTERNET RESOURCES

www.courtinfo.ca.gov/rules/index

www.law.cornell.edu/rules

www.quojure.com/samples/archives

CHAPTER **11**

Provisional Remedies

CHAPTER OBJECTIVES

This chapter introduces you to the various remedies that may be obtained by a plaintiff prior to trial. In this chapter you will learn:

♦ When you would use claim and delivery
♦ Why a temporary restraining order or preliminary injunction may be necessary
♦ How to obtain a temporary restraining order
♦ When a plaintiff can make a motion for a preliminary injunction
♦ When a writ of attachment may be obtained
♦ How to obtain a lis pendens

A. INTRODUCTION

Provisional remedies
Under proper circumstances, these remedies allow a plaintiff to essentially obtain the relief requested from the defendant before going to trial.

Provisional remedies are those remedies that may be obtained by a plaintiff prior to trial. Under the proper circumstances they allow a plaintiff to essentially obtain the relief the plaintiff is requesting from the defendant without the necessity of trial. Of course, the plaintiff must still go to trial, and if the plaintiff should lose at trial, the plaintiff may be responsible to the defendant for any damages that the defendant may have suffered as a result of the plaintiff receiving a provisional remedy from the court.

There are a number of provisional remedies that you and the lawyer will want to consider at the commencement of a lawsuit. The type of remedy you choose to seek depends on the nature of the action against the defendant and the type of remedy the plaintiff ultimately wishes to recover from the defendant. For example, if the plaintiff brings a lawsuit against a defendant to stop the defendant from taking some action, such as building a house that destroys the plaintiff's view, the plaintiff will probably want to obtain an injunction against the defendant from building the house. However, if the plaintiff were to wait two or three years for the lawsuit to be tried before the plaintiff could receive an injunction, the defendant would probably have sufficient time to build the house before any injunction could stop the defendant. In this situation the plaintiff will want to receive an injunction prohibiting the building of the house until such time as the lawsuit can be tried and the case decided by the judge or jury. This chapter explains how to obtain an injunction in such a situation. There are also a number of other situations that might be right for some provisional relief. In addition to injunctions, the most common remedies available to the plaintiff before trial are claim and delivery, attachments, writs of possession, and lis pendens. Each of these remedies is explained in this chapter.

B. CLAIM AND DELIVERY

Claim and delivery of personal property is governed by CCP §§512.010 through 516.050. After the filing of a complaint in which the plaintiff seeks possession of personal property, the plaintiff may apply for a **writ of possession.**[1] A writ of possession is an order to the sheriff of the county where the writ is issued to obtain possession of the property and deliver the property to the plaintiff. In order to obtain a writ of possession the plaintiff must show two things:

Writ of possession
Order to sheriff to obtain possession of property and deliver to plaintiff

1. The plaintiff is entitled to possession of the property
2. The property is wrongfully detained by the defendant

Common situations include property that has been pledged as collateral for a debt that is in default, or when there is a dispute as to the true owner of the property.

Most of the forms that you will need to apply for a writ of possession are judicial council forms. These forms include a notice of application, the application for writ of possession, and the writ of possession. See Exhibit 11.1, and the Litigation File at the end of the text. The Code requires that specific items be stated in the application in order for a writ of possession to be issued. These items include a description of the property and approximate value, the location of the property, and a statement of the facts as to why the plaintiff is entitled to immediate possession. By using the forms, you will ensure that you have followed all of the statutory requirements.

Upon filing the application, the defendant will have an opportunity to file a response to the application, and appear at the hearing on the application to defend against issuance of the writ of possession. If a writ of possession is issued, the court will order that the property be turned over to the plaintiff during the pendency of the lawsuit. The plaintiff will need to post a bond to provide some monetary protection to the defendant in the event the plaintiff ultimately loses at trial.

In some cases, it may be possible to obtain an **ex parte** writ of possession. Ex parte means without notice to the other side. An ex parte writ of possession is used if the plaintiff believes that if the defendant learns of the notice of application, the defendant may cause the property to be damaged, destroyed, or removed from the jurisdiction.

Ex parte
Without notice to the other party

1. These sections also apply to a cross-complaint.

Exhibit 11.1. Judicial Council Forms—Notice of Application, Application for Writ of Possession, Writ of Possession

CD-100

ATTORNEY OR PARTY WITHOUT ATTORNEY *(Name, State Bar number, and address)*:	*FOR COURT USE ONLY*

TELEPHONE NO.:   FAX NO. *(Optional)*:

E-MAIL ADDRESS *(Optional)*:

ATTORNEY FOR *(Name)*:

SUPERIOR COURT OF CALIFORNIA, COUNTY OF

STREET ADDRESS:

MAILING ADDRESS:

CITY AND ZIP CODE:

BRANCH NAME:

PLAINTIFF:

DEFENDANT:

APPLICATION FOR WRIT OF POSSESSION ☐ **AFTER HEARING** ☐ **EX PARTE** ☐ **AND FOR TEMPORARY RESTRAINING ORDER**	CASE NUMBER:

1. Plaintiff* has filed a complaint and makes claim for delivery of property in the possession of the defendant named in b.
   a. Plaintiff *(name)*:
   b. Defendant *(name)*:

2. Plaintiff applies for *(check all that apply)*:
   a. ☐ Writ of possession after hearing (Code Civ. Proc, (C.C.P.), § 512.010).
   b. ☐ Ex parte writ of possession (C.C.P., § 512.020). *(File Declaration for Ex Parte Writ of Possession, form CD-180.)*
   c. ☐ Temporary restraining order (C.C.P., § 513.010). *(File Application for Temporary Restraining Order, form CD-190.)*

3. The basis of the plaintiff's claim and right to possession of the claimed property is specified in ☐ a written document, a copy of which is attached. ☐ the verified complaint. ☐ the attached declaration. ☐ the following facts *(specify)*:

4. Claimed property *(Describe, state value, and further identify any property that is a farm product (Code Civ.Proc., § 511.040) or inventory held for sale or lease (Code Civ. Proc., § 511.050))*:

☐ Continued on Attachment 4.

* "Plaintiff" includes cross-complainant, "defendant" includes cross-defendant, and "complaint" includes cross-complaint.

Page 1 of 2

Form Adopted for Mandatory Use
Judicial Council of California
CD-100 [Rev. January 1, 2006]

APPLICATION FOR WRIT OF POSSESSION
(Claim and Delivery)

Code Civ. Proc. § 512.010
www.courtinfo.ca.gov

American LegalNet, Inc.
www.USCourtForms.com

Exhibit 11.1. Continued

CD-100

| PLAINTIFF: | CASE NUMBER: |
| DEFENDANT: | |

5. A showing that the claimed property is wrongfully detained by defendant, of how the defendant came into possession of the claimed property, and, according to Plaintiff's best knowledge, information, and belief, of the reason for the defendant's detention of the claimed property, is made ☐ in the verified complaint. ☐ in the attached declaration. ☐ as follows *(specify):*

6. To Plaintiff's best knowledge, information, and belief the claimed property or some part of it is located as stated
   ☐ in the verified complaint. ☐ in the attached declaration. ☐ as follows (specify):
   (Include in this statement whether any part of the claimed property is within a private place that may have to be entered to take possession. If so, complete item 7.)

7. ☐ Facts showing probable cause for belief that the claimed property or some part of it is located in the private place referred to in item 6 are specified ☐ in the verified complaint. ☐ in the attached declaration. ☐ as follows:

8. The claimed property has not been taken for a tax, assessment, or fine, pursuant to statute, and *(check one):*
   a. ☐ has not been seized under an execution against the plaintiff's property.
   b. ☐ has been seized under an execution against the plaintiff's property, but is exempt from such seizure under
      (code section):

9. ☐ This action is subject to the ☐ Unruh Retail Installment Sales Act (Civ. Code, §§ 1801-1812.10);
      ☐ Rees-Levering Motor Vehicle Sales and Finance Act (Civ. Code, §§ 2981-2984.4).
      Facts showing that this is the proper court are specified in the ☐ verified complaint. ☐ attached declaration.

10. Total number of pages attached: _____

I declare under penalty of perjury under the laws of the State of California that the foregoing is true and correct.

Dated:

▶

_____
(TYPE OR PRINT NAME)

_____
(PLAINTIFF'S SIGNATURE)

CD-100 [Rev. January 1, 2006]

Page 2 of 2

APPLICATION FOR WRIT OF POSSESSION
(Claim and Delivery)

C. TEMPORARY RESTRAINING ORDERS AND PRELIMINARY INJUNCTIONS

Injunction
Equitable remedy used by the plaintiff to stop certain conduct or actions by the defendant

Temporary restraining order
An order from the court temporarily prohibiting a party from doing some act until a hearing for an injunction can be heard

An **injunction** is "a writ or order requiring a person to refrain from a particular act." CCP §525. Injunctions are of three types: temporary restraining orders, preliminary injunctions, and permanent injunctions. A **permanent injunction** is a remedy that can be ordered only after a trial on the merits of the case. **Temporary restraining orders** and **preliminary injunctions**, governed by CCP §527, are provisional remedies whose purpose is to maintain the **status quo** (i.e., the positions of the parties as they presently exist) and to avoid irreparable injury to the plaintiff until the rights of the parties can be adjudicated. A temporary restraining order can be granted **ex parte** (i.e., without notice to the other side) and can be granted only until a hearing for a preliminary injunction can be held. Its purpose is to avoid an immediate irreparable injury to the petitioning party. A preliminary injunction, by contrast, can be issued only after an adversarial hearing; it maintains the status quo until the case is tried.

Both preliminary injunctions and temporary restraining orders are forms of injunctions. Since an injunction is an equitable remedy—a remedy designed to prevent some future harm—it can only be granted if the legal remedies are inadequate. Accordingly, make sure that the underlying complaint asks for injunctive relief and that such relief would be proper if the complaint's allegations are ultimately proved. While CCP §527 governs temporary restraining orders and preliminary injunctions, local rules often have additional requirements that must be met.

1. Temporary restraining orders

a. Law

A **temporary restraining order (TRO)** is governed by CCP §527(c). Its purpose is to maintain the status quo until a hearing upon notice can be held. Since this is an extraordinary procedure, the Code's requirements must be followed precisely.

First, a TRO can be granted without notice to the opposing party, but only if two requirements are met. The motion must be supported by affidavit or a verified complaint alleging specific facts that show that "great or irreparable injury will result" unless the order is issued before the opposing side can be heard. In addition, the attorney representing the applicant must file an affidavit stating the efforts, if any, which have been made to give notice or the reasons why "the applicant should not be required" to give notice. Both of these requirements must be met.

Although CCP §527(c) expressly requires only that an applicant for a TRO show a "great or irreparable injury," case law generally holds that the applicant must make the same showing, at least on a preliminary basis, as that required for a preliminary injunction. That is, the applicant must show, in addition to an irreparable injury, that there is a likelihood of success on the merits of the case, that the threatened injury to the applicant exceeds any foreseeable injury to the adverse party if the order is granted, and that any order will not be against the public interest. As a practical matter, a court will not enter a TRO unless these considerations, taken as a whole, appear to weigh heavily in the applicant's favor.

Second, if a TRO is granted, the court will set a date for a hearing on an order to show cause why a preliminary injunction should not issue. The TRO will remain in effect until the hearing on the preliminary injunction.

b. *Practice approach*

Apply for a TRO only under appropriate circumstances. There is a great deal of work involved, and the court cannot properly issue a TRO unless a great or irreparable injury will occur without it. Since a TRO is a powerful and extraordinary judicial remedy, courts are necessarily reluctant to grant it except in the most compelling of circumstances. When drafting an application for a TRO, consider the following steps.

First, you must demonstrate in the moving papers a great and irreparable injury and an inadequate remedy at law. Common situations involve threatened damage to unique property and proprietary interests. For example, if someone is about to cut down mature elm trees on another's property, if a magazine is about to release personal photographs of a private person without authorization, or if a former employee is about to sell trade secrets to a business competitor, a TRO may be appropriate because in these situations the wronged party cannot be made whole through money damages.

Second, make sure that the court has both subject matter jurisdiction over the claim and personal jurisdiction over the defendant. Lack of subject matter jurisdiction will result in dismissal of the complaint. Lack of personal jurisdiction will make any injunctive relief ordered unenforceable.

Third, moving for a TRO requires that you prepare, file, and ultimately serve several things at nearly the same time. These include:

♦ Complaint and summons
♦ Application for TRO and preliminary injunction

- ◆ Attorney's certificate of attempted notice
- ◆ Witness affidavits
- ◆ Security for costs and damages
- ◆ Court order

i. Complaint and Summons

Where a TRO is being sought, the allegations in the complaint will form the factual basis for the motion and must be coordinated with it. The relief requested should include a TRO, preliminary injunction, and permanent injunction. The factual allegations should, like any complaint, show that the pleader is entitled to the relief requested if the allegations are proved. Finally, the allegations should be verified by the party, since this has the same evidentiary effect as an affidavit. A complaint is verified when it contains a statement that the party has read the complaint, personally knows the facts, and states that the facts are true.

The complaint is usually filed at the same time as the application for the TRO. This means that the summons will not yet have been served. However, since the Code requires that the attorney state how notification on the adverse party has been attempted, try to have service of the complaint and summons expedited.

ii. Application for TRO and Preliminary Injunction

The application for a TRO should be combined with a request for a preliminary injunction, since a hearing on a preliminary injunction must be scheduled as soon as possible after a TRO without notice is granted.

The application must allege that a great and irreparable injury will occur unless the TRO is granted. Since the application must be supported by facts, it usually refers to the verified complaint and accompanying witness affidavits for factual support. As with motions generally, the application itself is usually drafted briefly and refers to the supporting material for the substance.

iii. Attorney's Certificate Regarding Notice

CCP §527(c)(2) requires that the attorney for the moving party certify under oath the efforts that have been made to give the notice or the reasons supporting his claim that notice should not be required. Notice here includes informal as well as formal notice. The court will clearly prefer any notice to none at all, such as a telephone call to the adverse party, his lawyer if known, or an agent. Accordingly, the lawyer's certificate should show all the reasonable steps she took to give some advance notice to the adverse party. Exhibit 11.2 shows a sample certificate.

Exhibit 11.2. Sample Certificate

[Caption]

CERTIFICATE OF ATTORNEY IN SUPPORT OF APPLICATION FOR TEMPORARY RESTRAINING ORDER WITHOUT NOTICE

I, Terry Anton, attorney for plaintiff, make this certificate in support of plaintiff's application for a temporary restraining order without notice to the defendant.

1. On June 1, 2006, at approximately 1:00 P.M. I was first informed of defendant's imminent conduct as set forth in the complaint. I immediately began drafting the complaint, this application, and the supporting documents.

2. At the same time I telephoned defendant at his place of business to advise him of this application, but could not personally contact him. I left a message with his answering service, but have received no call from him.

3. I have attempted to locate the defendant's residence and present whereabouts without success.

4. I have no knowledge of any attorney who may presently represent the defendant, and have attempted to learn this without success.

_____
Attorney for Plaintiff

iv. Witness Declarations

The applicant for a TRO must show specific facts, through a verified complaint or witness declarations, that demonstrate the required "great or irreparable injury." Accordingly, you should review the verified complaint and determine what additional facts must be shown, and put them in declaration form. The declaration should show who the witness is and demonstrate that the witness has first-hand knowledge of all the facts in the affidavit. A declaration for this purpose is shown in Exhibit 11.3.

v. Security for Costs

Unlike the Federal Rules, there is no requirement under state law that the applicant post a bond as security for any of the defendant's costs and damages that may be incurred by the defendant if the TRO is wrongfully issued. However, since the posting of a bond is discretionary with the court, you should always have the plaintiff prepared to deposit the likely cash bond immediately if the TRO is granted, and the court requires a

Exhibit 11.3. Witness Declaration Supporting Temporary Restraining Order

---

<u>DECLARATION</u>

I, William Jones, having been first duly sworn, state:
    1. I am the plaintiff in this action, I live at 123 Maple Lane, Denver, and am the owner of that property.
    2. On June 1, 2006, at approximately 8:30 A.M. I saw . . .
    3. . . .
    4. . . .

I declare under penalty of prejury that the foregoing is true and correct.

                                    _____
                                    Name of Declarant

---

bond. Check with the clerk's office to determine its requirements for receiving bonds and other security.

vi. Order and Service

It is the usual procedure for the judge or his clerk to issue orders, either minute or full written orders. However, since with a TRO time is critical, it is useful to prepare a draft order for the judge in advance so that it can be immediately signed if the judge grants the TRO.

Since the court's order is not enforceable until the defendant receives actual notice of it, you should attempt to notify the defendant by telephone of the court's order and arrange for immediate proper service of the order.

2. Preliminary injunctions

a. Law

Preliminary injunction
An injunction granted after a hearing; maintains the status quo until trial

Preliminary injunctions are also governed by CCP §527. The purpose of a preliminary injunction is to maintain the status quo until a trial on the merits can be held. The requirements for obtaining a preliminary injunction are similar to those for issuing a TRO.

First, the Code provides that no preliminary injunction may issue without notice to the adverse party. Also, notice of the motion must include service of the complaint and summons.

Second, the **movant**—that is, the party making the motion—must post a bond in an amount the court deems proper for the payment of costs and damages that may be incurred if the party is found to have been wrongly enjoined. CCP §529.

Third, the movant has the burden of showing, through verified pleadings or testimony and other evidence at the hearing, that (1) if the injunction is not ordered, the movant will suffer an irreparable injury; (2) the movant will likely succeed on the merits of his claims at trial; and (3) on balance, the threatened injury to movant exceeds any threatened injury to the adverse party.

Fourth, if the court orders a preliminary injunction, the order must be specific and state in reasonable detail what acts are enjoined.

b. Practice approach

A preliminary injunction can come before the court in two ways. First, it can be set by the judge as part of an order granting an application for a TRO. Second, the plaintiff can move for a preliminary injunction without requesting a TRO first.

Regardless of how a motion for a preliminary injunction comes before the court, several considerations must be remembered. First, the adverse party must have notice of the motion, which must be given in accordance with the usual notice requirements. Second, the hearing is an adversarial one, with the opposing party having a right to submit timely opposition to the motion. Third, the plaintiff has the burden of proving that an irreparable injury will occur unless the status quo is maintained during the pendency of the action, that there is a likelihood of ultimate success on the merits, and that the threatened injury to the plaintiff exceeds any threatened injury to the defendant. Fourth, the plaintiff must post a bond for costs and damages before a preliminary injunction can be issued. Fifth, if a preliminary injunction is granted, it is in effect until a final trial on the merits, although the court can modify or vacate the order if warranted.

The critical point to remember is that the hearing on the preliminary injunction is, as a practical matter, often the determinative proceeding in an injunction case. Furthermore, in the event an injunction is granted, the court will give priority in trial setting. Since it is likely that your case will be set on an accelerated schedule, all discovery will need to proceed expeditiously. The court will frequently order that discovery be expedited. Thus, the plaintiff's lawyer must be prepared to go to trial quickly and present her entire case on short notice.

If the lawyer asks you to draft a motion for a preliminary injunction, it should be drafted both to allege the legal requirements for such relief and to specify precisely what acts are sought to be enjoined. Such a motion is shown in Exhibit 11.4.

3. Permanent injunctions

Permanent injunctions are granted only after a trial on the merits. While it is not necessary to first obtain a preliminary injunction, in practice a permanent injunction usually only follows after a preliminary injunction has been granted. If you are seeking injunctive relief as a remedy, be sure to include in the prayer of the complaint a request for a permanent injunction.

Exhibit 11.4. Motion for a Preliminary Injunction

[Caption]

MOTION FOR PRELIMINARY INJUNCTION

Plaintiff moves for a preliminary injunction enjoining defendant, his officers, employees, agents, and any persons working with him, until a trial on the merits is held and final order is entered in this action. In support of his motion plaintiff states:

1. Defendant will act in the manner alleged in the complaint unless enjoined.

2. Defendant's threatened action if carried out will result in irreparable injury, loss, and damage, as more fully alleged in the complaint.

3. The injury to plaintiff, if defendant is not enjoined, will substantially exceed any foreseeable injury to the defendant.

WHEREFORE, plaintiff requests that the court enter a preliminary injunction enjoining defendant from [specify and describe conduct sought to be enjoined].

_____
Attorney for Plaintiff

D. WRITS OF ATTACHMENT

Attachment is the legal process in which someone's property is seized to satisfy a judgment not yet rendered. The purpose of any attachment is to seize sufficient property or money of the defendant to satisfy any future judgment the plaintiff may obtain against the defendant. This is a powerful remedy for the plaintiff who naturally does not want to wait until a judgment to obtain relief against the defendant. In addition, the remedy protects the plaintiff against a defendant who may have sufficient assets now, but may not have sufficient assets two or three years later once the plaintiff does have a judgment against him. There are remedies for wrongful attachment, however, so caution is in order.

Attachment
Pretrial order of the court seizing property of the defendant for later satisfaction of any judgment received by the plaintiff

1. The law

The rules for obtaining an attachment are detailed, and can be complex. They are found in CCP §§481.010-493.060. These sections define the circumstances and specify the procedures, including service of process and bonds that must be followed. Use the checklist below to determine if the plaintiff has a right to an attachment. Only after determining that all grounds for an attachment exist should you seek to obtain an attachment against the defendant.

- ☐ An attachment is available only on contract claims. Thus, if the plaintiff is seeking damages for both contract and tort claims, unless the contract claim is based on separate and distinct facts, the attachment remedy may not be available.
- ☐ The contract claim must be for a specific sum of money. If the amount is not known or cannot be easily ascertained, the plaintiff cannot seek an attachment.
- ☐ The amount owed to the plaintiff must be **unsecured.** This means that there is no security for the obligation that the defendant has to the plaintiff. If the plaintiff otherwise had security for the obligation, plaintiff's remedy would be to obtain the security from the defendant, not seek an attachment.
- ☐ The claim against an individual must arise out of the individual's trade or profession. This means that a party cannot seek an attachment on any money claim personally owed by the defendant, but only for those claims involving an individual's business.

Once you have determined that there are proper grounds for an attachment, talk with the lawyer to determine whether an attachment should be brought against the defendant.

2. Practice approach

Once you and the lawyer have decided that there are sufficient grounds to seek an attachment, the next step is to draft the attachment papers. In general, the papers will require a motion with notice given to the other side. In the papers you should demonstrate to the court that all of the grounds for an attachment exist and show that it is likely that the plaintiff will prevail at trial. Fortunately, the Judicial Council has developed forms for the application for right to attach, the right to attach order, and the writ of attachment. See Exhibit 11.5.

In rare situations the court may grant an attachment ex parte. However, in these situations you must demonstrate to the court that there is great or irreparable injury that might occur to the plaintiff if relief is not granted immediately. Such cases might include those with attached property in danger of being destroyed or sold.

If your client has a motion for a writ of attachment served against her, there are several grounds for opposing the attachment. First, if any of the grounds for an attachment are not met, the defendant should point this out to the court in the opposing papers. If all the grounds are not satisfied, then an attachment will be denied.

Another ground for opposing an attachment is demonstrating to the court that the plaintiff is not likely to prevail at trial. If there are sufficient defenses to the plaintiff's claim, the court will not allow the plaintiff to have provisional relief before trial. This does not mean that the plaintiff will not ultimately prevail at trial, only that based on the information presented to the court at this time the plaintiff will probably not prevail. The decision of the court on the writ of attachment, however, cannot be introduced at trial and has no bearing on the outcome of the trial.

Finally, there are certain exemptions for the type of property that may be attached to satisfy a writ of attachment. These exemptions include homestead exemptions, which apply to the defendant's personal residences, life insurance policies, motor vehicles, tools of the defendant's trade, and property necessary for the support of the defendant and her family. The Judicial Council has also developed forms to be used by the opposition. The opposition forms include a notice of opposition to right to attach order, and an order to set aside the attachment. See Exhibit 11.6.

Lis pendens
A notice that is recorded against particular real property alerting potential purchasers that there is a pending dispute

E. LIS PENDENS

A **lis pendens** places a lien on real property owned by the defendant. Pursuant to CCP §405.5, the procedure for a lis pendens, referred to in the Code as a notice of pending action, applies to an action pending in federal court in the same manner as applied in state courts. Consider

Exhibit 11.5. Judicial Council Forms for Right to Attach, Right to Attach Order, Writ of Attachment

---

AT-105

ATTORNEY OR PARTY WITHOUT ATTORNEY *(Name, state bar number, and address)*:	*FOR COURT USE ONLY*

TELEPHONE NO.:　　　　　　　FAX NO.:

ATTORNEY FOR *(Name)*:

NAME OF COURT:
STREET ADDRESS:
MAILING ADDRESS:
CITY AND ZIP CODE:
BRANCH NAME:

PLAINTIFF:

DEFENDANT:

APPLICATION FOR	CASE NUMBER:
☐ **RIGHT TO ATTACH ORDER** ☐ **TEMPORARY PROTECTIVE ORDER** ☐ **ORDER FOR ISSUANCE OF WRIT OF ATTACHMENT** ☐ **ORDER FOR ISSUANCE OF ADDITIONAL WRIT OF ATTACHMENT** ☐ **After Hearing** ☐ **Ex Parte** ☐ **Against Property of Nonresident**	

1. Plaintiff *(name)*:
   applies ☐ after hearing ☐ ex parte　for
   a. ☐ a right to attach order and writ of attachment.
   b. ☐ an additional writ of attachment.
   c. ☐ a temporary protective order.
   d. ☐ an order directing the defendant to transfer to the levying officer possession of
   　　(1) ☐ property in defendant's possession.
   　　(2) ☐ documentary evidence in defendant's possession of title to property.
   　　(3) ☐ documentary evidence in defendant's possession of debt owed to defendant.

2. Defendant *(name)*:
   a. ☐ is a natural person who
   　　(1) ☐ resides in California.
   　　(2) ☐ does not reside in California.
   b. ☐ is a corporation
   　　(1) ☐ qualified to do business in California.
   　　(2) ☐ not qualified to do business in California.
   c. ☐ is a California partnership or other unincorporated association.
   d. ☐ is a foreign partnership that
   　　(1) ☐ has filed a designation under Corporations Code section 15800.
   　　(2) ☐ has not filed a designation under Corporations Code section 15800.
   e. ☐ is other *(specify)*:

3. Attachment is sought to secure recovery on a claim upon which attachment may issue under Code of Civil Procedure section 483.010.

4. Attachment is not sought for a purpose other than the recovery on a claim upon which the attachment is based.

5. Plaintiff has no information or belief that the claim is discharged or the prosecution of the action is stayed in a proceeding under Title 11 of the United States Code (Bankruptcy).

(Continued on reverse)　　　　　　　　　　　　　　　　　Page one of three

Form Approved for Optional Use Judicial Council of California AT-105 [Rev. January 1, 2000]	**APPLICATION FOR RIGHT TO ATTACH ORDER, TEMPORARY PROTECTIVE ORDER, ETC. (Attachment)**	Code of Civil Procedure, §§ 482.030, 484.010 et seq. American LegalNet, Inc. www.USCourtForms.com

Exhibit 11.5.   Continued

SHORT TITLE:	CASE NUMBER:

6. ☐ Plaintiff's claim or claims arise out of conduct by the defendant who is a natural person of a trade, business, or profession. The claim or claims are not based on the sale or lease of property, a license to use property, the furnishing of services, or the loan of money where any of the foregoing was used by the defendant primarily for personal, family, or household purposes.

7. The facts showing plaintiff is entitled to a judgment on the claim on which the attachment is based are set forth with particularity in the
   a. ☐ verified complaint.
   b. ☐ attached affidavit or declaration.
   c. ☐ following facts *(specify)*:

8. The amount to be secured by the attachment is: $
   a. ☐ which includes estimated costs of: $
   b. ☐ which includes estimated allowable attorney fees of: $

9. Plaintiff is informed and believes that the following property sought to be attached for which a method of levy is provided is subject to attachment:
   a. ☐ Any property of a defendant who is **not** a natural person.
   b. ☐ Any property of a nonresident defendant.
   c. ☐ Property of a defendant who is a natural person that is subject to attachment under Code of Civil Procedure section 487.010 described as follows *(specify)*:

   d. ☐ Property covered by a bulk sales notice with respect to a bulk transfer by defendant on the proceeds of the sale of such property *(describe)*:

   e. ☐ Plaintiff's pro rata share of proceeds from an escrow in which defendant's liquor license is sold *(specify license number)*:

10. Plaintiff is informed and believes that the property sought to be attached is not exempt from attachment.

11. ☐ The court issued a Right to Attach Order on *(date)*:
   (Attach a copy.)

12. ☐ Nonresident defendant has not filed a general appearance.

(Continued on page three)

AT-105 [Rev. January 1, 2000]	**APPLICATION FOR RIGHT TO ATTACH ORDER, TEMPORARY PROTECTIVE ORDER, ETC. (Attachment)**	**Page two of three**

Exhibit 11.5. Continued

SHORT TITLE:	CASE NUMBER:

13. a. Plaintiff ☐ alleges on ex parte application for order for writ of attachment
      ☐ is informed and believes on application for temporary protective order
  that plaintiff will suffer great or irreparable injury if the order is not issued before the matter can be heard on notice because
    (1) ☐ it may be inferred that there is a danger that the property sought to be attached will be
        (a) ☐ concealed.
        (b) ☐ substantially impaired in value.
        (c) ☐ made unavailable to levy by other than concealment or impairment in value.
    (2) ☐ defendant has failed to pay the debt underlying the requested attachment and is insolvent as defined in Code of Civil
        Procedure section 485.010, subdivision (b)(2).
    (3) ☐ a bulk sales notice was recorded and published pursuant to Division 6 of the Commercial Code with respect to a bulk
        transfer by the defendant.
    (4) ☐ an escrow has been opened under the provisions of Business and Professions Code section 24074 with respect to
        the sale by the defendant.
    (5) ☐ other circumstances *(specify)*:

  b. The statements in item 13a are established by ☐ the attached affidavit or declaration
    ☐ the following facts *(specify)*:

14. ☐ Plaintiff requests the following relief by temporary protective order *(specify)*:

15. Plaintiff
  a. ☐ has filed an undertaking in the amount of: $
  b. ☐ has not filed an undertaking.

Date:

_____ ▶ _____
(TYPE OR PRINT NAME OF PLAINTIFF OR PLAINTIFF'S ATTORNEY)   (SIGNATURE OF PLAINTIFF OR PLAINTIFF'S ATTORNEY)

DECLARATION

I declare under penalty of perjury under the laws of the State of California that the foregoing is true and correct.

Date:

_____ ▶ _____
(TYPE OR PRINT NAME)   (SIGNATURE OF DECLARANT)

16. Number of pages attached: _____

AT-105 [Rev. January 1, 2000]	**APPLICATION FOR RIGHT TO ATTACH ORDER, TEMPORARY** **PROTECTIVE ORDER, ETC. (Attachment)**	Page three of three

Exhibit 11.6. Judicial Council Opposition Form

ATTORNEY OR PARTY WITHOUT ATTORNEY *(Name and Address)*: TELEPHONE NO.: *FOR COURT USE ONLY*

ATTORNEY FOR *(Name)*:

NAME OF COURT:

STREET ADDRESS:

MAILING ADDRESS:

CITY AND ZIP CODE:

BRANCH NAME:

PLAINTIFF:

DEFENDANT:

NOTICE OF

☐ **OPPOSITION TO APPLICATION FOR RIGHT TO ATTACH ORDER**
☐ **CLAIM OF EXEMPTION**
☐ **MOTION (AFTER ISSUANCE OF WRIT) FOR CLAIM OF EXEMPTION**
☐ **AND MOTION FOR CLAIM OF EXEMPTION**

CASE NUMBER:

1. To plaintiff *(name)*:

2. You are notified that a hearing will be held in this court as follows:

   date: time: ☐ dept.:   ☐ div.:   ☐ rm.:

3. This opposition or claim of exemption is filed by
   a. ☐ defendant *(specify name)*:

   b. ☐ nondefendant *(specify name and mailing address where service of opposition may be made)*:

   (name and last known address of defendant):

4. Opposing party
   a. ☐ will oppose the issuance of a right to attach order upon the following grounds *(specify grounds of opposition)*:

   b. ☐ objects to the amount sought to be secured by the attachment upon the following grounds *(specify grounds of opposition)*:

(Continued on reverse)

Form Approved by the
Judicial Council of California
AT-155 [Rev. July 1, 1983]

**NOTICE OF OPPOSITION TO RIGHT TO ATTACH ORDER
AND CLAIM OF EXEMPTION**
(Attachment)

CCP 482.030

American LegalNet, Inc.
www.USCourtForms.com

Exhibit 11.6. Continued

SHORT TITLE:	CASE NUMBER:

4. c. ☐ will claim exemption.
☐ will move the court for an exemption from attachment of the following property:
    (1) ☐ Property exempt from execution under CCP 703.010 et seq. *(specify code section and describe property)*:

        (a) ☐ Property exempt under CCP 704.010 [motor vehicles] or 704.060 [tools of a trade] *(describe all other property of the same type, including exempt proceeds of property of the same type, owned by defendant alone or in combination with others on the date of levy and identify the property to which the exemption is to be applied, regardless of whether it was levied upon)*:

        (b) ☐ Property exempt under CCP 704.100 life insurance policies] *(state the nature and amount of all other property of the same type owned by defendant or defendant's spouse alone or in combination with others on the date of levy)*:

    (2) ☐ Property which is necessary for the support of a defendant who is a natural person and the family of the defendant supported in whole or in part by the defendant (CCP 487.020(b) *(describe the property and attach a financial statement executed under oath as required in CCP 703.530)*:

    (3) ☐ Compensation paid or payable to a defendant employee by an employer for personal services performed by the employee whether denominated as wages, salary, commission, bonus, or otherwise (CCP 487.020(c)) *(describe compensation)*:

    (4) ☐ Property not subject to attachment pursuant to CCP 487.010 *(describe property)*:

    (5) ☐ Other *(describe property and specify grounds for exemption)*:

5. Defendant's affidavit supporting any factual issues and points and authorities supporting any legal issues is attached.

6. Total number of pages attached:

Date:

. . . .   ▶ _____
        (TYPE OR PRINT NAME)   *(SIGNATURE OF DEFENDANT OR ATTORNEY)*

By . . . .
               (NAME AND TITLE)

AT-155 [Rev. July 1, 1983]
**NOTICE OF OPPOSITION TO RIGHT TO ATTACH ORDER
AND CLAIM OF EXEMPTION (Attachment)**
Page two

filing and recording a notice of pending action whenever a suit involves an interest in real property. This gives notice of the pending litigation to parties having an interest in the property because prior to purchasing real estate, potential buyers usually have a title search done to ensure that no one else has an interest in the property they are purchasing. Thus, if anyone purchases the property with notice of the pending litigation, that person must take the property subject to any judgment that may be entered in the litigation.

If the suit involves title to real property, follow the requirements stated in CCP §§405.21 and 405.22. Following these sections requires you to do the following:

1. Prepare a notice of pending action and have the attorney of record sign the notice (see Exhibit 11.7).
2. Serve a copy of the notice by registered or certified mail, return receipt requested to all known addresses of the parties to whom the property claim is adverse and to all owners of record of the real property prior to recording the document
3. Prepare a proof of service
4. Record the notice of pending action with the proof of service in the county where the property is located
5. File a copy of the notice with the court where the action is pending

This is a powerful remedy for the plaintiff as it effectively puts a cloud on the defendant's title to the real property, virtually prohibiting the defendant from being able to sell the property. Few people are going to want to purchase property from a defendant that may lose title to the property due to a lawsuit. However, there are remedies for the defendant to remove the lis pendens.

After a lis pendens has been recorded, the defendant, or any party with an interest in the real property, may move the court to expunge the lis pendens. The court may expunge a lis pendens on two grounds. First, if the complaint does not contain a claim to the real property that is subject to the notice, the court may expunge the lis pendens.

Exhibit 11.7.   Notice of Pending Action

PLEASE TAKE NOTICE THAT the above-entitled action by the Plaintiff against the Defendant affects title to and/or possession of real property in that the Plaintiff seeks to recover possession of the real property located in Alameda County, at 445 N. Burke Street, Oakland, California and legally described as follows:

(Give legal description of the property)

See CCP §405.31. Second, if the court finds that the plaintiff cannot establish by a "preponderance of the evidence the probable validity of the real property claim" the lis pendens may also be expunged. *See* CCP §405.32. Finally, the court may expunge a lis pendens if the defendant can post a sufficient bond to secure the rights of the plaintiff. *See* CCP §405.33.

CHAPTER SUMMARY

Provisional remedies are important tools for a plaintiff. In this chapter you have learned the most common provisional remedies available to plaintiffs in civil litigation. One of the most frequently used provisional remedies is injunctions. Injunctions can only be granted under limited circumstances, and you must be familiar with the injunction rules so the papers are drafted correctly. You also may be responsible for arranging for posting a bond in the event a preliminary injunction is granted.

Other provisional remedies that you need to be familiar with are attachments, writs of possession, and notices of lis pendens. Writs of possession are used when the plaintiff has security in the personal property of the defendant. This remedy allows the plaintiff to obtain the personal property from the defendant prior to trial.

An attachment is available to a plaintiff when the plaintiff is seeking damages based on a breach of contract. The contract claim must be for a specific sum of money and be unsecured. The defendant may oppose a request for attachment. These grounds include demonstrating that the grounds for a writ of attachment are not satisfied, showing that the plaintiff is not likely to prevail at trial, and claiming exemptions for the type of property that may be used to satisfy a writ of attachment.

Finally, you may be asked to file a notice of pending action (lis pendens), or if a notice is filed against your client, to make a motion to expunge the lis pendens. A lis pendens places a lien on real property owned by the defendant. There are limited circumstances under which a defendant may expunge a lis pendens.

KEY TERMS

Attachment
Ex parte
Lis pendens
Movant
Permanent injunction
Preliminary injunction

Provisional remedies
Status quo
Temporary restraining order
Unsecured
Writ of possession

REVIEW QUESTIONS

1. Why might a plaintiff want to seek a provisional remedy?

2. Identify the three types of injunctions. What is the purpose of each type of injunction?

3. What are the grounds for seeking an attachment?

4. When is it appropriate to seek a writ of possession as a provisional remedy?

5. What is the purpose of filing a lis pendens?

INTERNET RESOURCES

www.courtinfo.ca.gov/cgi-bin/forms.cgi
www.law.cornell.edu/wex/index.php/Injunction
www.lectlaw.com
www.lectlaw.com/def/i046.htm
www.legal-database.com

CHAPTER **12**

Evidence

A. Introduction
B. The Paralegal's Role
C. Relevance
D. Hearsay
E. Hearsay Exceptions
F. Witnesses, Exhibits, Judicial Notice, and Objections
G. Privileges

CHAPTER OBJECTIVES

This chapter provides you with an overview of the law of evidence. You will learn:

- What constitutes evidence
- Why paralegals must be familiar with the rules of evidence
- How to determine what evidence is relevant
- What evidence is excluded based on the hearsay rules
- Whether hearsay evidence may be admissible under a hearsay exception
- When a witness is competent to testify
- What evidence is protected from disclosure based on a claim of privilege

A. INTRODUCTION

Federal Rules of Evidence
Rules applicable in federal courts that govern what evidence is admissible

The law of evidence determines which "facts" may be presented to the jury during a trial. It is important for you to be familiar with the law of evidence so that you may assist the attorney in preparing the facts for the case. In addition, familiarity with the rules will help you in determining what evidence is discoverable. Discovery is further explained in Chapter 10. In California state courts you will follow the evidence rules as codified in the California Evidence Code ("Evid. Code"). The **Federal Rules of Evidence** were enacted in 1975 and the rules are very similar to state court rules. Hence, once you know the California evidence rules, you will also generally know the rules that apply in federal courts.

Evidentiary issues are **questions of law**—that is, evidentiary issues that raise legal questions and not factual questions. Thus, the trial judge will make rulings on evidentiary issues. By ruling on motions and objections, the trial judge determines what evidence may be presented to and considered by the jury, the finder of facts during a trial. The law of evidence is the tool the judge uses to filter **testimony** (i.e., oral statements given at trial by witnesses under oath) or **exhibits** (tangible evidence offered at trial) and to determine which will be admissible or inadmissible.

The law of evidence permits only that which is deemed sufficiently pertinent and trustworthy to be received by the jury. The jury is still free to accept or reject the evidence, in whole or in part. A convenient way to consider this filtration process is to remember the three "Rs." All evidence, to be admissible must be:

1. **Relevant** (must prove or disprove something in issue)
2. **Reliable** (must be first-hand or otherwise trustworthy information)
3. **Real** (the information must be what it purports to be)

B. THE PARALEGAL'S ROLE

While paralegals are not responsible for making evidentiary objections at trial, as indicated previously, a paralegal must still be familiar with the rules of evidence. Paralegals are charged with significant responsibility during the discovery process and may also assist in preparing declarations and affidavits in support of, or in opposition to, pretrial motions. In addition, paralegals often assist with the preparation of evidence for trial. Accordingly, to adequately perform these tasks, a paralegal must know what evidence is properly admissible.

Familiarity with the rules of evidence in discovery is particularly important. During the course of discovery, numerous documents may be exchanged between the parties. Written responses to interrogatories also will be supplied to the opposing parties. If the documents or any response to discovery contains information that would otherwise be subject to an evidentiary objection, such as the attorney-client privilege or the work product doctrine, the objection may be waived by disclosure of the information to the other parties. Thus, evidence may be admissible against the client at trial that would not otherwise have been admissible if a timely objection had been made.

Declarations and affidavits also must comply with all evidentiary requirements and contain only admissible evidence. As discussed in earlier chapters, **declarations** are written statements made by a witness and signed under penalty of perjury, while **affidavits** are written statements by a witness made under oath and acknowledged by a notary public. Declarations or affidavits that contain inadmissible evidence are subject to a motion to strike and will not be considered by the court. Paralegals drafting these documents should be careful to include only admissible evidence to avoid any motion to strike by the other parties.

Finally, when assisting in trial preparation, the paralegal must be able to discern the difference between what the court will likely allow to be admitted and what the court will clearly rule inadmissible under the rules of evidence. A paralegal familiar with the rules of evidence will be able to simplify evidentiary issues and to assist the lawyer in resolving evidentiary problems in advance of trial.

C. RELEVANCE

To be properly admissible, all evidence must first meet the general relevance test. This test can be summarized by asking yourself three questions:

1. Is the offered evidence "of consequence" to the issues in the action? For example, in a negligence action, plaintiff's contributory

negligence is relevant to the amount of damages plaintiff can recover.

2. Does the offered evidence have "any tendency" to make a fact "more or less probable"? For example, in a personal injury action, where the plaintiff is trying to prove that the defendant-driver of an automobile was negligent, the fact that the driver previously lived in Florida or is a Vietnam veteran is irrelevant to the negligence claim and has no tendency to make the fact "more or less probable."

3. Even if relevant, is the **probative** value of the evidence—that is, the ability to prove or disprove a fact—"substantially outweighed" by other considerations? For example, in a wrongful death case, the only contested issue may be the cause of death. If the plaintiff offers color photographs of the victim's body, the photographs should not be admitted because they have minimal probative value (showing only the fact of death, a fact undoubtedly established by other evidence) and are inflammatory.

Consider a breach of contract action where the contract required that the defendant install an outdoor sprinkler system at the plaintiff's home. The plaintiff will need to show that the defendant breached the contract. Evidence from the plaintiff showing that two days after its installation the sprinkler system stopped working is relevant evidence to show breach of the contract. First, the evidence is "of consequence" to an issue in the case. That is, the evidence relates to the issue to be proven. Second, the evidence has some tendency to prove that the installation done by the defendant was not adequate, therefore making the breach of the contract "more or less probable." Finally, the probative value is outweighed by any other considerations since there is little risk here that the jury could be confused, misled, or prejudiced by the introduction of this evidence.

However, assume on the other hand that the plaintiff wishes to introduce evidence on the issue of breach that the defendant had installed a sprinkler system for a neighbor and had given the neighbor a refund for the price paid for the installation based on the neighbor's claim that the installation was faulty. If the plaintiff tried to use this evidence during the litigation, it would probably not meet the relevance test. First, an allegation of the faulty work by a third person does not necessarily mean that the defendant breached the contract to the plaintiff in this instance. The evidence is not "of consequence" to an issue in this case. Moreover, even if the first test is met, the plaintiff would have a hard time meeting the second and third tests. The fact that the defendant gave a refund to another person does not tend to prove or disprove the fact that there was a breach in the contract between the plaintiff and defendant. In addition, this evidence could confuse a jury and lead the jury to believe that the defendant does poor work on all jobs. For this reason, also, the minimum probative value of the evidence is substantially outweighed by the evidence's potential to confuse and mislead a jury.

If evidence is irrelevant under the general relevance test, the evidence is inadmissible. However, even if the evidence is relevant under the general relevance test, there may be special rules that preclude the introduction of the evidence. Evidence of a person's character or habits, for example, is subject to special evidence rules; in addition, some evidence, while relevant, can be excluded for policy reasons. These rules are found in Evid. Code §§1100 through 1109, and 1150 et. seq. The key exclusions are discussed below.

1. Character traits

Common sense and experience tell us that a person is likely to act consistently with the kind of person he really is, that is, with his **"character traits."** However, evidence of someone's character traits (such as whether he is honest, aggressive, trustworthy, and so on), although perhaps relevant under the general test, will only be admissible if character is an essential element of a claim or defense. For example, in an action for libel, where the defendant stated that the plaintiff is a chronic liar and the defendant's defense is "truth," an essential element of that defense is the plaintiff's truth-telling character. Thus, if the character trait evidence is offered to prove conduct on a specific occasion, it will not be admitted. This means that the plaintiff cannot show that she is honest and therefore must be telling the truth when plaintiff testifies that defendant ran the red light.

Character traits
A person's distinctive qualities; admissible as evidence only if character is an essential element of a claim or defense

2. Habit evidence

The "habit" of a person may be relevant to prove that the conduct of the person on a particular occasion was in conformity with the habit or routine practice of that person. Evidence of conduct that is routine enough to be considered a "habit" will be admissible.[1] Thus, a routine business practice in handling and processing outgoing mail will be habit evidence admissible to prove circumstantially that a particular letter was actually put in the mail.

3. Policy exclusions

Certain evidence automatically is inadmissible to prove negligence or fault based on policy reasons: Three of the more common exclusions are

1. Evid. Code §1105.

evidence of subsequent remedial repairs, payment (or offer of payment) of medical expenses, and liability insurance.[2] Evidence of subsequent remedial repairs is excluded because a party may not make a repair if the fact that he made such a repair can be used against him to prove negligence or fault. Thus, by excluding the evidence, the policy promotes repairs and improvements. Moreover, such repairs and improvements do not necessarily show negligence, but there is a danger that the jury will think that they do.

Payment or the offer of payment of medical expenses also is excluded because such offers or payments may be motivated by reasons other than fault, but again the jury will think the payment or offer shows fault.

Finally, evidence that a person had liability insurance is not admissible to prove negligence or fault. The rationale is that the existence of liability insurance is simply not relevant to the issue of negligence.

D. HEARSAY

Hearsay represents the second of the three "Rs"—"reliable" evidence. The Evidence Code, and the rules of most states, define hearsay as "a statement that was made other than by a witness while testifying at the hearing and that is offered to prove the truth of the matter stated."[3]

The hearsay rules filter offered evidence and permit only that which is sufficiently reliable to be admitted. You must distinguish between hearsay and nonhearsay. If evidence is nonhearsay, it is admissible. If evidence is hearsay, it is inadmissible unless a hearsay exception applies. Hearsay can be a very complex area. The intent of this chapter is to simplify the hearsay rules as much as possible, without going into too much detail. Fully understanding the hearsay rules and exceptions takes time and an opportunity to work with the concepts.

The simplest way to determine if a statement is hearsay is to break down the Rule quoted above into three elements:

1. a statement
2. made out of court
3. offered to prove the truth of the matter asserted in the statement

2. The Evidence Code prohibits introduction of evidence to prove negligence or fault; however, such evidence may be introduced for purposes *other* than showing negligence or fault. For example, the Code does not bar the use of the evidence of subsequent repairs in order to prove ownership, control, or feasibility of precautionary measures, if controverted.

3. Evid. Code §1200.

If the statement fulfills all three elements, it is considered hearsay and subject to exclusion in court unless an exception applies.[4]

1. Is it a "statement"?

Think of "statements" as falling into one of three categories: oral assertions, written assertions, and assertive conduct (nonverbal conduct that is intended as an assertion). The following examples of testimony by witness in court are illustrative of the rules.

Example

1. "I saw the defendant run the red light." Under the hearsay rules this is not a statement; the witness on the stand is merely saying what he previously saw rather than making an assertion.

2. "John told me he saw the defendant run the red light." This is an oral assertion and considered a statement.

3. "John gave me a note that said: 'I saw the defendant run the red light.'" This is a written assertion and considered a statement.

4. "I met John and asked him: 'Did you see the defendant run the red light?' John nodded his head." This is an example of assertive conduct, since John's nodding his head is the functional equivalent of John saying "yes." This too is considered a statement.

2. Was the statement made "out of court"?

The hearsay rule does not apply to the actual oral testimony of the witness in court. Obviously, if it did, witnesses could not say anything on the witness stand. The hearsay rule does apply whenever the witness, while on the witness stand, repeats any "statement" that either he or another person made at any other time or place. The following are examples of out-of-court statements.

Example

1. "Yesterday I saw John and he said 'Tom, your car needs a tune-up.'" This is a statement of John, made out of court.

2. "Yesterday I saw John, and I said 'John, my car needs a tune-up.'" This is also an out-of-court statement even though the out-of-court declarant is the same person as the witness testifying in court.

---

4. Exceptions are discussed in section E.

3. Is the out-of-court statement "offered to prove the truth of the matter asserted in the statement"?

This final element merely requires you to determine what it is you want to prove by using a particular statement. In the examples above, if you are trying to prove that the defendant ran a red light or that Tom's car needs a tune-up, you would be using the statements to prove the truth of the matter asserted. However, what if you were using the statements to prove something else? For example, what if you were trying to prove that John could speak, or write, or was present at a certain location? Then the statements would not be used to prove the matter asserted in the statements, but used to prove something else. Under such circumstances, the statements do not fulfill the third element, and the statements would not be considered hearsay.

E. HEARSAY EXCEPTIONS

The hearsay rule traditionally guarantees reliability by the personal presence of the declarant at trial, under oath, and subject to cross-examination by the opposing parties. The basic reasons for testimonial unreliability are lack of perception, poor memory, inability to communicate, and motive to fabricate. Remember, if evidence is deemed to be hearsay, it is inadmissible unless a hearsay exception applies. Since the hearsay rule is designed to admit only reliable evidence, it may seem strange at first to have any hearsay exceptions. Yet the hearsay exceptions are based, in part, on the premise that the particular circumstances eliminate one or more of the reasons for testimonial unreliability. Thus, after you have determined that a statement is hearsay, you must next determine whether there is any exception to the hearsay rules. If such an exception exists, then the statement will be admitted into evidence. Ten of the most common exceptions are discussed below.

1. Admission of a party opponent

The most common exception to the hearsay rules is an admission of a party opponent. This is one place where the federal rules differ. Under the Federal Rules of Evidence, such an admission is not even considered hearsay.[5] However, in California the statement is considered hearsay, but it is admitted into court under the exception.[6] An **admission of a party opponent** is any statement made by an adverse party in the lawsuit. The rationale for admitting the statement is that the adverse party is

---

5. Fed. R. Evid. 801(d)(2).
6. Evid. Code §1220.

in court and can hardly complain about the inability to cross-examine himself. In addition, the adverse party can certainly testify in court to either deny or explain the statement that was made. The following are examples of admission of a party opponent.

Example

1. In an automobile negligence action, the plaintiff may offer the testimony of a bystander that the defendant-driver said: "I don't know, but perhaps the light was red."
2. In a breach of contract action, the plaintiff testifies that the defendant told her "I am not going to pay for the goods that were delivered."

2. Prior statements by witnesses

Evidence Code §1235 provides that, under certain circumstances, prior statements by witnesses that were made at a previous hearing or deposition may be admitted. The purpose is to allow prior inconsistent statements to be used to impeach a witness.

Example

The defendant states at an earlier deposition that he knew that his brakes were bad before the accident. During trial the defendant now says that he cannot remember whether he knew that his brakes were bad, or he says that the brakes were not bad prior to the accident. The previous out-of-court statement may come into evidence as an exception to the hearsay rule.

3. Declarations against interest[7]

When the declarant is unavailable to testify at trial, certain statements of the declarant may be admitted under an exception to the hearsay rule.[8] A statement made by a declarant that is against his interest is admissible as an exception to the hearsay rule. The statement may be against the declarant's pecuniary or proprietary interest. The statement must be

7. Evid. Code §1230.
8. Some exceptions to the hearsay rule require that a witness be unavailable in order for the exception to apply. Under the Evidence Code "unavailable" means that the witness is exempted by the court from testifying on the grounds of privilege, disqualified from testifying, unable to be present or testify at the hearing because of death, illness or infirmity, or that the proponent of the statement is unable to compel the declarant's attendance at the hearing by process or other reasonable means.

within the declarant's personal knowledge and against the declarant's interest when it is made. It is not enough that the statement became against the declarant's interest at a later time.

The rationale for this hearsay exception is that a witness is not likely to make a statement against his interest unless it is true. In addition, because the witness is unavailable to testify at trial, the evidence is necessary.

The following are examples of declarations against interest.

Example

1. In an automobile negligence action, plaintiff claims that defendant was the driver of the other car involved in the accident. Defendant denies this allegation. Defendant calls a witness who testifies that he heard Al Jones say the following a few days after the accident: "I was actually driving the car that was in the accident the defendant is getting blamed for." If Jones is now unavailable, the statement is admissible since it is a statement by Jones against his interest.

2. Defendant is on trial for slander. Susan Bailey testifies that she heard Al Jones say: "Poor defendant is being sued for slander when I am the one who slandered the plaintiff." Again, if Jones is now unavailable, the statement is admissible.

The declarations against interest are not the same as admissions by party opponents. The differences are illustrated in the following chart:

Admissions by a Party Opponent	*Declarations Against Interest*
a. only by a party opponent	a. by any witness
b. need not be unavailable	b. witness must be unavailable
c. need not be against interest when made	c. must be against interest of witness when made
d. need not be within personal party	d. must be within personal knowledge of declarant

4. Former testimony[9]

If a witness is unavailable, former testimony of the witness may be admissible. To be admissible, the following requirements must be met. First, the witness must be unavailable. Second, the former testimony must have been given under oath in another action or at a former hearing or trial in the same action. Former testimony also includes depositions

9. Evid. Code §§1290 through 1294.

taken in another action. Third, the former testimony must have been offered by the adversary in the former proceeding, or if it was offered against the adversary in the former proceeding, the adversary must have had an opportunity to examine the witness with the same opportunity and motive as he does now. If the adversary was not a party to the former proceeding, then the former testimony may be used in civil cases only if the person against whom the testimony was offered in the former proceeding has the same motive and interest as the adversary now.

When faced with a former testimony situation, one should analyze the statement by asking four questions:

1. Is the witness unavailable?
2. Was the testimony under oath in a former action or proceeding?
3. Was the former testimony offered against the same party you wish to offer the evidence against now or the party's predecessor in interest?
4. Did the opposing party or the predecessor in interest have the same motive and opportunity to examine the witness then as now?

The following example shows how to determine whether former testimony is admissible.

Example

Plaintiff Smith sues Jones, the defendant-driver, for negligence arising from an automobile accident. During the trial plaintiff called Williams as a witness, and defendant called Franklin as a witness. Both Williams and Franklin were eyewitnesses to the accident.

In a separate action, Roberts, a passenger in Smith's car, also sues Jones. Neither Williams nor Franklin is now available. Plaintiff Roberts wants to introduce into the trial the former testimony of Williams, and Jones wants to introduce the transcript of Franklin's former testimony. Can they introduce the testimony?

The answer depends on which witness is involved:

1. Williams' former testimony is admissible. He is presently unavailable, the testimony is being offered against Jones, the same party, and Jones would have had a similar motive and opportunity to develop the witness' testimony in the earlier trial.

2. Franklin's former testimony is inadmissible. He is presently unavailable, but his testimony is not being offered against the same party or a predecessor in interest. The current plaintiff, Roberts, is not the same party as Smith, nor is Roberts a predecessor in interest of Smith.

5. Contemporaneous statements[10]

A statement made during or immediately after an event that explains or makes understandable the conduct of the declarant is admissible. The rationale for this exception is that reliability is reasonably assured because the statement is made contemporaneously with the conduct.

Example

After seeing another car pass them on a highway, the driver of the passed car says to his passenger: "The way they're speeding, they'll crash for sure." The statement is admissible as an exception to the hearsay rule.

6. Spontaneous statements[11]

A statement made under the stress of excitement relating to a startling event or condition and made while the declarant is perceiving the event or condition, or immediately thereafter, is admissible. The rationale for this exception is that these statements are considered reliable because the declarant has no time to fabricate.

Example

A pedestrian sees a car coming toward the intersection and yells: "Look out! He ran the red light!" Thus, a witness could testify as to the statement made by the pedestrian.

Keep in mind that there are differences between contemporaneous statements and spontaneous statements. The following chart illustrates the differences:

Contemporaneous Statements	*Spontaneous Statements*
a. statement made while engaged in conduct	a. statement relates to a startling event or condition
b. describe or explain conduct	b. made under the "stress of excitement"

10. Evid. Code §1241.
11. Evid. Code §1240.

7. Statements for purposes of medical diagnosis[12]

Statements about a patient's condition are admissible. The rationale behind this exception is that these statements are reliable because a patient, presumably interested in getting well, will not deliberately falsify his medical history or present symptoms. Thus, both doctors and related parties, such as nurses and clerks, can testify about the statement made by the declarant.

Example

A patient, brought to the hospital after an accident, says to the nurse: "I broke my arm, I ache all over, my head hurts, and I think I have a concussion. The other driver went right through the red light and rammed me with his car going about 35 miles per hour."

If the nurse is called to testify, she may testify to everything the patient-declarant told her, with the exception of the last sentence. The last sentence does not relate to the declarant's present or past condition and is not necessary for diagnosis. Thus, the last sentence would be hearsay and excluded from the testimony at trial.

8. Statement of present mental or physical state[13]

A statement made by a declarant about her present state of mind, emotion or physical sensation is admissible. The rationale for this exception is that the declarant knows best what is going on in her mind.

Example

Witness testifies at trial that the declarant told her: "I intend to go to Baker's house tonight." To prove that the declarant actually went to Baker's house, this testimony will be admissible as a statement of the present state of mind of the declarant.

9. Dying declarations[14]

A statement by a declarant is admissible if made while the declarant believes that he or she is about to die and the statement is about the

12. Evid. Code §1253.
13. Evid. Code §1250.
14. Evid. Code §1242.

circumstances of the declarant's death. Under California law, the declarant must actually die. The rationale for this exception is that persons who believe they are dying are likely, as their last act, to tell the truth. Under the Federal Rules, the declarant does not have to die. If the declarant recovers from the injury, the dying declaration may be admitted so long as the declarant is now unavailable.

Example

In a wrongful death action, a witness testifies that Jones stated, just before he died, that the car driven by Smith went through the red light. The statement of Jones is admitted as a dying declaration.

10. Records exceptions

There are several exceptions to the hearsay rule that allow records to be admitted into evidence. Remember that statements may be oral, nonverbal, or written. Accordingly, written records may be admitted under a number of exceptions identified in the Evidence Code.[15] The three most common exceptions are discussed in this section.

Business records
Records made by employees in the course of their employment and made on behalf of the business

The first record exception is the **business records** exception.[16] The complexity of modern commerce requires that business records be admitted into evidence to prove the occurrence of certain business transactions. Moreover, since businesses need accurate records to conduct their affairs and the records are made by employees who have a duty to create accurate records, the records are considered reliable. Business records include memoranda, reports, or data compilations in any form. Use the following checklist of elements to determine whether a proper foundation can be laid for the admission of the business record:

- ☐ a writing made in the regular course of the business
- ☐ made at or near the time of the events recorded on the record
- ☐ a custodian or other qualified witness testifies to the identity of the record and how it was prepared, and
- ☐ the sources of the information and preparation of the record appear trustworthy.

To use this exception, an appropriate witness will need to testify to each of the four elements identified. Accordingly, if a business record needs to be admitted into evidence, you may be asked to contact the

15. Evid. Code §§1270 through 1284.
16. Evid. Code §§1270 through 1272.

custodian of records for the business who will probably be able to testify to each requirement.

Second, **public records** and reports are admissible.[17] This exception is similar to the business records exception. Under this exception, however, a witness does not need to testify in court in order to lay a foundation for the document. It is sufficient if a certified copy of the public document or report is made available in court.

Public records
Business records generated by governmental entities

Finally, **past recorded recollections** are admissible.[18] If a witness has forgotten an earlier event, but made an accurate record of the event, the record is considered reliable. It is preferable to admit the record than lose the evidence altogether. This exception requires that some foundation be laid before the document will be read into evidence. Use the following as a checklist to determine whether a proper foundation for the document can be made:

Past recorded recollections
A record made of events at about the time the events occurred

☐ A writing made at the time facts occurred or while still fresh in the witness' memory
☐ Made by the witness or under witness' direction
☐ Offered after witness testifies statement made was true statement of the facts
☐ Offered after authenticated as being accurate
☐ The writing may be read into evidence, but the document itself may not be admitted.

11. Other exceptions

Other hearsay exceptions also may be available. The more common exceptions have been identified in this chapter. However, if faced with a hearsay problem, review the evidence carefully to determine whether another exception may apply.[19]

F. WITNESSES, EXHIBITS, JUDICIAL NOTICE, AND OBJECTIONS

Up to this point we have been examining the nature of relevant and reliable evidence. We are now involved with the third "R"—"real" evidence. Evidence otherwise admissible under relevance and hearsay rules must also be real; that is, the presentation of the evidence must pass certain standards. The three areas of concern for real evidence involve witnesses, exhibits, and judicial notice.

17. Evid. Code §1280 through 1284.
18. Evid. Code §1237.
19. See Evid. Code §§1220 through 1370 for all the exceptions.

1. Witnesses

A person called to testify at trial is either a "lay" witness or an "expert" witness. A lay witness is any witness who has not been qualified as an expert in a particular area. Almost all witnesses are considered lay witnesses; these are the witnesses who, based on their personal knowledge, will testify to the facts as they have observed or perceived them. Lay witnesses are sometimes referred to as "percipient" witnesses.

Two principal issues arise with respect to every witness who testifies at trial. These issues are whether the witness is "competent" to testify and, if the witness does testify, how that witness may be "impeached."

a. Competency

The threshold issue with any witness is whether the witness is competent to testify.[20] In general, a witness is competent to testify if she has the ability to communicate either orally or by gestures. Even a child may testify, so long as the judge is satisfied that the child can observe, recollect, and communicate.

To be competent to testify, a witness also must have personal knowledge. It is not sufficient that the witness knows of the facts because they were related by someone else to the witness.[21] The witness must have independent knowledge of the facts.

b. Impeachment

Impeachment
Refers to the discrediting of a witness' testimony

Impeachment refers to the discrediting of a witness' testimony so that the statements made by the witness will not be believed by the trier of fact. Impeachment evidence can be divided into two types: cross-examination of the witness or the introduction of other evidence, called extrinsic evidence, that serves to discredit the witness. A witness may be impeached by a number of methods.

One method of impeaching a witness is to show that the witness is biased or has an interest in the outcome of the lawsuit.[22] For example, on cross-examination the attorney may ask the following questions of the witness to show bias or interest:

---

20. Evid. Code §§700 through 703.
21. The only exception to this rule is in the case of expert witnesses. Evid. Code §720.
22. Evid. Code §780(f).

Example

Bias

Q: Aren't you the plaintiff's brother?
Q: Weren't you fired last year by the defendant?

Interest

Q: Aren't you an equal partner with the plaintiff in this construction venture?
Q: If this will is held invalid, you'll inherit half the estate, won't you?

A witness also may be impeached by a prior inconsistent statement.[23] For example, if a witness previously has testified at a deposition inconsistent with the testimony at trial, the prior inconsistent statement may be used to impeach the witness. This prior inconsistent statement detracts from the credibility of the witness.

Whenever any witness testifies, her credibility is an issue. Accordingly, at trial the opponent can call a reputation witness who will testify that the earlier witness' character for truthfulness is bad.[24] Of course, the proponent can thereafter present contrary testimony of the witness' good reputation for telling the truth. This scenario could be played out as in the example that follows.

Example

Plaintiff in a personal injury case calls Clifford as a witness in plaintiff's case-in-chief. Plaintiff then rests. Defendant in his case-in-chief calls Davis, who testifies that Clifford has a bad reputation for truthfulness. Defendant then rests. Plaintiff in rebuttal calls Adams, who testifies that Clifford has a good reputation for truthfulness.

Example

Prior Bad Acts

Q: Didn't you fill out a false employment application last year?
Q: Didn't you file a false state income tax return two years ago?

In some states that do not follow the Federal Rules, evidence of prior bad acts to attack a witness' credibility is not allowed. Accordingly, if

23. Evid. Code §770.
24. Evid. Code §780(e).

Contradiction
Method of
impeachment that
shows that the true
facts are different
from those stated by
the witness

your case is in state court, be certain to always check your state rules of evidence.

Another method of impeachment is by **contradiction.** Under certain circumstances a cross-examiner may wish to show that the true facts are different from those the witness claims. This is often called impeachment by contradiction.

Example

Impeachment by Contradiction

The witness in an automobile negligence action testifies that he was 10 feet from the accident when it happened. On cross-examination the witness is asked, "Weren't you 100 feet from the accident?" and the witness denies this fact. Here the cross-examiner can bring in other evidence to prove that the witness was indeed 100 feet from the accident to "contradict" the witness' testimony.

---

2. Expert witnesses[25]

Expert testimony is proper whenever it will assist the trier of fact (either the judge or jury) to understand the evidence or determine a fact in issue.

Experts are almost essential in personal injury cases or in any case involving a large amount of technical information. The expert can explain the medical or technical terms to the jury and render an opinion as to a particular issue. For example, in an automobile negligence action, a doctor may be asked to give an opinion as to the chances of plaintiff completely recovering from injuries. Such an opinion will assist the judge or jury in determining how much compensation to award the plaintiff if the defendant is found liable.

Any person having specialized knowledge can be qualified as an expert. Unlike a lay witness, an expert witness does not need to have first-hand knowledge of all the facts on which she bases her opinion. Rather, she also can give an opinion if facts are conveyed to her (as when she sits in court and hears all the evidence presented), or if the facts come from a source relied on by persons in her field (such as where a doctor relies on lab tests actually performed by a hospital laboratory).

---

25. Evid. Code §§720 through 730.

3. Exhibits

Exhibits are tangible items of evidence. Common examples are photographs, diagrams, and business records. To be admissible, exhibits must be relevant. In addition, the proponent of the evidence must show that the offered exhibit is what it appears to be.[26] Thus, it is often said that the exhibit must be **authenticated.** To authenticate an exhibit, a witness must testify who can "establish a foundation" for the offered exhibit. Once the judge determines that sufficient credible evidence has been submitted so a foundation for admission has been established, the exhibit may be admitted into evidence and considered by the **trier of fact**—that is, either the judge or the jury who will decide questions of fact. The kind of foundation required to have an exhibit admitted into evidence depends on the type of exhibit involved. There are five basic types of exhibits which are discussed below.

Authenticate
Establish through witness testimony a foundation for the evidence presented before the trier of fact

a. Real evidence

Real evidence refers to physical objects. Here the exhibit is the actual piece of evidence. The foundation necessary for admissibility from a competent witness is:

1. The exhibit is the actual physical object
2. The exhibit is in substantially the same condition now as when it was first obtained

b. Demonstrative evidence

Demonstrative evidence refers to exhibits that represent real things, such as photographs, diagrams, models, and maps. Here the exhibit is only a representation of the actual object. The foundation necessary for admissibility from a competent witness is:

1. The exhibit is a representation of the real thing as it was at the pertinent date
2. The exhibit is reasonably accurate or to scale

c. Writings

Certain types of writings have independent legal significance. Common examples are wills, contracts, promissory notes, and checks. The only foundation requirement for these kinds of writings is whether the

---

26. Evid. Code §1400.

writing was in fact signed or written by the undersigned person. In other words, the signatures or handwriting must be authenticated. This can be done through any witness who saw the document being signed or written or is familiar with the signature or handwriting and can identify it. If such a witness is unavailable, handwriting comparisons may be used or any other method that identifies the maker of the document.

d. Business records

As discussed previously, business records are obviously hearsay and must therefore be qualified as an exception to the hearsay rules. The foundation for the business records may properly be laid by using the following checklist:

- ☐ a writing made in the regular course of the business
- ☐ made at or near the time of the events recorded on the record
- ☐ a custodian or other qualified witness testifies to the identity of the record and how it was prepared, and
- ☐ the sources of the information and preparation of the record appear trustworthy.

e. Public records

Public records are simply business records generated by governmental entities. Such records are self-authenticating and need no qualifying witness to lay a foundation. A properly certified copy of the public records will be admissible.

4. Best evidence rule

Best evidence rule
Under the common law, a requirement that an original writing had to be produced if the writing was going to be used as evidence

The **best evidence rule** is more accurately called the original document rule, since it applies principally to writings. The common law rule stated that whenever a writing's contents were to be introduced into evidence, the original had to be produced. The rule was a response to the errors and inaccuracies of handmade copies. If there is a genuine dispute over authenticity or it would be unfair to admit a duplicate, the original must still be produced.

5. Judicial notice[27]

Judicial notice is an evidentiary procedure in which the trial judge is asked to rule that certain facts are true. The purpose is to promote trial

---

27. Evid. Code §450 through 460.

efficiency, sharpen issues, and permit the introduction of indisputable evidence where formal proof would be difficult and lengthy. There are a number of matters in which the court must take judicial notice and several when the court may take judicial notice.

Pursuant to Evidence Code §452, there are three common types of facts that may be judicially noticed:

1. Facts generally known within the particular geographical area
2. Facts capable of accurate and readily available determination from an unquestionably accurate source
3. Scientific basis for accepted scientific tests

G. PRIVILEGES

The Evidence Code contains a number of **privileges**,[28] which are rules providing that certain communications are inadmissible because of confidentiality issues, and are based on policy considerations. Under certain situations a higher social good is obtained (promoting open and candid conversations between specified persons) that outweighs the evidentiary cost of losing relevant evidence. Privileges were developed through the common law and, more recently, by statutes. The following are the more common privileges you should be familiar with in your practice.

1. Lawyer-client privilege[29]

The **lawyer-client privilege** applies to confidential communications between a client and a lawyer and the lawyer's representatives relating to the rendering of legal services. The client is the holder of the privilege, and the privilege can be asserted by the client or the client's personal representative, and by the lawyer on behalf of the client.

Lawyer-client privilege
Protection that allows communications between a lawyer and client to remain confidential

As with most things in the law, there are exceptions to the privilege. While there are a number of exceptions, three of the most frequently used exceptions are explained here.

First, there is no lawyer-client privilege if the services of the lawyer are sought to enable or aid one to commit or plan a crime or fraud. Obviously, no social good is advanced by keeping such communications privileged.

Second, when a client claims a breach of duty by the lawyers, the lawyer-client privilege may not be invoked. The rationale is that it would be unfair to permit a client to accuse the attorney of a breach of duty and to thereafter invoke the privilege to prevent the attorney from bringing forth evidence in the attorney's defense.

---

28. Evid. Code §§900 through 1070.
29. Evid. Code §§950 through 962.

Most important, the privilege may be waived if the "confidential communication" is disclosed to others. This is why, when responding to interrogatories or document requests, a paralegal must be certain not to disclose any such communication (whether the communication is oral or in writing) to the adverse party.

2. Work product privilege[30]

Work product
Work performed by an attorney during the course of representing a client

The **work product** privilege is a qualified privilege for the workpapers, notes, memoranda, and reports gathered or prepared by attorneys in anticipation of litigation. This qualified privilege is intended to encourage an attorney to pursue an exhaustive pretrial investigation and analysis of facts without fear that the fruits of this labor will be discoverable by the other side.

The privilege is qualified because in some instances the attorney's work product may be discoverable. In cases where the work product does not contain the lawyer's opinion, mental impression, or legal theories, a party seeking disclosure may be able to demonstrate that there is a substantial need for such materials, and there is no other way to obtain the materials. In such a case, the court may order that such materials be produced to the other side. However, in cases where the materials contain the lawyer's opinion, mental impressions, or legal theories, the materials are never discoverable.

Although the privilege is referred to as the "attorney work product," the privilege applies equally to materials prepared by a legal assistant or agents of the lawyer working under the direction of the lawyer.

3. Physician-patient privilege

Pursuant to Evidence Code §§990 through 1007, a patient, whether or not a party, has a privilege to not disclose—and to prevent the physician from disclosing—any information acquired by the physician in confidence while attending to the patient. Again, there are exceptions. For example, if the patient puts her health in issue, such as in the case of a personal injury action, the physician-patient privilege will not apply.

California also recognizes a psychotherapist-patient privilege.[31] Confidential communications between a psychotherapist and patient for purposes of diagnosing or treating a mental condition of the patient will be privileged. However, if the patient has placed her mental condition in evidence, the privilege may not be asserted.

---

30. Although considered a privilege, the privilege is found in the Code of Civil Procedure and not the Evidence Code. See CCP §2018.

31. Evid. Code §1010 through 1016.

4. Marital privileges[32]

Confidential communications made by one spouse to the other during a legally valid marriage are protected from disclosure. The policy behind allowing such a privilege is to promote candid conversations between spouses. Either spouse may prohibit the other spouse from disclosing the privileged communication. The privilege continues even after the marriage has ended in divorce, so long as the communication itself was made during the marriage.

In addition, a spouse has a privilege not to testify against the other spouse even if the communication is made before the marriage. The privilege provides that a spouse can refuse to testify as a witness against the other spouse. The policy behind this privilege is to promote marital harmony between spouses.

CHAPTER SUMMARY

This chapter has provided an overview of the law of evidence. A paralegal must be familiar with the rules of evidence so that the paralegal can adequately assist the lawyer in determining what evidence can or cannot be admitted into evidence at trial. Familiarity with the rules of evidence is also essential for assisting with pretrial motions and preparing responses to discovery requests.

To be admissible, all evidence must be relevant, reliable, and real. Some evidence, even though relevant, will be excluded under special circumstances. In addition, even though some evidence may not be considered reliable because the evidence is hearsay, there may be exceptions to the hearsay rule. The exceptions still are designed to guarantee reliability by the personal presence of the declarant at trial, under oath, and subject to cross-examination by the opposing parties, or because the exceptions acknowledge other indications of reliability.

Real evidence principally involves issues concerning witnesses, exhibits, and judicial notice. A witness must be competent to testify. A witness' testimony can be impeached by opposing parties. There are several methods of impeachment, including bias, prior inconsistent statements, and contradiction.

Exhibits must be authenticated to show that the exhibit is what it purports to be before the exhibit may be introduced into evidence. An exhibit may be authenticated by a witness who can establish a foundation for the exhibit.

Finally, as a paralegal, you must be aware of privileges that may exist. A privilege protects certain communications from being disclosed to opposing parties. These privileges include communications between

---

32. Evid. Code §970 through 987.

an attorney and client, and documents generated by the attorney in the course of representing the client.

KEY TERMS

Admission of a party opponent

Affidavit

Authenticated

Best evidence rule

Business records

Character traits

Contradiction

Declaration

Demonstrative evidence

Exhibits

Hearsay

Impeachment

Judicial notice

Lawyer-client privilege

Past recorded recollections

Privileges

Probative

Public records

Question of law

Real evidence

Testimony

Trier of fact

Work product

REVIEW QUESTIONS

1. What do we mean by the term "relevant evidence"?

2. What types of relevant evidence are excluded based on policy reasons? What are the policy reasons behind excluding such evidence?

3. What are the three elements necessary for determining whether a statement is "hearsay"?

4. There are several exceptions to the hearsay rule. Identify at least three exceptions and give an example of each.

5. Why are communications between a lawyer and the client subject to the lawyer-client privilege?

6. What does "judicial notice" mean? Can you give an example of a fact that the court may be able to take judicial notice of?

7. How might a witness' statement be impeached?

8. What is the best evidence rule?

INTERNET RESOURCES

http://caselaw.lp.findlaw.com/cacodes/evid.html

http://info.sen.ca.gov

www.leginfo.ca.gov/calaw.html

CHAPTER 13

Introduction to Discovery

A. Introduction
B. Discovery Overview
C. Scope of Discovery
D. Discovery Strategy: A Seven-Step Process

CHAPTER OBJECTIVES

Discovery is one of the primary tools that a paralegal uses to ascertain facts during the course of a lawsuit. In this chapter you will learn:

- ◆ What discovery devices you may use to obtain facts
- ◆ How you may use computers for litigation support
- ◆ What the paralegal's role is in discovery
- ◆ When to use different discovery devices
- ◆ What is the scope of the discovery

A. INTRODUCTION

Discovery is the principal fact-gathering method in the formal litigation process. In today's litigation environment the discovery stage is where most of the battles are fought and where the war is largely won or lost. Consequently, understanding discovery so that you can effectively use the permissible discovery methods as tactical and strategic tools is critical for every litigation paralegal.

Discovery has three main characteristics. First, for the most part, you may conduct discovery without judicial approval, participation, or regulation. Second, the discovery rules are flexible and permit any sequence—and repeated use—of the various discovery methods subject only to court protection against abuse. Third, orders regulating discovery are usually not appealable orders. Since discovery issues will often be moot by the time a final judgment is entered in the case, appeals are relatively infrequent. This means that issues concerning discovery are principally resolved at the trial court level. Many cases are won or lost at the discovery stage because this is where you are most likely to find out the strengths and weaknesses of your case.

B. DISCOVERY OVERVIEW

1. Types of discovery

Discovery is designed to prevent trial by surprise. The purpose is to allow each party to find out the other side's facts supporting the various issues in the litigation so that each party may prepare his or her case for trial. However, in civil actions, where the majority of cases are resolved without trial, it is obvious that discovery has its advantages in the settlement context as well. Properly used, discovery highlights the strengths and weaknesses of one's case. Once these strengths and weaknesses are fully exposed, the parties are usually able to discover the true "value" of the case and come to a settlement.

There are six methods of discovery permitted against any other party:

- ◆ Interrogatories
- ◆ Requests to produce
- ◆ Depositions
- ◆ Physical and mental examinations
- ◆ Requests for admission
- ◆ Exchange of expert trial witness information

Nonparties may be deposed by issuance of a subpoena. In addition the subpoena may request nonparties to bring documents.

Interrogatories are written questions sent by one party to another party. This sending of interrogatories to another party is sometimes referred to as "propounding" interrogatories. The party receiving the interrogatories must give a written response under oath to each question. Under California law, the responding party has 30 days to respond.

Interrogatories are most effective for obtaining basic factual data from other parties, such as the identity of proper parties, agents, employees, witnesses, and experts and the identity and location of documents, records, and tangible evidence. They are also useful in obtaining other parties' positions on disputed facts and experts' opinions and bases for opinions. On the other hand, interrogatories are not usually effective instruments for getting detailed facts, impressions, or versions of events.

A **request to produce** is a written request by one party to another seeking formal permission to obtain copies of records, documents, and other tangible items for inspection, copying, and testing. Such a request also permits entry onto another party's land or property to inspect, photograph, and analyze things on the land or property. By using this discovery device, a party can force the opponent to produce records and other evidence and to permit entry onto property to copy, photograph, or study evidence that is within the opponent's possession, custody, or control.

Depositions are oral questions by one party to another. Although depositions are often taken in a conference room in an attorney's office, the testimony given by the witness (referred to as the **deponent**) is under oath and taken down by a shorthand reporter who is usually a notary public. The oral questions and answers are then transcribed in a booklet form that the deponent is asked to read and sign. The deponent may be cross-examined, and the deponent's attorney may make objections to the questions that are asked.

Depositions are most effective in tying down parties and witnesses to details and in discovering everything they know pertinent to the case. It

Interrogatories
Written questions sent from one party to another party

Depositions
Oral questions asked by one party to another during the discovery stage

is the only discovery vehicle that permits your side to assess how good a witness a person is likely to be at trial. It is an excellent vehicle to secure admissions or other evidence favorable to your side and it is the only one that can be used on nonparty witnesses. Furthermore, a deposition is the only method to preserve testimony if a witness becomes unavailable for trial.

A **physical or mental examination** of a party can be obtained if the party's physical or mental condition is in issue. This is often the case in personal injury cases. The examination can only be done if a court order is obtained or if the party agrees to voluntarily submit to an examination. The examination is usually conducted by a doctor chosen by the party requesting the examination. While other discovery methods can be used to get records of past examinations, this is the only means of forcing a party to be examined and tested for proof of her current condition. It is the best method for evaluating a party on such damages elements as permanence, extent of injury, and medical prognosis.

Requests for admission are written statements that force a party to admit or deny a fact or a document's genuineness. An admitted fact is deemed conclusively admitted for the purpose of the pending trial. This discovery method is effective if limited to simple factual data, such as someone's employment on a specific date or the genuineness of signatures on a contract. It is not a good method for dealing with opinions or evaluative information.

Finally, an **exchange of expert trial witness information** allows any party, after the initial trial date is set, to obtain a list of the names of expert witnesses, the reports and writings of the expert and information concerning the testimony of the expert witness.

All of these methods will be discussed in greater detail later in this chapter.

2. The paralegal's role

As a litigation paralegal, you can expect to have significant involvement in the discovery process. In addition to preparing discovery requests to the other side, you will often be responsible for obtaining information and responding to the discovery the other side serves upon your client. For example, you may be asked to prepare interrogatories and document requests to ascertain facts from the opposing side. This requires that you not only have a complete understanding of the nature of the case but also know and understand the rules for when and how the discovery should be prepared.

Similarly, you may be asked to obtain information or documents from your client in order to properly respond to the discovery requests served by the other side. Knowing when and how to respond to the discovery are essential paralegal skills.

Lawyers frequently rely on paralegals to prepare witnesses for deposition, to digest documents, and to summarize deposition testimony. Since depositions are frequently scheduled at the convenience of the attorneys and the deponent, you may be responsible for scheduling a date for the deposition and selecting a court reporter to attend.

You also may be asked to select a physician to conduct a medical examination, arrange for the examination, and obtain the medical reports prepared as a result of the examination. In summary, other than appearing on behalf of a deponent at a deposition, there is virtually no part of the discovery process in which you will not be involved.

3. Computerized litigation support

Computers have become a significant tool in the litigation process. With respect to the discovery process, there are three areas where computers are valuable.

♦ Conducting research
♦ Locating information about parties and witnesses
♦ Organizing discovery

a. Conducting research

Computers have been used for years to assist lawyers and paralegals in conducting research for their litigation cases. Two of the major computer services available are LEXIS and WESTLAW. However, there are others that your firm may subscribe to that work in a similar fashion. These services provide computerized access to virtually every primary legal resource available, including court cases, statutes, and codes. By inputting a request for particular information, the computer will locate the materials available in that area. In addition, the California state bar website, as well as the Judicial Council website, provides many links to free research sites.

Of course, knowing how to research using the computer is important so that you can properly design a computer search that fits your particular area of inquiry. In addition, your law firm may also have financial restrictions on how much time can be spent in computer research. Accordingly, being able to narrow your search to the relevant inquiry is important. Most paralegal schools now have at least one computer service that the school uses to train paralegals. If your school does not have such a service and the law firm you work for does use a computer service, training will be provided to you (usually for free) by a representative of the computer service. The Internet now offers many legal sites that are available free of charge (see Internet Resources, Chapter 2) and should be consulted where possible.

b. Locating information about parties and witnesses

A second area in which computers are now being used in the discovery stage is the location of information about parties or witnesses. Some computer services give you access to records of the secretary of state or other corporate information such as Dun & Bradstreet reports. By accessing this information, you may be able to find out who the officers and directors of a particular business are, who the corporation's agent for service of process is, and the nature of the business. In addition to LEXIS and WESTLAW, other software vendors for this type of service are also available and should be explored. The Internet also offers many websites devoted to locating witnesses and businesses, done for a fee, and others free of charge. Also consider, if the name you are searching for is not common, doing a search at google.com.

c. Organizing discovery

Finally, in large litigation matters, you may need to input discovery information into your firm's computer or even scan the produced documents into the computer. There are also numerous software programs for document management. If your firm does a lot of litigation, you will probably have a document management program that is used by the firm. A computer is a valuable tool for keeping track of documents and quickly locating specific information. A deposition transcript is also available on computer disk. This allows you to search for particular testimony without having to read the entire transcript. The court reporter who took the deposition can give you a disk that is formatted for the type of computer software your firm uses.

Computer use in law firms is rapidly increasing, and paralegals should learn to utilize a computer not only for word processing but for litigation support as well. Numerous litigation support programs are available, and your law firm will probably have one of these. Some of these programs are available from Aspen Litigation Support, American Legal Systems, and Techlaw Systems, Inc. Again, in most instances, training on the job is available. However, if you are unfamiliar with computers, you should consider enrolling in a basic computer class. Paralegal schools, as well as continuing education programs, often offer these classes.

C. SCOPE OF DISCOVERY

Code of Civil Procedure §2017.010 controls the scope of discovery. The Code provides that a party may discover "any matter, not privileged, that is relevant to the subject matter involved in the pending action." This section discusses what "relevance" means in the discovery context.

1. Relevance

Relevance for discovery purposes is exceptionally broad. Information sought need not be admissible at trial, nor need the information itself be relevant. If the information sought to be discovered "appears reasonably calculated to lead to the discovery of admissible evidence" on the subject matter of the lawsuit, it is discoverable. In short, a "fishing expedition" is proper if it might unveil probative evidence.

CCP §2017.010 expressly permits discovery of potential witnesses, and documents or other tangible items. The Code provides for discovery of the "identity and location of persons having knowledge of any discoverable matter." This includes the names and addresses of those persons. In addition, discovery of the "existence, description, nature, custody, condition and location of any documents, tangible things or land or other property" is also permitted.

2. Insurance agreements

CCP §2017(b) expressly permits the discovery of a liability insurance policy held by any party that may satisfy, in part or in whole, a judgment. This information is critical for assessing the "value" of a case and the defendant's ability to pay a judgment. However, under Evidence Code §1155, the disclosure of insurance information does not necessarily make it admissible as evidence.

3. Experts

There are three basic kinds of experts: testifying experts, consulting experts, and informally consulted experts. CCP §2034.410 governs the discoverability of the identity, opinions, and reports of testifying experts. The experts consulted by a party, who will not be called as trial witnesses are usually not discoverable and are considered a party's work product. The discovery of expert witness information is discussed in Chapter 14.

4. Privileges

As discussed in Chapter 12, there are various privileges that may protect the disclosure of certain evidence to the other parties. If a party objects to disclosure of information or documents on the grounds of privilege, the party must provide enough information to allow the other parties to evaluate the applicability of the claimed privilege. Withholding materials without such notification subjects the party to sanctions and may constitute a waiver of the privilege.

5. Trial preparation materials

Code of Civil Procedure §2018.020(a) specifically states that it is the policy of this state to "preserve the rights of attorneys to prepare cases for trial with that degree of privacy necessary to encourage them to prepare their cases thoroughly and to investigate not only the favorable but the unfavorable aspects of those cases; and . . . to prevent attorneys from taking undue advantage of their adversary's industry and efforts." This is referred to as the attorney's work product.

There are two types of attorney work product. The first type concerns trial preparation materials, which include documents and tangible things that were prepared in anticipation of litigation. Under this type of work product, the trial preparation materials are not discoverable unless a court determines that the denial of discovery will unfairly prejudice the party seeking discovery. This issue most frequently arises in the area of witness statements. For example, if an attorney takes an informal statement of a witness, and the witness later dies, the adverse party may be able to compel the attorney to produce the statement since there is no other way to obtain another statement from the witness.

The second type of work product privilege is the one covering the lawyer's mental impressions, conclusions, and opinions on legal theories. The work product of this type is absolutely protected by the privilege. Hence, disclosure can never be compelled.

D. DISCOVERY STRATEGY: A SEVEN-STEP PROCESS

The discovery rules are both broad and extensive, and in most cases they permit more discovery than either party will wish to make. Consequently, the overriding concern at the discovery stage is: What will be an effective discovery strategy for this particular case? As outlined previously, discovery planning is essentially a seven-step process.

1. What facts are needed in order to establish a winning case on the client's claims (or to defeat the opponent's claims)?

2. What facts already have been obtained through informal fact investigation?

These questions should already be answered in your developing litigation chart.

3. What "missing" facts must still be obtained through formal discovery?

Discovery is the vehicle your side will use to force other parties, and nonparties, to disclose information they have pertinent to the litigation. Your first question, therefore, should be, What additional information do I need to know to assist in preparing the case for a possible trial? While the answer will vary with each case, use the following checklist to ascertain whether you already have information as a result of informal investigation or whether further discovery is necessary:

CHECKLIST OF INFORMATION OBTAINED

- ☐ Identity of proper parties
- ☐ Defendant's ability to pay a judgment
- ☐ Identity of agents and employees
- ☐ Opponent's factual basis for legal claims
- ☐ Opponent's position on factual issues
- ☐ Identity and location of witnesses
- ☐ Prospective testimony of adverse parties, agents, and employees
- ☐ Prospective testimony of important witnesses
- ☐ Identity, opinions, and reasoning of experts
- ☐ Prospective testimony of experts
- ☐ Tangible evidence
- ☐ Documents
- ☐ Records
- ☐ Statements of parties and witnesses
- ☐ Testimony of favorable witnesses that may become unavailable for trial

Not all of this information is necessarily discoverable. However, you should always compile a similar roster for each case because it will control the information you will try to discover. On your litigation chart you will have noted information that can only be found through discovery. Your chart will help lead you through the checklist above for each case.

4. What discovery methods are most effective for obtaining the missing facts?

Although there is some overlap in the discovery methods you may use to obtain the missing information, each method is particularly well suited for certain kinds of information. However, occasionally, there will be information about certain facts that are missing. Oftentimes, these "missing facts" can be obtained by using some of the non-traditional forms of discovery. For example, under CCP §2034.410 a party may depose a person who has been identified as an expert whose opinions may be presented at trial. Accordingly, once you have exchanged expert witness lists, you may find that by deposing the other party's experts you will obtain some of the key facts you are missing.

Also, recall from earlier in the chapter that attorney work product that includes trial preparation materials, can be obtained from an opponent only upon showing that a party will be unfairly prejudiced. This exception to the attorney's work product rule arises most often in regard to witness statements, which are not automatically discoverable. When one side has taken a statement from a witness who now refuses to talk to other lawyers, who cannot be subpoenaed, or who has a lapse of memory, and the substantial equivalent of the statement cannot be obtained, the court may order the production of the statement.

5. What facts and witnesses, already identified through informal investigation, must be pinned down by formal discovery?

There is little point in using formal discovery methods with the favorable witnesses, unless those witnesses are infirm or are likely to move away. If this is the case, the lawyer will want to take the witness' deposition to preserve the testimony for trial.

With unfavorable, hostile, or adverse witnesses and parties, however, there are good reasons for deposing them, even if your side already knows from the informal fact investigation what these witnesses will say at trial. First, there are always benefits in learning in detail what those witnesses will say. Second, witnesses may testify inconsistently with their previous statements or with each other. Third, it may be possible to limit the witnesses' trial testimony by getting the witnesses to admit to topics they have no first-hand knowledge of, are not sure of, or are only approximating or guessing at.

6. What restrictions does the client's litigation budget place on the discovery plan?

Information gathering, especially formal discovery, is expensive, and any discovery strategy must necessarily consider the expenses involved. Accordingly, always consult with the lawyer responsible for the litigation before you prepare any discovery requests.

In addition, responding to discovery, particularly interrogatories and document requests, can become expensive because of the time involved in researching and preparing responses and reviewing the necessary documents. Before you begin preparing any responses, discuss with the lawyer the time you expect will be necessary to properly prepare the responses.

7. In what order should the discovery proceed?

Formal discovery should be used as a progressive device in which each discovery method is utilized as a sequential building block. In federal court, Federal Rules of Civil Procedure Rule 26 attempts to accelerate the exchange of basic information about the case and to eliminate the paperwork involved in requesting such information. Rule 26 imposes on the parties a duty to disclose basic information without waiting for formal discovery requests. However, in California state courts because the discovery process is largely governed by the parties, the relevant questions are: When should discovery start? In what order should discovery be carried out?

a. When should discovery start?

If the prefiling investigation and preparation work are done, discovery may begin during the pleading stage. For instance, defendants frequently serve interrogatories with their answers and sometimes serve notice to take the plaintiff's deposition at the same time. Doing this shows the plaintiff that the defendant intends to litigate vigorously and gives the defendant a head start on any discovery cut-off dates.

b. In what order should discovery be carried out?

The following is a common discovery sequence:

1. Interrogatories
2. Requests to produce and subpoenas
3. Depositions of parties, witnesses, and experts
4. Physical and mental examinations
5. Requests to admit

This sequence uses the building block approach to discovery. Interrogatory answers should identify the opponent's witnesses, documents, and positions on the facts. Once the answers are received, serving requests to produce on parties and subpoenas on nonparty witnesses is useful to obtain the documents, records, and other evidence identified in the interrogatory answers. After receiving this information it is time to take depositions of parties, witnesses, and, if permitted, experts. In personal injury cases, the physical and mental examinations of parties are ordinarily conducted later in the litigation process because these examinations usually focus on such issues as permanence of injury, prognosis, and loss of earning capacity. Once these steps have been completed, requests to admit can further pinpoint areas of dispute and eliminate the need to prove uncontested facts at trial.

This sequence, of course, can be modified. Amended, supplemental, or additional pleadings may be filed that will necessarily alter the course of discovery. In addition, there may be tactical benefits in changing the usual sequence or in serving more than one discovery device at the same time. Because the discovery process educates the opponent as well as the party requesting the discovery, lawyers sometimes take the deposition of an adverse party first on the theory that the adverse party will have neither the time nor the inclination to prepare thoroughly by collecting and reviewing all the pertinent records beforehand. Also, lawyers frequently schedule depositions of the adverse party and that party's employees and agents back to back so that successive deponents cannot review the testimony of earlier deponents before being deposed themselves. Furthermore, lawyers frequently couple interrogatories requesting the existence of documents with a request to produce the documents identified, and use early requests to admit facts in order to narrow the scope of discovery.

There is no magic formula for deciding on the best sequence for discovery. Discovery may be tailored to the specific needs and circumstances of each case. An important point to remember, however, is that discovery should not be used simply because it is available. Each step must have a specific purpose and be part of an overall discovery strategy.

CHAPTER SUMMARY

This chapter has discussed the formal tools for obtaining facts in a lawsuit. Basically, there are six discovery devices that you may use: interrogatories, requests to produce, depositions, medical examinations, requests to admit facts, and exchange of expert trial witness information. Each of these devices serves a different purpose. Interrogatories are beneficial for obtaining basic factual information. Requests to produce allow you to obtain documents and other tangible items that are in the control of other parties. Depositions are an effective method for tying down parties and witnesses to details. A physical and/or mental examination helps a party assess medical damages. A request to admit provides a way to have a fact conclusively established without having to prove the fact at trial. When an initial trial date is set, a demand may be made to exchange information about what the other party's trial experts will state at trial.

Each discovery device serves a different purpose, and deciding the type of discovery, the order of discovery, and when to take discovery are important considerations. This chapter has provided you with a seven-step process that can be used to determine the discovery strategy to use depending on the needs of the case and the client.

KEY TERMS

Deponent	Physical and mental examinations
Deposition	Requests for admission
Interrogatories	Request to produce

REVIEW QUESTIONS

1. Identify the six different discovery devices. What is the purpose of each device?

2. How can computers be used to assist in the litigation process?

3. What does "relevance" mean in the context of discovery?

4. Why are insurance policies held by the parties discoverable?

5. Identify the seven steps for discovery planning.

INTERNET RESOURCES

www.californiadiscovery.findlaw.com/admissions.htm
www.dicarlolaw.com/DiscoveryTechniques.htm
www.iaf.net (Internet address finder)
www.whowhere.com

CHAPTER **14**

Written Discovery

CHAPTER OBJECTIVES

In Chapter 13 you learned the basic discovery devices used to conduct formal fact-finding investigations. The discovery devices are either sent to the opposing parties in written form or, sometimes, testimony is taken by oral depositions. In this chapter you will learn:

♦ How to draft the different forms of written discovery
♦ When to use interrogatories
♦ What type of documents can be obtained through document requests
♦ When to exchange expert witness information
♦ When a discovery motion may be necessary

A. INTRODUCTION

Written discovery is an important part of the formal investigation process. Each discovery device is designed to solicit different information. It is important, as a paralegal, for you to know how the different discovery devices work together and how to use the different devices to obtain the information you want from the other side.

As you learned in Chapter 2, finding and assimilating information is an important process to prove the elements of your client's claim or defense. At trial, a judge or jury will allow you to introduce facts as evidence of your client's claim. If you cannot get the facts through your client or other informal discovery, and the possibility of obtaining all the facts that you need to prove your case is rare, then you must obtain the facts through the information held by other parties. This is the purpose of the formal discovery methods. In addition, often times it is impossible to assess the value of a client's case without knowing how strong the client's case is and what the other side's strengths and weaknesses are. Accordingly, engaging in discovery is often an important tool in helping to settle a case without the necessity of further litigation.

B. INTERROGATORIES

Submitting interrogatories—that is, a list of written questions—to the opposing parties is usually the first step in the discovery process because interrogatories are the best method for getting basic facts about the other side's case. Once interrogatory answers have been received, further discovery can develop this basic information in greater detail.

In addition to the forms included in this chapter, additional sample interrogatories and answers are included in the Litigation File at the end of this book and in the accompanying workbook.

1. Law

Although interrogatories are governed by CCP §2030, the Code is often supplemented by local rules because discovery abuse tends to be more extensive with interrogatories than with other discovery methods. These local rules frequently impose additional constraints, most commonly placing limits on the number of interrogatories that can be served and requiring court approval for additional sets of interrogatories. Hence, one should always check the rules for the particular court.

The Judicial Council has approved **form interrogatories** for common cases such as personal injury suits. Usually taking the form of pre-printed questions that relate to a specific area of the law, form interrogatories seek information commonly requested in all cases in that particular area. For example, in personal injury cases, recurring interrogatory questions include identification of past injuries, the treating physicians, and the amount of damages sustained. One example of form interrogatories is shown in Exhibit 14.1. In cases involving less than $25,000, the Judicial Council also approves a form, a sample of which is contained in the workbook, to exchange basic information about the case without the necessity of spending a lot of money on discovery.

Interrogatories may be used to identify witnesses and experts; to obtain the subject matter, opinions, and bases for the opinions of experts; and to identify documents and other tangible things. Also, they can be used to inquire about any claim or defense and about any relevant matter that is not privileged.

The number of interrogatories each party can serve on another is limited to 35 specially prepared interrogatories and as many relevant interrogatories that are contained in the official forms. However, if a party can show either (a) the "complexity or the quantity of the existing and potential issues in the particular case"; or (b) the "financial burden on a party entailed in conducting the discovery by oral deposition" the party may propound a greater number of interrogatories. The Code specifically sets out the Declaration that needs to be filed for additional discovery. A sample declaration is shown in Exhibit 14.2. A party cannot avoid the number limit on interrogatories by using distinct subparts. For example, an interrogatory such as the following would count as three separate interrogatories:

Exhibit 14.1. Judicial Council Form Interrogatories

DISC-001

ATTORNEY OR PARTY WITHOUT ATTORNEY *(Name, State Bar number, and address)*:

TELEPHONE NO.:
FAX NO. *(Optional)*:
E-MAIL ADDRESS *(Optional)*:
ATTORNEY FOR *(Name)*:

SUPERIOR COURT OF CALIFORNIA, COUNTY OF

SHORT TITLE OF CASE:

FORM INTERROGATORIES—GENERAL

Asking Party:

Answering Party:
Set No.:

CASE NUMBER:

Sec. 1. Instructions to All Parties

(a) Interrogatories are written questions prepared by a party to an action that are sent to any other party in the action to be answered under oath. The interrogatories below are form interrogatories approved for use in civil cases.

(b) For time limitations, requirements for service on other parties, and other details, see Code of Civil Procedure sections 2030.010–2030.410 and the cases construing those sections.

(c) These form interrogatories do not change existing law relating to interrogatories nor do they affect an answering party's right to assert any privilege or make any objection.

Sec. 2. Instructions to the Asking Party

(a) These interrogatories are designed for optional use by parties in unlimited civil cases where the amount demanded exceeds $25,000. Separate interrogatories, Form *Interrogatories—Limited Civil Cases (Economic Litigation)* (form DISC-004), which have no subparts, are designed for use in limited civil cases where the amount demanded is $25,000 or less; however, those interrogatories may also be used in unlimited civil cases.

(b) Check the box next to each interrogatory that you want the answering party to answer. Use care in choosing those interrogatories that are applicable to the case.

(c) You may insert your own definition of **INCIDENT** in Section 4, but only where the action arises from a course of conduct or a series of events occurring over a period of time.

(d) The interrogatories in section 16.0, Defendant's Contentions–Personal Injury, should not be used until the defendant has had a reasonable opportunity to conduct an investigation or discovery of plaintiff's injuries and damages.

(e) Additional interrogatories may be attached.

Sec. 3. Instructions to the Answering Party

(a) An answer or other appropriate response must be given to each interrogatory checked by the asking party.

(b) As a general rule, within 30 days after you are served with these interrogatories, you must serve your responses on the asking party and serve copies of your responses on all other parties to the action who have appeared. See Code of Civil Procedure sections 2030.260–2030.270 for details.

(c) Each answer must be as complete and straightforward as the information reasonably available to you, including the information possessed by your attorneys or agents, permits. If an interrogatory cannot be answered completely, answer it to the extent possible.

(d) If you do not have enough personal knowledge to fully answer an interrogatory, say so, but make a reasonable and good faith effort to get the information by asking other persons or organizations, unless the information is equally available to the asking party.

(e) Whenever an interrogatory may be answered by referring to a document, the document may be attached as an exhibit to the response and referred to in the response. If the document has more than one page, refer to the page and section where the answer to the interrogatory can be found.

(f) Whenever an address and telephone number for the same person are requested in more than one interrogatory, you are required to furnish them in answering only the first interrogatory asking for that information.

(g) If you are asserting a privilege or making an objection to an interrogatory, you must specifically assert the privilege or state the objection in your written response.

(h) Your answers to these interrogatories must be verified, dated, and signed. You may wish to use the following form at the end of your answers:

I declare under penalty of perjury under the laws of the State of California that the foregoing answers are true and correct.

_____   _____
(DATE)   *(SIGNATURE)*

Sec. 4. Definitions

Words in **BOLDFACE CAPITALS** in these interrogatories are defined as follows:

(a) *(Check one of the following):*

☐ (1) **INCIDENT** includes the circumstances and events surrounding the alleged accident, injury, or other occurrence or breach of contract giving rise to this action or proceeding.

Page 1 of 8

Form Approved for Optional Use
Judicial Council of California
DISC-001 [Rev. January 1, 2007]

FORM INTERROGATORIES—GENERAL

Code of Civil Procedure,
§§ 2030.010-2030.410, 2033.710
www.courtinfo.ca.gov

American LegalNet, Inc.
www.FormsWorkflow.com

Exhibit 14.1. Continued

☐ **(2)** **INCIDENT** means *(insert your definition here or on a separate, attached sheet labeled "Sec. 4(a)(2)"):*

(b) **YOU OR ANYONE ACTING ON YOUR BEHALF** includes you, your agents, your employees, your insurance companies, their agents, their employees, your attorneys, your accountants, your investigators, and anyone else acting on your behalf.

(c) **PERSON** includes a natural person, firm, association, organization, partnership, business, trust, limited liability company, corporation, or public entity.

(d) **DOCUMENT** means a writing, as defined in Evidence Code section 250, and includes the original or a copy of handwriting, typewriting, printing, photostats, photographs, electronically stored information, and every other means of recording upon any tangible thing and form of communicating or representation, including letters, words, pictures, sounds, or symbols, or combinations of them.

(e) **HEALTH CARE PROVIDER** includes any **PERSON** referred to in Code of Civil Procedure section 667.7(e)(3).

(f) **ADDRESS** means the street address, including the city, state, and zip code.

Sec. 5. Interrogatories

The following interrogatories have been approved by the Judicial Council under Code of Civil Procedure section 2033.710:

CONTENTS

1.0 Identity of Persons Answering These Interrogatories

☐ 1.1 State the name, **ADDRESS**, telephone number, and relationship to you of each **PERSON** who prepared or assisted in the preparation of the responses to these interrogatories. (*Do not identify anyone who simply typed or reproduced the responses.*)

2.0 General Background Information—individual

☐ 2.1 State:
(a) your name;
(b) every name you have used in the past; and
(c) the dates you used each name.

☐ 2.2 State the date and place of your birth.

☐ 2.3 At the time of the **INCIDENT,** did you have a driver's license? If so state:
(a) the state or other issuing entity;
(b) the license number and type;
(c) the date of issuance; and
(d) all restrictions.

☐ 2.4 At the time of the **INCIDENT,** did you have any other permit or license for the operation of a motor vehicle? If so, state:
(a) the state or other issuing entity;
(b) the license number and type;
(c) the date of issuance; and
(d) all restrictions.

☐ 2.5 State:
(a) your present residence **ADDRESS;**
(b) your residence **ADDRESSES** for the past five years; and
(c) the dates you lived at each **ADDRESS.**

☐ 2.6 State:
(a) the name, **ADDRESS,** and telephone number of your present employer or place of self-employment; and
(b) the name, **ADDRESS,** dates of employment, job title, and nature of work for each employer or self-employment you have had from five years before the **INCIDENT** until today.

☐ 2.7 State:
(a) the name and **ADDRESS** of each school or other academic or vocational institution you have attended, beginning with high school;
(b) the dates you attended;
(c) the highest grade level you have completed; and
(d) the degrees received.

☐ 2.8 Have you ever been convicted of a felony? If so, for each conviction state:
(a) the city and state where you were convicted;
(b) the date of conviction;
(c) the offense; and
(d) the court and case number.

☐ 2.9 Can you speak English with ease? If not, what language and dialect do you normally use?

☐ 2.10 Can you read and write English with ease? If not, what language and dialect do you normally use?

FORM INTERROGATORIES—GENERAL

Exhibit 14.1. Continued

2.11 At the time of the **INCIDENT** were you acting as an agent or employee for any **PERSON?** If so, state:
(a) the name, **ADDRESS,** and telephone number of that **PERSON:** and
(b) a description of your duties.

2.12 At the time of the **INCIDENT** did you or any other person have any physical, emotional, or mental disability or condition that may have contributed to the occurrence of the **INCIDENT?** If so, for each person state:
(a) the name, **ADDRESS,** and telephone number;
(b) the nature of the disability or condition; and
(c) the manner in which the disability or condition contributed to the occurrence of the **INCIDENT.**

2.13 Within 24 hours before the **INCIDENT** did you or any person involved in the **INCIDENT** use or take any of the following substances: alcoholic beverage, marijuana, or other drug or medication of any kind (prescription or not)? If so, for each person state:
(a) the name, **ADDRESS,** and telephone number;
(b) the nature or description of each substance;
(c) the quantity of each substance used or taken;
(d) the date and time of day when each substance was used or taken;
(e) the **ADDRESS** where each substance was used or taken;
(f) the name, **ADDRESS,** and telephone number of each person who was present when each substance was used or taken; and
(g) the name, **ADDRESS,** and telephone number of any **HEALTH CARE PROVIDER** who prescribed or furnished the substance and the condition for which it was prescribed or furnished.

3.0 General Background Information—Business Entity

3.1 Are you a corporation? If so, state:
(a) the name stated in the current articles of incorporation;
(b) all other names used by the corporation during the past 10 years and the dates each was used;
(c) the date and place of incorporation;
(d) the **ADDRESS** of the principal place of business; and
(e) whether you are qualified to do business in California.

3.2 Are you a partnership? If so, state:
(a) the current partnership name;
(b) all other names used by the partnership during the past 10 years and the dates each was used;
(c) whether you are a limited partnership and, if so, under the laws of what jurisdiction;
(d) the name and **ADDRESS** of each general partner; and
(e) the **ADDRESS** of the principal place of business.

3.3 Are you a limited liability company? If so, state:
(a) the name stated in the current articles of organization;
(b) all other names used by the company during the past 10 years and the date each was used;
(c) the date and place of filing of the articles of organization;
(d) the **ADDRESS** of the principal place of business; and
(e) whether you are qualified to do business in California.

3.4 Are you a joint venture? If so, state:
(a) the current joint venture name;
(b) all other names used by the joint venture during the past 10 years and the dates each was used;
(c) the name and **ADDRESS** of each joint venturer; and
(d) the **ADDRESS** of the principal place of business.

3.5 Are you an unincorporated association?
If so, state:
(a) the current unincorporated association name;
(b) all other names used by the unincorporated association during the past 10 years and the dates each was used; and
(c) the **ADDRESS** of the principal place of business.

3.6 Have you done business under a fictitious name during the past 10 years? If so, for each fictitious name state:
(a) the name;
(b) the dates each was used;
(c) the state and county of each fictitious name filing; and
(d) the **ADDRESS** of the principal place of business.

3.7 Within the past five years has any public entity registered or licensed your business? If so, for each license or registration:
(a) identify the license or registration;
(b) state the name of the public entity; and
(c) state the dates of issuance and expiration.

4.0 Insurance

4.1 At the time of the **INCIDENT,** was there in effect any policy of insurance through which you were or might be insured in any manner (for example, primary, pro-rata, or excess liability coverage or medical expense coverage) for the damages, claims, or actions that have arisen out of the **INCIDENT?** If so, for each policy state:
(a) the kind of coverage;
(b) the name and **ADDRESS** of the insurance company;
(c) the name, **ADDRESS,** and telephone number of each named insured;
(d) the policy number;
(e) the limits of coverage for each type of coverage contained in the policy;
(f) whether any reservation of rights or controversy or coverage dispute exists between you and the insurance company; and
(g) the name, **ADDRESS,** and telephone number of the custodian of the policy.

4.2 Are you self-insured under any statute for the damages, claims, or actions that have arisen out of the **INCIDENT?** If so, specify the statute.

5.0 [Reserved]

6.0 Physical, Mental, or Emotional Injuries

6.1 Do you attribute any physical, mental, or emotional injuries to the **INCIDENT?** *(If your answer is "no," do not answer interrogatories 6.2 through 6.7).*

6.2 Identify each injury you attribute to the **INCIDENT** and the area of your body affected.

Exhibit 14.1. Continued

6.3 Do you still have any complaints that you attribute to the **INCIDENT?** If so, for each complaint state:
(a) a description;
(b) whether the complaint is subsiding, remaining the same, or becoming worse; and
(c) the frequency and duration.

6.4 Did you receive any consultation or examination (except from expert witnesses covered by Code of Civil Procedure sections 2034.210–2034.310) or treatment from a **HEALTH CARE PROVIDER** for any injury you attribute to the **INCIDENT?** If so, for each **HEALTH CARE PROVIDER** state:
(a) the name, **ADDRESS**, and telephone number;
(b) the type of consultation, examination, or treatment provided;
(c) the dates you received consultation, examination, or treatment; and
(d) the charges to date.

6.5 Have you taken any medication, prescribed or not, as a result of injuries that you attribute to the **INCIDENT?** If so, for each medication state:
(a) the name;
(b) the **PERSON** who prescribed or furnished it;
(c) the date it was prescribed or furnished;
(d) the dates you began and stopped taking it; and
(e) the cost to date.

6.6 Are there any other medical services necessitated by the injuries that you attribute to the **INCIDENT** that were not previously listed (for example, ambulance, nursing, prosthetics)? If so, for each service state:
(a) the nature;
(b) the date;
(c) the cost; and
(d) the name, **ADDRESS**, and telephone number of each provider.

6.7 Has any **HEALTH CARE PROVIDER** advised that you may require future or additional treatment for any injuries that you attribute to the **INCIDENT?** If so, for each injury state:
(a) the name and **ADDRESS** of each **HEALTH CARE PROVIDER;**
(b) the complaints for which the treatment was advised; and
(c) the nature, duration, and estimated cost of the treatment.

7.0 Property Damage

7.1 Do you attribute any loss of or damage to a vehicle or other property to the **INCIDENT?** If so, for each item of property:
(a) describe the property;
(b) describe the nature and location of the damage to the property;

(c) state the amount of damage you are claiming for each item of property and how the amount was calculated; and
(d) if the property was sold, state the name, **ADDRESS**, and telephone number of the seller, the date of sale, and the sale price.

7.2 Has a written estimate or evaluation been made for any item of property referred to in your answer to the preceding interrogatory? If so, for each estimate or evaluation state:
(a) the name, **ADDRESS**, and telephone number of the **PERSON** who prepared it and the date prepared;
(b) the name, **ADDRESS**, and telephone number of each **PERSON** who has a copy of it; and
(c) the amount of damage stated.

7.3 Has any item of property referred to in your answer to interrogatory 7.1 been repaired? If so, for each item state:
(a) the date repaired;
(b) a description of the repair;
(c) the repair cost;
(d) the name, **ADDRESS**, and telephone number of the **PERSON** who repaired it;
(e) the name, **ADDRESS**, and telephone number of the **PERSON** who paid for the repair.

8.0 Loss of Income or Earning Capacity

8.1 Do you attribute any loss of income or earning capacity to the **INCIDENT?** *(If your answer is "no," do not answer interrogatories 8.2 through 8.8).*

8.2 State:
(a) the nature of your work;
(b) your job title at the time of the **INCIDENT;** and
(c) the date your employment began.

8.3 State the last date before the **INCIDENT** that you worked for compensation.

8.4 State your monthly income at the time of the **INCIDENT** and how the amount was calculated.

8.5 State the date you returned to work at each place of employment following the **INCIDENT.**

8.6 State the dates you did not work and for which you lost income as a result of the **INCIDENT.**

8.7 State the total income you have lost to date as a result of the **INCIDENT** and how the amount was calculated.

8.8 Will you lose income in the future as a result of the **INCIDENT?** If so, state:
(a) the facts upon which you base this contention;
(b) an estimate of the amount;
(c) an estimate of how long you will be unable to work; and
(d) how the claim for future income is calculated.

Exhibit 14.1. Continued

9.0 Other Damages

☐ 9.1 Are there any other damages that you attribute to the **INCIDENT?** If so, for each item of damage state:
(a) the nature;
(b) the date it occurred;
(c) the amount; and
(d) the name, **ADDRESS,** and telephone number of each **PERSON** to whom an obligation was incurred.

☐ 9.2 Do any **DOCUMENTS** support the existence or amount of any item of damages claimed in interrogatory 9.1? If so, describe each document and state the name, **ADDRESS,** and telephone number of the **PERSON** who has each **DOCUMENT.**

10.0 Medical History

☐ 10.1 At any time before the **INCIDENT** did you have complaints or injuries that involved the same part of your body claimed to have been injured in the **INCIDENT?** If so, for each state:

(a) a description of the complaint or injury;
(b) the dates it began and ended; and
(c) the name, **ADDRESS,** and telephone number of each **HEALTH CARE PROVIDER** whom you consulted or who examined or treated you.

☐ 10.2 List all physical, mental, and emotional disabilities you had immediately before the **INCIDENT.** *(You may omit mental or emotional disabilities unless you attribute any mental or emotional injury to the INCIDENT.)*

☐ 10.3 At any time after the **INCIDENT,** did you sustain injuries of the kind for which you are now claiming damages? If so, for each incident giving rise to an injury state:

(a) the date and the place it occurred;
(b) the name, **ADDRESS,** and telephone number of any other **PERSON** involved;
(c) the nature of any injuries you sustained;
(d) the name, **ADDRESS,** and telephone number of each **HEALTH CARE PROVIDER** who you consulted or who examined or treated you; and
(e) the nature of the treatment and its duration.

11.0 Other Claims and Previous Claims

☐ 11.1 Except for this action, in the past 10 years have you filed an action or made a written claim or demand for compensation for your personal injuries? If so, for each action, claim, or demand state:

(a) the date, time, and place and location (closest street **ADDRESS** or intersection) of the **INCIDENT** giving rise to the action, claim, or demand;
(b) the name, **ADDRESS,** and telephone number of each **PERSON** against whom the claim or demand was made or the action filed;

(c) the court, names of the parties, and case number of any action filed;
(d) the name, **ADDRESS,** and telephone number of any attorney representing you;
(e) whether the claim or action has been resolved or is pending; and
(f) a description of the injury.

☐ 11.2 In the past 10 years have you made a written claim or demand for workers' compensation benefits? If so, for each claim or demand state:
(a) the date, time, and place of the **INCIDENT** giving rise to the claim;
(b) the name, **ADDRESS,** and telephone number of your employer at the time of the injury;
(c) the name, **ADDRESS,** and telephone number of the workers' compensation insurer and the claim number;
(d) the period of time during which you received workers' compensation benefits;
(e) a description of the injury;
(f) the name, **ADDRESS,** and telephone number of any **HEALTH CARE PROVIDER** who provided services; and
(g) the case number at the Workers' Compensation Appeals Board.

12.0 Investigation—General

☐ 12.1 State the name, **ADDRESS,** and telephone number of each individual:
(a) who witnessed the **INCIDENT** or the events occurring immediately before or after the **INCIDENT;**
(b) who made any statement at the scene of the **INCIDENT;**
(c) who heard any statements made about the **INCIDENT** by any individual at the scene; and
(d) who **YOU OR ANYONE ACTING ON YOUR BEHALF** claim has knowledge of the **INCIDENT** (except for expert witnesses covered by Code of Civil Procedure section 2034).

☐ 12.2 Have **YOU OR ANYONE ACTING ON YOUR BEHALF** interviewed any individual concerning the **INCIDENT?** If so, for each individual state:
(a) the name, **ADDRESS,** and telephone number of the individual interviewed;
(b) the date of the interview; and
(c) the name, **ADDRESS,** and telephone number of the **PERSON** who conducted the interview.

☐ 12.3 Have **YOU OR ANYONE ACTING ON YOUR BEHALF** obtained a written or recorded statement from any individual concerning the **INCIDENT?** If so, for each statement state:
(a) the name, **ADDRESS,** and telephone number of the individual from whom the statement was obtained;
(b) the name, **ADDRESS,** and telephone number of the individual who obtained the statement;
(c) the date the statement was obtained; and
(d) the name, **ADDRESS,** and telephone number of each **PERSON** who has the original statement or a copy.

Exhibit 14.1.   Continued

DISC-001

☐ 12.4   Do **YOU OR ANYONE ACTING ON YOUR BEHALF** know of any photographs, films, or videotapes depicting any place, object, or individual concerning the **INCIDENT** or plaintiff's injuries? If so, state:

(a) the number of photographs or feet of film or videotape;
(b) the places, objects, or persons photographed, filmed, or videotaped;
(c) the date the photographs, films, or videotapes were taken;
(d) the name, **ADDRESS,** and telephone number of the individual taking the photographs, films, or videotapes; and
(e) the name, **ADDRESS,** and telephone number of each **PERSON** who has the original or a copy of the photographs, films, or videotapes.

☐ 12.5   Do **YOU OR ANYONE ACTING ON YOUR BEHALF** know of any diagram, reproduction, or model of any place or thing (except for items developed by expert witnesses covered by Code of Civil Procedure sections 2034.210–2034.310) concerning the **INCIDENT?** If so, for each item state:

(a) the type (i.e., diagram, reproduction, or model);
(b) the subject matter; and
(c) the name, **ADDRESS,** and telephone number of each **PERSON** who has it.

☐ 12.6   Was a report made by any **PERSON** concerning the **INCIDENT?** If so, state:

(a) the name, title, identification number, and employer of the **PERSON** who made the report;
(b) the date and type of report made;
(c) the name, **ADDRESS,** and telephone number of the **PERSON** for whom the report was made; and
(d) the name, **ADDRESS,** and telephone number of each **PERSON** who has the original or a copy of the report.

☐ 12.7   Have **YOU OR ANYONE ACTING ON YOUR BEHALF** inspected the scene of the **INCIDENT?** If so, for each inspection state:

(a) the name, **ADDRESS,** and telephone number of the individual making the inspection (except for expert witnesses covered by Code of Civil Procedure sections 2034.210–2034.310); and
(b) the date of the inspection.

13.0 Investigation—Surveillance

☐ 13.1   Have **YOU OR ANYONE ACTING ON YOUR BEHALF** conducted surveillance of any individual involved in the **INCIDENT** or any party to this action? If so, for each surveillance state:

(a) the name, **ADDRESS,** and telephone number of the individual or party;
(b) the time, date, and place of the surveillance;
(c) the name, **ADDRESS,** and telephone number of the individual who conducted the surveillance; and
(d) the name, **ADDRESS,** and telephone number of each **PERSON** who has the original or a copy of any surveillance photograph, film, or videotape.

☐ 13.2   Has a written report been prepared on the surveillance? If so, for each written report state:
(a) the title;
(b) the date;
(c) the name, **ADDRESS,** and telephone number of the individual who prepared the report; and
(d) the name, **ADDRESS,** and telephone number of each **PERSON** who has the original or a copy.

14.0 Statutory or Regulatory Violations

☐ 14.1   Do **YOU OR ANYONE ACTING ON YOUR BEHALF** contend that any **PERSON** involved in the **INCIDENT** violated any statute, ordinance, or regulation and that the violation was a legal (proximate) cause of the **INCIDENT?** If so, identify the name, **ADDRESS,** and telephone number of each **PERSON** and the statute, ordinance, or regulation that was violated.

☐ 14.2   Was any **PERSON** cited or charged with a violation of any statute, ordinance, or regulation as a result of this **INCIDENT?** If so, for each **PERSON** state:

(a) the name, **ADDRESS,** and telephone number of the **PERSON;**
(b) the statute, ordinance, or regulation allegedly violated;
(c) whether the **PERSON** entered a plea in response to the citation or charge and, if so, the plea entered; and
(d) the name and **ADDRESS** of the court or administrative agency, names of the parties, and case number.

15.0 Denials and Special or Affirmative Defenses

☐ 15.1   Identify each denial of a material allegation and each special or affirmative defense in your pleadings and for each:
(a) state all facts upon which you base the denial or special or affirmative defense;
(b) state the names, **ADDRESSES,** and telephone numbers of all **PERSONS** who have knowledge of those facts; and
(c) identify all **DOCUMENTS** and other tangible things that support your denial or special or affirmative defense, and state the name, **ADDRESS,** and telephone number of the **PERSON** who has each **DOCUMENT.**

16.0 Defendant's Contentions—Personal Injury

☐ 16.1   Do you contend that any **PERSON,** other than you or plaintiff, contributed to the occurrence of the **INCIDENT** or the injuries or damages claimed by plaintiff? If so, for each **PERSON:**
(a) state the name, **ADDRESS,** and telephone number of the **PERSON;**
(b) state all facts upon which you base your contention;
(c) state the names, **ADDRESSES,** and telephone numbers of all **PERSONS** who have knowledge of the facts; and
(d) identify all **DOCUMENTS** and other tangible things that support your contention and state the name, **ADDRESS,** and telephone number of the **PERSON** who has each **DOCUMENT** or thing.

☐ 16.2   Do you contend that plaintiff was not injured in the **INCIDENT?** If so:
(a) state all facts upon which you base your contention;
(b) state the names, **ADDRESSES,** and telephone numbers of all **PERSONS** who have knowledge of the facts; and
(c) identify all **DOCUMENTS** and other tangible things that support your contention and state the name, **ADDRESS,** and telephone number of the **PERSON** who has each **DOCUMENT** or thing.

Exhibit 14.1. Continued

☐ 16.3 Do you contend that the injuries or the extent of the injuries claimed by plaintiff as disclosed in discovery proceedings thus far in this case were not caused by the **INCIDENT**? If so, for each injury:

(a) identify it;
(b) state all facts upon which you base your contention;
(c) state the names, **ADDRESSES,** and telephone numbers of all **PERSONS** who have knowledge of the facts; and
(d) identify all **DOCUMENTS** and other tangible things that support your contention and state the name, **ADDRESS,** and telephone number of the **PERSON** who has each **DOCUMENT** or thing.

☐ 16.4 Do you contend that any of the services furnished by any **HEALTH CARE PROVIDER** claimed by plaintiff in discovery proceedings thus far in this case were not due to the **INCIDENT**? If so:

(a) identify each service;
(b) state all facts upon which you base your contention;
(c) state the names, **ADDRESSES,** and telephone numbers of all **PERSONS** who have knowledge of the facts; and
(d) identify all **DOCUMENTS** and other tangible things that support your contention and state the name, **ADDRESS,** and telephone number of the **PERSON** who has each **DOCUMENT** or thing.

☐ 16.5 Do you contend that any of the costs of services furnished by any **HEALTH CARE PROVIDER** claimed as damages by plaintiff in discovery proceedings thus far in this case were not necessary or unreasonable? If so:

(a) identify each cost;
(b) state all facts upon which you base your contention;
(c) state the names, **ADDRESSES,** and telephone numbers of all **PERSONS** who have knowledge of the facts; and
(d) identify all **DOCUMENTS** and other tangible things that support your contention and state the name, **ADDRESS,** and telephone number of the **PERSON** who has each **DOCUMENT** or thing.

☐ 16.6 Do you contend that any part of the loss of earnings or income claimed by plaintiff in discovery proceedings thus far in this case was unreasonable or was not caused by the **INCIDENT**? If so:

(a) identify each part of the loss;
(b) state all facts upon which you base your contention;
(c) state the names, **ADDRESSES,** and telephone numbers of all **PERSONS** who have knowledge of the facts; and
(d) identify all **DOCUMENTS** and other tangible things that support your contention and state the name, **ADDRESS,** and telephone number of the **PERSON** who has each **DOCUMENT** or thing.

☐ 16.7 Do you contend that any of the property damage claimed by plaintiff in discovery Proceedings thus far in this case was not caused by the **INCIDENT**? If so:

(a) identify each item of property damage;
(b) state all facts upon which you base your contention;
(c) state the names, **ADDRESSES,** and telephone numbers of all **PERSONS** who have knowledge of the facts; and
(d) identify all **DOCUMENTS** and other tangible things that support your contention and state the name, **ADDRESS,** and telephone number of the **PERSON** who has each **DOCUMENT** or thing.

☐ 16.8 Do you contend that any of the costs of repairing the property damage claimed by plaintiff in discovery proceedings thus far in this case were unreasonable? If so:

(a) identify each cost item;
(b) state all facts upon which you base your contention;
(c) state the names, **ADDRESSES,** and telephone numbers of all **PERSONS** who have knowledge of the facts; and
(d) identify all **DOCUMENTS** and other tangible things that support your contention and state the name, **ADDRESS,** and telephone number of the **PERSON** who has each **DOCUMENT** or thing.

☐ 16.9 Do **YOU OR ANYONE ACTING ON YOUR BEHALF** have any **DOCUMENT** (for example, insurance bureau index reports) concerning claims for personal injuries made before or after the **INCIDENT** by a plaintiff in this case? If so, for each plaintiff state:

(a) the source of each **DOCUMENT**;
(b) the date each claim arose;
(c) the nature of each claim; and
(d) the name, **ADDRESS,** and telephone number of the **PERSON** who has each **DOCUMENT.**

☐ 16.10 Do **YOU OR ANYONE ACTING ON YOUR BEHALF** have any **DOCUMENT** concerning the past or present physical, mental, or emotional condition of any plaintiff in this case from a **HEALTH CARE PROVIDER** not previously identified (except for expert witnesses covered by Code of Civil Procedure sections 2034.210–2034.310)? If so, for each plaintiff state:

(a) the name, **ADDRESS,** and telephone number of each **HEALTH CARE PROVIDER**;
(b) a description of each **DOCUMENT**; and
(c) the name, **ADDRESS,** and telephone number of the **PERSON** who has each **DOCUMENT.**

17.0 Responses to Request for Admissions

☐ 17.1 Is your response to each request for admission served with these interrogatories an unqualified admission? If not, for each response that is not an unqualified admission:

(a) state the number of the request;
(b) state all facts upon which you base your response;
(c) state the names, **ADDRESSES,** and telephone numbers of all **PERSONS** who have knowledge of those facts; and
(d) identify all **DOCUMENTS** and other tangible things that support your response and state the name, **ADDRESS,** and telephone number of the **PERSON** who has each **DOCUMENT** or thing.

18.0 *[Reserved]*
19.0 *[Reserved]*

20.0 How the Incident Occurred—Motor Vehicle

☐ 20.1 State the date, time, and place of the **INCIDENT** (closest street **ADDRESS** or intersection).

☐ 20.2 For each vehicle involved in the **INCIDENT**, state:

(a) the year, make, model, and license number;
(b) the name, ADDRESS, and telephone number of the driver;

Exhibit 14.1. Continued

(c) the name, **ADDRESS,** and telephone number of each occupant other than the driver;

(d) the name, **ADDRESS,** and telephone number of each registered owner;

(e) the name, **ADDRESS,** and telephone number of each lessee;

(f) the name, **ADDRESS,** and telephone number of each owner other than the registered owner or lien holder; and

(g) the name of each owner who gave permission or consent to the driver to operate the vehicle.

20.3 State the **ADDRESS** and location where your trip began and the **ADDRESS** and location of your destination.

20.4 Describe the route that you followed from the beginning of your trip to the location of the **INCIDENT**, and state the location of each stop, other than routine traffic stops, during the trip leading up to the **INCIDENT**.

20.5 State the name of the street or roadway, the lane of travel, and the direction of travel of each vehicle involved in the **INCIDENT** for the 500 feet of travel before the **INCIDENT**.

20.6 Did the **INCIDENT** occur at an intersection? If so, describe all traffic control devices, signals, or signs at the intersection.

20.7 Was there a traffic signal facing you at the time of the **INCIDENT?** If so, state:

(a) your location when you first saw it;

(b) the color;

(c) the number of seconds it had been that color; and

(d) whether the color changed between the time you first saw it and the **INCIDENT**.

20.8 State how the **INCIDENT** occurred, giving the speed, direction, and location of each vehicle involved:

(a) just before the **INCIDENT;**

(b) at the time of the **INCIDENT;** and (c) just after the **INCIDENT**.

20.9 Do you have information that a malfunction or defect in a vehicle caused the **INCIDENT**? If so:

(a) identify the vehicle;

(b) identify each malfunction or defect;

(c) state the name, **ADDRESS,** and telephone number of each **PERSON** who is a witness to or has information about each malfunction or defect; and

(d) state the name, **ADDRESS,** and telephone number of each **PERSON** who has custody of each defective part.

20.10 Do you have information that any malfunction or defect in a vehicle contributed to the injuries sustained in the **INCIDENT?** If so:

(a) identify the vehicle;

(b) identify each malfunction or defect;

(c) state the name, **ADDRESS,** and telephone number of each **PERSON** who is a witness to or has information about each malfunction or defect; and

(d) state the name, **ADDRESS,** and telephone number of each **PERSON** who has custody of each defective part.

20.11 State the name, **ADDRESS,** and telephone number of each owner and each **PERSON** who has had possession since the **INCIDENT** of each vehicle involved in the **INCIDENT**.

25.0 *[Reserved]*

30.0 *[Reserved]*

40.0 *[Reserved]*

50.0 Contract

50.1 For each agreement alleged in the pleadings:

(a) identify each **DOCUMENT** that is part of the agreement and for each state the name, **ADDRESS,** and telephone number of each **PERSON** who has the **DOCUMENT;**

(b) state each part of the agreement not in writing, the name, **ADDRESS,** and telephone number of each **PERSON** agreeing to that provision, and the date that part of the agreement was made;

(c) identify all **DOCUMENTS** that evidence any part of the agreement not in writing and for each state the name, **ADDRESS,** and telephone number of each **PERSON** who has the **DOCUMENT;**

(d) identify all **DOCUMENTS** that are part of any modification to the agreement, and for each state the name, **ADDRESS,** and telephone number of each **PERSON** who has the **DOCUMENT;**

(e) state each modification not in writing, the date, and the name, **ADDRESS,** and telephone number of each **PERSON** agreeing to the modification, and the date the modification was made;

(f) identify all **DOCUMENTS** that evidence any modification of the agreement not in writing and for each state the name, **ADDRESS,** and telephone number of each **PERSON** who has the **DOCUMENT**.

50.2 Was there a breach of any agreement alleged in the pleadings? If so, for each breach describe and give the date of every act or omission that you claim is the breach of the agreement.

50.3 Was performance of any agreement alleged in the pleadings excused? If so, identify each agreement excused and state why performance was excused.

50.4 Was any agreement alleged in the pleadings terminated by mutual agreement, release, accord and satisfaction, or novation? If so, identify each agreement terminated, the date of termination, and the basis of the termination.

50.5 Is any agreement alleged in the pleadings unenforceable? If so, identify each unenforceable agreement and state why it is unenforceable.

50.6 Is any agreement alleged in the pleadings ambiguous? If so, identify each ambiguous agreement and state why it is ambiguous.

60.0 *[Reserved]*

Exhibit 14.2. Declaration

DECLARATION OF EMMA JACOBSON FOR
ADDITIONAL DISCOVERY

I, Emma Jacobson, declare:

1. I am the attorney for Defendant Becker Medical Supplies, a party to this action.

2. I am propounding to the Plaintiff the attached set of interrogatories.

3. This set of interrogatories will cause the total number of specially prepared interrogatories propounded to the party to whom they are directed to exceed the number of specially prepared interrogatories permitted by paragraph (1) of subdivision (c) of Section 2030.050 of the Code of Civil Procedure.

4. I have previously propounded a total of 42 interrogatories to this party, of which 32 were not official form interrogatories.

5. This set of interrogatories contains a total of 8 specially prepared interrogatories.

6. I am familiar with the issues and the previous discovery conducted by all the parties in the case.

7. I have personally examined each of the questions in the set of interrogatories.

8. This number of questions is warranted under paragraph (2) of subdivision (c) of Section 2030.050 of the Code of Civil Procedure because this case involves a series of six complicated contracts between the parties concerning licenses for use of medical devices that extend over a five-year period, and the facts concerning each of the contracts cannot be adequately ascertained without propounding additional interrogatories.

9. None of the questions in this set of interrogatories is being propounded for any improper purpose, such as to harass the party, or the attorney for the party, to whom it is directed, or to cause unnecessary delay or needless increase in the cost of litigation.

I declare under penalty of perjury under the laws of the State of California that the foregoing is true and correct, and that this declaration was executed on March 4, 2006.

Emma Jacobson
Attorney for Defendant

Example

1. State all facts upon which you base your contention that the defendant was negligent.

    (a) For each fact, identify all documents to support your contention.
    (b) For each fact, identify all witnesses.

To avoid this problem, CCP §2030.060(f) specifically admonishes against using subparts.

Interrogatories can be served by any party on any other party. However, a plaintiff must wait at least 10 days after service of the summons and complaint to serve the interrogatories, unless the plaintiff makes a motion in court to allow the interrogatories to be served earlier.

Answers are due within 30 days of service of the interrogatories. The answer must respond to each interrogatory separately with either an answer or an objection. An answer must be a "full" answer that fairly meets the substance of the interrogatory. The answering party has an obligation to find the information if it is within the party's possession, even if not within the personal knowledge of the actual person answering.

The answering party may specify business records from which an answer may be derived or ascertained instead of giving a direct answer, if the burden of deriving or ascertaining the answer is substantially the same for the party serving the interrogatory as for the party served. When this is the case, the answer should specify the records in sufficient detail to allow the requesting party to locate and identify the records, and to give the requesting party a reasonable opportunity to inspect and copy them.

An answer must be signed under oath by the person making it. If any interrogatories are objected to, the lawyer making the objection must sign as well.

Sometimes an answer may be correct when made, but the party later discovers or acquires additional information. To avoid being surprised by changed answers based upon the changed information, a party may propound an additional interrogatory twice before the initial setting of a trial date and once before trial that asks the responding party to supplement any previous interrogatory response. However, at all times if a previous answer is later found to be incorrect or false when it was made, there is a duty to correct the inaccurate information.

2. Practice approach

When you are asked by the lawyer to send interrogatories to another party, ask yourself two basic questions: What kind of information should

I seek? How should I organize and draft interrogatories to get the desired information?

The Litigation File at the end of the book shows an example of a defendant's interrogatories to a plaintiff.

a. Topics: what information should I seek?

Before drafting the interrogatories, ask yourself: What information do I want now so that I can use subsequent discovery methods to develop the information more fully? If you have thought through and discussed with the lawyer the discovery strategy, you should know what information you need that is well suited to obtaining thorough interrogatories. This initial information usually includes the following topics that you can use as a checklist to assist in drafting the interrogatories.

☐ Identity of parties, agents, and employees

Identifying the parties, agents, and employees is not as straightforward as it sounds. Frequently in commercial litigation you will not know the proper formal names of parties, parent corporations, subsidiaries; where they are incorporated or licensed to do business; or the type of legal entities they are or their relationships to other parties. You will also need to learn the identity of all agents and employees and their relationships to the party. Interrogatories are the best method for getting this information.

☐ Identity of witnesses

Most lawsuits will have witnesses to the events and transactions on which the claims are based. Interrogatories are a good method for obtaining the witnesses' identities, locations, and relationships to the parties.

☐ Identity of documents and tangible things

Similarly, most lawsuits will have certain documents, records, and other tangible things on which the claims are based or that are relevant to the claims. Interrogatories are the best method for identifying and locating these and for determining who has custody or control of them.

☐ Identity of facts

The facts upon which a party bases its causes of action or defenses upon is important information to obtain early in the litigation. This is also one way of pinning the other side down to their version of the facts.

☐ Details and sequences of events and transactions

Interrogatories are a useful method for obtaining concrete facts underlying vague or generalized claims. For this reason they are particularly useful in the commercial litigation area where lawsuits are frequently based on a series of events and transactions spread out over time but not detailed in any way in the pleadings.

☐ Damages information and ability to pay

The plaintiff's complaint will often contain only a general request for damages or whatever the minimum jurisdictional amount is. Damages interrogatories to the plaintiff are useful for drawing out the specific legal theories of recovery the plaintiff is asserting, the dollar amount claimed for each element of damages, and the basis for each claim.

☐ Identity of persons who prepared answers and of sources used

When interrogatories are served on a corporate party, they should ask for the identity of each person who participated in preparing the answers and the identity of the documents used to prepare each answer. This information will be important in deciding whom to depose and what documents to request.

☐ Positions on issues and opinions of fact

Interrogatories that ask for "opinions," "contentions relating to facts," or the "application of law to facts" are proper under CCP §2030.010. On the other hand, interrogatories that ask for matters directly about the law are objectionable. The dividing line is unclear, and a great many discovery motions deal with this problem. Where a pleading is vague, however, a proper interrogatory can prove to be a useful request. For example, it is proper in a negligence action to ask what specific conduct plaintiff claims constituted the negligence, just as in a contract action it is proper to ask what conduct plaintiff claims constituted a breach.

b. Drafting the interrogatories

When you draft interrogatories, your principal task is to prepare a set of interrogatories that will successfully elicit the desired information. The questions must be drafted so as to force the answering party to respond to them squarely and to eliminate the possibility of evasive, though superficially responsive, answers. In addition, the questions should be organized sequentially to make sure that all desired topics are covered.

Basic interrogatories for recurrent types of actions are frequently stored in word processors, making them easy to modify for a specific case.

i. Headings

An interrogatory, like any court document, must contain a caption showing the court, parties, and civil case number. Furthermore, the interrogatories should include a heading that identifies which party is raising the interrogatories to which other party. It is also a good practice to label interrogatories "First Set," "Second Set," and so on and to number them sequentially, with a later set picking up where the previous set left off. This avoids confusion when references are later made to interrogatories and answers. Exhibits 14.3 and 14.4 show sample headings.

ii. Definitions and Instructions

While you will still see prefaces, definitions and instructions in the front of interrogatories propounded in federal court cases, in California state courts no preface, instructions or definitions shall be included with the interrogatories. Rather, each interrogatory must be complete within itself. If a word is defined in an interrogatory so that it can be used as an abbreviated version in later interrogatories, the word should be capitalized in all subsequent interrogatories. The following is an example:

Exhibit 14.3.   Interrogatory Headings

[Caption]

PLAINTIFF JOHNSON'S INTERROGATORIES TO DEFENDANT ACME CORPORATION

(First Set)

Plaintiff Johnson requests that defendant Acme Corporation, through an officer or authorized agent of the corporation, answer the following interrogatories under oath and serve them upon plaintiff within 30 days, pursuant to Code of Civil Procedure Section 2030.010:

1. . . .
2. . . .
3. . . .

Exhibit 14.4. Answer Heading

[Caption]

PROPOUNDING PARTY: Plaintiff Johnson
RESPONDING PARTY: Defendant ACME Corporation
SET NO: Two (Interrogatory Nos. 23-25)

Plaintiff Johnson requests that. . . .
   23. . . .
   24. . . .
   25. . . .

Example

1. State all facts upon which you base your contention that the defendant Becker Medical Supplies Corporation ("BECKER") was negligent.
2. Identify all documents to support your contention that BECKER was negligent.
3. Identify all witnesses who support your contention that BECKER was negligent.

iii. Interrogatory Style

Interrogatories must be clear and must adequately cover the necessary subjects. They are usually drafted as imperative statements, not as actual questions, since the imperative form affirmatively requires the answering party to supply information. Keep in mind that clear, simple interrogatories are more likely to yield clear, simple answers that will provide useful information. The more complex the interrogatories, the more complex and less useful the answers are likely to be. It is usually better to err on the side of simplicity.

The first purpose of interrogatories is to identify parties, witnesses, documents, and experts. Exhibits 14.5 through 14.7 show how to draft interrogatories requesting this information.

Note that rather than ask for witnesses in a general way, the interrogatories in Exhibit 14.6 first focus on witnesses to a particular transaction or event, then expand the scope in subsequent questions to ensure that all possible known witnesses are identified. This organizes the information into useful categories.

Exhibit 14.5. Interrogatories: Request to Identify Parties and Agents

> 1. State the full name of the defendant, where and when incorporated, where and when licensed to do business, where it has its principal place of business, and all names under which it does business.
> 2. Identify each officer and director of the defendant during the time period of June 1, 2007, through the date answers to these interrogatories are signed.
> 3. Identify each company, subdivision, and subsidiary in which the defendant has any ownership, control, or interest of any amount for the period referred to in Interrogatory #2 above.

Exhibit 14.6. Interrogatories: Request to Identify Witnesses

> 1. Identify each person who was present during the execution of the contract that forms the basis of the first cause of action of plaintiff's complaint.
> 2. Identify each person who was present during any of the negotiations of the contract executed by plaintiff and defendant on June 1, 2007.
> 3. State the full name of each person who witnessed the collision between vehicles driven by the plaintiff and defendant occurring on June 1, 2007.
> 4. State the full name of each person who was present at the scene of the collision during and after the collision, other than the persons identified in Interrogatory #3 above.
> 5. State the full name of each person who has any knowledge of the facts of the collision, other than those persons already identified in Interrogatories #3 and #4 above.

Exhibit 14.7. Interrogatories: Request to Identify Documents

> 1. Identify each document that relates to the contract executed by plaintiff and defendant on June 1, 2007.
> 2. Identify each document in your possession and control that relates to the accident that is the basis for plaintiff's complaint.

The categories of interrogatories in Exhibits 14.5 through 14.7 are a part of almost every interrogatory set. These questions obtain the hard data that will provide the springboard for further investigation and discovery.

Interrogatories should also ask for the specific facts on which the pleadings are based. This is particularly important since the pleadings frequently contain general conclusory language that gives little information about the facts on which claims, defenses, or damages are based. Interrogatories should develop the basic facts so that the parties can focus on specific facts underlying the legal claims. Exhibit 14.8 shows a request for this type of information.

Complaints commonly allege that the defendant "breached the contract" or "negligently operated a motor vehicle." An interrogatory is an effective means of developing the facts that the other party claims support the legal contentions. The following are examples of how to further develop facts through interrogatories:

Example

Developing Facts

1. State the facts upon which you base your claim that defendant acted negligently.
2. State the conduct by the plaintiff and any of its officers, employees, or agents that you claim constituted a breach of the contract.
3. Do you contend that Samuel Jones lacked authority to enter into a contract on behalf of the defendant corporation?
4. If you contend that Samuel Jones lacked authority to enter into a contract, state the facts on which you base this contention.

iv. Signing, Serving, and Filing

The interrogatories must be signed by the attorney and served on each party. However, you do not need to file the interrogatories with the court. Service is made by any permitted method, most commonly by mailing a copy to the lawyers for the other parties. The original interrogatories, with an attached proof of service statement, should be served

Exhibit 14.8. Interrogatories: Request for Specific Facts

1. Describe the personal injuries you sustained as a result of the accident that occurred on April 14, 2006 (the "ACCIDENT").
2. Were you hospitalized as a result of the ACCIDENT?

on the party propounding the interrogatories, and a copy kept for your firm's files. A sample set of interrogatories is shown in Exhibit 14.9.

c. Responses to interrogatories

A party must usually answer interrogatories within 30 days of service of the interrogatories. Since they frequently require a substantial amount of work, information necessary to prepare the answers must be obtained reasonably quickly. If the client is out of town or unavailable, or the interrogatories are lengthy, it may be necessary for your side to move for additional time to respond. It is usually a good idea for you or the

Exhibit 14.9.   Sample Interrogatories

[Caption]

PROPOUNDING PARTY: Plaintiff Ruth Dorsey
RESPONDING PARTY: P.W. Dell Enterprises
SET NO: One (Interrogatory Nos. 1-6)

Plaintiff Ruth Dorsey requests that defendant P.W. Dell Enterprises answer the following interrogatories in writing and under oath pursuant to CCP §2030.010:

1. State the full name of the defendant.

2. Identify each officer of the defendant during the time period of June 1, 2004 through the date answers to these interrogatories are signed.

3. Identify each person who was present during the execution of the contract that forms the basis of the first cause of action of the plaintiff's complaint.

4. Identify each person who was present during any of the negotiations of the contract executed by plaintiff and defendant on June 1, 2004.

5. Identify each document that relates to the contract executed by plaintiff and defendant on June 1, 2004.

6. State all facts that support your denial of the claim stated by plaintiff in the first cause of action of the plaintiff's complaint.

Dated: January 18, 2007

_____
J.J. Rayson
Attorney at Law

lawyer to call the opposing lawyer, explain the problem, and ask the opposing lawyer to agree to stipulate to allow additional time.

i. Researching and Preparing Answers

A common procedure in answering interrogatories is to send the interrogatories to the client and ask her to respond to the request for information from her own records and from personal recall and to then return the information to you or the lawyer. After you receive the responses back, you can then draft the actual answers by incorporating the client's responses and making any appropriate objections. After you prepare the answers, the client should review the answers for accuracy and completeness, then sign the verification and return the document to you. This procedure works best with individual clients.

Corporate parties and other artificial entities, however, present special considerations. First, you must ascertain who in the corporation should answer the interrogatories. Ordinarily a corporate officer who has personal knowledge of the transactions involved or who has knowledge of the corporate recordkeeping system is an appropriate choice. The selection of the person is more significant than might first appear, however, because although whoever provides the answer will be bound by it, the answer will also be binding on the corporate party.

Second, the corporate party has an obligation to investigate files that are in its possession or control, to collect the requested information, and to put that information in the answer. Records are considered in a party's possession or control if they are records that are kept at the company's offices, or if they are physically in the possession of another, such as an accountant or a storage company, but the party has the power to get the records returned. The corporation's duty to investigate is limited only by the extent of its own records, but there is no duty to conduct an independent outside investigation. A corporate party cannot avoid answering a proper interrogatory through the device of selecting someone to answer the interrogatories who has no personal knowledge of any relevant facts.

Third, a party can answer an interrogatory by specifying the business records from which the requested information can be derived if the burden of obtaining the desired information from those records is substantially the same for either party. This is a most useful device because it avoids "doing the homework" for the requesting party and permits answers to be made more quickly.

ii. Objections

A party on whom interrogatories have been served has two possible responses: an answer or an **objection.** If the response is an objection, simply state the objection as your answer to a particular interrogatory.

Objection
Statement made by the responding party in an interrogatory that indicates a reason for not answering the question asked

Each objection must be specifically stated; unstated or untimely grounds for objection will generally be considered to be waived. However, the responding party still has a duty to provide "answers to the extent the interrogatory is not objectionable."

There are several bases for objecting. First, a party may object on the basis that the information sought is irrelevant. However, since the definition of relevance for discovery purposes is quite broad, such an objection is difficult to make successfully. In addition, the court can grant sanctions for frivolous objections.

Second, a party may object on the ground of privilege, relying on either the privilege for attorney work product or one of the privileges under the Evidence Code as discussed in Chapter 12.

Third, an objection can be made to interrogatories that ask for information that cannot be obtained by interrogatories, such as an interrogatory that demands the production of records.

Fourth, an objection can be made on the basis that the interrogatory is annoying, embarrassing, oppressive, or unduly burdensome and expensive. This is probably the most frequently raised objection, one that has generated a substantial body of case law. When such an objection is raised, the answering party should move for a protective order. The claim that an interrogatory is unduly burdensome and expensive requires that the court balance the burden of collecting the information requested with the benefit to the requesting party. When the work involved in obtaining the information is enormous and the benefit to the requesting party is small in light of the issues in the case, an objection to the interrogatory should be sustained.

Where an objection exists, it should be made on the interrogatory answer. Exhibit 14.10 shows examples of objections.

iii. Answers

The other possible response is to answer the interrogatory. There are three basic types of responses.

First, the party can answer the interrogatory by supplying the requested information if it is either known or ascertainable from the party's personal knowledge or records. The answer should be as brief as possible, since you ordinarily don't want to volunteer information that has not been requested. On the other hand, you must answer with the essential facts at your disposal, since failing to disclose can subject your side to serious sanctions.

In addition, if your side has a strong case and the attorney is looking toward a favorable settlement, you may want to volunteer information. The goal in answering interrogatories is to strike an appropriate balance between the advantages of brevity and a full, detailed answer. Exhibit 14.11 shows appropriate answers.

Exhibit 14.10. Objections to Interrogatories

Interrogatory No. 8: State which officers were involved in the sale of forklift trucks to the XYZ Corporation on August 1, 2007.

Answer: Defendant objects to Interrogatory No. 8 on the ground that it asks for information that is not relevant to the subject matter of this action, nor likely to lead to the discovery of admissible evidence because it pertains to a transaction with a nonparty, the XYZ Corporation, that has no relevance to the controversy between the plaintiff and defendant.

Interrogatory No. 9: Identify all conversations between defendant's employees and defendant's corporate counsel between August 1, 2006, and the present date.

Answer: Defendant objects to Interrogatory No. 9 on the ground that it asks for material that is privileged under the attorney-client privilege.

When the interrogatory asks for information on which the answering party has some personal knowledge but not to the detail requested, and no records exist that can supply those details, the answer should accurately reflect this situation. In this instance you might reply as follows:

Example

Interrogatory No. 6: Identify each communication between John Marlowe and Phillip Johnson that relates to the contract that forms the basis of the First Cause of Action of plaintiff's complaint.

Answer to Interrogatory No. 6 : There were several telephone conversations between Marlowe and Johnson during a period of approximately four weeks preceding the execution of the contract. The exact dates and substance of each of these conversations are unknown.

This type of answer is satisfactory when the answer cannot state facts that are not within the knowledge or recall of the answering party and no records exist to supply the details. The better practice is to follow up on this type of response through depositions, which allow the extent and details of the party's recall to be explored and developed.

When an interrogatory asks for a party's contentions, a more complete answer is called for since the answering party does not wish to limit its

Exhibit 14.11. Answers Supplying the Requested Information

Interrogatory No. 2: Identify each person who was present during the execution of the contract that forms the basis of the first cause of action of plaintiff's complaint.

Answer to Interrogatory No. 2: John Marlowe and Phillip Johnson.

Interrogatory No. 3: Identify each physician who treated you as a result of the accident that occurred on October 3, 2004.

Answer to Interrogatory No. 3: Dr. William Jackson, Mercy Hospital, Carlsbad, California; Dr. Erica Olson, 3420 Cascades Highway, Carlsbad, California; possibly other physicians at Mercy Hospital whose names are unknown at this time. Investigation is continuing.

Interrogatory No. 4: State the name of each person who was present or claims to have been present during the collision.

Answer to Interrogatory No. 4: Mary Carter. Frank Wilson. In addition, there were several other pedestrians in the vicinity, but the names and addresses of such persons are presently unknown, investigation continues.

proof or theories of liability. This more complex response might be framed as follows:

Example

Interrogatory No. 4: State all the facts on which you claim that defendant acted negligently.

Answer to Interrogatory No. 4 : Defendant (1) drove in excess of the posted speed limit; (2) drove in excess of a reasonable speed under the existing conditions and circumstances; (3) failed to keep a proper lookout to ensure the safety of others; (4) failed to keep his vehicle in the proper lane; (5) failed to yield the right of way; and (6) failed to obey traffic signals, markers, and "rules of the road." Investigation continues.

In this type of answer, the "investigation continues" response is important because additional investigation and discovery may develop additional facts to support the negligence claim.

A second type of response (see below) is simply to state "no knowledge" when this is accurate.

Example

Interrogatory <u>No. 4</u>: State if any witnesses to the collision prepared written reports of any kind regarding the collision.
<u>Answer to Interrogatory No. 4</u> : No knowledge.

Keep in mind that an answering party must search her own records to determine if the information exists and, if it does, use the information to answer the interrogatory.

The third type of answer is to identify business records that provide the information. The answer should specify the records and give the requesting party a reasonable opportunity to examine and copy them. Actual production with the interrogatory answer is not required; however, such records are always discoverable through a **request to produce.** For this reason, there may be times when you will want to simply attach copies of the pertinent documents as exhibits to the interrogatory answers. Below are examples of answers to requests to identify records.

Example

<u>Interrogatory No. 5</u>: Identify each communication between Phillip Johnson and Jane East between June 1, 2008, and August 4, 2009, relating to the contract that forms the basis of the First Cause of Action of plaintiff's complaint.

<u>Answer to Interrogatory No. 5</u>: Any such communications are kept in the defendant's telephone logbook, the pertinent dates of which may be examined and copied at a reasonable time at the defendant's place of business.

<u>Interrogatory No. 6</u>: Identify each sales transaction entered into between plaintiff and defendant for the period of January 1, 2008, through August 4, 2009.

<u>Answer to Interrogatory No. 6</u>: These transactions are recorded in the defendant's sales records, which are computerized after sales transactions are completed. A printout of these transactions is attached as Exhibit A.

---

iv. Signing, Serving, and Filing

The format for interrogatory answers, like any other court document, should include a case caption and document title. The answers must be signed under oath by the person making them.[1] If any interrogatories are objected to, the attorney must sign them as well.

---

1. The statement under oath is often referred to as the verification (since the person is verifying the accuracy of the statements). The verification may be sworn to under oath and acknowledged by a notary public, or stated under penalty of perjury under the laws of the State of California.

The completed interrogatory answers must then be served on each party. The original should be mailed to the party propounding the interrogatories and copies mailed to the lawyers for the other parties. Be sure to keep a copy for your firm's files.

C. REQUESTS TO PRODUCE DOCUMENTS AND SUBPOENAS

After answers to interrogatories have been received, you will usually have enough detailed information to ask for copies of identified documents through a request to produce. Hence, requests to produce are usually the second step in the discovery process, although simple requests to produce documents are also frequently served with interrogatories and ask for the production of all documents identified in the interrogatory answers.

In addition, do not forget the ability to obtain public records from government entities. If a government entity is involved in the litigation, you may be able to obtain any records kept by the entity by simply making a public records request.

1. Law

Requests to produce documents and other physical or tangible evidence and for entry upon land to inspect are governed by CCP §2031.010. A request to produce can be served upon another party and also nonparties if served as a subpoena to attend a deposition and produce documents. The scope of the request, like other discovery, is controlled by CCP §2017.010, which permits discovery of any relevant matter that is not privileged.

Requests to produce generally fall into one of three categories:

1. Documents for inspection and copying
2. Tangible things for inspection, copying, and testing
3. Entry on land or property for inspection and testing

Of these, production of documents is the principal use of requests. Documents include all writings, drawings, graphs, charts, photographs, phonorecords, and other data compilations from which information can be obtained.

The Code requires a party to produce all documents that are in that party's "possession, custody or control." This obligates a party to produce all relevant documents, even those not in the party's actual possession, if the party has a lawful right to get them from another person or entity. In short, a party cannot avoid production through the simple device of transferring the documents to another person or entity such as the party's lawyer, accountant, insurer, or corporate subsidiary. When this avoidance device is used, the party is deemed to have retained "control" of the documents and is required to get them returned in order to comply with the production request.

A request to produce must describe each item or category to be produced with reasonable particularity. This is usually read to require that, in the context of the case and the overall nature of the documents involved, a responding party must reasonably be able to determine what particular documents are called for. (Sample requests with particularity are shown later in this chapter.) This is obviously a flexible standard that varies from case to case.

The documents produced for inspection must be produced in either the same order as they are normally kept or in the order, with labels, that corresponds to the categories of the request. The producing party cannot purposefully disorganize documents and records to make them more difficult to comprehend. Furthermore, the request to produce must specify a reasonable time and place for the inspection. The responding party must serve a written response for each category requested, usually within 30 days of service of the request, stating whether he objects, with reasons for the objection, or will comply.

2. Practice approach

a. Timing

Before serving a request to produce documents or a request for entry upon land to inspect, you need to know what documents you want produced and what things you want to inspect. If you have drafted your interrogatories carefully and have asked for descriptions of relevant documents and for the identity of those whose custody those documents are in, answers to the interrogatories should provide sufficient detail to meet the particularity requirement for production requests. Hence, requests to produce should normally be served as soon as possible after the answers to interrogatories have been received. Sometimes, as previously mentioned, production requests are served at the same time as interrogatories.

This timetable presumes that the party has adequately, and in a timely fashion, answered your interrogatories. If the answering party has objected, failed to answer, or served evasive or incomplete answers, these problems must be resolved through appropriate discovery motions. Doing this, however, will necessarily delay serving the requests to produce. In this situation you should consider serving a request to produce anyway, since you can ordinarily determine in a general way what documents the other party is likely to have and describe them sufficiently by topic or subject matter to meet the particularity requirement. It is easy for discovery to become sidetracked or to stall completely. In these situations you must weigh the benefits and liabilities of waiting or going ahead in light of the overall discovery strategy for the case.

b. Organization

Before actually drafting the request to produce, you need to organize your thoughts on what you want from the other party. If you have thoroughly discussed the discovery strategy with the supervising attorney, intelligently thought it through, and put forth your interrogatories to and received answers from that party, then the bulk of your work is already done. You will know in sufficient detail what documents you want, what documents the answering party admits having, how those documents are described or labeled, and who their custodian is.

If you have not yet received interrogatory answers but are asked by the lawyer to send out requests to produce anyway, you will have to evaluate what documents the other party is likely to have, how they are likely to be labeled and organized, and who their custodian is. Some of this information may be within the client's knowledge. Accordingly, you should check with the client before serving the document request.

c. Drafting requests to produce

i. Heading

A request to produce should be drafted like any other court document. It must have a caption showing the court, case title, and docket number and be properly labeled. When a case has several parties, it is useful to designate which party is sending the request to which other party; otherwise, the simple title "DEMAND TO INSPECT DOCUMENTS" will suffice. A sample heading is shown in Exhibit 14.12.

ii. Definitions

Requests to produce, just like interrogatories, may not contain definitions. Accordingly, terms and phrases frequently used, such as "document," "record," "relating to," "transaction," and "occurrence," should be defined within the specific document request and then capitalized in all subsequent requests to produce.

Exhibit 14.12.   Request to Produce: Heading

[Caption]

PLAINTIFF JOHNSON'S REQUESTS TO PRODUCE DOCUMENTS TO DEFENDANT ACME CORPORATION

Plaintiff Johnson requests defendant Acme Corporation to produce the documents and things listed below, pursuant to Code of Civil Procedure Section 2031.010:

1. . . .
2. . . .
3. . . .

iii. Requests Format

There are three basic requests permitted: to inspect and copy documents, to inspect and examine tangible things, and to enter upon land to inspect and examine things. The requests should follow a basic format.

The requests to produce must specify a reasonable date, time, and place for the production. What is "reasonable," should take into account the volume and complexity of the records sought. Since the Code requires a response within 30 days of service, the date set for the production should be a longer time period. Exhibit 14.13 shows the request format.

Most requests to produce involve documents. There are several ways to draft requests that will meet the reasonable particularity requirement.

First, you can use the interrogatory answers. If those answers have listed and described a variety of documents, referring to the descriptions should be adequate. The responding party will be in a poor position to claim that a description it furnished is now suddenly insufficient.

Example

Request Based on Interrogatory Answer

1. Each document identified in defendant's answer to Interrogatory No. 6 in plaintiff's first set of interrogatories.

Second, ask for all documents that relate to a specific transaction or event. By making the request specific, it should not be challenged on the grounds of being too vague.

Exhibit 14.13. Request to Produce: Request Format

A. Plaintiff requests that defendant produce the following documents for inspection and copying at the offices of Mary Anton, plaintiff's attorney, 200 Main Street, Suite 400, Monterey Park, California, on August 22, 2006, at 2:00 P.M.:
    1. . . .
    2. . . .
B. Plaintiff requests that defendant produce the following things for inspection, copying, and testing at the offices of Independent Testing, 2000 Main Street, Cypress, California, on August 23, 2006, at 9:00 A.M.:
    1. . . .
    2. . . .
C. Plaintiff requests that defendant permit plaintiff to enter defendant's lumberyard located at 4000 Monroe Street, La Miranda, California, for the purpose of inspecting, photographing, and measuring the premises on August 24, 2006, at 2:00 P.M.

Example

Request Based on Specific Transaction

2. All documents relating to the sale of property located at 4931 Sunrise St., Fresno, California, entered into between plaintiff and defendant on July 31, 2006.

Third, you can ask for specific types of documents that relate to a more general time frame or course of conduct.

Example

Request for Specific Types of Documents

3. All bills of lading, invoices, and shipping confirmation notices relating to all goods shipped from plaintiff to defendant during the period from January 1, 2006, through April 30, 2006.

In each of the above examples, the party responding to the request to admit should not have difficulty in either understanding the request or identifying the documents requested. In contrast, a request calling for the production of "all documents relating to the allegations in plaintiff's complaint" or similarly vague language is defective and unenforceable because it does not meet the specificity requirement.

It is possible that the responding party will not object to a general request, but, regardless, it is usually not an effective approach for discovery. Requests to produce should balance the safety of inclusiveness with the utility of a more focused request. A request that is too broad may result in a huge volume of paperwork being deposited in your office; you may have neither the time nor assistance to review all of it in order to extract the few documents that are relevant to the case.

Fourth, it is always useful to ask for the identity of any documents that existed at one time but have since been destroyed. This prevents the literally true but misleading response that there are "no records" of the description requested.

iv. Signing, Serving, and Filing

The request to produce should be signed by the lawyer, and served on each party. The request does not need to be filed with the court. Service is made by any permitted method, commonly by mailing a copy to the lawyers for the other parties. The original requests to produce, with an attached proof of service statement, are then retained in the firm's files. A sample request to produce is shown in Exhibit 14.14, as well as in the Litigation File at the end of the book.

d. Responses to requests to produce

A party served with a request to produce usually must respond within 30 days of service of the request. Even though the lawyers for the requesting and responding parties frequently reach an informal agreement on how and when to produce documents and conduct inspections, the responding party should serve and file a response since this is required by CCP §2031.210.

i. Researching and Preparing Responses

If the preliminary investigation has been done and answers to interrogatories have been prepared and served, you already will have done most of the initial work involved in responding to requests to produce. In addition, you should always send the requests to the client and ask the client a couple of questions about the requests. First, does the client know what the requests actually call for? If not, your side may want to object on grounds of vagueness. Second, how much effort will be required to collect the documents requested? If it is substantial and the case is not

Exhibit 14.14.   Request to Produce

[Caption]

PLAINTIFF JOHNSON'S REQUESTS TO PRODUCE DOCUMENTS TO DEFENDANT ACME CORPORATION

Pursuant to Code of Civil Procedure Section 2031.010, Plaintiff Johnson requests defendant Acme Corporation to produce for inspection and copying the documents and things listed below, on August 22, 2006 at 2:00 P.M. at the law offices of Mary Anton, located at 200 Main Street, Suite 400, Bakersfield, California.

Request No. 1: All documents reflecting, referring, or otherwise relating to any communications between Defendant and anyone else concerning the contract entered into between the Plaintiff Johnson and Defendant Acme Corporation on, or about June 1, 2004.

Request No. 2: All bills of lading, invoices, and shipping confirmation notices relating to all goods shipped from Plaintiff to Defendant during the period from June 1, 2004 through and including December 15, 2004.

Request No. 3: All documents identified in Defendant's answer to Interrogatory No. 5 in Plaintiff's First Set of Interrogatories.

Dated: May 3, 2005

Jacob Marker

---

complex, your side may be able to object on the grounds that the requests are unduly burdensome and move for a protective order or at least for additional time to respond.

After the client has collected the documents, review the material to determine if all of it is relevant. If there are any privileged communications, now is the time to object, since privileges are waived unless timely asserted. Finally, make sure that those documents are in fact all the available documents the client has in his possession, custody, or control. You can be sure that the client and other witnesses will be questioned about the completeness of the tendered documents during their depositions. Now is the time to review the documents with the client for completeness. Also be sure to check your firm's files because documents responsive to the request may be in the files.

ii. Objections

As with interrogatories, a party who has been served with a request to produce has two possible responses: an answer or an objection. An objection to a part, item, or category must be specific, and production should still be allowed for the portions that are unobjectionable.

If the response is an objection, there are several possible bases. First, an objection may be made on the ground that the documents sought are irrelevant. However, since the Code of Civil Procedure has such a broad definition of relevance for discovery purposes, this is a difficult ground on which to prevail. Moreover, this ground will probably have been ruled on if the same objection was made to the interrogatory that asked for the identity of the documents. Second, an objection can be based on a privilege, either the privilege for attorney work product, or the privileges under the Evidence Code. Third, an objection can be based on the request being annoying, embarrassing, oppressive, or unduly burdensome and expensive. Here the answering party should seek a protective order; still, an objection to a request to produce should be made on the response. A response with an objection is shown in Exhibit 14.15.

As noted above, a request can frequently be objectionable in part. When this is so, the response should make clear what part is being objected to and what the responding party agrees to produce. Such an objection is a common response to a broad request asking for a variety of documents, some of which may be privileged. In this case you might phrase the objection as follows:

Example

2. Defendant objects to plaintiff's Request No. 2 to the extent it asks for privileged communications protected by the attorney-client privilege. Plaintiff's Request No. 2 asks for the production of "memoranda by defendant's subsidiary, Acme Productions, relating to a bid on U.S. Government Contract No. 04-3287, commonly known as the 'Tri-star Contract.'" These memoranda include documents prepared by Acme Productions officers and employees, documents prepared at the request of and sent to Acme Corporation's General Counsel, which relate to the pending litigation and are protected from disclosure by the attorney-client privilege.

iii. Answers

If a request to produce is not objected to, it must be answered. An answer involves two considerations: the formal response and the

Exhibit 14.15. Response to Request to Produce: Objection

[Caption]

RESPONSE TO PLAINTIFF'S REQUESTS TO PRODUCE

Defendant Acme Corporation responds to plaintiff's Requests to Produce Documents as follows:

    1. Defendant objects to plaintiff's Request No. 1 on the ground that it requests documents the disclosure of which would violate the attorney-client privilege, since the request on its face asks for the production of "all correspondence from corporate officers to corporate counsel regarding the contract dated July 1, 2006."

practical concerns involved in arranging for the actual production of the documents. There should be a formal answer even if, as is often the case, the production is worked out informally between the attorneys because CCP §2031 requires a response. Exhibit 14.16 shows a typical answer.

Exhibit 14.16. Response to Request to Produce: Answer

[Caption]

RESPONSE TO PLAINTIFF'S REQUESTS FOR PRODUCTION AND INSPECTION

Defendant Acme Corporation responds to plaintiff's requests for production of documents and inspection as follows:

    1-8. Defendant has agreed to produce the documents requested in plaintiff's Request Nos. 1 through 8 at the offices of plaintiff's attorney on or before August 15, 2006.

    9. Defendant has agreed to permit the inspection of the items described in plaintiff's Request No. 9 at its manufacturing plant located at 9000 Main St., Davis, California, at a mutually agreed-upon date and time, but not later than August 31, 2006.

                            Attorney for Defendant
                                Acme Corporation

If records requested do not exist, the response should clearly establish this fact. In this case your response would be phrased like the following example:

Example

3. There are no documents in the possession, custody, or control of defendant Acme Corporation requested by plaintiff's Request No. 3.

Most production requests are worked out informally between the lawyers, who usually call each other and agree on the mechanics of delivering and copying the pertinent records. This will usually include when and where the documents will be produced, how the documents will be organized, and who will perform and pay for the actual copying. The usual procedure is for the documents to be produced at, or delivered to, the requesting attorney's offices on an agreed-upon date. The responding party has the option of producing the records either in the order in which they are ordinarily kept or labeled to correspond to the categories of the request. Since most production requests overlap on particulars to ensure completeness, a common approach in responding is to produce the documents in their usual order because this is easier for the responding party.

Regarding an informal agreement on the mechanics of reproducing the records, the Code requires only production—not copying—by the responding party. However, it is usually desirable for the responding party to make copies so as to retain possession of the original documents. For this reason it is common for the responding party to make copies of the records that comply with the requests; the cost of reproduction is then paid by the requesting party.

When the documents involved are so voluminous that copying all of them would be prohibitively expensive, a common solution is to have the lawyer for the requesting party review the documents at the offices of either the answering party or the answering party's lawyer. The requesting lawyer can then select the relevant documents for photocopying.

If your client is the answering party, make sure that you keep a copy of everything submitted to the opposing side so that no issue arises later over what was actually delivered. In addition, all documents produced should be stamped in the lower right-hand corner with a number so that an exact count of the documents can be made. The number also makes it easier to identify the documents for depositions and trial preparation.

In addition, the numbers can serve to identify which party produced the document. For example, the parties may agree that the plaintiff will number her documents as numbers 1-1,000, while the defendant will use numbers 2,000-3,000. Alternatively, you may simply set up a code to identify the documents, such as placing a "p" in front of all documents produced by the plaintiff. Whichever method you use, be consistent in the numbering. Sometimes you will hear the term **Bate Stamp** used in numbering documents. This is a general way of referring to the stamp that is used to number the documents. The stamp, similar to date stamps, automatically advances each time it is used so that you have an easy way of labeling the documents. For large productions, document services exist that will copy and number the documents for you.

iv. Signing, Serving, and Filing

The written response to requests to produce must be signed, and then served on every other party. Service is commonly by mailing a copy to the lawyers for the other parties. The original response, with an attached proof of service, is served on the party requesting the documents and a copy should be maintained in the firm's files.

3. Document subpoenas to nonparties

Deposition subpoena for production of records
An order of the court requiring a witness to appear and produce documents

To obtain documents against a nonparty a **deposition subpoena for production of records** is the only discovery method permitted. Under CCP §§1985 through 1987.5 a subpoena can be issued to command any person to attend a deposition and to produce and permit inspection of designated records and tangible things.

The deposition subpoena for production of records is issued by the attorney or, if a person is representing herself, can be issued by the court clerk or the judge. A copy of the approved Judicial Council form for production of business records is shown in Exhibit 14.17.

4. Document productions

Every litigation paralegal will undoubtedly be called on at some point to attend a production of documents. Usually, in document-intensive cases, documents are produced to the other party by making the documents available for photocopying and inspection at either the office of the lawyer of the party producing the documents or, if they are too voluminous to transport, the place where the documents are located. As a litigation paralegal, you may be asked to attend a production of documents produced by the other side or be asked to review documents that are going to be produced by your side to the other side.

Exhibit 14.17. Form Deposition for Business Records

SUBP-010

ATTORNEY OR PARTY WITHOUT ATTORNEY *(Name, State Bar number, and address):*	*FOR COURT USE ONLY*
TELEPHONE NO.: FAX NO. *(Optional)*: E-MAIL ADDRESS *(Optional)*: ATTORNEY FOR *(Name)*:	

SUPERIOR COURT OF CALIFORNIA, COUNTY OF
STREET ADDRESS:
MAILING ADDRESS:
CITY AND ZIP CODE:
BRANCH NAME:

PLAINTIFF/PETITIONER:

DEFENDANT/RESPONDENT:

DEPOSITION SUBPOENA **FOR PRODUCTION OF BUSINESS RECORDS**	CASE NUMBER:

THE PEOPLE OF THE STATE OF CALIFORNIA, TO *(name, address, and telephone number of deponent, if known)*:

1. YOU ARE ORDERED TO PRODUCE THE BUSINESS RECORDS described in item 3, as follows:

To *(name of deposition officer)*:
On *(date)* :   At *(time)*:
Location *(address)*:

Do not release the requested records to the deposition officer prior to the date and time stated above.

a. ☐ by delivering a true, legible, and durable **copy** of the business records described in item 3, enclosed in a sealed inner wrapper with the title and number of the action, name of witness, and date of subpoena clearly written on it. The inner wrapper shall then be enclosed in an outer envelope or wrapper, sealed, and mailed to the deposition officer at the address in item 1.

b. ☐ by delivering a true, legible, and durable **copy** of the business records described in item 3 to the deposition officer at the witness's address, on receipt of payment in cash or by check of the reasonable costs of preparing the copy, as determined under Evidence Code section 1563(b).

c. ☐ by making the **original** business records described in item 3 available for inspection at your business address by the attorney's representative and permitting **copying** at your business address under reasonable conditions during normal business hours.

2. *The records are to be produced by the date and time shown in item 1 (but not sooner than 20 days after the issuance of the deposition subpoena, or 15 days after service, whichever date is later). Reasonable costs of locating records, making them available or copying them, and postage, if any, are recoverable as set forth in Evidence Code section 1563(b). The records shall be accompanied by an affidavit of the custodian or other qualified witness pursuant to Evidence Code section 1561.*

3. **The records to be produced are described as follows:**

☐ Continued on Attachment 3.

4. **IF YOU HAVE BEEN SERVED WITH THIS SUBPOENA AS A CUSTODIAN OF CONSUMER OR EMPLOYEE RECORDS UNDER CODE OF CIVIL PROCEDURE SECTION 1985.3 OR 1985.6 AND A MOTION TO QUASH OR AN OBJECTION HAS BEEN SERVED ON YOU, A COURT ORDER OR AGREEMENT OF THE PARTIES, WITNESSES, *AND* CONSUMER OR EMPLOYEE AFFECTED MUST BE OBTAINED BEFORE YOU ARE REQUIRED TO PRODUCE CONSUMER OR EMPLOYEE RECORDS.**

DISOBEDIENCE OF THIS SUBPOENA MAY BE PUNISHED AS CONTEMPT BY THIS COURT. YOU WILL ALSO BE LIABLE FOR THE SUM OF FIVE HUNDRED DOLLARS AND ALL DAMAGES RESULTING FROM YOUR FAILURE TO OBEY.

Date issued:

_____   ▶ _____
(TYPE OR PRINT NAME)   (SIGNATURE OF PERSON ISSUING SUBPOENA)

_____
(TITLE)

(Proof of service on reverse)   Page 1 of 2

Form Adopted for Mandatory Use
Judicial Council of California
SUBP-010 [Rev. January 1, 2007]

DEPOSITION SUBPOENA FOR PRODUCTION
OF BUSINESS RECORDS

Code of Civil Procedure, §§ 2020.410–2020.440;
Civil Code, § 15(a)(e);
Government Code § 68097.1
www.courtinfo.ca.gov

American LegalNet, Inc.
www.FormsWorkflow.com

Exhibit 14.17. Continued

	SUBP-010
PLAINTIFF/PETITIONER:	CASE NUMBER:
DEFENDANT/RESPONDENT:	

PROOF OF SERVICE OF DEPOSITION SUBPOENA FOR PRODUCTION OF BUSINESS RECORDS

1. I served this *Deposition Subpoena for Production of Business Records* by personally delivering a copy to the person served as follows:

   a. Person served *(name)*:

   b. Address where served:

   c. Date of delivery:

   d. Time of delivery:

   e. (1) ☐ Witness fees were paid.
          Amount: . . . . $ _____
      (2) ☐ Copying fees were paid.
          Amount: . . . . $ _____

   f. Fee for service: . . . . $ _____

2. I received this subpoena for service on *(date)*:

3. Person serving:
   a. ☐ Not a registered California process server.
   b. ☐ California sheriff or marshal.
   c. ☐ Registered California process server.
   d. ☐ Employee or independent contractor of a registered California process server.
   e. ☐ Exempt from registration under Business and Professions Code section 22350(b).
   f. ☐ Registered professional photocopier.
   g. ☐ Exempt from registration under Business and Professions Code section 22451.
   h. Name, address, telephone number, and, if applicable, county of registration and number:

I declare under penalty of perjury under the laws of the State of California that the foregoing is true and correct.

Date:

▸ _____
          (SIGNATURE)

(For California sheriff or marshal use only)
I certify that the foregoing is true and correct.

Date:

▸ _____
          (SIGNATURE)

SUBP-010 [Rev. January 1, 2007]   **PROOF OF SERVICE OF DEPOSITION SUBPOENA FOR PRODUCTION OF BUSINESS RECORDS**   Page 2 of 2

If you are asked to attend a production of documents produced by the other party, take the following steps before reviewing the documents:

1. Review the request for production of documents and the response to ascertain what documents need to be produced.
2. Discuss with the lawyer the type of documents you should look for that may be of particular interest.
3. Decide on the method of photocopying and the client's budget for photocopying.

With respect to the latter point, in an ideal situation you will want to photocopy all documents that have even the slightest relevance to the case at issue. However, large volumes of photocopying can become expensive, especially if it is necessary to bring in a mobile copy machine and have someone undo stapled pages and copy each document individually. On the other hand, if the opposing side will release the documents to an outside copy service and the documents can be automatically fed into the copy machine, the cost is much less. Accordingly, it is important to discuss with the lawyer the type of copy service you will use and any limits on costs of production.

Once you are at the location where the documents are being produced, you will need to review the documents carefully and determine which documents should be copied. If you are unsure about certain documents, you may wish to tab the documents and verify with the attorney the significance of the particular document. If cost is not an object, when you are in doubt the document should be copied.

After the documents have been copied, you will need to devise a method for indexing the documents. As with the documents you produce to the other side, all pages of each document should be number stamped. Avoid the temptation of listing every document produced with the corresponding number. Although this method may work in cases where few documents are produced, in larger cases the sheer volume of documents makes it impractical to review such a list for a specific document. Rather, the documents can be set up chronologically, by subject matter, or by type of document (i.e., correspondence, draft contracts, executed contracts, memoranda). Choose the method that works best for you and ensures that you will be able to quickly locate a document when needed.

If your side is producing the documents, you may be asked to review the documents prior to the production. This review is essential since you must be careful to remove any documents that are subject to an attorney-client or work product privilege. Failure to remove the privileged document may result in a waiver of the privilege. In addition, you will want to remove any documents that are not relevant to the request made by the opposing party.

Sometimes documents will contain both privileged and unprivileged or relevant and irrelevant matter. In this situation, you will need to **redact** the portion of the document that is privileged or nonresponsive. "Redacting" refers to the covering up of the portions of the document that should not be produced. To redact a document, photocopy the document first, then use white-out or white tape to cover up the portions of the photocopied document that should not be produced. After you have redacted all necessary parts of the document, photocopy the document again. This latter photocopy document will be produced. This document should contain a notation that it has been redacted and the reason for the redaction, such as "Document Redacted—Attorney-Client Privilege."

If you are producing a small number of documents, you may wish simply to send photocopies of the documents to your adversary without engaging in a formal document production. If the attorney agrees that the documents may be produced informally, send a transmittal letter along with the documents produced. This will act as a record that the documents were sent and a record of the day the documents were sent

Exhibit 14.18. Sample Transmittal Letter

Dear Mr. Jones:

Pursuant to Defendant's Response to Plaintiff's First Request for Production of Documents, enclosed are copies of documents number stamped 1,000 to 1,200. The number represents a control number placed by our office to identify the documents as coming from our client. The documents being produced are as follows:

Description	Number
Invoices	1,000-1,075
Correspondence	1,076-1,196
Contract dated June 1, 2003	1,197-1,200

If you find any document to be missing, or if any document is illegible and you would like to review the original, please notify me immediately.

Sincerely,

_____

Thomas Flannery
Legal Assistant

and of the documents that were produced. A sample transmittal letter is shown in Exhibit 14.18.

D. PHYSICAL AND MENTAL EXAMINATIONS

In some cases, primarily personal injury cases, the physical and mental condition of a party is a critical fact affecting both liability and damages. Under those circumstances, that party should be examined to evaluate the genuineness of the condition, its extent and causes, and to develop a prognosis. Section 2032 of the Code of Civil Procedure governs this process.

1. Law

Code of Civil Procedure §2032.220 applies to physical and mental examinations of a party, of an agent of any party, and of a "person in the custody or under the legal control of a party." The law clearly applies to minors and other legally incapacitated persons who are not the actual named parties but are the real parties in interest.

A court order is not required in a personal injury action where the plaintiff is claiming damages so long as the examination does not include any test or procedure that is "painful, protracted, or intrusive" and is conducted at a location within 75 miles of the plaintiff's residence. In all other cases, a court order is required. The court's order must specify the date, time, place, manner, conditions, and scope of the examination, as well as the person or persons who will perform it. The scope of the examination is determined by the nature of the claims, defenses, and facts and issues in controversy.

2. Practice approach

If the action involves personal injuries where an examination can be required without leave of court, the defendant must simply serve a demand for a physical examination upon the plaintiff, and all other parties who have appeared in the action. The examination should be set for a date at least 30 days after the demand. A sample demand for medical examination is shown in Exhibit 14.19.

The plaintiff must serve a written statement within 20 days after service of the demand. The plaintiff has three choices in responding to the demand: (1) comply with the demand as stated; (2) comply with the demand as specifically modified by the plaintiff, or (3) indicate that the plaintiff refuses to comply. If the defendant disagrees with the plaintiff,

Exhibit 14.19. Sample Demand for Medical Examination

[Caption]

TO PLAINTIFF AND HER ATTORNEY OF RECORD:

Demand is hereby made requiring the Plaintiff to submit to a medical examination pursuant to the provisions of Code of Civil Procedure Section 2032. The examination will be performed by Dr. Gottfried and such assistants and colleagues as Dr. Gottfried may call upon to assist her in such examination. The examination will take place on March 15, 2007, at 9:00 A.M. at 123 Oak Street, Tarzana, California. The examination will consist of patient history, x-rays, and diagnostic examination and manipulation necessary to ascertain the existence and nature of bodily injuries allegedly suffered when the defendant's car rear-ended the plaintiff on August 3, 2006.

Exhibit 14.20. Sample Order Granting Request for Physical Examination

[Caption]

ORDER

This matter being heard on defendant's motion to compel the physical examination of plaintiff, all parties having been given notice, and the court having heard arguments, it is hereby ordered that:

1. Plaintiff John Williams be examined by William B. Rudolf, M.D., at 200 Main Street, Suite 301, San Francisco, California, on August 15, 2007, at 4:00 P.M., unless the plaintiff and Dr. Rudolf mutually agree to an earlier date and time.

2. Plaintiff shall submit to such orthopedic examinations and tests as are necessary to diagnose and evaluate the plaintiff's back and legs, so that Dr. Rudolf may reach opinions and conclusions about the extent of any injuries, their origin, and prognosis.

3. Dr. Rudolf shall prepare a written report detailing his findings, test results, diagnosis, and opinions, along with any earlier similar reports on the same conditions, and deliver it to defendant's attorneys on or before September 15, 2007.

Entered:

Dated: _____

_____
Superior Court Judge

the defendant can make a motion to compel the medical examination. A sample notice of motion for an order to compel physical examination is shown in the Litigation File at the end of the book. If the court grants the motion, an order must be entered. A sample order granting request for physical examination is shown in Exhibit 14.20.

E. REQUESTS TO ADMIT FACTS

A **request to admit facts** and the genuineness of documents is the fifth method of discovery permitted under the Code of Civil Procedure and is usually one of the last employed during the litigation process. Its purposes are to sharpen trial issues, streamline trials, and eliminate the need to formally prove controverted facts.

1. Law

Requests to admit are governed by CCP §2033.010 and apply only to parties. Admissions made in response to the requests are admissions for the purposes of the pending action only and cannot be used for any other purposes. This encourages a party to admit facts without worrying about collateral consequences.

Requests may be made by the defendant at any time. However, a plaintiff must wait to make requests for admissions until at least ten days after service of the summons and complaint. Other than this hold period at the beginning of the case, like other discovery provisions, requests can be employed essentially at any time during the litigation process.

A request can be directed to three categories:

♦ Genuineness of documents
♦ Truth of facts
♦ "Application of law to fact"

The general scope of these requests is the same as for discovery in general; they apply to anything that is relevant but not privileged. Each request must be separately stated.

After a request has been served on a party, that party must serve a response within 30 days or the party waives any objection to the requests, including objections based upon privileged. Accordingly, it is extremely important to calendar requests to admit when they come into your office to make sure a response is filed timely.

There are four basic responses permitted. First, the party can object to a matter in the request, in which case the party must state the reasons for the objection. Second, the party can admit the matter; if admitted, the matter is deemed conclusively established, unless the court allows withdrawal or amendment. Third, the party can deny the matter. Fourth, the party can neither admit nor deny because the matter is genuinely in dispute or because, after reasonable inquiry, the party does not have sufficient information to determine if the matter is true or not, setting forth the reasons.

Once a response has been received, your side can move the court to review the adequacy of the objections and responses pursuant to CCP §2033(l). The court can enter an order compelling an answer or amended answer if appropriate, or order that the matter be deemed admitted. The court shall also impose a monetary sanction against any party that either unsuccessfully makes or opposes a motion to compel unless the court finds the party acted with "substantial justification."

2. Practice approach

Since the scope of requests to admit facts is so broad, using and responding to the requests are principally tactical concerns that must be discussed thoroughly with the lawyer in coordinating the overall discovery strategy. Requests for admissions are best seen not as a method for getting additional facts but as a technique for eliminating the need for formal proof and for determining what facts opposing parties intend to contest at trial.

a. Timing

Other than the limitation on the plaintiff at the beginning of a case, when to use requests for admission is usually controlled by practical considerations. Frequently, however, the requests are used at the end of the discovery stage. Discovery is essentially complete when the interrogatory answers and records pursuant to document requests have been received, the parties and necessary witnesses have been deposed, and, when appropriate, physical and mental examinations have been conducted. Requests for admissions are most commonly served at this point because the existing discovery will identify what still remains in issue. The requests should focus on the remaining facts still in issue and be served after other discovery has been completed. Requests to admit served at that time will help determine what facts the other side will concede or contest if the case goes to trial.

Another approach is to serve requests to admit early in the discovery process. This forces the opponent to decide what facts and issues she intends to dispute and allows later discovery to become more focused. If a party denies a fact in a request to admit without a substantial basis for the denial, and that fact is later proved at trial, the party proving the fact can receive as court costs the reasonable expense of proving the denied fact at trial, including attorney's fees. In addition, if there is a belief that the opposing party will use dilatory tactics or avoid serious settlement discussions on a case that should be settled quickly, making a request to admit early raises the risks for the party using those tactics. This can be effective in forcing the opponent to admit facts.

b. *What to request*

To determine what to request, look first at the elements of your side's claims. Second, analyze each "fact" that the client will need to prove to meet the burden of proof at trial on each element. Once this is accomplished, you can organize those "facts" into the three categories permitted under CCP §2033: (1) genuineness of documents, (2) truth of facts, and (3) application of law to facts. Third, review the pleadings to see what has been admitted, and review your side's discovery results to see what facts are conceded. Reviewing the discovery is critical because a fact, when admitted in interrogatory answers or by a party deposition, is only an admission by a party opponent. This means that the party admitting a fact can still present contrary evidence at trial. However, if a party admits facts in a request to admit, this is a conclusive admission. This means that a party cannot present contrary evidence at trial unless the court permits amendment or withdrawal of the admission. Thus, look for admissions to your previous discovery requests, and ask for the same admission of facts in the requests to admit.

c. *Drafting the requests*

The cardinal rule for drafting requests to admit facts is to keep them simple. A lengthy, complicated request practically begs to be denied, objected to, or responded to with a lengthy, equivocal response. This will merely generate further motions and probably achieve nothing.

Simplicity requires that a request be short and contain a single statement of fact. Such requests are difficult to quibble with, and they stand the best chance of being admitted outright. They should also comply with admissibility rules, such as those concerning relevance and hearsay.

Organize your requests into the three permitted categories:

♦ Genuineness of documents
♦ Truth of facts
♦ Opinions of fact and application of law to facts

Examples of requests for each of these categories are shown in Exhibits 14.21 through 14.23. In addition, the Judicial Council has an approved form as shown in Exhibit 14.24. See also the Litigation File at the end of this book.

Requests to admit regarding "opinions of fact" and the "application of law to fact" are a problematic area because questions of "pure law" cannot be asked. For instance, a request that asks a party to admit negligence or culpability is objectionable. Where the line is between "opinions of fact" and "application of law to fact," as against "pure law," remains unclear. Regardless of where that line is, treading close to it will probably draw objections. Accordingly, it is usually better to be on the safe side and leave the legal disputes for resolution at trial. Common situations in which the application of law to fact is raised are issues of title, ownership, agency, and employment.

The requests to admit should be signed by the lawyer, and served on each party. As with other discovery devices, service is made by any permitted method, but most commonly by mailing a copy to the lawyers of the other parties.

d. Choosing a response

A party who has been served with a request for admissions must respond within 30 days of receiving the requests, or else the objections will be deemed waived. There are four basic responses to a request.

First, your side can object to the request. As with discovery generally, you can object that the matter requested is irrelevant or privileged. In addition, you can object and seek a protective order if the request is unduly burdensome or harassing.

Second, your side can admit the request. When you do so, you conclusively admit the matter for the purpose of the pending action only. Such an admission prevents you from presenting contrary evidence at trial.

Third, your side can deny the request. The denial must be based on good faith. If the requesting party later proves the denied matter at trial, that party may get expenses involved in proving the matter. The response can, of course, admit to some parts of a request and deny others.

Fourth, under certain circumstances your side can neither admit nor deny. This is allowed if the answering party has made a "reasonable

Exhibit 14.21. Request to Admit Facts: Genuineness of Documents

[Caption]

<u>REQUESTS TO ADMIT FACTS AND GENUINENESS OF DOCUMENTS</u>

Plaintiff Ralph Johnson requests defendant Marian Smith to make the following admissions, within 30 days after service of this request, for the purposes of this action only:
That each of the following documents is genuine:
    1. A contract, attached as Exhibit A, is a true and accurate copy of the contract signed by plaintiff and defendant on August 1, 2007.

Exhibit 14.22. Request to Admit Facts: Truth of Facts

That each of the following facts is true:
    1. The signature on the contract, attached as Exhibit A, purporting to be that of the defendant, is in fact that of the defendant.
    2. The defendant signed the original of Exhibit A.
    3. Defendant signed the original of Exhibit A on August 1, 2007.

Exhibit 14.23. Request to Admit Facts: Opinions of Fact and Application of Law to Fact

That each of the following statements is true:
    1. Defendant was the legal titleholder of a lot commonly known as 3401 Fifth Street, Sylmar, California, on August 1, 2007.
    2. On August 1, 2007, William Oats was an employee of XYZ Corporation.
    3. On August 1, 2007, William Oats was authorized to enter into sales contracts on behalf of XYZ Corporation.

inquiry" in an effort to acquire necessary information for responding to the request but is still unable to respond. In addition, if the answering party considers the requested matter to be a genuine trial issue, it can either deny or set forth reasons for neither admitting nor denying.

When you and the lawyer have decided what the appropriate response should be, drafting the response is similar to drafting answers

Exhibit 14.24.   Judicial Council Request for Admissions

DISC-020

ATTORNEY OR PARTY WITHOUT ATTORNEY *(Name, State Bar number, and Address)*:	FOR COURT USE ONLY

TELEPHONE NO.:   FAX NO. *(Optional)*:

E-MAIL ADDRESS *(Optional)*:

ATTORNEY FOR *(Name)*:

SUPERIOR COURT OF CALIFORNIA, COUNTY OF

STREET ADDRESS:

MAILING ADDRESS:

CITY AND ZIP CODE:

BRANCH NAME:

SHORT TITLE:

REQUEST FOR ADMISSIONS ☐ **Truth of Facts** ☐ **Genuineness of Documents** **Requesting Party:** **Responding Party:** **Set No.:**	CASE NUMBER:

You are requested to admit within thirty days after service of this *Request for Admissions* that

1. ☐   each of the following facts is true *(number each fact consecutively)*:

☐   Continued on Attachment 1

2. ☐   the original of each of the following documents, copies of which are attached, is genuine *(number each document consecutively)*:

☐   Continued on Attachment 2.

▶

_____   _____
(TYPE OR PRINT NAME)   (SIGNATURE OF PARTY OR ATTORNEY)

Page 1 of 1

Form Approved by the Judicial Council of California DISC-020 [Rev. January 1, 2007]	**REQUEST FOR ADMISSIONS**	Code Civil Procedure, §§ 2033.010–2033.420, 2033.710 www.courtinfo.ca.gov

American LegalNet, Inc.
www.FormsWorkflow.com

to complaints. However, the better format is that used for interrogatory answers, where the answers and interrogatories both appear together. A sample response to requests for admission is shown in Exhibit 14.25.

The response to a request for admissions should be signed by the party under oath, unless the response contains only objections in which case the response may be signed by the party's lawyer. The original response, with an attached proof of service statement, should be served on the party requesting the admissions and copied for all other parties. Be sure to keep a copy for your firm's files.

e. Requesting party's responses

When a party has made and served responses to requests to admit facts on the requesting party, the requesting party can do two things:

Exhibit 14.25. Response to Request for Admissions

[Caption]

RESPONSE TO REQUESTS FOR ADMISSIONS

Defendant Marian Smith responds to plaintiff Ralph Johnson's requests for admissions as follows:

Request No. 1: A contract, attached as Exhibit A, is a true and accurate copy of the contract signed by plaintiff on August 1, 2007.

Answer: Admit.

Request No. 2: Plaintiff performed all his obligations under the contract.

Answer: Deny.

Request No. 3: On August 1, 2007, William Oats was authorized to enter into sales contracts on behalf of XYZ Corporation.

Answer: Objection. Responding to this request would disclose the substance of conversations between William Oats, an attorney, and the XYZ Corporation, which are protected from disclosure by the attorney-client privilege.

Request No. 4: Mary Doyle was the sole titleholder of a lot commonly known as 3401 Fifth Street, Sacramento, California.

Answer: Defendant can neither admit nor deny this request. Public records neither confirm nor deny, and defendant has no access to any documents that could confirm or deny it.

first, move to review the sufficiency of an answer; second, move to review the validity of an objection. Both of these are directed to the court's discretion. The court can enter any appropriate order, such as deeming a matter admitted, or requiring an amended answer.

When the answering party denies a request to admit facts, a good approach is to send the answering party interrogatories that ask for the basis of the denial. You should discuss this strategy with the attorney responsible for the matter.

F. EXCHANGE OF EXPERT WITNESS INFORMATION

The simultaneous exchange of information concerning expert trial witnesses is governed by CCP §2034.210. This provision provides that after setting the initial trial date, any party may demand that all parties simultaneously exchange information about their respective expert trial witnesses. The demand may request the following exchange:

♦ The names and address of any natural person whose testimony the party expects to use as an expert at trial
♦ Production of all discovery reports and writings made by the expert

The date identified for the exchange shall be 50 days before the initial trial date, or 20 days after the service of the demand, whichever is closest to the trial date. This date applies even if the initial trial date is later postponed or continued. This allows the party sufficient time to depose the expert witnesses in advance of trial to ascertain and further explore the basis for their expert opinion.

If a party who has been served with the demand does not wish to comply with the demand for some reason, then the party served must move for a protective order. The grounds for such a protective order include, that a timely demand was not made, that the date for exchange be either earlier or later than specified, that the exchange be subject to certain terms and conditions, or that the exchange occur at a different place or time.

G. DISCOVERY MOTIONS

Discovery under both federal and state rules is largely undertaken without judicial intervention, except for the specific areas discussed here. Generally, courts become involved only when there is a discovery dispute.

Three points should be remembered when making any discovery motion. First, prior to making a motion the moving party's lawyer must certify what good faith efforts have been made to resolve a dispute before the court will intervene.

Second, discovery abuse has probably been the subject of more controversy and proposals than any other aspect of the litigation process. Courts have responded to the problem by becoming more involved in discovery, particularly by having discovery plan conferences and by dealing more actively with abuses and imposing stiffer sanctions.

Third, courts have the power to limit discovery where it is unnecessarily cumulative or duplicative, or is obtainable from other sources with less effort and expense. There are two principal types of discovery motions, those for protective orders and those for orders compelling discovery.

1. Protective orders

Code of Civil Procedure §2019(b) governs **protective orders** in general. Whenever an entity or person from whom discovery is sought feels that they are being subjected to cumulative or duplicative discovery, or the relevant information is more easily and less expensively obtained from another source, or that the discovery is unduly burdensome, or expensive, the appropriate procedure is to move for a protective order. Before filing a motion for a protective order, the Code requires that the moving party meet and confer with the other party and make a good faith effort to resolve the discovery dispute without the need for court intervention. Both parties and nonparty deponents can seek protective orders.

Protective orders
An order from the court restricting or limiting discovery by one party to another

The moving party must show **good cause.** While grounds for protection are numerous, the most common grounds are that the discovery requested is so lengthy and detailed that it is unduly oppressive and expensive—for example, discovery involving lengthy or repetitive interrogatories and depositions, and overly detailed document requests and requests to admit. Another common ground is the serving of notice for depositions on high corporate officers who have no firsthand knowledge of any relevant facts. If the dominant purpose of the discovery is not to develop information reasonably necessary to prepare for trial or settlement, but to bend the opposition into submission, a protective order is appropriate. Other motions frequently seek to limit disclosure, such as restricting persons present at depositions and preventing the disclosure of business secrets to persons outside the litigation.

Good cause
The grounds the court looks at to determine whether the requested relief should be granted

Keep in mind that many discovery matters come up by motions to compel after a party has objected to discovery requests. Objections are permitted in answers to interrogatories, document requests, and requests for admissions. In these circumstances the objection protects the responding party. The requesting party must move for an order compelling discovery, and there is no need for the responding party to move for a protective order.

If a protective order is appropriate, a court has a variety of remedies that it can utilize to protect a party or person. These include barring the requested discovery; regulating the terms, conditions, methods, and scope of discovery; limiting persons present at the discovery; requiring the sealing of depositions and documents; and regulating or barring disclosure of trade secrets and confidential information.

The motion for a protective order must be prepared like any other motion and must include statements of the facts as well as a request for the relief sought. The motion must be accompanied by a notice of motion indicating the date, time, and place of the hearing on the motion, and include a supporting memorandum of points and authorities and a declaration or affidavit from someone with personal knowledge of the facts stated in the motion.

A common practice is to prepare a proposed order and attach it to the motion. The proposed order should parallel the motion by setting out what information needs to be protected and how it will be protected. However, always check the local rules of the court where the motion will be heard to see if additional requirements or procedures must be met.

2. Orders compelling discovery

If a party fails to respond to certain discovery, or the response is inadequate, the party requesting the discovery may file a motion to compel. As with protective orders, the Code provides that litigants make a good faith effort to resolve discovery disputes informally before filing motions to compel discovery or disclosure with the court. The attorney must attach a declaration to the motion showing what steps were taken to attempt to resolve the dispute. A sample declaration is shown in Exhibit 14.26.

A party can move for an order compelling discovery whenever a party fails to answer or gives evasive or incomplete answers to proper discovery. Frequently the issue arises when a party responds by objecting to an interrogatory, request to produce, or request to admit facts. A motion to compel must then be made to determine whether the objection is proper. The issue also frequently arises when a party fails to answer interrogatories, fails to produce documents after being served with a request to

Exhibit 14.26. Sample Declaration

I, Allen Smith, attorney of record for defendant Alfred Jenkins, declare as follows:

1. On July 15, 2007, I sent a letter to plaintiff's attorney reminding her that her interrogatory answers were overdue. I received no response to this letter. A true and correct copy of my letter is attached hereto as Exhibit A.

2. Approximately three times during the past month I have called plaintiff's attorney and left messages requesting the overdue answers.

3. Three days ago I left a message with plaintiff's attorney advising her that I would make a motion to compel unless I received answers within 48 hours. I received no response of any kind from plaintiff's attorney or her office.

I declare under penalty of perjury under the laws of the State of California that the foregoing is true and correct.

Executed this 4th day of September, 2007.

_____
Attorney for Defendant

produce, refuses to designate a deponent on behalf of a corporate party, or, in the case of deponents, refuses to appear, be sworn, or answer questions.

The steps to follow with the motion to compel are the same as those for a motion for a protective order: After the motion is prepared and signed, a copy along with a notice of motion must be served on every other party. The originals of the motion and notice of motion, with a proof of service, must be filed with the clerk of the court. Keep in mind that many courts delegate discovery matters to special discovery judges, so make sure that your notice of motion correctly specifies who will hear the motion.

In addition, Rule 3.1020 of the California Rules of Court provides a specific format for discovery motions and provides that in cases where a response has been served, but is inadequate, a separate statement is required to be filed with the discovery motion. The separate statement must include all of the following in order for the court to make a decision on the sufficiency of the response:

1. The text of the request, interrogatory, question, or inspection demand;
2. The text of each response, answer, or objection, and any further responses or answers;

3. A statement of the factual and legal reasons for compelling further responses, answers, or production as to each matter in dispute;
4. If necessary, the text of all definitions, instructions, and other matters required to understand each discovery request and the responses to it;
5. If the response to a particular discovery request is dependent on the response given to another discovery request, or if the reasons a further response to a particular discovery request is deemed necessary are based on the response to some other discovery request, the other request and the response to it must be set forth; and
6. If the pleadings, other documents in the file, or other items of discovery are relevant to the motion, the party relying on them must summarize each relevant document.

No separate statement is required if a party fails to completely respond to the discovery request.

CHAPTER SUMMARY

This chapter has discussed the formal tools for obtaining facts in a lawsuit. Basically, there are six discovery devices that you may use: interrogatories, requests to produce, depositions, medical examinations, requests to admit facts, and exchange of expert trial witness information. Each of these devices serves a different purpose. Interrogatories are beneficial for obtaining basic factual information. Requests to produce allow you to obtain documents and other tangible items that are in the control of other parties. A physical and/or mental examination helps a party assess medical damages. A request to admit provides a way to have a fact conclusively established without having to prove the fact at trial. When an initial trial date is set, a demand may be made to exchange information about what the other party's trial experts will state at trial.

Each discovery device has its own format requirements and timing requirements that must be followed. If the party responding to the discovery believes that the discovery is unduly burdensome, or unduly expensive, the responding party may move for a protective order to limit or restrict the discovery. If a protective order is not sought, the responding party must answer and/or assert a valid objection to the discovery.

While for the most part discovery is conducted without court intervention, it sometimes becomes necessary to make a discovery motion before the court. Thus, the paralegal must be familiar with how to obtain a protective order from the court and how to compel a party to respond to discovery requests.

Finally, this chapter has detailed the various ways a computer can be utilized for litigation support. This includes using a computer to organize documents and to locate key testimony in a deposition transcript.

KEY TERMS

Bate Stamp

Deposition subpoena for
  production of records

Form interrogatories

Good cause

Interrogatories

Physical and mental
  examinations

Protective order

Redact

Request to admit facts

Request to produce

REVIEW QUESTIONS

1. Identify the six different discovery devices. What is the purpose of each device?

2. How can computers be used to assist in the litigation process?

3. Identify at least three grounds a party may have for objecting to interrogatories.

4. What is a protective order? Why is it important to move for a protective order as quickly as possible?

5. Why is it sometimes necessary to serve a subpoena for production of documents?

6. Why is it necessary to sometimes "redact" portions of a document that is produced to the opposing side?

7. What items of information must be included in a notice of deposition?

8. If you are preparing a client for a deposition, what rules for responding to deposition questions should you review with the client?

INTERNET RESOURCES

www.courtinfo.ca.gov/cgi-bin/forms.cgi

www.law.cornell.edu

www.lawsource.com/also

www.washlaw.edu

CHAPTER **15**

Depositions

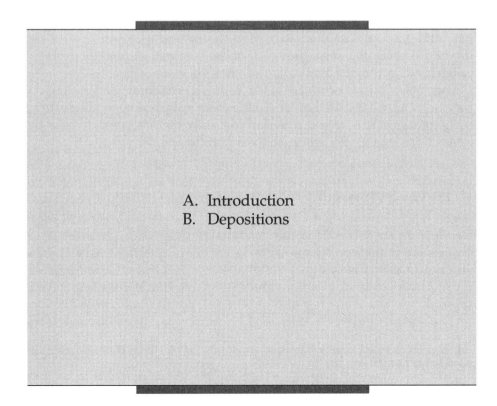

A. Introduction
B. Depositions

CHAPTER OBJECTIVES

Depositions are the discovery tool that is used to directly ask questions and receive answers from other parties and witnesses. In this chapter you will learn:

♦ Why a party may want to take a deposition
♦ How to prepare a witness for deposition
♦ What questions to ask a witness in a deposition
♦ Who can attend a deposition
♦ How to prepare a deposition summary in different ways
♦ When it is necessary to serve a deposition subpoena

A. INTRODUCTION

Depositions are usually taken after both interrogatory answers and responses to document requests have been received, since those answers and documents will usually be used to plan an intelligent deposition. Although depositions are both expensive and time consuming, they are quite useful in assessing witness credibility, learning what witnesses know, and pinning witnesses down. Other than a subpoena for documents, they are the only discovery method that can be used on nonparties, and the only method in which the opposing counsel does not directly control the responses. For these reasons, depositions play a critical role in the discovery plan of virtually every case.

Code of Civil Procedure §2025.010 governs oral depositions of parties,[1] and §2020.010 governs deposition subpoenas of nonparties.[2] Although you may attend a deposition, only the lawyer may take the deposition or defend a witness at a deposition.

B. DEPOSITIONS

Depositions are a way to obtain testimony, under oath, from the other parties and witnesses. A deposition is a series of questions asked by the attorney of the witness similar to what occurs in a trial. The witness will give answers to each question, and everything that the witness says is taken down by a court reporter and later typed up in booklet form for review and signing by the witness. Depositions are useful because if the

---

1. Deposition based upon written questions is also a potential way of taking depositions, but is rarely used.
2. The rules discussed herein are specific to party depositions. However, with the exception of requiring a subpoena, as opposed to simply noticing the deposition of a party, the rules are the same.

witness answers a question and then later changes his testimony at trial, the deposition testimony can be used to impeach the witness. Thus, depositions serve dual purposes of ascertaining information and pinning witnesses down so that they do not change their mind at trial and testify differently.

1. Law

a. Timing

Oral depositions may be taken of any party or nonparty. Leave of court is not necessary to take the deposition, however, there are requirements limiting when a deposition may be taken. The defendant may serve a deposition notice any time after the defendant has been served with the summons and complaint. However, the plaintiff must wait at least 20 days after service of the complaint upon the defendant before the plaintiff may serve a deposition notice. This is to give the defendant time to review the complaint and consider the facts prior to responding to questions at a deposition.

b. Notice

The notice of deposition must state a date for the deposition at least ten days in advance. In the case of a deposition subpoena of a nonparty that requires the production of documents at the deposition, the deposition must be scheduled at least 20 days in advance. It is common courtesy to check with the opposing counsel to determine dates that are mutually convenient for the parties and attorneys.

The notice must state the address where the deposition will be taken, the date of the deposition, and the name of the deponent. If the deponent is a nonparty, the address, if known, of the deponent must be stated. If the name of the deponent is not known, the notice must describe the person to be deposed in sufficient detail to identify that person individually or as part of a class or group. This is frequently the case with corporations and other artificial entities where the actual name of the proper person to be deposed is unknown. In such a case, the corporation or other entity must designate an officer, director, managing agent or other person to testify on its behalf.

In addition to the notice to other parties, the person to be deposed must also be notified. A sample notice of deposition appears in the Litigation File at the end of the book. When the deponent is also a party, the notice of deposition is sufficient. When the deponent is a nonparty, he must be subpoenaed in accordance with CCP §2020.010.

Unlike a subpoena that requests documents at the deposition, a subpoena that only requests the nonparty to appear and testify at the deposition does not need to be accompanied by an affidavit showing good cause. Witness fees and mileage costs must accompany the subpoena, as set forth in Title 8 of the Government Code. A problem that frequently arises concerns the amount of fees and costs that the witness is entitled to receive. A common practice is to tender the witness a check for the probable mileage and one day's witness fees, and to take care of any differences after the deposition.

Finally, the deponent can be commanded to produce records, documents, and tangible things for inspection and copying at the deposition. With parties, this is simply achieved by serving on the deponent a request to produce for the same date and place on which the deposition will be held. Nonparties can also be commanded to produce records by serving a subpoena for production of records as discussed in the section regarding document request.

c. Location

Code of Civil Procedure §2025.250 governs where a deposition may be conducted. The deposition must be at a location "either within 75 miles of the deponent's residence, or within the county where the action is pending and within 150 miles of the deponent's residence, unless the court orders otherwise."

d. Persons present

Who may be present at a deposition? The usual persons are the person being deposed, the parties' lawyers, and the court reporter. If the deposition will be videotaped, a videotape operator will also be there.

Often you, as the paralegal, will also be present to assist the lawyer in taking notes or handling exhibits during the deposition. In some cases, if your client is not being deposed and another party is taking the deposition of a witness, you may be asked to attend the deposition in place of the lawyer who represents your client. In these cases you may be present to take notes for the lawyer and observe the proceedings. However, since you are not authorized to practice law, you will not be allowed to make any objections or statements for the record. In addition, you must be certain to represent to all parties present that you are a paralegal and not a lawyer, so that no one will have the misimpression that you are there in the capacity of a lawyer representing a client.

Parties usually have the right to be present at any deposition, although they appear infrequently. However, if a party's appearance is for an improper purpose, such as intimidation or harassment of a deponent, a protective order can be obtained to prohibit the party from attending. Nonparties and members of the media are usually held to have no right to attend depositions, since a deposition, unlike a trial, is not considered to be a public forum.

e. Recording

The predominant means of recording remains the court reporter, since this method produces a written transcript. Videotaping is often done to make a more vivid re-creation of the deponent's testimony. Video depositions are also a good idea if the opposing counsel is unduly interfering when the counsel for your side is taking the deposition, such as by repeatedly making objections that serve no proper purpose and are made only to coach the witness on a desirable response.

f. Signing, correcting, and filing

Unless the parties agree otherwise, the deposition must be transcribed. This is called a **deposition transcript**, which is the written record of the questions, answers, and objections made during the deposition. The witness has the right to review the transcript for accuracy and sign it. The deponent has 30 days after receiving notice that the transcript is ready to review it and, if there are any changes to make, sign a statement noting the changes and the reasons for them. That statement will then be appended to the deposition transcript.

The reporter must certify that the witness was sworn and that the transcript is accurate. The reporter should then seal the original, which should include any exhibits that were marked and used during the deposition, and file it with the clerk of the court, unless local rules provide otherwise.

g. Objections

Code of Civil Procedure §2025.410 identifies the objections that may be made during a deposition. The court reporter will note in the deposition transcript all objections to the qualifications of the reporter or other officer, to the procedure, evidence, and conduct of parties, as well as any other objections. The Code states that testimony objected to "shall proceed subject to the objection," the intent being that the witness should answer the questions asked with all objections being noted. This permits a judge to rule on the objections later, in the event that any party wishes to use the transcript at trial.

Objections to a witness' competency, or to the materiality or relevance of the testimony, need not be made during the taking of the deposition, unless the ground for the objection could have been eliminated if made known at that time. However, objections to the form of questions and other errors that might have been corrected if the objection had been made are waived unless timely made.

If the answer is privileged, providing the answer will constitute a waiver of the privilege. Therefore, a timely objection must be made, and if the deponent is a party, the deponent's lawyer should instruct the deponent not to answer. The party taking the deposition then has the option of moving for an order to compel discovery if he does not agree that the question calls for privileged information.

If the examination is being conducted in bad faith to annoy, embarrass, or harass the deponent, then a party or the deponent can demand that the deposition be suspended so that the party or deponent can move for a protective order to terminate or limit the examination.

2. Practice approach

Although as a paralegal you are not permitted to take the deposition of any witnesses, you will nevertheless have several responsibilities with respect to the deposition process. You may be asked to

- Schedule the deposition
- Prepare an outline of questions and issues for the lawyer to use at the deposition
- Prepare your witnesses for the taking of their depositions
- Attend the deposition to assist the lawyer in taking notes
- Summarize the deposition transcripts for future reference Each of these areas is discussed in detail below.

a. Scheduling the deposition

Scheduling a deposition involves two decisions: when and where. When is determined primarily by tactical considerations that the lawyer will make. Where depends on the lawyer's personal preference and what the Code allows. Since paralegals are often responsible for scheduling depositions, you must be familiar with the rules on choosing a location discussed above. If possible, the preferred location for deposing a party is in your office. The lawyer will have files there—which can be useful should the lawyer need to refer to them during the deposition—and the deponent will be away from familiar surroundings.

To depose an expert, it is usually better to schedule the deposition at the expert's office. It will be convenient for the expert, and the lawyer will have access to the expert's reports, records, and reference material. This will avoid what otherwise is a common problem: the expert who, for one reason or another, fails to bring all necessary paperwork, thereby making a thorough deposition impossible.

After you and the lawyer have selected a time and place for the depositions, take the following steps:

1. Send notices to parties
2. Serve subpoenas on witnesses
3. Send notices to produce or serve subpoenas for production of records
4. Reserve a suitable room for the deposition
5. Arrange for a court reporter
6. Reconfirm deposition date and attendance

The notices to parties and subpoenas to witnesses, along with any notices to produce or subpoenas for production of records, should be served with a reasonable lead time, even greater than the ten days required. Given the busy schedules of most people, 20 or 30 days' notice is certainly appropriate. When your side is deposing a party, the lawyer may ask you to call that party's lawyer and select a mutually convenient time before preparing the notices. This avoids delays, avoids motions to reset deposition dates, and generally helps create good working relationships between opposing sides, which benefits everyone. With nonparty witnesses, it is frequently a good idea to serve a subpoena first, and subsequently try to arrange for the witness to travel to your office.

The notices must be sent to every party to the action. If the deposition is for a party, nothing else need be done, unless you also need to send a notice to produce records. If the deposition is for a nonparty, you must serve a subpoena on that witness or, if necessary, a subpoena for production of records.

If your side wishes to have the party deponent produce records, simply add, "The deponent shall produce the following documents and records," and attach a list describing the relevant documents. If the deposition is of a nonparty, the notice should have a copy of the subpoena attached if possible. It is also a good practice to send a copy of the notice to the court reporter who is scheduled to take the deposition. The subpoena for a nonparty will be on a standard form that is presigned and sealed and issued by the appropriate clerk's office. A copy of the Judicial Council form is shown in Exhibit 15.1, and a sample form is provided in the Litigation File at the back of the book. Make sure you attach a check for the necessary witness and mileage fees.

Exhibit 15.1. Deposition Subpoena

SUBP-015

ATTORNEY OR PARTY WITHOUT ATTORNEY *(Name, State Bar number, and address):*	FOR COURT USE ONLY
TELEPHONE NO.: FAX NO. *(Optional):* E-MAIL ADDRESS *(Optional):* ATTORNEY FOR *(Name):*	

SUPERIOR COURT OF CALIFORNIA, COUNTY OF
STREET ADDRESS:
MAILING ADDRESS:
CITY AND ZIP CODE:
BRANCH NAME:

PLAINTIFF/ PETITIONER:

DEFENDANT/ RESPONDENT:

DEPOSITION SUBPOENA FOR PERSONAL APPEARANCE	CASE NUMBER:

THE PEOPLE OF THE STATE OF CALIFORNIA, TO *(name, address, and telephone number of deponent, if known):*

1. YOU ARE ORDERED TO APPEAR IN PERSON TO TESTIFY AS A WITNESS in this action at the following date, time, and place:

     Date: Time: Address:

     a. ☐ As a deponent who is not a natural person, you are ordered to designate one or more persons to testify on your behalf as to the matters described in item 2. (Code Civ. Proc., § 2025.220(a)(6).)

     b. ☐ This deposition will be recorded stenographically ☐ through the instant visual display of testimony, and by ☐ audiotape ☐ videotape.

     c. ☐ This videotape deposition is intended for possible use at trial under Code of Civil Procedure section 2025.620(d).

2. ☐ If the witness is a representative of a business or other entity, the matters upon which the witness is to be examined are as follows:

3. *At the deposition, you will be asked questions under oath. Questions and answers are recorded stenographically at the deposition; later they are transcribed for possible use at trial. You may read the written record and change any incorrect answers before you sign the deposition. You are entitled to receive witness fees and mileage actually traveled both ways. The money must be paid, at the option of the party giving notice of the deposition, either with service of this subpoena or at the time of the deposition.*

DISOBEDIENCE OF THIS SUBPOENA MAY BE PUNISHED AS CONTEMPT BY THIS COURT. YOU WILL ALSO BE LIABLE FOR THE SUM OF FIVE HUNDRED DOLLARS AND ALL DAMAGES RESULTING FROM YOUR FAILURE TO OBEY.

Date issued:

▶

_____   _____
     (TYPE OR PRINT NAME)   (SIGNATURE OF PERSON ISSUING SUBPOENA)

     _____
     (TITLE)

(Proof of service on reverse)   **Page 1 of 2**

Form Adopted for Mandatory Use Judicial Council of California SUBP-015 [Rev. January 1, 2007]	**DEPOSITION SUBPOENA** **FOR PERSONAL APPEARANCE**	Code of Civil Procedure, §§ 2020.310, 2025.220, 2025.620 Government Code, § 68097.1 *www.courtinfo.ca.gov*

American LegalNet, Inc.
www.FormsWorkflow.com

Exhibit 15.1. Continued

SUBP-015

PLAINTIFF/PETITIONER:	CASE NUMBER:
DEFENDANT/RESPONDENT:	

PROOF OF SERVICE OF DEPOSITION SUBPOENA FOR PERSONAL APPEARANCE

1. I served this *Deposition Subpoena for Personal Appearance* by personally delivering a copy to the person served as follows:
   a. Person served *(name)*:

   b. Address where served:

   c. Date of delivery:

   d. Time of delivery:

   e. Witness fees and mileage both ways *(check one)*:
      (1) ☐ were paid. Amount: . . . . $ _____
      (2) ☐ were not paid.
      (3) ☐ were tendered to the witness's
          public entity employer as
          required by Government Code
          section 68097.2. The amount
          tendered was *(specify)*: . . . . $ _____

   f. Fee for service: . . . . $ _____

2. I received this subpoena for service on *(date)*:

3. Person serving:
   a. ☐ Not a registered California process server.
   b. ☐ California sheriff or marshal.
   c. ☐ Registered California process server.
   d. ☐ Employee or independent contractor of a registered California process server.
   e. ☐ Exempt from registration under Business and Professions Code section 22350(b).
   f. ☐ Registered professional photocopier.
   g. ☐ Exempt from registration under Business and Professions Code section 22451.
   h. Name, address, telephone number, and, if applicable, county of registration and number:

I declare under penalty of perjury under the laws of the State of California that the foregoing is true and correct.

Date:

▶ _____
(SIGNATURE)

(For California sheriff or marshal use only)
I certify that the foregoing is true and correct.

Date:

▶ _____
(SIGNATURE)

After the notice and subpoena have been served, arrange for a suitable place in which the deposition can be taken. Make sure a court reporter is scheduled and told where and when the deposition will be held. Those who should be present include the deponent, the court reporter, the lawyers for the parties, and perhaps the parties themselves. A conference room or private office in your law office suite is usually the best place for the lawyer to take the deposition. The lawyer will be comfortable there and have all necessary files available. However, if your side wants to be particularly accommodating to a witness for tactical reasons, use a location convenient for the witness. If the deponent is required to produce documents and you are afraid she will not fully comply, depose her where the records are kept.

Finally, it is always a good idea to reconfirm the deposition with the parties, lawyers, witnesses, and court reporter involved. When a witness cannot be served and the deposition must be canceled, promptly notify all other persons involved.

b. Preparing for the deposition

A good deposition obviously requires preparation. The attorney may ask you to collect all the documentation in the firm's files that has any bearing on the witness' anticipated testimony, review it, and have copies available for use during the deposition. A copy can be marked by the witness during the deposition, and the lawyer can give the copy to the court reporter to attach as an exhibit to the deposition transcript.

When you have reviewed the available material, you and the lawyer should begin to discuss and outline how the lawyer will take the particular deposition. This depends on several considerations:

♦ Is the deponent an adverse party, unfavorable witness, or friendly witness?
♦ What information does your side need to obtain?
♦ What foundations for exhibits does the lawyer want to establish?
♦ What admissions or impeachment should the lawyer try to obtain?
♦ Is the lawyer taking the deposition only to discover information, or taking the deposition with an eye toward preserving the witness' testimony for possible later use?
♦ What are the risks in deposing this person?

These considerations must be evaluated so that you and the lawyer have good answers to the fundamental question that must be resolved: Why is this deposition important?

These considerations affect how the lawyer will take a particular deposition. Regardless of the approach, the questioning should be thorough because a basic purpose for depositions is to find out what the deponent knows. It is usually a good practice to make an outline of the anticipated topics with suitable references to the exhibits that the attorney will want to use. Paralegals are often asked to draw up this formal outline. While such an outline must obviously be tailored to the facts of each case, certain general topics should usually be explored. A sample outline is shown in Exhibit 15.2.

The background topics shown in Exhibit 15.2 should be pursued regardless of the deponent. When the deponent is a party, most of this information should already have been received in the interrogatory answers, but the lawyer should have the deponent reconfirm the information and explain it in greater detail where necessary.

There are also numerous books available that contain checklists for various types of cases and witnesses. These are useful for considering the types of topics that can be explored and the sensible order for them, but such checklists should never be a substitute for the lawyer tailoring questions to the particular deponent.

Exhibit 15.2. Deposition Outline: Preliminary Matters

1. Background
   Name and address
   Personal and family history
   Education
   Job history
2. Documents and records
   Notice to produce and subpoenas
   Record-keeping
   Record search
   Identifying produced records
   Names and addresses of other persons and entities that may have
      records related to case
3. Identity of party
   Officers, directors, employees, agents
   Parent corporation and subsidiaries, licensees
   Incorporation and places of business
   Residence
   Place where licensed to do business
   Names used in business
4. Witnesses
   Names and addresses of persons witnessing events and transactions
   Names and addresses of persons deponent has communicated with
   Names and addresses of persons who may know something about
      case

Once you organize the preliminary matters, outline the substantive areas, which depend on the type of case, legal and factual issues, and the witness' relationship to them. The key to the deposition here is detail. You need to make sure that the outline covers all the topics and is logically organized, usually chronologically. Sample outlines for different substantive areas are shown in Exhibits 15.3 through 15.5.

The deposition should extract from the witness everything the deponent knows that is pertinent to the case. Absent agreement from the parties or court order, there is usually only one opportunity to depose a person so the lawyer must be prepared, with the help of your outline, to get the most out of that opportunity.

A sample deposition appears in the Litigation File at the end of the book.

c. Preparing the client for deposition

When your office receives a notice for deposition of your client, you may be asked to prepare the client for the deposition. Preparing the client for the upcoming deposition may well be the most important single event in the litigation process. The opposing lawyers will use the deposition to determine what the client knows, develop admissions and impeachment, pin the client down to details about what he does or does not know, and generally size up the client as a trial witness. If the deposition goes well, the settlement value of the case will rise as well. Hence, preparation for the deposition is critical.

Shortly before the deposition date, have the client come to your office with enough time allocated to prepare him thoroughly. Scheduling this for the afternoon, as the last appointment for the day, is a good idea so you will not be rushed by other appointments. On the other hand, you may prefer to schedule such interviews in the morning, when you and the client are fresh. Take all of the following steps when preparing a client for deposition.

First, have the pleadings, discovery, documents, records, reports, photographs, diagrams, and sketches available for the client to review. However, show the client only his statements, not those of others. Showing the client other persons' statements will always create the impression, particularly at trial, that the client has tailored his testimony to be consistent with other witnesses or has used the other statements to acquire information he himself does not personally have. This may also make such statements disclosable at trial because under evidence rules an adverse party may be able to obtain any documents used to refresh the witness' recollection, even if used before trial; the adverse party may be able to use them during the witness' cross-examination and to introduce in evidence relevant portions of the documents. It is usually better

Exhibit 15.3. Deposition Outline: Substantive Issues (Personal Injury Case)

Deponent: Plaintiff in Personal Injury Case

1. Background questions
   (Preliminary matters as outlined above)
   Health history before accident
2. Vehicles involved
   Make, year, registration
   Insurance
   Condition, inspection, repair records
3. Scene of collision
   Neighborhood
   Roads
   Traffic markings and controls
4. Weather and road conditions
5. Events before accident
   Activities earlier in day
   Food, alcohol, drugs
   Physical condition at time
   Earlier activities
6. Events immediately before collision
   Location and direction of vehicles
   Passengers
   Traffic conditions
   Visibility and weather conditions
   Other distractions
   Where first saw defendant's car
   Marking diagrams and photographs
7. Collision
   Speed of cars before impact
   Traffic signals
   Braking and other conduct of plaintiff
   Braking and other conduct of defendant
   Point of impact
   Where cars ended up
   Marking diagrams and photographs
8. Events after collision
   Bystander activities
   Police activities
   What plaintiff and defendant did
   What plaintiff and defendant said
   Plaintiff's and defendant's condition after collision
   Ambulance

Exhibit 15.3. Continued

9. Medical treatment
   At hospital—diagnosis and treatment
   Doctors' visits after discharge—treatments
   Medication, therapy
10. Present physical condition
    Any physical limitations
    Medication
11. Damages
    Vehicle
    Hospital expenses
    Doctors' bills
    Lost wages
    Insurance payments
    Other claimed losses

to avoid this problem by not showing the client other witnesses' statements.

Second, review with the client what a deposition is, what its purpose is, why it is so critical, and what the procedure will be. Explain to the client that once the deposition begins, the lawyer representing the client will be relatively inactive, except to make objections in order to preserve error when necessary, or to instruct him not to answer if critical to do so. Make sure that the client knows to dress appropriately. There are commercial videotapes on deposition preparation available, and some are very useful to show what actually goes on during a deposition.

Third, review how your client should answer questions accurately. Impress upon him that even though the atmosphere will probably be informal, he must answer carefully. Standard suggestions given to the client include the following:

1. Make sure that you understand the question. If you don't, say so and ask that the question be rephrased.
2. If you know the answer, give it. If you don't know, say so. If you know but can't remember just then, say so. If you can only estimate or approximate, say so. However, give positive, assertive answers whenever possible.
3. Don't volunteer information. Answer only what the question specifically calls for. Don't exaggerate or speculate. Give the best short, accurate, truthful answer possible.
4. Answer questions only with what you personally know, saw, heard, or did, unless the question asks otherwise.

Exhibit 15.4. Deposition Outline: Substantive Issues (Contract Breach Case)

Deponent: Corporate Plaintiff in Contract Breach Case

1. Background questions
   (Preliminary matters as outlined above)
2. First contact with defendant
   Reasons—how came about
   Persons involved
3. Course of dealing up to contract
   Types of business conducted
   Business practices
   Specific contracts entered into
   Performance history
4. Negotiations leading up to contract
   Dates, times, places, participants
   All communications
5. Contract execution
   Date, time, place, participants
6. Conduct following execution
   Performance by each party
7. Breach claimed
   When, what
   Witnesses
8. Conduct following breach
   Attempts to mitigate
9. Damages claimed
   Breach damages
   Consequential damages

5. Read every document the questioner shows to you before answering any questions about the document.
6. Be calm at all times. Avoid arguing with the lawyers or getting upset over the questions. Your lawyer will be there to protect you from unfair questions and procedures by making objections and instructing you on what to do and say.

Fourth, discuss how objections will be handled. Explain that many objections are made "for the record," and that usually the witness must answer despite the objection, which is made for possible later use at trial. However, be sure that the client knows not to answer when an objection is made and the client's attorney tells him not to answer. This will be the case if the objection is based on privilege or harassment grounds, when answering the question may waive any error.

Exhibit 15.5. Deposition Outline: Substantive Issues (Personal Injury Case)

Deponent: Physician in Personal Injury Case

1. Professional background
   Education
   Internship and residency
   Licenses and specialty boards
   Description of practice
   Experience in type of injury involved here
2. Physician's medical records and reports
   Identify them
   Treatises he relies on
   Consultations
3. First contact with plaintiff at hospital
   Where and when
   History
   Symptoms
   Examination and findings
   Tests
   Diagnosis
   Treatment
4. Subsequent contacts with plaintiff
   Where and when
   Symptoms
   Examinations and findings
   Tests
   Prognosis
5. Opinions and conclusions
   Extent of injuries
   Permanence of injuries
   Effect on plaintiff
   Causation
   Why physician disagrees with other experts
6. Fees
   How much
   Future fees

Fifth, review with the client what questions the lawyers are likely to ask. This involves creating a short outline as discussed previously. Make sure that the client can accurately respond to those expected questions in a positive, convincing manner whenever possible. Let the client know that other lawyers present may ask additional questions, but that the client's lawyer will probably not ask questions unless necessary to correct a mistake or clarify something ambiguous.

Finally, explain that the client has a right to review the deposition if it is transcribed, noting any corrections and the reasons for them, and to sign it. However, you should also explain that, in the event any corrections are made, the attorneys will be able to comment on that fact at the time of trial. Accordingly, it is best to give the best testimony possible now, and not rely on the ability to correct errors in the transcript later.

d. Taking notes at the deposition

Although the deposition transcript will provide a written record of the statements made by the witness during the deposition, you may still be asked to be present during the deposition to take notes. Notes taken during a deposition are important in cases where several witnesses will be deposed within a short period of time, or a motion is pending or planned in which the deposition testimony is needed. In these cases, the transcript, if not specially ordered on an expedited basis, may not be ready in sufficient time to use for preparing for depositions of the other witnesses or for preparing or opposing a motion. The transcript usually will not be prepared for two to three weeks, thus requiring reference to the notes taken during the deposition. In addition, if the client does not attend the deposition, you may be asked to send a letter or memorandum to advise the client of the substance of the deposition testimony.

When taking notes, try not to take down everything. The transcript will contain all the questions and answers. Your task is to simply write down the important information that the witness gives. If you are not familiar with the issues in the case, discuss the issues with the lawyer in advance of the deposition and decide which questions and answers require particular attention.

After the deposition, promptly prepare a memorandum summarizing your notes. The memorandum should be in a narrative form and provide only the facts, not the questions that are given. The first two paragraphs of a sample memorandum are provided in Exhibit 15.6.

e. Summarizing the deposition

Summarizing depositions based on the deposition transcript is one of the more important roles you will undertake as a paralegal. A good summary will assist the lawyer in easily locating key deposition testimony for depositions of other witnesses or for trial. There are several types of deposition summaries. You should choose the type based on the importance of the particular witness to the issues in the case and the

Exhibit 15.6. Sample Memorandum Summarizing Deposition Notes

To: Litigation Attorney
From: Litigation Paralegal

Re: Smith v. Alliance Realty Company

On September 1, 2006, I attended the deposition of the plaintiff David Smith ("Smith"). The following is a summary of my notes taken during the deposition.

Smith was born on April 3, 1956, in Pasadena, California. He graduated from Pepper High School in 1974, and graduated from the University of Southern California in 1978 with a degree in business administration. He immediately went to work for the Alliance Realty Company as a bookkeeper. He remained in that position until 1982, at which time he was promoted to senior bookkeeper. In 1985 Smith was given the job title of Vice President of Accounting. However, his duties did not change. During the entire time of his employment, Smith was never informed of any problems with his work product, was never disciplined for any reason, and always received year-end bonuses. Smith was terminated on October 10, 2006, without any advance warning.

purpose for which the deposition summary will be used. For example, a deposition summary for a primary witness in the case will need to be more detailed than a summary for a witness whose testimony may be relevant to only one or two minor issues. A summary prepared for use at trial will need to be organized to quickly locate specific topics and page numbers where the topics are found. Discuss with the lawyer in advance the type of deposition summary that she wants you to prepare.

The different types of deposition summaries are identified below, along with a sample of each type.

i. Chronological Summary

Chronological summary
A deposition summary organized sequentially

The most common type of summary is the **chronological summary.** This type of summary starts at the beginning of the deposition and continues through to the end of the deposition. On the left-hand side of the page, general topic headings and line and page numbers are given. On the right-hand side of the page, a summary of the testimony is given. This type of summary will be the most detailed and should contain enough information that anyone who did not attend the deposition will still know what was stated at the deposition without having to read the entire transcript. However, remember that all deposition summaries are "summaries," and you should avoid including the witness'

Exhibit 15.7. Format: Chronological Deposition Summary

<u>Personal Background</u> pgs 1-6	Born April 3, 1956, in Pasadena, California. Graduated U.S.C. in 1978 with B.S. in Business Administration. Married. Two children.
<u>Employment</u> pg 6, lines 10-25	Alliance Realty Company. 1978 to October 10, 2006.
<u>Promotions</u> pgs 7-10	Started as bookkeeper. Promoted to senior bookkeeper in 1982. Vice President of Accounting 1985.

testimony word for word. The format of a chronological summary is shown in Exhibit 15.7.

ii. Subject Matter Summary

The **subject matter summary** does not digest the deposition in the order in which the topics appear chronologically. Rather, each subject matter is dealt with separately regardless of where the subject appears in the deposition. The advantage of this type of summary is that if questioning has skipped around to various topics, the summary helps to organize the topics. This summary is probably the most useful in preparing for depositions of other witnesses and for trial since the lawyer will not need to read through the entire summary in order to locate all the testimony on a particular issue. The format for this type of summary is shown in Exhibit 15.8.

Subject matter summary
A deposition summary that categorizes each topic by subject matter

Exhibit 15.8. Format: Subject Matter Deposition Summary

<u>Discussions with Other Employees</u> pg 14, lines 10-15 pg 18, lines 12-14 pg 50, lines 22-24	 Jay Becker Kevin McDonald Marcia Sawyer
<u>Employment After Termination</u> pg 22, lines 3-23 pg 28, lines 14-18	 Office clerk BBB Cable Company 12/1-3/14 Accountant Aerial Business Systems 3/20 to present

Exhibit 15.9. Format: Deposition Topic Index

Page	Topic
pg 10, lines 23-24	Educational background
pg 15, lines 12-15	Employment background
pg 18, lines 8-14	Present employment

iii. Topic Index

Topic index
A type of deposition summary that is an outline of the general topic areas

The **topic index** provides a quick reference for the lawyer on particular areas covered within the deposition. No attempt is made to completely summarize the deposition. Rather, it is merely an outline of the general. This type of summary may be used in addition to one of topic areas the other summaries to provide easy access at trial to specific testimony. The topic index may be arranged chronologically or by subject matter. A sample is shown in Exhibit 15.9.

iv. Narrative Summary

Narrative
A type of deposition summary that is in memorandum form with no reference to particular page and line numbers

The final type of summary is the **narrative** format. This summary is similar to the memorandum you may do immediately following the deposition. The only difference is that you will now have the benefit of the deposition transcript to prepare your summary. This type of summary is generally not useful for trial preparation. However, it is a useful summary to send to the client since the client will be more interested in the substance of the testimony than the page and line numbers where the testimony can be located. A sample narrative summary is shown in Exhibit 15.10.

Exhibit 15.10. Format: Narrative Deposition Summary

David Smith ("Smith") is 50 years old, married with two children. He was terminated from his employment at Alliance Realty Company on October 10, 2006. Since his termination, he has worked for two different companies: BBB Cable Company and Aerial Business Systems. He is presently earning $53,000 a year, which is $30,000 less than what he was earning at Alliance when he was terminated.

Smith does not know why he was terminated. He claims not to have been advised of any problems with his work during his 28 years of employment. In addition, he was never disciplined for any reason, and always received year-end bonuses based on his work performance. Smith testified that his immediate supervisor, Marcia Sawyer, always spoke very highly of him.

CHAPTER SUMMARY

This chapter has discussed the method by which you can obtain oral testimony of a party or witness before trial. Depositions are an effective method for tying down parties and witnesses to details. There are specific rules that must be followed in terms of timing and notice. In addition, the paralegal must perform many tasks with respect to depositions. These tasks include preparing a witness for deposition, taking notes during the deposition, and summarizing the transcript of the deposition. Different methods are available for summarizing the deposition transcript; you must choose a method that fits your particular needs and purposes.

KEY TERMS

Chronological summary

Deponent

Deposition

Deposition transcript

Narrative summary

Subject matter summary

Topic index

REVIEW QUESTIONS

1. What are the different ways a deposition summary may be prepared?

2. What items of information must be included in a notice of deposition?

3. If you are preparing a client for a deposition, what rules for responding to deposition questions should you review with the client?

4. What are the six steps you should take as a paralegal to prepare for the deposition?

5. What are the two purposes of taking a deposition?

6. What are the advantages and disadvantages of taking a deposition?

INTERNET RESOURCES

www.courtinfo.ca.gov

http://depositions.businesschaos.com

www.ifsmarketing.com/questions_to_ask_in_medical_depositions.htm

www.lacba.org/drs

PART III

Settlement, Trial, and Post-Trial

CHAPTER 16

Settlements

CHAPTER OBJECTIVES

Since most cases are settled before trial, it is important for a paralegal to be thoroughly familiar with the settlement process. This chapter provides details on:

♦ When to use a settlement brochure
♦ How to draft a settlement agreement
♦ What the different types of settlement agreements are
♦ How to enforce a settlement agreement

A. INTRODUCTION

Pretrial conference
A meeting between the parties before the court after litigation has commenced, but before trial begins

More than 90 percent of civil cases filed in court settle before trial. The law prefers settlement and has created several methods to accomplish it. Judges prefer settlement, and the trend has been toward greater judicial involvement, principally by using **pretrial conferences** to get the adversaries together to discuss settlement possibilities. Finally, most clients ultimately prefer settlement over the increased expenses and uncertainties of a trial. Small wonder, then, that lawyers settle most cases before trial.

Settling a case involves three basic steps:

♦ Determining the case's settlement value
♦ Selling such assessment to the opposing side
♦ Getting the client to agree

While a case can be settled at any time, settlement possibilities are almost always explored when a case nears the pretrial conference stage and a trial is just around the corner. Discovery will be complete at this point, and there is sufficient information to accurately assess the case.[1]

As a paralegal, you are not authorized to engage in the practice of law and, accordingly, do not have authority to negotiate a settlement. However, you may be requested by the lawyer to prepare a settlement brochure to send to the opposing party or to draft the settlement agreement.

---

1. Obviously, settlement is sometimes explored earlier as well, for instance, just before or just after filing suit or after the plaintiff's deposition has been taken, when the costs both in terms of time delay and litigation expenses can be held down.

B. PREPARING A SETTLEMENT BROCHURE

In recent years it has become fashionable among plaintiffs' personal injury lawyers to prepare **settlement brochures** in major cases. These brochures essentially set out the background of the plaintiff and the plaintiff's family along with the evidence showing liability and damages. The fact summaries are usually supplemented by photographs and documents such as employment records, hospital and other medical records, bills, and medical and economic expert reports detailing the extent of injuries, the degree of permanent physical losses, and the plaintiff's economic future. Some lawyers believe that developing such a brochure is the most effective way of presenting the plaintiff's case before trial and obtaining a favorable settlement. The settlement brochure should graphically show the nature and extent of the injuries, summarize the quality of the plaintiff's case, and demonstrate the jury appeal of a plaintiff.

Settlement brochure
A brochure that sets out the background of the plaintiff along with the evidence showing liability and damages

C. SETTLEMENT CONTRACTS

Since settlements are simply agreements between parties, general contract law principles apply. Good practice generally requires that the agreement be in writing and signed by each party, and some local rules require it.

Settlements are generally made using either a release, a covenant not to sue, or a loan receipt. The agreement is then presented to the court, and the case is dismissed with prejudice. It is critical to understand the legal differences between the various settlement methods. The choice of method is influenced by the types of legal claims and the number of parties involved, whether the settlement is intended to be complete or partial, the type of court action or approval that may be necessary, and the applicable law of contribution. You must know the law of the jurisdiction that governs the settlement contract because statutes and case law concerning releases, covenants not to sue, and loan receipts vary among the jurisdictions.

Also, the drafting of the agreement is important, since you need to ensure that it is treated under the applicable law in the way you and the lawyer want it treated, and that it has the effect you intend. This is particularly important in cases with **joint tortfeasors,** when two or more persons are liable to plaintiff for the same injury. In cases with joint tortfeasors the issue of contribution among the tortfeasors may arise. **Contribution** is a theory for apportioning liability among joint tortfeasors, so that the paying party may receive a proportionate sum from the other nonpaying joint tortfeasors.

1. Releases and covenants not to sue

Release
A discharge of all claims against the parties as well as against any persons against whom the same claims are or could have been asserted

A basic common law **release** is a complete discharge, or satisfaction, of an action. It operates as a discharge of all claims against the parties to the release as well as against any persons against whom the same claims are or could have been asserted. A release is used only when there is a settlement of the entire lawsuit involving every claim and every party.

A **covenant not to sue** does not discharge any parties. It is simply a contract between two or more parties in which the plaintiff agrees not to sue or to pursue an existing claim against one or more defendants. For this reason a covenant not to sue is used when there is a partial settlement not involving every party.

2. Drafting the agreement

Regardless of which type of settlement is used, care obviously must be taken in drafting the agreement to ensure that it is tailored to the case involved.

◆ The agreement should clearly state whether it is a release, covenant not to sue, or loan receipt, and state what matters it does and does not resolve
◆ The agreement should describe the events involved in the case, since the discharge will only be for those events
◆ The agreement should state the claims of liability and damages and the defendant's denial of them, since it is the compromise of these disputed claims that constitutes the mutual consideration in the agreement
◆ The agreement should specify how the pending court case is to be terminated

Exhibits 16.1 and 16.2 are simple examples of a release and a covenant not to sue. They should be modified to fit the facts of any particular situation. The Litigation File at the end of the book contains another sample release.

If you are requested by the lawyer to draft the settlement contract, you must keep the following basic concepts clear.

First, a common law release terminates all of plaintiff's claims against all existing and potential defendants, not just the settling defendant. A plaintiff must never agree to a release unless the plaintiff intends to terminate all present and future litigation.

Second, a covenant not to sue, first created to avoid the effect of the common law release rule, technically keeps the claims alive against

Exhibit 16.1. Sample Release

<u>RELEASE</u>

In consideration of the sum of $ _____ , which Plaintiff acknowledges receiving, Plaintiff _____ agrees to release Defendants _____ and _____ _____ and their heirs, survivors, agents, and personal representatives from all claims, suits, or actions in any form or on any basis, because of anything that was done or not done at any time, on account of the following:

All claims for personal injuries, property damage, physical disabilities, medical expenses, lost income, loss of consortium, and all other claims that have been or could be brought, including all claims now known or which in the future might be known, which arise out of an occurrence on or about _____*[date]*_____ , at _____*[location]*_____ , when Plaintiff claims to have sustained injuries as a result of a collision between an automobile driven by Plaintiff and automobiles driven by the Defendants.

As a result of this collision, Plaintiff has brought suit against the Defendants for damages. The Defendants have denied both liability and the claimed extent of damages. This release is a compromise settlement between Plaintiff _____ and the Defendant _____ _____ and Defendant _____ .

This agreement is a release and shall operate as a total discharge of any claims Plaintiff has or may have arising out of the above occurrence against these Defendants and any other persons.

Plaintiff _____ and Defendant _____ _____ and Defendant _____ also expressly agree to terminate any actions that have been filed, particularly a claim by this Plaintiff against these Defendants currently filed as civil action no. _____ in The Superior Court of the State of California for the County of _____ , in _____ . Plaintiff and these Defendants agree to execute a Stipulation of Dismissal, with prejudice, and file it with the Clerk of the above Court, thereby terminating that action in its entirety, within seven days of the execution of this agreement.

Date: _____

_____
Plaintiff

_____
Defendant

_____
Defendant

Exhibit 16.2.   Sample Covenant Not to Sue

<u>COVENANT NOT TO SUE</u>

In consideration of the sum of $ _____ , which Plaintiff acknowledges receiving, Plaintiff _____ agrees not to institute, pursue, or continue any claim, suit, or action in any form or on any basis, because of anything that was done or not done at any time, against Defendant _____ and his heirs, survivors, agents, or personal representatives on account of the following:

Any claims against Defendant _____ for personal injuries, property damage, physical disabilities, medical expenses, lost income, loss of consortium, and any other claims that have been or could be brought, including all claims now known or which in the future might become known, which arise out of an occurrence on or about _____ *[date]* , at _____ *[location]* , when Plaintiff claims to have sustained injuries as a result of a collision between an automobile driven by Plaintiff and an automobile driven by Defendant.

As a result of this collision, Plaintiff has brought suit against Defendant for damages. Defendant has denied both liability and the claimed extent of damages. This covenant not to sue is a compromise settlement between Plaintiff _____ and Defendant _____ _____ .

This agreement is a covenant not to sue, and not a release or an accord and satisfaction. Nothing in this agreement shall operate as a discharge against any other persons, and Plaintiff _____ expressly reserves the right to pursue any claims against any other persons other than Defendant _____ and his heirs, survivors, agents, and personal representatives.

Plaintiff _____ and Defendant _____ _____ also expressly agree to terminate any actions between them, particularly a claim by Plaintiff against this Defendant currently filed as civil action no. _____ in The Superior Court of the State of California for the County of _____ , in _____ . Plaintiff and Defendant agree to execute a Stipulation of Dismissal, with prejudice, and file it with the Clerk of the above Court, to terminate that action against this Defendant only, within seven days of the execution of this agreement.

Date: _____   _____
                                                        Plaintiff

                                                        _____
                                                        Defendant

the settling defendant since the plaintiff only agrees not to enforce the claims against that defendant. As a result, a settling defendant is still exposed to contribution claims by the other defendants who are still in the lawsuit. A defendant should never agree to a covenant not to sue unless the defendant has adequate protection against later contribution claims, either by statute or by the settlement agreement.

Third, contribution among joint tortfeasors is not the same thing as **indemnification,** which allows one party who has paid for a liability to recover completely from another party.[2] Contribution does not affect valid indemnification claims against any parties.

Indemnification
A claim allowing one party who has paid for a liability to recover completely from another party

It should be apparent that the drafting of a settlement can be complex, particularly in situations involving multiple joint tortfeasors. In general, every plaintiff wants a guaranteed dollar amount from the settling defendant, wants to keep claims alive against the nonsettling defendants, and wants no relief from contribution for the settling defendant. Every settling defendant, by contrast, wants to get out of the case with a guaranteed dollar amount to cap his exposure, and wants adequate protection from later contribution claims if a statute does not already provide it. Accordingly, you should confer with the lawyer in charge about the legal effect of these settlement devices and the contribution law that applies to the tort claims. This way you will be able to prepare a carefully drafted instrument that fits the particulars of the case so that the final agreement achieves what the lawyer needs in order to adequately protect the client.

3. Structured and installment settlements

In recent years so-called structured settlements have become common, particularly in the personal injury area when plaintiffs have been seriously and permanently injured. A **structured settlement** is simply a settlement under which the plaintiff receives periodic payments rather than one lump sum. The benefit to the plaintiff is that she is assured of support over a period of years. Defendant's insurance companies are also benefited, since paying a settlement over a number of years reduces the true cost of the settlement. Socially, structured settlements help ensure that the plaintiff will not become indigent and depend on the state for support. Under §104(a)(2) of the Internal Revenue Code, periodic payments receive the same tax treatment as lump sum payments.[3]

---

2. Contribution may exist when one party to a joint and several obligation pays more than his share of the obligation. In this situation, the paying party may be entitled to receive a proportionate contribution from the other jointly liable parties. Indemnification exists to completely save another from any legal consequences.

3. Tax laws change regularly. You should always advise the client to consult with a tax lawyer or the client's accountant to determine the taxable affect of any settlement.

The most frequently used approach in structured settlements is to provide for an initial lump sum and a series of periodic payments. The lump sum is large enough to cover the plaintiff's attorney's fee, other legal expenses, and the plaintiff's unpaid bills. The periodic payments cover either a fixed period of years or the lifetime of the plaintiff; the periods are either annual or a shorter time. If the payments may extend over a number of years, they may be tied to the inflation rate by providing for increases based on the Consumer Price Index or other measure of inflation rates. The defendant's insurer usually funds the periodic payments by purchasing an annuity from an established life insurance company that will automatically make the payments required under the agreement.

Even if the action does not involve personal injury claims, it is possible that the parties may agree to have the settlement funds paid in installments. This is often the case when the settling defendant may not be able to afford to pay a lump sum settlement, but can afford to make monthly payments and pay the settlement amount in installments.

Although uncommon, a party may sometimes breach a settlement. Since a settlement agreement is a contract, the settlement can always be enforced in a separate contract action. However, this is not the preferred method as it would require a party having to wait until the termination of the separate lawsuit before enforcing a judgment.

The best way to enforce a settlement is to include a separate provision in the settlement for immediate entry of a judgment in the event of a default in the settlement. Some courts may require the injured party to make a motion to enforce the settlement, even if there is a provision for entry of judgment in the settlement agreement. If a motion is required, the motion should be brought in the same court and preferably before the same judge to whom the case had been assigned. At the hearing on the motion, the settling party must be prepared to prove the breach of the settlement agreement. Once the motion is granted, a judgment can be entered against the defendant, and the judgment enforced using the methods discussed in Chapter 18. A sample of an installment settlement agreement is found in Exhibit 16.3.

4. Terminating the suit

After a settlement agreement has been reached, the lawsuit must be terminated. The standard method is to file a motion to dismiss with the clerk of the court.

Make sure the dismissal is with prejudice as to the settling defendant, since this bars the plaintiff from refiling the claim later. If the settlement is only partial, as is the case with a covenant not to sue, the dismissal must clearly show which party is being dismissed and which parties remain in the case.

Exhibit 16.3. Sample Structured Settlement

WHEREAS, plaintiff _____ , and defendant _____ , are parties to a civil action Case Number 224435, presently pending in the [identify court] (hereinafter referred to as the "Civil Action"); and

WHEREAS, the parties to the Civil Action are desirous of avoiding the time and expense associated with the further prosecution and defense of the Civil Action; and

WHEREAS, said parties are desirous of being released of any and all claims with respect to the Civil Action;

NOW THEREFORE, in consideration of the releases and covenants contained herein, Plaintiff and Defendant agree as follows:

1. Except with respect to the obligations under this Agreement Plaintiff, hereby forever and fully releases and discharges the Defendant from all liabilities, losses, cost, expenses (including, without limitation, attorneys' fees), and damages related to all or any part of the subject matter of the Civil Action, or the prosecution or defense thereof.

2. Except with respect to the obligations under this Agreement Defendant, hereby forever and fully releases and discharges the Plaintiff from all liabilities, losses, cost, expenses (including, without limitation, attorneys' fees), and damages related to all or any part of the subject matter of the Civil Action, or the prosecution or defense thereof.

3. With respect to the covenants contained in paragraphs 1 and 2 of this Agreement, each of the parties hereby expressly waives all benefits under any code, statute or rule of law which provides, in essence, that a general release does not extend to unknown or unsuspected claims which, if known by the creditor would have materially affected the settlement with the debtor. The parties understand and acknowledge the significance and consequence of such a waiver and assume full responsibility for any damages or losses sustained by them of any sort or nature which might otherwise have been or be assertable as claims.

4. In consideration of Plaintiff dismissing its complaint in the Civil Action and the releases, representations, and agreements as set forth in this Agreement, the Defendant will pay to Plaintiff the sum of Sixty Thousand Dollars ($60,000.00), said sum to be payable by cashier's check to Plaintiff as follows:

    a. $10,000 to be paid at the time of execution of this Agreement;

    b. $10,000 to be paid on or before March 1, 2006;

    c. $10,000 to be paid on or before December 1, 2006;

    d. The balance of $30,000 to be paid on or before March 1, 2007.

5. The parties agree that no interest is to accrue on the above amounts.

6. The parties agree that in the event that the defendant defaults

Exhibit 16.3. Continued

in the payment of any of the above amounts, that the plaintiff has the right to obtain by ex parte application, and without any further notice to the defendant, a judgment for the entire amount that remains due and owing, plus interest on said amount at the rate of 10% from the date of the breach of this settlement agreement.

7. If an action is commenced between the parties to this Agreement in connection with the enforcement of any provision of this Agreement, the prevailing party shall be entitled to reasonable costs and expenses, including attorneys' fees.

8. This Agreement shall be interpreted in accordance with the laws of the State of [name].

IN WITNESS WHEREOF, the parties hereto have each approved and executed this Agreement on the dates set forth opposite their signatures.

In certain types of cases court approval is needed for any settlement. Settlements in class actions must have court approval. Also, settlements involving decedents' estates or incapacitated parties such as minors and incompetents usually require court approval. In these situations the action will be brought in the name of the representative party, such as a guardian, guardian ad litem, conservator, administrator, or executor. Local statutes and rules must always be checked to ensure compliance with technical requirements. The usual procedure is to present a petition to the court having jurisdiction over the party, usually a probate or family court, and to serve notice to all parties and other interested persons. A hearing is then conducted on the proposed settlement and, if approved, an appropriate court order authorizing the settlement will be entered.

5. Offers of judgment

Offer of judgment
An offer by a party defending a claim to have judgment entered in a specific amount

Code of Civil Procedure §998 provides that either party can serve an **offer of judgment** upon the opposing party more than ten days before the trial. The purpose of this Code section is to encourage settlements when reasonable offers to settle have been made. If the offer is refused and a judgment following trial is the same or less favorable to the refusing party than the pretrial offer of judgment, the refusing party becomes responsible for the offering party's "costs" incurred from the time of the offer.

In the past few years CCP §998 offers have become a prominent weapon in the settlement stage of the litigation process. Parties must

Exhibit 16.4. *Sample Offer of Judgment*

[Caption]

<u>OFFER OF JUDGMENT TO PLAINTIFF AND HER ATTORNEY
OF RECORD:</u>

Defendant Johnson Corporation, pursuant to CCP §998, offers to allow judgment to be entered against it, in favor of Francine Jones, in the amount of fourteen thousand ($14,000) dollars, which amount includes costs of suit and attorney's fees incurred herein.

This offer is made under CCP §998 and is made as a settlement offer, and is not to be taken as an admission of, or any indication of liability on the part of this defendant.

Date: _____   _____
                                Attorney for Defendant
                                Johnson Corporation

consider carefully their chances of obtaining a more favorable judgment before refusing any offer.

If a party wishes to make an offer of judgment to the opposing party, this must be done more than ten days before trial begins. Make sure that the offer is actually delivered to the opposing party's attorney within the permissible time. A sample offer of judgment is shown in Exhibit 16.4.

Parties usually make settlement offers under CCP §998 when settlement negotiations have broken down and a trial is to begin soon. However, the offer can be made at any time, and should be made earlier if the value of the case can realistically be assessed.

If the plaintiff elects to accept the offer of judgment, he simply sends a notice to the defendant that he accepts the offer. Judgment can then be entered on the accepted offer.

6. Evidence rules

Under Evidence Code §1152 offers to compromise are not admissible to prove liability or damages. The law is broadly drafted to bar settlement discussions from being introduced at trial on those issues. The law, however, does not prevent admission of such evidence for other purposes, principally to expose bias and interest of a testifying witness. Accordingly, a party that has settled and later becomes a witness at the trial of the same case can be cross-examined on the existence and content of the settlement.

7. Insurer good faith requirements

In civil litigation a defendant will often have some insurance coverage. The insurance contract normally has language under which the insurer reserves the right to manage the defense and negotiate a settlement. However, courts have usually imposed a duty on the insurer to deal fairly and in good faith to protect the interests of the insured. This duty comes about because the interests of the insurer sometimes conflict with those of the insured. The insured naturally wants the company to stand behind her and defend vigorously or, if a settlement is reached, to settle within the policy limits. The insurer also has an interest in defending vigorously, but in a settlement situation only has a financial interest in settling the case under the policy limit. Hence, the insurer and insured's interests come most sharply in conflict when there is a risk of exposure over the policy limits since, once the policy limit is reached, only the insured has additional exposure. Because of this conflict, courts have imposed a good faith obligation on the insurer to manage the case fairly and to adequately protect the insured's interests. In other words, the insurer has a fiduciary duty and must conduct the defense in the best interests of the insured as though there were no policy limits.

Any settlement offer from the plaintiff should be communicated to the insured's lawyer, since the insured is the actual party. When a duty to defend in good faith has been breached, the insurer is generally liable for the entire judgment, regardless of policy limits.

For the defense counsel the message from case law should be clear. The defense counsel's client is the insured, and counsel's professional and ethical obligation is to serve the best interests of the client. That counsel was selected and will have fees paid by the insurance company does not alter the professional obligations. When settlement negotiations are in progress, both the insured and insurer must be kept informed of their progress. Whenever possible, the insured and insurer should both agree in writing to any settlement. Since the lawyer serves the client, not the insurer, the lawyer must accept a reasonable settlement, even when it involves the policy limits, if it is in the best interests of the client. When exposure above the policy limits is involved and the lawyer cannot get both the insured and the insurer to agree to a settlement, attention must be given to what the rights, duties, and liabilities of the insured and the insurer are in such circumstances.

CHAPTER SUMMARY

There are several methods available to settle a lawsuit. One method that is popular in encouraging settlement in personal injury actions is the preparation of a settlement brochure. The settlement brochure sets out the plaintiff's background, along with evidence showing liability and damages. The purpose is to graphically show the nature and extent of the injuries and to demonstrate the appeal the plaintiff's case will have to a jury.

If a settlement is reached, the settlement must be reduced to writing. The settlement may use a release, or a covenant not to sue. Under California law, the defendant may also make an offer of judgment that will be entered against the defendant if accepted by the plaintiff. If you are drafting a settlement agreement, care must be taken to ensure that the settlement is tailored to the case involved.

After the settlement agreement is reached, the lawsuit must be terminated. The standard method is to file a request for dismissal with the court. If one party breaches the settlement, the settlement can be enforced in a separate contract action, or the wronged party may be able to make a motion to enforce the settlement.

KEY TERMS

Contribution

Covenant not to sue

Indemnification

Joint tortfeasors

Offer of judgment

Pretrial conference

Release

Settlement brochure

Structured settlement

REVIEW QUESTIONS

1. What are the three basic steps involved in settling a case? How can the paralegal assist the lawyer with each of these steps?

2. What is included in a settlement brochure? Why is such a brochure popular in personal injury actions?

3. What are the differences between a "release" and a "covenant not to sue"?

4. What are the advantages to making a CCP §998 offer?

5. How can a plaintiff enforce a settlement agreement made by the defendant?

INTERNET RESOURCES

The following resources are just a few of many that can be consulted for sample forms and settlement agreements:

http://contracts.onecle.com
www.findlegalforms.com
www.formsguru.com
www.lawdepot.com

CHAPTER **17**

Trial Preparation, Trial, and Appeal

CHAPTER OBJECTIVES

Paralegals are involved in all aspects of trial preparation and may also assist at trial and with any appeal. In this chapter you will learn:

- ◆ How to draft a pretrial memorandum
- ◆ How to organize litigation files for trial
- ◆ What items must be included in a trial notebook
- ◆ Why developing a theory of the case is important
- ◆ How to prepare witnesses for trial
- ◆ How to prepare exhibits for trial
- ◆ What the paralegal's role is during trial
- ◆ What tasks must be performed if a party files an appeal

A. INTRODUCTION

Even though only a small percentage of civil cases filed will actually go to trial, preparation for trial is an integral part of the litigation. Trial preparation usually starts once discovery is complete, and well in advance of the actual trial. It is during this phase of the litigation that the emphasis shifts from gathering the facts to applying the facts to the issues for presentation to a judge or jury. Since the parties' attention is drawn to the issues in dispute and to the evidence available to support or refute the issues, it is no wonder that many cases settle during this stage of the litigation. Accordingly, proper preparation of the case serves two purposes: evaluation of the case for settlement purposes and presentation of the case at trial in the event there is no settlement.

This chapter discusses the important steps in properly preparing a case for trial and also the significant role you will play in this preparation as a paralegal. The conduct of the trial is noted to give you some advance familiarity with the trial process before you must actually attend a trial.

B. THE PARALEGAL'S ROLE

As a paralegal you are an essential member of the litigation team as the case progresses from the fact-gathering and discovery stage to trial. Paralegals are often responsible for organizing all of the data that have been collected throughout the course of the litigation and for ensuring that the data are readily available during the trial. In addition, paralegals assist with preparing and marking exhibits for trial, preparing witnesses, developing a theory of the case, preparing direct and cross-examination questions, and preparing any final pretrial motions.

During the trial the paralegal must ensure that all exhibits are properly in place and anticipate any documents that the attorney may need during the examination of witnesses. All trials are different and, regardless of the amount of planning and preparing that is done in advance, surprises often occur at trial. Part of your responsibility is to assist in responding to any unexpected developments during the trial and to help ensure that the presentation of your client's case goes smoothly.

C. PRETRIAL CONFERENCES

Depending upon the practice of the court, pretrial conferences may be held. Trial judges vary widely in their use of these conferences. Many counties and individual judges have adopted local rules and instructions regulating pretrial conferences. Hence, in assisting the lawyer in preparing for one, you must comply with applicable local rules and your judge's special instructions on, and attitude toward, pretrial conferences. The following is a brief description of how pretrial conferences generally work.

The pretrial conference is a meeting held before trial between the attorneys and the judge. The pretrial conference is usually informal and held in the judge's chambers. The purpose is to identify the issues in dispute and the evidence that will be presented. Local rules vary on whether any memoranda must be filed in advance of the pretrial conference. Some courts require a short general memorandum on the case, some require that the parties meet in advance to prepare a joint pretrial memorandum, and still others require no memorandum at all. Even if no memorandum is required, it is still a good idea to prepare a pretrial memorandum because it provides an opportunity to brief the judge in writing about the nature of the case in advance of the trial. The pretrial memorandum generally contains the following sections: uncontested facts, contested issues of fact and law, exhibit list, witness list, and jury instructions. A sample is shown in Exhibit 17.1.

After the pretrial conference, a pretrial order will be prepared, either by the judge or the parties, and signed by the judge. The **pretrial order** is a guide for the trial; it identifies the issues, witnesses, exhibits, and order of proof. The pretrial order must be complete, since no deviations are allowed from the pretrial order at trial. If any omissions or inaccuracies are made in the pretrial order, they must be promptly corrected. A sample pretrial order is shown in Exhibit 17.2.

Pretrial order
Order that acts as a guide for the trial

D. ORGANIZATION OF FILES

Ours is an age of records, and the field of law is no exception. Everything is routinely recorded and duplicated. By the time it approaches trial, even a simple case can, and invariably will, generate an extensive collection of paperwork. Consequently, one of the first steps to take in

Exhibit 17.1. Pretrial Memorandum

[Caption]

JOINT PRETRIAL MEMORANDUM

Counsel for plaintiff Frances Johnson and defendants Robert Jones and Lisa Roberts submit the following Joint Pretrial Memorandum:

I

Uncontested Facts

The accident occurred on June 1, 2006, at approximately 2:00 P.M. Plaintiff Frances Johnson was a passenger in a 1998 Honda Accord owned and driven by defendant Robert Jones. Jones was driving north on Kolb Road intending to turn left (west) on 22d Street. As he was executing this turn, the defendant Lisa Roberts, who was driving her 2000 Buick Skylark southbound on Kolb Road, struck Jones' vehicle. The intersection is controlled by a traffic light. Both defendant Roberts and defendant Jones claim to have had a green light favoring their direction of travel. At the time of the accident, the plaintiff Johnson was employed as a bank teller by the First National Bank.

II

Contested Issues of Fact and Law

1. Which of the defendants, if either, was negligent?
2. Were both defendants negligent?
3. If the plaintiff was injured as a result of the negligence of one or both defendants, what amount of money is she entitled to recover for her damages?

Exhibit 17.1. Continued

III

Exhibits

A. <u>Plaintiff Johnson's Exhibits:</u>	<u>Objections to Admissibility, if any:</u>
1. Medical expenses totaling $1571.04 as evidenced by vouchers in support of each expenditure contained in a blue brochure with a cover sheet listing the medical expenses.	
2. The Police Department official report of the accident.	Objected to by defendant Jones.
3. St. Mary's Hospital emergency room records of the plaintiff.	
4. Photographs of the plaintiff showing her shoulder deficit.	
5. X-rays taken of the plaintiff.	
6. Photographs and diagrams of the intersection involved.	
B. <u>Defendant Jones' Exhibits:</u>	<u>Objections to Admissibility, if any:</u>
1. Plaintiff's hospital and medical records.	
2. X-rays.	
3. Plaintiff's employment records.	
4. Bills concerning property damage.	
5. Time sequence of signal lights.	
6. Photographs of the vehicles.	
7. The police report as far as it is admissible.	
C. <u>Defendant Roberts' Exhibits:</u>	<u>Objections to Admissibility, if any:</u>
1. Police report of accident.	
2. Photographs of vehicles involved.	Objected to by plaintiff and by defendant Jones, for the reasons stated in the attached Memorandum of Law.
3. Plaintiff's medical records.	

Exhibit 17.1.   Continued

IV

Witnesses

A. Plaintiff Johnson's Witnesses:
1. Plaintiff.
2. Richard Martin, M.D.
3. Ernest Jackson, M.D.
4. Philip Wigmore, a bystander.
5. Bernie Sullivan, plaintiff's supervisor at First National Bank.
6. Investigating police officer Frank Johnson.
7. Defendants.

B. Defendant Jones' Witnesses:
1. The parties to this action.
2. Investigating police officer Frank Johnson.

C. Defendant Roberts' Witnesses:
1. The parties to this action.
2. Doctors who have seen or treated plaintiff.
3. Richard Hollister, a bystander.
4. Officer Horn, Police Department.
5. Glenda Sylvester, accident reconstruction expert.

V

Jury Instructions

Plaintiff and defendants' proposed jury instructions are attached.

1. Plaintiff Johnson objects to Jones' instructions numbers 4, 7, and 9, and objects to Roberts' instruction number 6 for the reasons stated in the attached Memorandum of Law.

2. Both defendants object to plaintiff Johnson's instructions numbers 6, 7, 8, and 13 for the reasons stated in the attached Memorandum of Law.

RESPECTFULLY SUBMITTED this 1st day of May, 2007.

By _____
Attorney for Plaintiff
Johnson

By _____
Attorney for Defendant
Jones

By _____
Attorney for Defendant
Roberts

Exhibit 17.2. Pretrial Order

[Caption]

FINAL PRETRIAL ORDER

The following are the results of pretrial proceedings in this cause held pursuant to Rule 16 and IT IS ORDERED:

I

This is an action for damages arising out of a collision involving vehicles driven by defendant Jones and defendant Roberts, which occurred on June 1, 2006, at the intersection of Kolb Road and 22d Street.

II

The following facts are admitted by the parties and require no proof:

1. The collision occurred on June 1, 2006, at the intersection of Kolb Road and 22nd Street.

2. Defendant Jones was the owner and operator of a 1997 Honda Accord that was involved in the collision.

3. Defendant Roberts was the owner and operator of a 2000 Buick Skylark that was involved in the collision.

4. Plaintiff Johnson was a passenger in defendant Jones' vehicle at the time of the collision.

III

The following facts, though not admitted, will not be contested at trial by evidence to the contrary:

1. Plaintiff was absent from work on June 1, 2006, through June 14, 2006.

2. Plaintiff was admitted to St. Mary's Hospital Emergency Room on June 1, 2006, and was discharged from the hospital on June 3, 2006.

3. Plaintiff's hospital bill was $592.83.

4. Plaintiff's doctor bills to date total $978.21.

Exhibit 17.2. Continued

IV

The following are the issues of fact to be tried and determined upon trial:

Issue: Whether the defendants used due care in operating their vehicles?

Plaintiff contends that both defendants were speeding, not driving safely, and were not keeping a proper lookout.

Defendant Jones contends that he was driving within the speed limit and operating his vehicle safely.

Defendant Roberts contends that she was driving within the speed limit and operating her vehicle safely, and that defendant Jones failed to yield the right of way.

V

The following are the issues of law to be tried and determined upon trial:

Issue: Whether the defendants, or either one of them, were negligent?

Plaintiff contends that both defendants were negligent and that their negligence jointly and directly caused plaintiff's injuries.

Defendant Jones contends that he was not negligent, and that his conduct caused no injuries to plaintiff.

Defendant Roberts contends that she was not negligent, that she did not violate any statutes, and that her conduct caused no injuries to plaintiff.

VI

a. The following exhibits are admissible in evidence in this case and may be marked in evidence by the Clerk:

(1) Plaintiff's exhibits: (see attached List number 1)

(2) Defendants' exhibits: (see attached Lists numbers 2 and 3)

b. As to the following exhibits, the party against whom the same will be offered objects to their admission upon the grounds stated:

(1) Plaintiff's exhibits: (see attached List number 4)

(2) Defendants' exhibits (see attached Lists numbers 5 and 6)

Exhibit 17.2. Continued

VII

The following witnesses will be called by the parties upon trial:
    (a) On behalf of plaintiff: (see attached List number 7)
    (b) On behalf of defendants: (see attached Lists numbers 8 and 9)

VIII

A jury trial has been requested, and was timely requested. It is anticipated that the case will require three trial days.

APPROVED AS TO FORM:

_____
Attorney for Plaintiff Johnson

_____
Attorney for Defendant Jones

_____
Attorney for Defendant Roberts

The foregoing constitutes the Final Pretrial Order in the above case. All prior pleadings in the case are superseded by this Order, which shall not be amended except by consent of the parties and by order of this court.

_____
Superior Court Judge

Dated: _____

preparing for trial is to ensure that the files are in order. All files must be organized, divided, and indexed to provide immediate and accurate access to the contents at any time during trial. The litigation team that is organized will appear prepared, confident, and professional to both the court and jury.

Files should usually include the following indexed folder categories:

COMMON FILE CATEGORIES

◆ *Court papers.* These should normally be bound in the order filed or entered:

  ☐ Pleadings
  ☐ Discovery
  ☐ Motions and responses
  ☐ Orders
  ☐ Subpoenas

◆ *Evidence.* Records should be placed in clear plastic document protectors and have evidence labels attached. While records will depend on the specific case, the following are commonly involved:

  ☐ Bills, statements, and receipts
  ☐ Correspondence between parties
  ☐ Photographs, maps, diagrams
  ☐ Business records

◆ *Attorney's records*

  ☐ Running case history (log of attorney's activities in the case)
  ☐ Retainer contract, bills, costs
  ☐ Correspondence
  ☐ Legal research
  ☐ Miscellaneous

There is no magic in organizing files. Everyone develops their own systems for the types of cases they routinely handle. The important point to remember is that your system must be logical, clearly indexed, and bound whenever possible, so that records can be retrieved quickly and accurately.

In some large cases you may have the ability to store the records on the computer. CD-ROM technology has been developed that can store all trial records and exhibits (including transcripts, pleadings, and so on) in a computer. Simply moving an electronic wand over a bar code, which instantly projects the appropriate exhibit on the computer screen, can retrieve these records. For trial purposes, the computer can be hooked up to a large-screen monitor. The exhibits can be retrieved at trial by the computer and projected on the screen. The exhibit then can be marked, highlighted, and enlarged by either the lawyer or witness at trial.

E. TRIAL MATERIALS

As the trial date approaches, it will be necessary to organize the material that will be used during trial. Trial material should be organized in a way that is the most efficient and useful at trial. This is different from organizing case files, discussed above in section D. Each part of a trial—jury selection, opening statements, direct and cross-examinations, and closing arguments—requires separate organization and preparation. Paperwork generated during the preparation of each phase of the trial should be organized in a logical, easily retrievable, way.

Two methods, the **divider method** and the **trial notebook method**, are most commonly used. Usually either of the two methods is used but they can also effectively be used in conjunction, especially in large cases. In such instances the notebook can be used as a working trial notebook that keys into a larger divider system. This is frequently done, particularly in large commercial litigation cases.

1. Divider method

Under this method each part of the trial receives a separate, labeled file divider, which has in it all papers pertinent to that phase of the trial. By merely pulling out the appropriate section, both you and the lawyer will have at your disposal during trial all necessary materials.

The advantage of the divider method is that it is usually better suited to a long, complex case when the paperwork is so voluminous it cannot physically be organized and contained in a trial notebook.

The disadvantages are primarily logistical. A divider method is only as reliable as the person maintaining it. If a file is misfiled or its contents misplaced, it cannot be readily located and its utility is eliminated. If more than one person is using the files, the possibilities of disruption are much greater.

2. Trial notebook method

Under this method all necessary materials for each part of the trial are placed in a three-ring notebook in appropriately tabbed sections. The advantages are that once placed in the notebook, the materials cannot be lost or misplaced and are immediately located simply by turning to the appropriate section.

Notes taken during the trial, such as during the cross-examinations of your side's witnesses or the direct examinations of your opponent's witnesses, should be on letter-sized paper, prepunched for three-ring notebooks. (Legal pads of this sort are readily available.) The notes can then be placed in the appropriate section of the trial notebook.

While it should be organized to meet individual needs, the notebook system works best when it contains enough tabbed sections to make the contents easily accessible. The following sections are commonly incorporated in trial notebooks.

a. Facts

This section should contain all reports, witness statements, diagrams, charts, and other factual materials. It should also contain a summary sheet that recites the parties, attorneys (address and telephone), the counts of the complaint or indictment, and the essential facts and chronology of events involved.

b. Pleadings

This section should contain the complaint or indictment, answer, and other pleadings of each party to the suit. The pleadings should be in chronological order. If amended pleadings have been filed, only the currently operative pleadings should be here. When pleadings are sufficiently complex, a pleading abstract, or summary of the pleading, should be included in this section. When the indictment or complaint is based on a specific statute, a copy of the statute should also be included. Keeping the elements instructions for the claims and defenses in this section is also useful.

c. Discovery

Included in this section should be the following discovery documents:

1. Interrogatories and answers to interrogatories
2. Deposition abstracts, cross-indexed to tabbed and marked depositions
3. Requests to admit and responses
4. Requests to produce and responses
5. Other discovery

d. Motions

This section should contain all pretrial motions, responses, and orders that already have been made, as well as any that will be presented prior to or during the trial. It should also contain the pretrial memoranda and final pretrial order.

e. Jury selection

This section should contain:

1. A **jury chart** to record the basic background information about each juror obtained during the voir dire examination. In voir dire examination the judge and, in some courts, the lawyers ask specific questions of the prospective jurors to ascertain any bias, prejudice, or other information that would affect the decision of the prospective juror in the case. The type of chart or diagram you use depends on how jury selection will be conducted. In some courts a **strike system** is used. This means that each prospective juror will be questioned before any challenges are made. Under this system you can simply use a legal pad to record the basic information about each juror and then strike a juror's name if a challenge is made.

Jury chart
A diagram to be used during voir dire examination of the jury

If a more traditional system is used, jurors will usually be called into the jury box and only those in the box will be questioned. As challenges are made and prospective jurors are excused, others will replace them. Under this system it is obviously necessary to develop a system that keeps track of the jurors in the box. Most lawyers and paralegals use a jury box diagram to record the jurors' names and backgrounds. When a challenge (see section J) is exercised, you simply put a large "P" (plaintiff), "D" (defendant), or "C" (cause) through the appropriate box to record which party exercised the challenge. When blank, a jury chart will appear as follows:

JURY CHART

The diagram will cover most of a page. Then simply write down the basic background information of each juror in the appropriate box during the voir dire examination, as demonstrated on the next page.

2. A checklist for questions, if counsel is permitted to conduct the voir dire examination in whole or in part. In some courts the judge conducts the voir dire.

> **John Doe** — 40 — carpenter — self-emp. 10 yrs. — 3C in grade school — W part-time book-keeper 15 yrs. — owns home Chicago, N. side — 2 yrs. army

3. A list of questions the lawyer wants the court to ask, if the court does part or all of the voir dire examination.
4. A list that keeps track of the challenges exercised by each party.

f. Charts

This section should contain the following lists and charts, which can easily be made on standardized forms:

1. **Witness list**, showing each witness' name, home address and telephone number, work address and telephone number, a short synopsis of the witness' testimony, and other information necessary for locating and scheduling the witness during trial. If the list is long, it is useful to put it in alphabetical order. A sample witness list is shown in Exhibit 17.3.

2. An **exhibit chart** for your party as well as all other parties showing the exhibit number, exhibit description, and boxes to check if exhibit was offered, admitted, refused, reserved, or withdrawn. A sample chart is shown in Exhibit 17.4.

3. A **trial chart** showing each element of each claim or defense and the witnesses and exhibits that will prove each required element. A sample trial chart is shown in Exhibit 17.5.

g. Direct examinations (your case-in-chief)

For each witness that your side intends to call as part of the case, a separate sheet should be maintained that outlines the direct examination questions. The witness sheets should reflect what exhibits the witness will qualify and the location of all prior statements.

When completed, the witness sheets can be arranged in the same order as the order of proof. In this way putting on the case-in-chief becomes a

Exhibit 17.3. Witness List

Frank Miller	accountant who prepared defendant's tax returns
123 North, Woodland Hills — (works at home)	
H (818) 888-1123 W (same)	

Sharon Jones	bookkeeper at defendant's company
2300 N. Clark, Woodland Hills — (works 8-12)	
H (818) 888-9876 W (818) 726-8231	

H (   )   W (   )

Exhibit 17.4. Exhibit Chart

EXHIBIT CHART — PLAINTIFF						
#	Exhibits marked for identification	Offered	Admitted	Refused	Reserved	Withdrawn
1	Construction contract	x	x			
2	Final payment check	x		x		
3a-g	Monthly progress reports (7)	x	x			

matter of simply calling the witnesses according to their witness sheets. Cross-examination notes should be made on paper pre-punched for three-ring binders so that they can easily be put in the notebook behind the witness sheet for each witness.

Exhibit 17.5. Trial Chart

TRIAL CHART — PLAINTIFF

Elements of Claim	Witness and Exhibits
(Count I—Contract)	
1. Contract made	1. Contract (Plaintiff Exhibit #1)
2. Defendant executed contract	2. (a) Answer to complaint (b) Defendant admission in deposition
3. Plaintiff performed	3. Plaintiff testimony
4. Defendant breached contract	4. Plaintiff testimony
5. Plaintiff damages	5. (a) Plaintiff testimony (b) Contractor who completed job (c) Checks (Plaintiff Exhibit #4) (d) Records (Plaintiff Exhibit #6)

h. Cross-examinations (opponent's case)

Each witness that you and the lawyer anticipate the opponent will call should have a witness sheet outlining the cross-examination the lawyer plans to conduct. The outline should be placed on one side of the page so brief notes can be made during the direct examination on the other side. The outline should show the location of all prior statements that might be used during the cross-examination.

i. Closing arguments

The closing arguments section should initially contain several blank sheets. Throughout the trial, as certain testimony or other ideas arise that the lawyer may want to use in closing arguments, the lawyer will note them in this section.

j. Jury instructions

This section should contain a copy of all the jury instructions your side intends to offer at the instruction conference, which is usually held shortly before the closing arguments. The instructions should be drafted *before* trial. In civil cases the court will usually require each side to submit proposed jury instructions as part of the pretrial memoranda. This section will also eventually contain the other side's instructions, which the court will rule on. During the conference you can mark each instruction as being given, refused, or withdrawn.

k. Research

This section should contain a copy of trial memoranda, trial briefs, or other legal research on issues that are likely to arise during the course of the trial. It should also contain photocopies of the principal cases and other authority supporting your party's case so the lawyer can quote the authorities or give them to the judge if necessary. This is also a convenient place to keep a copy of the rules of evidence for the appropriate jurisdiction.

The trial notebook system enables you and the lawyer to locate any necessary information immediately and present the case in a well-organized, professional manner. All paperwork necessary for the trial will be in the notebook, except transcripts and exhibits.

In addition, you may wish to set up a file divider for each witness containing a copy of every prior statement this witness has made, such as in a police report or deposition. This folder will then contain all statements usable to refresh recollection on direct and to impeach during cross-examination.

F. THEORY OF THE CASE

Up to this point the trial preparation has included organizing the case files, preparing the trial notebook, drafting jury instructions, reviewing the elements of each count, preparing exhibits, and reviewing the probable testimony of all anticipated witnesses. In conjunction with these preparations, you may be asked to assist the lawyer in developing a theory of the case.

As discussed in section D of Chapter 3, it is essential for the lawyer to develop a theory of the case before trial and act in accordance with it throughout the trial. A **theory of the case** is simply the lawyer's position on, and approach to, all the undisputed and disputed evidence that will be presented at trial. The lawyer must integrate the undisputed facts with her version of the disputed facts to create a cohesive, logical position at trial. That position must remain consistent during each phase of the trial. At the conclusion of the trial this position must be the more plausible explanation of "what really happened" to the jury.

Theory of the case
The lawyer's position on, and approach to, all the undisputed and disputed evidence that will be presented at trial

The theory of the case must be developed before the trial begins because the approach to each phase of the trial is dependent on the theory. Consider the following:

Example

Theory of the Case

In an automobile negligence case Marcy Walters is struck by Robert Chen's car at an intersection. Some evidence will place Marcy, the plaintiff, within the crosswalk with the walk-light green. Other testimony will show she was outside the crosswalk, jaywalking across the intersection.

Is the theory, as plaintiff, that:

1. Marcy was on the crosswalk and had the right of way? (ordinary negligence)
2. Marcy was not on the crosswalk but was injured because Robert (the defendant) could have stopped his car but didn't? (last clear chance)

G. PREPARATION OF WITNESSES

Witness preparation for trial purposes is not discovery. This is not the time to learn "what the case is all about" or to obtain interesting information. Witnesses favorable to your side must be prepared for testifying in court to those facts that will support your side's theory of the case. Preparation involves reviewing those facts that each witness and exhibit can provide, and preparing the witnesses to testify to those facts in a convincing fashion. Although the lawyer conducting the trial will usually prepare the witnesses, you may be asked to sit in on the meetings with each witness or to conduct the initial preparation. The following checklist should be used in conducting the preparation:

STEPS IN WITNESS PREPARATION

☐ Prepare each witness for trial individually.

Only in this way can you realistically expect each witness to be adequately prepared for his or her particular role in the trial.

☐ Review with the witness all previous testimony, depositions, answers to interrogatories, written and oral statements, and any other material that could be used for impeachment.

Have the witness read these materials or read them to the witness. Determine if his present recollection differs in any way from his previous statements. If so, and the witness insists that his present recollection, not the prior statement, is accurate, explain that the opposing lawyer is allowed to impeach him with the prior statement and how this will be done in court.

☐ Review with the witness all exhibits he will identify or authenticate.

☐ Review the probable testimony of other witnesses to see if any inconsistencies exist.

If they do, look for explanations for the inconsistencies that can be used to explain them if opposing counsel raises the inconsistencies at trial.

☐ Review the direct examination with the witness—repeatedly.

Make sure the witness can actually testify to what the lawyer anticipates he can. Make sure he can establish the foundation for all necessary exhibits. Once the general outline of the direct examination has been established, go over the actual questions in light of evidentiary requirements. Explain why the lawyer cannot use leading questions. If possible, review the testimony in an empty courtroom as a dress rehearsal, using the actual questions and answers the lawyer intends to present before the jury. Preparation should continue until the witness is thoroughly familiar with the questions, and answers them in the clearest, most accurate way. However, preparation should not continue to the point where the testimony sounds memorized or rehearsed.

☐ After the direct examination has been prepared, review with the witness the areas that the lawyer anticipates the cross-examination will cover.

Explain the different rules that apply to cross-examination and the purposes of the examination. Do a practice cross-examination of the witness, raising the same points and using the demeanor the actual cross-examiner is likely to raise and use at trial. Emphasize that the witness should maintain the same demeanor and attitude on cross as he had on direct and answer only the question asked.

☐ Prepare the witness for his courtroom appearance.

Explain that he should dress neatly and conservatively. Explain how the courtroom is arranged; where the judge, lawyers, court reporter, clerk, bailiff, and spectators sit; how the witness will enter and leave the courtroom; where and how he will take the oath; where he will sit while giving his testimony; and how he should act while in court. If the witness is a party who will sit with the lawyer at counsel table, remind him that the jury will be watching and assessing him even when he is not testifying. Instruct him not to whisper to the lawyer or to you or interrupt the lawyer when court is in session. Instead, have him write on a notepad anything he wants to tell the lawyer or you when other witnesses are testifying.

☐ Prepare the witness for his courtroom testimony.

Explain that following these rules will favorably affect the way the jury will evaluate and weigh his testimony:

◆ Listen carefully to every question. Answer only that question. Do not ramble or volunteer information. Look at the jury when answering questions. Speak clearly and loudly so that the last juror can easily hear you. Don't look at the judge or lawyer for help on difficult questions.

◆ If you do not understand a question, say so and the lawyer will rephrase it. If you cannot remember an answer to a question, say "I can't recall" or "I can't remember." You will be allowed to review any of your statements to jog your memory. If you don't know an answer, say "I don't know." If you can only approximate dates, times, and distances, give only your best approximation. If you cannot answer a question "yes" or "no" say so and explain your answer. However, give positive, clear, and direct answers to every question whenever possible. Answer the questions with the words you normally use and feel comfortable with. Don't use someone else's vocabulary, "police talk," or other stilted speech.

◆ Be serious and polite at all times. Do not exaggerate or understate the facts. Don't give cute or clever answers. Never argue with the lawyers or the judge. Never lose your temper. The lawyer on cross-examination may attempt to confuse you, have you argue with him, or have you lose your temper. Resist these temptations.

◆ You will be allowed to testify only to what you personally saw, heard, and did. You generally cannot testify to what others know, or to conclusions, opinions, and speculations.

◆ If either side makes an objection to any question or answer, stop. Wait for the judge to rule. If he overrules the objections, answer the question. If he sustains the objection, simply wait for the next question. Never try to squeeze an answer in when an objection has been made.

◆ Explain the purposes of direct, cross, redirect, and recross and the forms of questions employed in each type of examination.

◆ Explain trick questions that the other side may ask, such as: "Have you talked to anyone about this case?" "What did your lawyer tell you to say in court?" and "Are you getting paid to testify?" Explain how such questions can be accurately and fairly answered.

◆ Above all, always tell the complete truth according to your best recollection of the facts and events involved.

If a witness is not a party to the lawsuit, the witness will need to be served with a subpoena to appear at trial. Part of your preparation of witnesses should be to ensure that a subpoena is served on all nonparty witnesses. Friendly witnesses can be served with the subpoena at the time of the meeting to prepare them for trial. Explain to witnesses that you are serving them with a subpoena because they are nonparties and a subpoena is necessary to secure their attendance. Even friendly witnesses can sometimes have second thoughts about testifying. If they are not served with a subpoena, there is nothing compelling witnesses to attend. Accordingly, it is best to protect your client's interests by serving the subpoena rather than running the risk that a witness does not appear at trial.

It is also a good idea to make sure parties to a lawsuit will attend if their testimony is necessary for the trial. Although most parties attend their own trials, there is no guarantee that this is the case. CCP §1987(b) provides that, a party to a lawsuit, or any officer, director or managing agent of a party, the service of a subpoena is not required. Rather, a notice to appear at trial served upon the party's attorney is sufficient to compel attendance of the party.

H. PREPARATION OF EXHIBITS

Trial exhibits are generally exchanged between the parties in advance of trial. However, even if the exhibits do not need to be exchanged between the parties, you should still ensure that all exhibits are in order before the commencement of trial.

Discuss with the lawyer the documents she wants to use as trial exhibits and the order in which you should mark the exhibits. Once you collect the necessary documents, organize them in the order they will be used at trial. Place each exhibit in a separate folder and mark the exhibit for identification. Although you will need to check your local court rules, generally numbers are used for the plaintiff and letters are used for the defendant when identifying exhibits.

Remember that the best evidence rule requires you to have the original document. Attempt to locate the originals of all documents. Place the original document, along with a copy of the document, in the exhibit folder. If you do not have the original, put a note in the exhibit file indicating where to locate the original if necessary.

Often certain exhibits are enlarged so they will be easier for the jury to see. This is especially true in the case of photographs. Identify the exhibits that need to be enlarged as soon as practical so you will have sufficient time to have the enlargements made and mounted.

Demonstrative evidence, sometimes referred to as graphic evidence, is particularly useful in jury trials. Demonstrative evidence, such as charts, models, and diagrams, assists the jury in understanding the issues and

Demonstrative evidence
Exhibits that represent real things

facts. All demonstrative evidence should be prepared in advance of trial. Discuss with the lawyer the types of demonstrative evidence that she needs, and then arrange for the preparation of the evidence. If videotapes or slides will be used, arrange to have the necessary equipment available for the trial.

I. ORDER OF TRIAL

Opening arguments
Statements made by lawyers at the beginning of the trial to explain their clients' version of the facts and evidence they expect to prove

To fully prepare for trial, you need to understand the various stages of the trial and when evidence will be presented. The first stage is the selection of the jury. After selection of the jury, the lawyer for each party will present **opening arguments.** Opening arguments are an opportunity for the lawyers to tell the jury (or in nonjury trials, the judge) their respective clients' versions of the facts and what they expect the evidence to prove.

Next, the plaintiff's lawyer will present her case-in-chief. The **case-in-chief** refers to the evidence that a party will present to support the party's position. There is no magic to the order the lawyer will use to call her witnesses. Rather, the witnesses should be called in an order that will logically and forcefully present the evidence. Above all, the jury must be able to easily follow and understand the story as it unfolds. The lawyer, along with your assistance, will determine the order of the witnesses in advance of trial. In this way you can make arrangements to have the witnesses available for trial on the day they will likely be called on to testify.

After the plaintiff's lawyer presents her case-in-chief, the defendant's lawyer will present his case-in-chief. Again, the witnesses should be called in an order that permits logical and forceful presentation of the story of defendant's version of the facts.

Rebuttal evidence
Evidence refuting the evidence presented by the defendant as part of the defendant's case-in-chief

The plaintiff has the opportunity to present **rebuttal evidence** after the defendant's case-in-chief. Rebuttal evidence is evidence the plaintiff produces to explain or contradict the defendant's evidence. The defendant also has an opportunity to present evidence that explains or denies the rebuttal evidence. This is called **surrebuttal.**

After both sides have presented their cases and any rebuttal or surrebuttal evidence, closing arguments will be heard. In **closing arguments** the lawyers summarize the evidence that has been presented and explain why the judge or jury should rule in a particular way.

Surrebuttal
Evidence presented by the defendant that explains or denies the rebuttal evidence

J. ASSISTANCE DURING TRIAL

1. Planning for the courtroom

While assisting at trial, you will be responsible for ensuring that all necessary files, documents, and equipment are in the courtroom at the start of trial. Planning the logistics of this responsibility takes time.

Accordingly, do not wait until the day of trial to determine the proper setup of your materials.

If possible, visit the courtroom a few days before the trial. You will need to determine if adequate space exists for the storage of files, the location of chalkboards and easels for exhibits, and the location of electrical outlets for tape recorders, video equipment, or projectors. If extension cords are necessary, determine the number and length of the cords needed and whether the cords can be placed to avoid anyone tripping over them. Also observe the location of counsel tables to determine where your files should be placed. You will need to arrange your files so they will not be in the way, but at the same time are close enough so you have easy access. If necessary, diagram the courtroom so when you return to the office you can draw a map for location of all your materials.

In addition to your trial exhibits and files, pack a **trial box** with necessary items for the trial. This trial box should contain the following:

- Pens and pencils
- Notepads
- Paper clips
- Post-it tabs
- A copy of the evidence code and rules of civil procedure for your jurisdiction
- Manila folders
- Business cards for you and the lawyer to give to the court reporter
- Scotch tape
- Stapler and staples
- Pleading paper
- Change for telephoning witnesses who are on call

Ascertain what time the courtroom opens so on the morning of trial you can arrive early to set up the materials. Everything should be ready to go before trial starts.

2. Voir dire

The procedure for jury selection varies from court to court. However, in general, the prospective jurors come into the courtroom and take their place in the jury box. At that time either the judge or lawyers, depending on each court's particular practice, will conduct a voir dire of the jury.

Voir dire refers to the method used to learn about the prospective jurors. The judge or lawyers will ask questions of each prospective juror in an attempt to ascertain information about the juror. This information can help the lawyer decide whether the prospective juror will be biased in favor or against one side.

Voir dire
Process of the judge and lawyers asking specific questions to learn information about prospective jurors

Peremptory challenge
Allows a lawyer to strike a juror from the panel without having any stated reason

If the lawyer wishes to strike a juror from the jury panel, a challenge to that juror can be made. A challenge may be peremptory or for cause. A **peremptory challenge** allows a lawyer to strike a juror from the panel without having any stated reason—for example, perhaps the lawyer believes the juror does not have the right personality or experience to render a decision favorable to the lawyer's client. However, recent case law prohibits the use of race and gender as the basis for exercising peremptory challenges.

To avoid too many challenges, the lawyers are each given only a limited number of peremptory challenges (usually no more than four or five). In most jurisdictions the number of challenges is contained in statutes and rules. The numbers vary widely, and you must read the applicable statutes and rules prior to trial to find out the exact number. If the juror is biased, or has some interest in the litigation, or personally knows any of the parties to the litigation, the juror may be stricken from the panel **for cause.**

For cause
When a juror is stricken from the jury panel because of a particular reason

Your role as a paralegal during the voir dire is to keep a chart of the names and information given by the prospective jurors. This information will then be reviewed with the lawyer to assist the lawyer in exercising the challenges. A sample chart is included in section E of this chapter. You should also keep track of the number of peremptory challenges that the lawyer uses so that you can advise the lawyer how many challenges remain. The lawyer will want to save at least one challenge until the complete jury is picked to avoid running out of challenges and having to accept a juror that may be detrimental to the client's case.

3. The trial

During trial, you must watch and listen to everything. Be alert for documents the lawyer needs for direct and cross-examination and for impeachment. Take notes during each witness' testimony so you can review the testimony with the lawyer during breaks and recesses. You also will be responsible for keeping the exhibit chart. You must note the identity of each document, and whether the exhibit was offered into evidence, admitted, refused, reserved, or withdrawn.

Nonparty witnesses generally will not sit through the entire trial. Rather, they will usually be **on-call**, requiring that you call them when it is time for them to appear and testify. It is essential that you telephone the on-call witnesses well in advance of the time their testimony is expected. You do not want there to be any unnecessary breaks in the trial because a witness is late. Moreover, if a witness chooses not to appear on time, the court may require the lawyer to call another witness to keep the trial moving. This could significantly alter the planned order of proof and presentation of the evidence.

At the conclusion of each day's evidence, determine with the lawyer whether a daily transcript or any portion of the transcript is needed. Many times the lawyer will want at least a portion of the transcript to use for examination of future witnesses or for the closing arguments. If a transcript is necessary, arrange with the court reporter for the portion you desire before you leave for the day. This will maximize the possibility that the reporter will have the transcript ready when you need it. However, remember that daily transcript copies are expensive and should be obtained only if genuinely needed.

At the end of each day of trial, you should meet with the lawyer, even if for only a few minutes, to discuss the day's events and what materials will be necessary for the next day.

K. THE PARALEGAL'S CONDUCT DURING TRIAL

No chapter on trial can be complete without mentioning some basic rules that govern paralegals' conduct during a trial, rules that are best reflected on each time you attend a trial.

The lawyers, as well as the parties, are on trial; that trial begins when you first enter the courtroom and ends when the court rules on the last post-trial motion. Remember that the lawyer's conduct and your conduct are constantly being evaluated and compared by everyone in the courtroom.

During the testimony of witnesses you should never appear worried or anxious. If the evidence is unfavorable, incorrect, or a surprise, never let your expression show any sign of your reaction. In short, you should maintain a "poker face" at all times. Also, avoid nodding or shaking your head or any other gestures that can be distracting to the jury.

Talking with the lawyer at the counsel table should be limited. Rather, make a note of anything you need to communicate. You should instruct the client also to make notes if he or she wants to communicate something to either you or the lawyer during the testimony of witnesses.

Finally, a couple of ethical reminders for trial. First, be careful not to speak with any of the jurors. Your inadvertent communication with a juror could lead to claims of impropriety by the adverse party and a mistrial. Second, avoid discussion of the case in the elevators, corridors, and restrooms. You never know who may overhear your conversation.

L. APPEAL

Simply because the trial is over does not mean that the litigation is put to rest. Rather, if there is a possibility of obtaining a reversal, the losing party will undoubtedly appeal the judgment. The paralegal can provide organizational, analytical, and substantive assistance during the appellate process.

1. The appellate process

The rules governing the appellate process are found in CCP §901 et seq. and CRC, Title Eight. These rules must be carefully followed to avoid forfeiture of your client's rights. A copy of the Judicial Council form explaining the appellate procedure is provided in the workbook.

Every party has an appeal as a matter of right from the trial court to an appellate court. This means that the losing party is permitted to appeal the trial court's judgment, and the appellate court must hear the appeal. Which court will act as the appellate court depends on which court was the trial court. Remember the chart from Chapter 1 that identified the appellate court for each trial court. The rules discussed in this chapter are those for appeals from the Superior Court to the Courts of Appeal.

If a party loses in the Courts of Appeal, there is no automatic right to another appeal. Rather, the losing party must petition the Supreme Court to hear the appeal; the Supreme Court will hear the appeal only if the petition is granted. This petition is called a **petition for review.** Since petitions to the Supreme Court are rare, this chapter will focus on the appeals from a trial court to the courts of appeal.

The losing party in the trial court may file an appeal by filing a document called a **notice of appeal.** This notice must contain the name of the party or parties making the appeal. The notice must also state the judgment, or part of the judgment, that the party is appealing from. For example, the plaintiff may have obtained a judgment in the trial court against the defendant for breach of contract and received damages in the amount of $30,000. However, even though the plaintiff won, the plaintiff may not have been satisfied with the amount of the judgment. Therefore, the plaintiff would specify in the notice of appeal that the plaintiff is appealing from the amount of damages that has been awarded.

If the defendant were filing the appeal in this case, the defendant would probably want to appeal the entire judgment since the defendant lost on both the issues of liability and damages. The appeal must also contain the name of the court to which the appeal is taken. A sample notice of appeal is shown in Exhibit 17.6.

In California, the party bringing the appeal is called the **appellant.** The party defending against the appeal is called the **respondent.** This differs from federal court, where the party bringing the appeal is called the appellant, but the party responding is called the **appellee.**

Exhibit 17.6. Notice of Appeal

APP-002

ATTORNEY OR PARTY WITHOUT ATTORNEY *(Name, state bar number, and address)*:	**FOR COURT USE ONLY**

TELEPHONE NO.:   FAX NO. *(Optional)*:

E-MAIL ADDRESS *(Optional)*:

ATTORNEY FOR *(Name)*:

SUPERIOR COURT OF CALIFORNIA, COUNTY OF

STREET ADDRESS:

MAILING ADDRESS:

CITY AND ZIP CODE:

BRANCH NAME:

PLAINTIFF/PETITIONER:

DEFENDANT/RESPONDENT:

☐ **NOTICE OF APPEAL** ☐ **CROSS-APPEAL**
(UNLIMITED CIVIL CASE)

CASE NUMBER:

Notice: Please read *Information on Appeal Procedures for Unlimited Civil Cases* (Judicial Council form APP-001) before completing this form. This form must be filed in the superior court, not in the Court of Appeal.

1. NOTICE IS HEREBY GIVEN that *(name)*:

   appeals from the following judgment or order in this case, which was entered on *(date)*:

   ☐ Judgment after jury trial

   ☐ Judgment after court trial

   ☐ Default judgment

   ☐ Judgment after an order granting a summary judgment motion

   ☐ Judgment of dismissal under Code of Civil Procedure sections 581d, 583.250, 583.360, or 583.430

   ☐ Judgment of dismissal after an order sustaining a demurrer

   ☐ An order after judgment under Code of Civil Procedure section 904.1(a)(2)

   ☐ An order of judgment under Code of Civil Procedure section 904.1(a)(3)–(13)

   ☐ Other *(describe and specify code section that authorizes this appeal)*:

2. For cross-appeals only:

   a. Date notice of appeal was filed in original appeal:

   b. Date superior court clerk mailed notice of original appeal:

   c. Court of Appeal case number *(if known)*:

Date:

▶

_____   _____
(TYPE OR PRINT NAME)   (SIGNATURE OF PARTY OR ATTORNEY)

Page 1 of 2

Form Approved for Optional Use Judicial Council of California APP-002 [Rev. January 1, 2007]	**NOTICE OF APPEAL/CROSS-APPEAL (UNLIMITED CIVIL CASE)** (Appellate)	Cal. Rules of Court, rule 8.100 www.courtinfo.ca.gov American LegalNet, Inc. www.FormsWorkflow.com

Exhibit 17.6. Continued

	APP-002
CASE NAME:	CASE NUMBER:

NOTICE TO PARTIES: A copy of this document must be mailed or personally delivered to the other party or parties to this appeal. A PARTY TO THE APPEAL MAY NOT PERFORM THE MAILING OR DELIVERY HIMSELF OR HERSELF. A person who is at least 18 years old and is not a party to this appeal must complete the information below and mail (by first-class mail, postage prepaid) or personally deliver the front and back of this document. When the front and back of this document have been completed and a copy mailed or personally delivered, the original may then be filed with the court.

PROOF OF SERVICE

☐ **Mail**   ☐ **Personal Service**

1. At the time of service I was at least 18 years of age and **not a party to this legal action.**

2. My residence or business address is *(specify):*

3. I mailed or personally delivered a copy of the *Notice of Appeal/Cross-Appeal (Unlimited Civil Case)* as follows *(complete either a or b):*

   a. ☐ **Mail.** I am a resident of or employed in the county where the mailing occurred.

      (1) I enclosed a copy in an envelope **and**

         (a) ☐ **deposited** the sealed envelope with the United States Postal Service, with the postage fully prepaid.

         (b) ☐ **placed** the envelope for collection and mailing on the date and at the place shown in items below, following our ordinary business practices. I am readily familiar with this business's practice for collecting and processing correspondence for mailing. On the same day that correspondence is placed for collection and mailing, it is deposited in the ordinary course of business with the United States Postal Service, in a sealed envelope with postage fully prepaid.

      (2) The envelope was addressed and mailed as follows:

         (a) Name of person served:

         (b) Address on envelope:

         (c) Date of mailing:

         (d) Place of mailing *(city and state):*

   b. ☐ **Personal delivery.** I personally delivered a copy as follows:

      (1) Name of person served:

      (2) Address where delivered:

      (3) Date delivered:

      (4) Time delivered:

I declare under penalty of perjury under the laws of the State of California that the foregoing is true and correct.

Date:

▶

(TYPE OR PRINT NAME)	(SIGNATURE OF DECLARANT)

The notice of appeal is filed with the superior court. The clerk of the court will then mail out notice of the appeal to each party or their counsel of record. The fee for filing a notice of appeal is $265.00.

The notice of appeal must be filed within 60 days after the date of mailing by the clerk of the "notice of entry" of judgment. You must keep careful track of the dates so that an appeal is timely.

2. The record on appeal

As discussed in Chapter 1, an appellate court is limited to reviewing the record of the court below. Thus, there are no witnesses called to give testimony. Instead, the parties must submit to the appellate court the transcript of the trial court proceedings and any documents and exhibits that were filed in the trial court. The transcript, original documents, exhibits, and a copy of the docket sheet that lists all the documents that were filed in the trial court are collectively referred to as the **record on appeal.**

Record on appeal
The transcript and any documents and exhibits filed in trial court, which are submitted to the appellate court for review

Under Rule 8.130 of the CRC, the appellant has ten days from the filing of the notice of appeal to order the written transcript of the trial court proceedings from the court reporter. If there has been a trial, the appellant will generally request a transcript of the entire trial, unless the parties stipulated that a portion of the transcript does not need to be transcribed. The request must be in writing. A sample notice to prepare transcript is shown in Exhibit 17.7.

Rule 8.130 also governs situations when there is no transcript. In that case, the appellant may serve notice of a motion for leave to file an agreed statement or settled statement. An agreed statement is explained in Rule 8.134 of the CRC and must delineate the nature of the action, the basis of the reviewing court's jurisdiction, and how the superior court decided the points to be raised on appeal. The statement should recite only those facts needed to decide the appeal and must be signed by the parties. A settled statement is a narrative statement of the proceedings and the requirements governing such a statement are found in Rule 8.137 of the CRC.

Pursuant to Rule 8.120 of the CRC, the appellant also has ten days from the filing of the notice of appeal to serve and file a notice designating the "papers or records on file or lodged with the clerk, including the clerk's minutes, any written opinion of the superior court, affidavits, and written instructions given or refused, to be incorporated into the clerk's transcript." Alternatively, any party may serve and file with the clerk of the court an election, under Rule 8.124, to prepare an appendix containing the items normally contained in the clerk's transcript. The Judicial Council form used to designate the record on appeal is shown in Exhibit 17.8.

Exhibit 17.7.   Notice to Prepare Reporter's Transcript

THE SUPERIOR COURT OF THE STATE OF CALIFORNIA
FOR THE COUNTY OF LOS ANGELES

AMY BALDWIN Plaintiff, v. LJJ MOTOR COMPANY Defendant.	No. CIV 043519 NOTICE TO PREPARE REPORTER'S TRANSCRIPT

Notice is hereby given that appellant Amy Baldwin requests that the court reporter prepare a transcript of the trial in the above matter which commenced on September 1, 2006 and continued until September 8, 2006.

Dated: October 7, 2006

Mark Jacobs
Attorney for Amy Baldwin

---

3. Written briefs

Rules 8.200 through 8.224 of the CRC govern the content and format of the written briefs. The appellant's brief, called the **opening brief**, should contain the following items:

- A table of contents, with page numbers
- A table of cases (arranged alphabetically) and a list of all statutes used and other authorities cited, with a reference to the page of the brief where the case, statute, or authority appears
- A statement of the issues presented in the appeal
- A statement that the appeal is from a judgment that finally disposes of all issues between the parties or a statement explaining why the order or nonfinal judgment is appealable.
- A statement of the case, which is the procedural history of the case and how it was decided in the trial court
- A statement of facts relevant to the issues in the appeal
- An argument that contains the contentions of the appellant, the reasons for the contentions, and citations to appropriate authority
- A short conclusion that states the relief that you want on the appeal

Exhibit 17.8. Notice Designating Record on Appeal

APP-003

ATTORNEY OR PARTY WITHOUT ATTORNEY *(Name, state bar number, and address):*	FOR COURT USE ONLY

TELEPHONE NO.:   FAX NO. *(Optional)*:

E-MAIL ADDRESS *(Optional)*:

ATTORNEY FOR *(Name)*:

SUPERIOR COURT OF CALIFORNIA, COUNTY OF

STREET ADDRESS:

MAILING ADDRESS:

CITY AND ZIP CODE:

BRANCH NAME:

PLAINTIFF/PETITIONER:

DEFENDANT/RESPONDENT:

NOTICE DESIGNATING RECORD ON APPEAL (UNLIMITED CIVIL CASE)	Superior Court Case Number:
RE: Appeal filed on *(date)*:	Court of Appeal Case Number *(if known)*:

Notice: Please read *Information on Appeal Procedures for Unlimited Civil Cases* (Judicial Council form APP-001) before completing this form. This form must be filed in the superior court, not in the Court of Appeal.

TO: Clerk of the Superior Court of California, County of *(name of county)*:

NOTICE IS HEREBY GIVEN that *(name)*:

The ☐ Appellant ☐ Respondent in the above case elects to proceed with the following record on appeal:

(check only one)

1. ☐ (Appendix Only; no Reporter's Transcript)
   a. elects under rule 8.124 of the California Rules of Court to prepare own transcript in lieu of a court-prepared clerk's transcript.
   AND
   b. elects to have no reporter's transcript. *(Date and sign only.)*

2. ☐ (Appendix and Reporter's Transcript)
   a. elects under rule 8.124 of the California Rules of Court to prepare own transcript in lieu of a court-prepared clerk's transcript.
   AND
   b. elects a reporter's transcript as designated on page 3. *(Fill out the reporter's transcript section on page 3.)*

3. ☐ (Clerk's Transcript Only; no Reporter's Transcript)
   a. elects under rule 8.120 of the California Rules of Court to proceed with a clerk's transcript as designated on page 2. *(Fill out the clerk's transcript section on page 2.)*
   AND
   b. elects to have no reporter's transcript.

4. ☐ (Clerk's and Reporter's Transcripts)
   a. elects under rule 8.120 of the California Rules of Court to proceed with a clerk's transcript as designated on page 2. *(Fill out the clerk's transcript section on page 2*
   AND
   b. elects a reporter's transcript as designated on page 3. *(Fill out the reporter's transcript section on page 3.)*

Date:

►

_____   _____
(TYPE OR PRINT NAME)   (SIGNATURE OF PARTY OR ATTORNEY)

Page 1 of 4

Form Approved for Optional Use Judicial Council of California APP-003 [Rev. January 1, 2007]	**NOTICE DESIGNATING RECORD ON APPEAL (UNLIMITED CIVIL CASE)** (Appellate)	Cal. Rules of Court, rules 8.120, 8.124, 8.128, 8.130 www.courtinfo.ca.gov

American LegalNet, Inc.
www.FormsWorkflow.com

Exhibit 17.8. Continued

	APP-003
CASE NAME:	CASE NUMBER:

NOTICE DESIGNATING CLERK'S TRANSCRIPT
(Cal. Rules of Court, rule 8.120)

A. It is requested that the following documents in the superior court file be included in the clerk's transcript *(give the specific title of each document, an accurate description, and the date of filing)*:

Document Title and Description   Date of Filing

(NOTE: Items 1–7 are required to be a part of the clerk's transcript and will automatically be included.)

1. Notice of appeal

2. Notice designating record on appeal *(this document)*

3. Judgment or order appealed from

4. Notice of entry of judgment *(if any)*

5. Notice of intention to move for new trial or motion to vacate the judgment, for judgment notwithstanding the verdict, or for reconsideration of an appealed order *(if any)*

6. Ruling on item 5

7. Register of actions *(if any)*

8.

9.

10.

11.

12.

13.

14.

15.

16.

17.

B. It is requested that the following EXHIBITS admitted into evidence or marked for identification be copied into clerk's transcript on appeal *(check only one box)*:

1. ☐ All Exhibits

2. ☐ Specific Exhibits *(give the exhibit number [for example, Plaintiff's #1, Defendant's B, Respondent's A), a brief description, and admission status.)*:

☐ See additional pages.

APP-003 [Rev. January 1, 2007]	**NOTICE DESIGNATING RECORD ON APPEAL (UNLIMITED CIVIL CASE)** **(Appellate)**	Page 2 of 4

Exhibit 17.8. Continued

APP-003

CASE NAME:	CASE NUMBER:

NOTICE DESIGNATING REPORTER'S TRANSCRIPT
(Cal. Rules of Court, rule 8.130)

Reporter's Name	Dept.	Date	Nature of Proceedings
1.			
2.			
3.			
4.			
5.			
6.			
7.			
8.			
9.			
10.			
11.			
12.			
13.			
14.			
15.			
16.			
17.			
18.			
19.			

☐ See additional pages.

APP-003 [Rev. January 1, 2007] **NOTICE DESIGNATING RECORD ON APPEAL (UNLIMITED CIVIL CASE)** Page 3 of 4
(Appellate)

Exhibit 17.8. Continued

APP-003

CASE NAME:	CASE NUMBER:

NOTICE TO PARTIES: A copy of this document must be mailed or personally delivered to the other party or parties to this appeal. A PARTY TO THE APPEAL MAY NOT PERFORM THE MAILING OR DELIVERY HIMSELF OR HERSELF. A person who is at least 18 years old and is not a party to this appeal must complete the information below and mail (by first-class mail, postage prepaid) or personally deliver the front and back of this document. When the front and back of this document have been completed and a copy mailed or personally delivered, the original may then be filed with the court.

PROOF OF SERVICE
☐ **Mail** ☐ **Personal Service**

1. At the time of service I was at least 18 years of age and **not a party to this legal action.**

2. My residence or business address is *(specify):*

3. I mailed or personally delivered a copy of the *Notice Designating Record on Appeal (Unlimited Civil Case)* as follows *(complete either a or b)*:

    a. ☐ **Mail.** I am a resident of or employed in the county where the mailing occurred.

        (1) I enclosed a copy in an envelope **and**

           (a) ☐ **deposited** the sealed envelope with the United States Postal Service, with the postage fully prepaid.

           (b) ☐ **placed** the envelope for collection and mailing on the date and at the place shown in items below, following our ordinary business practices. I am readily familiar with this business's practice for collecting and processing correspondence for mailing. On the same day that correspondence is placed for collection and mailing, it is deposited in the ordinary course of business with the United States Postal Service, in a sealed envelope with postage fully prepaid.

        (2) The envelope was addressed and mailed as follows:

           (a) Name of person served:

           (b) Address on envelope:

           (c) Date of mailing:

           (d) Place of mailing *(city and state):*

    b. ☐ **Personal delivery.** I personally delivered a copy as follows:

        (1) Name of person served:

        (2) Address where delivered:

        (3) Date delivered:

        (4) Time delivered:

I declare under penalty of perjury under the laws of the State of California that the foregoing is true and correct.

Date:

▶

_____   _____
(TYPE OR PRINT NAME)   (SIGNATURE OF DECLARANT)

APP-003 [Rev. January 1, 2007]   **NOTICE DESIGNATING RECORD ON APPEAL (UNLIMITED CIVIL CASE)**   Page 4 of 4
(Appellate)

One item in this list, the argument, requires explanation. The argument is very similar to a memorandum of points and authorities that accompanies a motion. However, in an appellate brief, the argument needs to include a section on the appropriate **standard of review**. A standard of review is how the appellate court should look at the issues in making a decision. For example, depending on the issues, the court may look to see whether there is substantial evidence to support the judgment of the court. If there is substantial evidence to support the judgment, the judgment will be affirmed. Another standard of review is to look to see if there was any procedural error that prejudiced your side. You will need to do legal research to determine what the standard of review is for your case. In many cases, treatises and handbooks on appeals will be helpful to you in determining the standard of review.

Standard of review Determines how an appellate court should look at the issues in deciding an appeal

After the appellant files and serves a written brief, the respondent has 30 days to serve and file a response to the appellant's brief. The respondent's brief should contain the following:

♦ A statement of the issues
♦ A statement of the case
♦ A statement of the standard of review
♦ An argument that responds to the contentions of the appellant.

Rule 8.212 provides specific rules on the type size that may be used in briefs, and the covers that must appear on each brief submitted.

4. The paralegal's role

As indicated in this chapter, the appellate process is governed by detailed court rules. To ensure that all deadlines and rules are met, keep a chart such as the one in Exhibit 17.9 for every case that identifies the deadline for any appeal, whether an appeal is filed, the deadline for filing cross-appeals, whether a cross-appeal is filed, and dates for filing written briefs. This chart should be kept regardless of whether you represent the party appealing the judgment or the responding party.

The chart should be expanded to include any special rules for your particular court, such as filing notices to the reporter to prepare the trial transcript, requests for extensions of time to file written briefs, and the time for filing any appellate motions.

If your side is appealing the judgment, you can assist in analyzing the trial transcript to locate any **prejudicial errors**. The prejudicial errors that may justify grounds for appeal include objections that were improperly ruled on by the judge, evidence that was improperly denied or admitted, or jury instructions improperly given or denied.

Prejudicial errors Errors that occur in the trial that, if such errors had not occurred, might have changed the outcome of the trial

Exhibit 17.9. Appellate Process Chart

Date judgment was entered	
Deadline for filing appeal	
Was appeal filed?	
Deadline for filing cross-appeal	
Was cross-appeal filed?	
Deadline for opening brief	
Deadline for responding brief	
Deadline for reply brief	

If your side is defending against the appeal, your analysis of the trial transcript will focus on locating trial excerpts that show that there were no errors or, at a minimum, the error claimed by the opposing side did not affect the trial outcome. For example, if the trial judge refused to allow a witness to testify to certain evidence, perhaps similar evidence was admitted through another witness. Thus, any error was harmless and should not justify a reversal.

In addition to analyzing the trial records, the paralegal can provide writing and research support to the lawyer. Written briefs by all parties will need to be submitted to the court. Thus, excerpts from the records will need to be woven into a statement of the facts. In addition, the paralegal can assist with conducting research for legal authority to support the client's position. In fact, the experienced paralegal can take full responsibility for the appellate process, leaving only minimal supervision and oral argument to the lawyer.

CHAPTER SUMMARY

This chapter has outlined all the essential steps for successful trial preparation. Adequate trial preparation is not only necessary for presentation of the case at trial but also to help evaluate the case for settlement purposes.

As part of the trial preparation, you may be asked to draft a pretrial memorandum. Many courts require a pretrial conference between the parties and the trial judge. If a pretrial conference is held, prepare a memorandum in advance of the conference. Even if such a memorandum is not required by the local rules, prepare a memorandum nevertheless for it will help familiarize the judge with the various issues in the lawsuit. The memorandum generally contains sections on uncontested facts, contested issues of fact and law, exhibits, witnesses, and jury instructions.

As the case proceeds to trial, organize the litigation files for easy access during trial. The files should include file folders for court papers, evidence, and attorney's records. The material to be used at trial should be organized using either the divider method or the trial notebook method.

During trial preparation the lawyer will develop a theory of the case. A theory of the case is the lawyer's position on, and approach to, all the evidence that will be presented at trial. The theory of the case will influence the approaches taken to each phase of the trial. To adequately assist with trial preparation, the paralegal should be familiar with the theory of the case.

Even though witnesses have been prepared for deposition during the discovery phase, trial preparation requires that witnesses be specifically prepared for testifying at trials. Use the checklist in this chapter in conducting the preparation of trial witnesses. Similarly, documents gathered in discovery must be marked as trial exhibits. Some exhibits may need to be enlarged and mounted for use at trial.

During trial the paralegal will be an integral part of the litigation team. Some of the paralegal responsibilities during trial include recording information during jury voir dire, taking notes of each witness' testimony, keeping the exhibit chart, arranging for on-call witnesses to be present at the appropriate time, and setting up any equipment for demonstrative evidence.

Once the trial is over, one or more parties may appeal the judgment. If an appeal is brought, trial transcripts must be carefully analyzed and written briefs prepared for submission to the appellate court.

KEY TERMS

Appellant

Appellee

Case-in-chief

Closing argument

Demonstrative evidence

Divider method

Exhibit chart

For cause

Jury chart

Notice of appeal

On-call witnesses

Opening argument

Opening brief

Peremptory challenge

Petition for review

Prejudicial errors

Pretrial order

Rebuttal evidence

Record on appeal

Respondent

Standard of review

Strike system

Surrebuttal

Theory of the case

Trial box

Trial chart

Trial notebook method

Voir dire

Witness list

REVIEW QUESTIONS

1. Identify the two ways that trial material may be organized. What are the advantages and disadvantages of each method?

2. What does the phrase "theory of the case" mean? Why is it important to develop a theory of the case in advance of trial?

3. Why is it necessary to serve nonparty witnesses with a subpoena to appear at trial?

4. How can a paralegal assist a lawyer with the voir dire of the jury?

5. What is the role of the paralegal during trial? What ethical considerations should govern your conduct during the trial?

6. What is the process for starting an appeal?

7. Why is it important to keep a chart of all deadlines during the appellate process?

INTERNET RESOURCES

www.chesslaw.com/freebriefs.htm
www.courtinfo.ca.gov/rules
www.findlegalforms.com
www.formsguru.com

CHAPTER **18**

Enforcement of Judgments

CHAPTER OBJECTIVES

This chapter provides a checklist of the various methods available for enforcing a judgment. You will become familiar with:

♦ How to draft a demand letter
♦ Why you should record an abstract of judgment
♦ When you should file a notice of lien
♦ When a writ of execution is required
♦ What the differences are between a till tap, a keeper, and a bank levy
♦ How to locate assets of the debtor

A. INTRODUCTION

Now that the trial is over and you have a judgment, what do you do next? The client obviously will be pleased if a favorable monetary judgment has been rendered in her favor, but complete satisfaction only will be had once the money is in the client's hand. Not surprisingly, many defendants against whom a judgment has been entered do not automatically turn over payment to the plaintiff without sufficient prodding. Once judgment is obtained, there are several steps you can take to see that your client's rights are protected and to maximize a quick payment on the judgment.

Use the steps in this chapter as a checklist to help identify what action you should take in enforcing money judgments. Other remedies, such as claim and delivery of specific property or injunctions, have been discussed in previous chapters.

B. DEMAND LETTER

Judgment debtor
The party that owes the money

The easiest and quickest step to take is to send a **demand letter** for payment on the judgment. Although the **judgment debtor**, the party that owes money, may not send a check for the entire amount, you may be able to elicit an offer to pay a reduced sum or to pay in installments. Both options should be considered by your client if you and the lawyer believe it may be difficult to ever collect the full amount of the judgment from the debtor. The letter may be sent to the judgment debtor directly or, if represented by counsel, the judgment debtor's counsel.

Although you may draft the demand letter, the lawyer should sign the letter. A typical demand letter is shown in Exhibit 18.1.

Exhibit 18.1. Demand Letter

Mr. J.J. Jones
123 Main Street
Los Angeles, California 93048

Re: Smith v. Jones

Dear Mr. Jones:

As you are aware, on June 1, 2006, a judgment was entered against you and in favor of our client Susan Smith. The amount of the judgment, plus interest to date, is $37,141.96. Interest continues to accrue at the daily rate of $10.14. Accordingly, demand is hereby made upon you to pay the entire sum due on or before July 1, 2006. Your personal check, cashier's check, or money order should be made payable to Susan Smith and sent to my attention at the above address. Once your check has cleared, we will file an acknowledgment of satisfaction of judgment and cease all further enforcement activities.

If we do not receive your payment, we will have no choice but to continue our enforcement activities, the cost of which will be charged against you.

We look forward to your prompt payment.

Sincerely,

_____
Ann Medcalf

C. ABSTRACTS OF JUDGMENT AND NOTICES OF LIEN

Pursuant to CCP §697.060, an **abstract of judgment** places a **lien** on all real property owned by the debtor. The lien continues for a period of 10 years and the lien will also attach to any property the debtor acquires for a period of time after the recording of the lien. When a lien is recorded, it places all buyers of the property on notice of your client's claim against the judgment debtor. The property cannot be sold until your client's judgment is satisfied. If it is sold, the buyer must take the property subject to the lien. Naturally, few buyers are willing to take on such obligations.

Lien
A claim by the creditor against property of the debtor as security for the debt

A **notice of judgment lien** also may be filed to create a lien on personal property of the debtor. The judgment lien will last for 5 years from the date of filing or until the judgment is satisfied or the judgment lien is released.

Although these remedies can be very effective in obtaining payment of your client's judgment, they also have their drawbacks. If the debtor is not paying your client, it is likely he has other creditors who are not being paid. If a senior lienholder forecloses on the property, your client's lien will be extinguished unless there is sufficient equity in the property to pay the junior liens. However, this drawback should never discourage you from recording an abstract of judgment, since an abstract of judgment is simple and inexpensive.

The form for the abstract of judgment is shown in Exhibit 18.2. The abstract of judgment will need to be recorded in all geographical areas in which the debtor owns property. The notice of judgment lien is also a Judicial Council form. A sample form is shown in Exhibit 18.3.

D. WRITS OF EXECUTION

Code of Civil Procedure §699.510 provides, in part, that "after entry of a money judgment, a writ of execution shall be issued by the clerk of the court upon application of the judgment creditor and shall be directed to the levying officer in the county where the levy is to be made and to any registered process server." A **writ of execution** is an order from the court empowering the sheriff, marshal, or other appropriate law enforcement agency to **levy** upon the assets of the debtor in order to satisfy the judgment. The writ of execution, although sounding impressive, is a form that is filled out by the judgment creditor and issued by the clerk of the court. Upon issuance of the writ of execution, the judgment creditor can transfer the writ to the sheriff, marshal, or other agency, with instructions to levy upon certain assets of the judgment debtor. A sample form is shown in Exhibit 18.4. There are primarily three types of levies: the till tap, the keeper, and the bank levy.

Levy
The procedure by which assets of the debtor are seized for satisfaction of a judgment

1. The till tap

If the judgment debtor is the owner of a business, or if the debtor is a business entity, a **till tap** is an effective method to collect the cash and checks on hand at the business. The law enforcement agent will go into the business and stay for a short period of time, usually no more than three or four hours. During this time, the agent will collect any cash or checks that are in the register or that come into the business while the law enforcement agent is present.

Till tap
Collection of cash and checks on hand at a business in order to satisfy a judgment

Exhibit 18.2. Abstract of Judgment

EJ-001

ATTORNEY OR PARTY WITHOUT ATTORNEY *(Name, address, State Bar number, and telephone number):*

Recording requested by and return to:

☐ ATTORNEY FOR ☐ JUDGMENT CREDITOR ☐ ASSIGNEE OF RECORD

SUPERIOR COURT OF CALIFORNIA, COUNTY OF

STREET ADDRESS:

MAILING ADDRESS:

CITY AND ZIP CODE:

BRANCH NAME:

FOR RECORDER'S USE ONLY

PLAINTIFF:

DEFENDANT:

CASE NUMBER:

ABSTRACT OF JUDGMENT—CIVIL AND SMALL CLAIMS ☐ **Amended**

FOR COURT USE ONLY

1. The ☐ judgment creditor ☐ assignee of record applies for an abstract of judgment and represents the following:
   a. Judgment debtor's

   ⌐ Name and last known address ⌐

   b. Driver's license No. and state: ☐ Unknown
   c. Social security No.: ☐ Unknown
   d. Summons or notice of entry of sister-state judgment was personally served or mailed to *(name and address):*

2. ☐ Information on additional judgment debtors is shown on page 2.

3. Judgment creditor *(name and address):*

4. ☐ Information on additional judgment creditors is shown on page 2.

5. ☐ Original abstract recorded in this county:
   a. Date:
   b. Instrument No.:

Date:

_____
(TYPE OR PRINT NAME)

▶ _____
(SIGNATURE OF APPLICANT OR ATTORNEY)

6. Total amount of judgment as entered or last renewed:
   $

7. All judgment creditors and debtors are listed on this abstract.

8. a. Judgment entered on *(date):*
   b. Renewal entered on *(date):*

9. ☐ This judgment is an installment judgment.

[SEAL]

This abstract issued on *(date):*

10. ☐ An ☐ execution lien ☐ attachment lien is endorsed on the judgment as follows:
    a. Amount: $
    b. In favor of *(name and address):*

11. A stay of enforcement has
    a. ☐ not been ordered by the court.
    b. ☐ been ordered by the court effective until *(date):*

12. a. ☐ I certify that this is a true and correct abstract of the judgment entered in this action.
    b. ☐ A certified copy of the judgment is attached.

Clerk, by _____ , Deputy

Form Adopted for Mandatory Use
Judicial Council of California
EJ-001 [Rev. January 1, 2006]

ABSTRACT OF JUDGMENT—CIVIL AND SMALL CLAIMS

Page 1 of 2
Code of Civil Procedure, §§ 488.480, 674, 700.190

American LegalNet, Inc.
www.USCourtForms.com

Exhibit 18.2. Continued

PLAINTIFF:	CASE NUMBER:
DEFENDANT:	

NAMES AND ADDRESSES OF ADDITIONAL JUDGMENT CREDITORS:

13. Judgment creditor *(name and address):*   14. Judgment creditor *(name and address):*

15. ☐ Continued on Attachment 15.

INFORMATION ON ADDITIONAL JUDGMENT DEBTORS:

16.   Name and last known address   17.   Name and last known address

Driver's license No. & state: ☐ Unknown   Driver's license No. & state: ☐ Unknown
Social security No.: ☐ Unknown   Social security No.: ☐ Unknown
Summons was personally served at or mailed to *(address):*   Summons was personally served at or mailed to *(address):*

18.   Name and last known address   19.   Name and last known address

Driver's license No. & state: ☐ Unknown   Driver's license No. & state: ☐ Unknown
Social security No.: ☐ Unknown   Social security No.: ☐ Unknown
Summons was personally served at or mailed to *(address):*   Summons was personally served at or mailed to *(address):*

20.   Name and last known address   21.   Name and last known address

Driver's license No. & state: ☐ Unknown   Driver's license No. & state: ☐ Unknown
Social security No.: ☐ Unknown   Social security No.: ☐ Unknown
Summons was personally served at or mailed to *(address):*   Summons was personally served at or mailed to *(address):*

22. ☐ Continued on Attachment 22.

EJ-001 [Rev. January 1, 2006]   **ABSTRACT OF JUDGMENT—CIVIL AND SMALL CLAIMS**   Page 2 of 2

Exhibit 18.3. Notice of Lien

AT-180/EJ-185

ATTORNEY OR PARTY WITHOUT ATTORNEY *(Name and Address):*	TELEPHONE NO.:	*FOR COURT USE ONLY*

ATTORNEY FOR LIEN CLAIMANT:

NAME OF COURT:
STREET ADDRESS:
MAILING ADDRESS:
CITY AND ZIP CODE:
BRANCH NAME:

PLAINTIFF:

DEFENDANT:

NOTICE OF LIEN **(Attachment—Enforcement of Judgment)**	CASE NUMBER:

ALL PARTIES IN THIS ACTION ARE NOTIFIED THAT

1. A lien is created by this notice under
   a. ☐ Article 3 (commencing with section 491.410) of Chapter 11 of Title 6.5 of Part 2 of the Code of Civil Procedure.
   b. ☐ Article 5 (commencing with section 708.410) of Chapter 6 of Title 9 of Part 2 of the Code of Civil Procedure.
2. The lien is based on a
   a. ☐ right to attach order and an order permitting the creation of a lien (copies attached).
   b. ☐ money judgment.
3. The right to attach order or the money judgment is entered in the following action:
   a. Title of court *(specify):*
   b. Name of case *(specify):*
   c. Number of case *(specify):*
   d. ☐ Date of entry of judgment *(specify):*
   e. ☐ Dates of renewal of judgment *(specify):*
4. The name and address of the judgment creditor or person who obtained the right to attach order are *(specify):*

5. The name and last known address of the judgment debtor or person whose property is subject to the right to attach order are *(specify):*

6. The amount required to satisfy the judgment creditor's money judgment or to secure the amount to be secured by the attachment at the time this notice of lien is filed is $
7. The lien created by this notice attaches to any cause of action of the person named in item 5 that is the subject of this action or proceeding and to that person's rights to money or property under any judgment subsequently procured in this action or proceeding.
8. No compromise, dismissal, settlement, or satisfaction of this action or proceeding or any of the rights of the person named in item 5 to money or property under any judgment procured in this action or proceeding may be entered into by or on behalf of that person, and that person may not enforce any rights to money or property under any judgment procured in this action or proceeding by a writ or otherwise, unless one of the following requirements is satisfied:

   a. the prior approval by order of the court in this action or proceeding has been obtained;
   b. the written consent of the person named in item 4 has been obtained or that person has released the lien; or
   c. the money judgment of the person named in item 4 has been satisfied.

> **NOTICE The person named in item 5 may claim an exemption for all or any portion of the money or property within 30 days after receiving notice of the creation of the lien. The exemption is waived if it is not claimed in time.**

Date:

▶

_____   _____
(TYPE OR PRINT NAME)   *(SIGNATURE OF LIEN CLAIMANT OR ATTORNEY)*

Form Approved by the Judicial Council of California AT-180/EJ-185 [New January 1, 1985]	**NOTICE OF LIEN** **(Attachment—Enforcement of Judgment)**	CCP 491.410. 708.410
		American LegalNet, Inc. www.USCourtForms.com

Exhibit 18.4.   Writ of Execution

EJ-130

ATTORNEY OR PARTY WITHOUT ATTORNEY *(Name, State Bar number and address):*	*FOR COURT USE ONLY*

TELEPHONE NO.:   FAX NO. *(Optional):*

E-MAIL ADDRESS *(Optional):*

ATTORNEY FOR *(Name):*

☐ ATTORNEY FOR   ☐ JUDGMENT CREDITOR   ☐ ASSIGNEE OF RECORD

SUPERIOR COURT OF CALIFORNIA, COUNTY OF

STREET ADDRESS:

MAILING ADDRESS:

CITY AND ZIP CODE:

BRANCH NAME:

PLAINTIFF:

DEFENDANT:

WRIT OF	☐ **EXECUTION (Money Judgment)** ☐ **POSSESSION OF** ☐ **Personal Property** ☐ **Real Property** ☐ **SALE**	CASE NUMBER:

1. **To the Sheriff or Marshal of the County of:**

   You are directed to enforce the judgment described below with daily interest and your costs as provided by law.

2. **To any registered process server:** You are authorized to serve this writ only in accord with CCP 699.080 or CCP 715.040.

3. *(Name):*

   is the ☐ judgment creditor ☐ assignee of record   whose address is shown on this form above the court's name.

4. **Judgment debtor** *(name and last known address):*

   ☐ Additional judgment debtors on next page

5. **Judgment entered** on *(date):*

6. ☐ **Judgment renewed** on *(dates):*

7. **Notice of sale** under this writ
   a. ☐ has not been requested.
   b. ☐ has been requested *(see next page)*.
8. ☐ Joint debtor information on next page.

[SEAL]

9. ☐ See next page for information on real or personal property to be delivered under a writ of possession or sold under a writ of sale.

10. ☐ This writ is issued on a sister-state judgment.

11. Total judgment . . . . $

12. Costs after judgment (per filed order or memo CCP 685.090) . . . . $

13. Subtotal *(add 11 and 12)* . . . . $

14. Credits . . . . $

15. Subtotal *(subtract 14 from 13)* . . . . . . $

16. Interest after judgment (per filed affidavit CCP 685.050) (not on GC 6103.5 fees). . . $

17. Fee for issuance of writ . . . . $

18. **Total** *(add 15, 16, and 17)* . . . . $

19. Levying officer:
   (a) Add daily interest from date of writ *(at the legal rate on 15)* (not on GC 6103.5 fees) of. . . . . . . $
   (b) Pay directly to court costs included in 11 and 17 (GC 6103.5, 68511.3; CCP 699.520(i)) . . . . $

20. ☐ The amounts called for in items 11–19 are different for each debtor. These amounts are stated for each debtor on Attachment 20.

Issued on *(date):* _____   Clerk, by _____ , Deputy

NOTICE TO PERSON SERVED: SEE NEXT PAGE FOR IMPORTANT INFORMATION.

Page 1 of 2

Form Approved for Optional Use
Judicial Council of California
EJ-130 [Rev. January 1, 2006]

WRIT OF EXECUTION

Code of Civil Procedure, §§ 699.520, 712.010,
Government Code, § 6103.5
www.courtinfo.ca.gov
American LegalNet, Inc.
www.USCourtForms.com

Exhibit 18.4. Continued

	EJ-130
PLAINTIFF:	CASE NUMBER:
DEFENDANT:	

— Items continued from page 1—

21. ☐ **Additional judgment debtor** *(name and last known address):*

22. ☐ **Notice of sale** has been requested by *(name and address):*

23. ☐ **Joint debtor** was declared bound by the judgment (CCP 989–994)
   a. on *(date):*   a. on *(date):*
   b. name and address of joint debtor: b. name and address of joint debtor:

   c. ☐ additional costs against certain joint debtors *(itemize):*

24. ☐ *(Writ of Possession* or *Writ of Sale)* **Judgment** was entered for the following:
   a. ☐ Possession of real property: The complaint was filed on *(date):*
      (Check (1) or (2)):
      (1) ☐ The Prejudgment Claim of Right to Possession was served in compliance with CCP 415.46.
         The judgment includes all tenants, subtenants, named claimants, and other occupants of the premises.
      (2) ☐ The Prejudgment Claim of Right to Possession was NOT served in compliance with CCP 415.46.
         (a) $ was the daily rental value on the date the complaint was filed.
         (b) The court will hear objections to enforcement of the judgment under CCP 1174.3 on the following
            dates *(specify):*
   b. ☐ Possession of personal property.
      ☐ If delivery cannot be had, then for the value *(itemize in 9e)* specified in the judgment or supplemental order.
   c. ☐ Sale of personal property.
   d. ☐ Sale of real property.
   e. Description of property:

NOTICE TO PERSON SERVED

WRIT OF EXECUTION OR SALE. Your rights and duties are indicated on the accompanying *Notice of Levy* (Form EJ-150).
WRIT OF POSSESSION OF PERSONAL PROPERTY. If the levying officer is not able to take custody of the property, the levying officer will make a demand upon you for the property. If custody is not obtained following demand, the judgment may be enforced as a money judgment for the value of the property specified in the judgment or in a supplemental order.
WRIT OF POSSESSION OF REAL PROPERTY. If the premises are not vacated within five days after the date of service on the occupant or, if service is by posting, within five days after service on you, the levying officer will remove the occupants from the real property and place the judgment creditor in possession of the property. Except for a mobile home, personal property remaining on the premises will be sold or otherwise disposed of in accordance with CCP 1174 unless you or the owner of the property pays the judgment creditor the reasonable cost of storage and takes possession of the personal property not later than 15 days after the time the judgment creditor takes possession of the premises.
► *A Claim of Right to Possession form accompanies this writ (unless the Summons was served in compliance with CCP 415.46).*

| EJ-130 [Rev. January 1, 2006] | **WRIT OF EXECUTION** | Page 2 of 2 |

The length of time you want to instruct the agent to remain on the premises depends on the type of business of the debtor. If the business is, say, a furniture store and does not have very much walk-in trade, you may want to instruct the law enforcement agent to collect the funds on hand when the agent arrives, but not stay on the premises. However, if the business is a fast-food restaurant, keeping the agent on the premises through the lunch hour may be enough to satisfy the debt owed to your client. Keep in mind that it is expensive to have a law enforcement agent stay on the premises. Accordingly, instruct the agent to stay only as long as you believe it is worthwhile. The judgment creditor usually can charge the expense by adding the expense to the judgment. However, this is little comfort if the judgment creditor is unlikely to recover the entire amount of the judgment from the debtor.

2. The keeper

Keeper
A law enforcement agent who stays on the premises of a business and collects cash or checks sufficient to satisfy a judgment

Similar to a till tap is the installation of a **keeper**. A keeper will stay at the business premises for a longer period of time, usually 24 to 48 hours. During this time, the keeper collects any money that comes into the business. At the end of the time, if sufficient funds have not been collected, the keeper will take possession of personal property. This property will be sold at an execution of sale, and proceeds sufficient to satisfy the judgment will be given to the judgment creditor. Any excess funds would, of course, go back to the judgment debtor.

The real value of this method is that once a keeper is installed, debtors are usually very anxious to negotiate a payment with the judgment creditor. Thus, it is likely that you will receive a telephone call from the debtor shortly after the keeper arrives on the premises.

As with a till tap, the keeper also is a member of a law enforcement agency. Since not all law enforcement agencies will install a keeper, check with the agency before sending instructions and the writ of execution.

3. The bank levy

Bank levy
A seizure of funds held in a debtor's bank account

If the judgment debtor is an individual who does not own his own business, the choices for enforcing the judgment are more limited. The most common enforcement technique is the **bank levy**. If you know the name and location of the debtor's bank, you can instruct the law enforcement agency to levy upon all funds in the debtor's bank account. It is not necessary that you know the account number. However, you will need to know the particular branch office if the bank has more than one office.

Upon notice of the levy, the bank will turn over to the law enforcement agency serving the notice all funds in the debtor's account on the date the notice is received, up to the amount necessary to satisfy the judgment. This procedure usually works only once. After the debtor learns of the levy, it is likely he will close his account or, at a minimum, not deposit any additional sums at that particular branch.

E. WAGE GARNISHMENTS

A **wage garnishment** is a direction to the employer of the judgment debtor to withhold a certain amount of money from each paycheck of the debtor for a limited period of time. The application for a wage garnishment, must be made on the official Judicial Council form. A sample form is shown in Exhibit 18.5. In California, there are exemptions for child support and taxes. Federal law also provides for certain exemptions. Unless the amount of judgment is small, it is unlikely that a wage garnishment will ever satisfy the full amount of the judgment.

F. LOCATING ASSETS

All the methods discussed for enforcement of judgments are fine, so long as you know what property and assets the debtor owns. If you do not know, you will need to attempt to locate the assets before you can give instructions to the law enforcement agency.

There are several steps you can take to locate assets of the debtor. The first step is to check with the client to see what information the client has about the debtor. For example, the client may have a returned check from the debtor, a financial application, or a report from a credit reporting agency.

If the client does not have sufficient information, your next step is to take discovery from the debtor. This discovery can be in the form of post-judgment written interrogatories or an oral examination of a debtor. The advantage of requiring the debtor to submit to a debtor's examination rather than responding to interrogatories is time. Obviously, you will be able to obtain quicker results if the debtor is required to respond orally to the location and identification of his assets. The disadvantage is that the debtor may state during the examination that he does not recall certain information. For this reason, you should always request that the debtor bring with him documents such as check ledgers, savings account numbers, and grant deeds so the debtor can refer to the documents to answer questions.

If you are still unable to locate assets of the debtor, either because you do not have sufficient information or you suspect the debtor is hiding assets, you may wish to hire a private investigator. A private investigator will locate real property and bank accounts of the debtor. Many

Exhibit 18.5.   Wage Garnishment

WG-001

ATTORNEY OR PARTY WITHOUT ATTORNEY *(Name, State Bar number, and address):* TELEPHONE NO.:	LEVYING OFFICER *(Name and Address):*

ATTORNEY FOR *(Name):*

NAME OF COURT, JUDICIAL DISTRICT, OR BRANCH COURT, IF ANY:

PLAINTIFF:

DEFENDANT:

APPLICATION FOR EARNINGS WITHHOLDING ORDER (Wage Garnishment)	LEVYING OFFICER FILE NO.:	COURT CASE NO.:

TO THE SHERIFF OR ANY MARSHAL OR CONSTABLE OF THE COUNTY OF
OR ANY REGISTERED PROCESS SERVER

1. The judgment creditor *(name):*

requests issuance of an Earnings Withholding Order directing the employer to withhold the earnings of the judgment debtor (employee).

    Name and address of employer   Name and address of employee

2. The amounts withheld are to be paid to   Social Security Number *(if known):*
   a. ☐ The attorney (or party without an attorney)   b. ☐ Other *(name, address, and telephone):*
   named at the top of this page.

3. a. Judgment was entered on *(date):*
   b. Collect the amount directed by the Writ of Execution unless a lesser amount is specified here:
   $

4. ☐ The Writ of Execution was issued to collect delinquent amounts payable for the **support** of a child, former spouse, or spouse of the employee.

5. ☐ Special instructions *(specify):*

6. *(Check a or b)*
   a. ☐ I have not previously obtained an order directing this employer to withhold the earnings of this employee.
      —OR—
   b. ☐ I have previously obtained such an order, but that order *(check one):*
       ☐ was terminated by a court order, but I am entitled to apply for another Earnings Withholding Order under the provisions of Code of Civil Procedure section 706.105(h).
       ☐ was ineffective.

_____ ▶ _____
     (TYPE OR PRINT NAME)   *(SIGNATURE OF ATTORNEY OR PARTY WITHOUT ATTORNEY)*

I declare under penalty of perjury under the laws of the State of California that the foregoing is true and correct.

Date:

  ▶

_____ _____
     (TYPE OR PRINT NAME)   *(SIGNATURE OF DECLARANT)*

Page 1 of 1

Form Adopted by the Judicial Council of California WG-001 [Rev. January 1, 2007]	**APPLICATION FOR EARNINGS WITHHOLDING ORDER** (Wage Garnishment)	Code Civ. Procedure, § 706.121 www.courtinfo.ca.gov American LegalNet, Inc. www.FormsWorkflow.com

investigators charge their fees based on the number of bank accounts or property they are able to locate. Since retaining an investigator can be expensive, this should be your last resort.

CHAPTER SUMMARY

There are several methods to enforce a judgment. The easiest and quickest method is to send a letter demanding payment. However, this method is rarely successful, and the paralegal's job is to be familiar with the other ways a judgment can be enforced. This chapter has described some of the more common methods of enforcement.

Abstracts of judgments place a lien on all real property owned by the debtor. This method can be very effective if the debtor owns real property and there are not many senior lienholders.

A writ of execution must be obtained before a sheriff, marshal, or other law enforcement agent can levy against any assets of the debtor. If a writ of execution is obtained, the judgment creditor may request a till tap, installation of a keeper, or a bank levy. The method chosen will depend on the nature of the assets held by the debtor. If the debtor is employed, the writ of execution can be used to obtain a garnishment of the debtor's wages.

Each of the enforcement of judgment methods requires that you know where the assets of the debtor are located. In attempting to locate assets, you can check with the client for information, propound post-judgment interrogatories, or conduct a debtor examination.

KEY TERMS

Abstract of judgment	Levy
Bank levy	Lien
Demand letter	Till tap
Judgment debtor	Wage garnishment
Keeper	Writ of execution

REVIEW QUESTIONS

1. What is the purpose of an abstract of judgment? Why is an abstract of judgment an effective way to enforce a judgment?

2. What is a "writ of execution"?

3. Identify the differences between a till tap and the installation of a keeper. What are the advantages and disadvantages of each?

4. How can a judgment creditor obtain funds in a judgment debtor's bank account?

5. Identify at least three ways you can obtain information about the location of the debtor's assets.

INTERNET RESOURCES

The sources below may be helpful to you in enforcing judgments or attempting to find information about assets of a judgment debtor:

www.abika.com/reports/samples/howtofindassets.htm
www.ask.com
www.ag.ca.gov/consumers/general/small.php
www.dca.ca.gov/legal/small_claims/index.html

CHAPTER **19**

Alternative Dispute Resolution

CHAPTER OBJECTIVES

This chapter introduces you to the alternatives to resolving disputes through the litigation process. You will learn:

◆ What the differences are between arbitration and mediation
◆ How to submit a claim to private arbitration
◆ Why parties may wish to arbitrate a claim
◆ When parties must arbitrate their disputes

A. INTRODUCTION

Arbitration
The submission by the parties of their dispute to an impartial tribunal for resolution

Neutrals
Term used for arbitrator in judicial arbitration cases by some courts

With the increasing costs of litigation, alternative dispute resolution is becoming a popular alternative to the court system. **Arbitration** is the parties' submission of their dispute to an impartial tribunal for resolution by one or more arbitrators. In some cases, arbitration will be required by the courts, or the parties may wish to stipulate to have the matter heard before an arbitrator. In other cases, the parties may prefer to attempt to reach a settlement of a case by referring the case to mediation.

In California any matter filed in the superior court in which the amount in controversy is less than $50,000 is subject to mandatory arbitration. Pursuant to California Rules of Court (CRC) Rule 3.221, the plaintiff must serve each defendant at the time of serving the complaint, an Alternative Dispute Resolution (ADR) packet. This packet can be obtained from the court at the time the complaint is filed. Local rules may also provide for arbitration in other cases. For example, Los Angeles Superior Court Local Rules provide for selection of ADR **neutrals** to hear the case, as well as the hearing process. Arbitration of smaller matters helps to ease the court backlog and can provide a quicker and less expensive forum for the parties. Arbitration through the court system is referred to as **judicial arbitration.** Unless otherwise agreed to by the parties, judicial arbitration is nonbinding. This means that the parties have a right to either appeal the arbitrator's decision to a court of law or in some cases obtain a new trial in the court.

In addition to arbitration through the court, nonjudicial arbitration is available through private agencies and is usually paid for by the parties. The most frequently used private agency is the **American Arbitration Association** (AAA), which has offices in over 38 cities. Arbitration administered through agencies such as the AAA is binding. Thus, the parties would have no right to appeal a decision by the arbitrator.

B. MEDIATION

Arbitration and mediation are not the same. **Mediation** is the informal resolution of a dispute between the parties.

In an arbitration proceeding, an arbitrator[1] will hear both sides of the dispute. The parties will present evidence, call witnesses, and conduct a proceeding that is very similar to a trial. At the conclusion of the arbitration, the arbitrator will make a ruling in favor of one party and against another. This ruling is similar to a judgment and is called the **arbitration award.**

In mediation, which is also available through the AAA and is also proscribed under CRC Rule 3.800 et seq., the **mediator** is a neutral person who will listen to both sides of the dispute. The mediator will not give any legal advice, nor will the mediator express a decision in favor of one party. Rather than rendering a decision for one side against the other, the mediator will help the parties attempt to reach an acceptable settlement. Thus, mediation can be especially useful if the parties have had difficulty communicating with one another or have not been able to work out an agreeable settlement on their own. The communications made to a mediator are confidential, and the mediator must not disclose any information revealed in confidence.

In some cases the parties may choose to mediate their dispute prior to an arbitration hearing. If the mediation is successful, the parties will simply confirm this through a written settlement agreement. If the mediation is not successful, the parties will then set a hearing for the arbitration and proceed as if no attempt at mediation had taken place. Any evidence of settlement negotiations during the course of the mediation cannot be used as evidence in a subsequent arbitration or trial.

The advantages of mediation are many. First, there is no winner or loser in mediation. Rather, the mediator facilitates the parties arriving at their own solution. Thus, the parties, with the assistance of the mediator, can be creative in coming up with a solution to the dispute. In arbitration and civil litigation, there is generally no opportunity for coming up with an acceptable middle position. For example, assume that a dispute exists over damage to a fence that divides the property line of two neighbors. If neighbor A brings a lawsuit against neighbor B, claiming that B is responsible to pay for the damage, absent a settlement, the court and any court-required arbitration is bound to determine whether B is required to pay the amount requested by A. However, in mediation, the parties may decide, during the mediation process, that they would like to share the cost of a new brick wall. Not only is the ability to fashion a creative solution a benefit, but also the parties are now more likely to

Mediation
A process in which a neutral person helps to facilitate communication between the parties to assist them in reaching a mutually acceptable agreement.

Arbitration award
The ruling arising from arbitration

---

1. Although the term *arbitrator* is used, the same rule applies to neutrals selected under Local Rules.

preserve their relationship rather than have it destroyed by the outcome of a lawsuit.

Second, mediation is often a less expensive alternative than a trial. Since mediation does not involve a hearing to determine who is liable and the amount of liability, the mediator will not hear from witnesses other than the parties or consider numerous evidentiary exhibits to determine an outcome. Rather, the parties will appear, give their side of the dispute, often out of the presence of the other side, and the mediator will attempt to facilitate a resolution from the information given, but without divulging any confidential information. Thus, the costs involved in preparing witnesses and preparing exhibits are eliminated. In addition, if the mediation occurs early in the process, the costs of discovery and trial preparation can also be greatly reduced.

Finally, having the benefit of a neutral party to listen to, and comment on, the information provided is often a useful way for parties to see both the strengths and the weaknesses of their individual case.

C. ARBITRATION

1. Judicial arbitration

Judicial arbitration is governed by CCP §1141.10 et seq. and CRC Rule 3.800 et seq. If the court determines that the amount in controversy will not exceed $50,000 for each plaintiff, the case must be submitted to judicial arbitration. Cases where equitable relief is requested are exempt from the arbitration process. Members of the State Bar shall be selected to serve as arbitrators and are encouraged to volunteer their services. Within five days of naming an arbitrator, any party may request disqualification of the arbitrator, and a new arbitrator will be appointed.

The arbitrator shall hear the case, including listening to oral argument and taking in evidence from the witnesses. The case will proceed just as if the case were in a court of law, with the exception that the case is usually heard in an informal office setting.

Once the matter is concluded, the arbitrator will file a written award with the court deciding the case. The arbitration award is final unless one party, within 30 days of filing the award, elects to have a **trial de novo.** A trial de novo is a new trial, which is why judicial arbitrations are considered non-binding.

There is some disincentive for parties to elect a trial de novo after receiving an adverse arbitration award. Pursuant to CCP §1141.21, if the judgment after the new trial is not more favorable to the party electing the new trial, the court can order that party to pay the other party certain costs and fees.

2. Arbitration by agreement

In addition to arbitration ordered by a court, arbitration may also be agreed to by the parties. Frequently, agreements to arbitrate are included in contracts between the parties prior to a dispute arising. There are three basic methods by which arbitration by agreement of the parties is handled. Judicial arbitration can proceed under CCP §1141.12 upon stipulation of the parties regardless of the amount in controversy. In addition, arbitration can proceed under the rules set forth in CCP §1280 et seq., and finally, by the rules established by the AAA. The CCP provides a method for appointing an arbitrator, the conduct of the arbitration proceedings, and time for making the arbitrator award. However, if the agreement provides for a different method, the agreement between the parties must control.

Arbitration is also available through the AAA whenever the parties either have a contract that has a provision in it for arbitration of disputes or if the parties agree to submit an existing dispute to arbitration. The AAA recommends that in drafting a contract to include an arbitration provision, you use the following language:

> Any controversy or claim arising out of or relating to this contract, or the breach thereof, shall be settled by arbitration administered by the American Arbitration Association in accordance with its Commercial Arbitration Rules, and judgment on the award rendered by the arbitrator(s) may be entered in any court having jurisdiction thereof.

This is the standard arbitration clause you will see in most business contracts. Arbitration clauses also appear in many other types of contracts. The AAA has specific rules and guidelines for arbitration of disputes concerning hospital and medical claims, construction claims, labor claims, and security claims. You should obtain from the AAA the specific rules for the type of claim that you are arbitrating.

Under the rules of the AAA, all types of arbitration are commenced by filing a **demand for arbitration**, along with the appropriate administrative fee, with the AAA. The demand also must be served upon all opposing parties. The party filing the demand is called the **claimant**. The party responding to the demand is the **respondent**. Once the demand is filed, the AAA takes care of all other details, including scheduling an arbitration date and arranging for the arbitration. An AAA arbitration demand form is shown in Exhibit 19.1.

Demand for arbitration
The form that a party files to commence arbitration through the AAA

D. PREPARING FOR ARBITRATION

If the parties are proceeding under a judicial arbitration, the matter will continue as any other case prior to the arbitration hearing. However, the

Exhibit 19.1. AAA Arbitration Demand Form

American Arbitration Association
Dispute Resolution Services Worldwide

_____**ARBITRATION RULES**
(ENTER THE NAME OF THE APPLICABLE RULES)
Demand for Arbitration

MEDIATION: If you would like the AAA to contact the other parties and attempt to arrange mediation, please check this box. ☐ There is no additional administrative fee for this service.

Name of Respondent	Name of Representative (if known)	
Address:	Name of Firm (if applicable):	
	Representative's Address	

City	State	Zip Code	City	State	Zip Code
Phone No.		Fax No.	Phone No.		Fax No.
Email Address:			Email Address:		

The named claimant, a party to an arbitration agreement dated _____, which provides for arbitration under the _____ Arbitration Rules of the American Arbitration Association, hereby demands arbitration.

THE NATURE OF THE DISPUTE

Dollar Amount of Claim $	Other Relief Sought: ☐ Attorneys Fees ☐ Interest ☐ Arbitration Costs ☐ Punitive/ Exemplary ☐ Other _____

AMOUNT OF FILING FEE ENCLOSED WITH THIS DEMAND (please refer to the fee schedule in the rules for the appropriate fee) $

PLEASE DESCRIBE APPROPRIATE QUALIFICATIONS FOR ARBITRATOR(S) TO BE APPOINTED TO HEAR THIS DISPUTE:

Hearing locale_____ (check one) ☐ Requested by Claimant ☐ Locale provision included in the contract

Estimated time needed for hearings overall: _____ hours or _____ days	Type of Business: Claimant _____ Respondent_____

Is this a dispute between a business and a consumer? ☐Yes ☐ No
Does this dispute arise out of an employment relationship? ☐Yes ☐ No

If this dispute arises out of an employment relationship, what was/is the employee's annual wage range? Note: This question is required by California law. ☐Less than $100,000 ☐ $100,000 - $250,000 ☐ Over $250,000

You are hereby notified that copies of our arbitration agreement and this demand are being filed with the American Arbitration Association's Case Management Center, located in (check one) ☐ Atlanta, GA ☐ Dallas, TX ☐ East Providence, RI ☐ Fresno, CA ☐ International Centre, NY, with a request that it commence administration of the arbitration. Under the rules, you may file an answering statement within the timeframe specified in the rules, after notice from the AAA.

Signature (may be signed by a representative) Date:	Name of Representative	
Name of Claimant	Name of Firm (if applicable)	
Address (to be used in connection with this case):	Representative's Address:	

City	State	Zip Code	City	State	Zip Code
Phone No.		Fax No.	Phone No.		Fax No.
Email Address:			Email Address:		

To begin proceedings, please send two copies of this Demand and the Arbitration Agreement, along with the filing fee as provided for in the Rules, to the AAA. Send the original Demand to the Respondent.

Please visit our website at www.adr.org if you would like to file this case online. AAA Customer Service can be reached at 800-778-7879

rules are slightly different in the case of an arbitration under the AAA. The procedure for an AAA hearing is discussed in this section.

Once the demand for arbitration has been received by the AAA, the AAA will assign the case to a staff member referred to as the **case administrator.** The case administrator will send out a list of potential arbitrators to the parties, as well as a request for dates when the parties will be available for the arbitration hearing. The parties have the right to strike any names of arbitrators that they object to and to rank in order of preference the remaining arbitrators. The case administrator will then review both lists submitted by the parties and choose an arbitrator who has not been objected to by either party.

The hearing will generally be held within a few months of filing the demand for arbitration. The case administrator will set a date for the arbitration hearing based on the request for dates received from the parties and the availability of the arbitrator.

Since the arbitration will proceed similarly to a trial and the arbitrator will render a binding decision at the conclusion of the hearing, it is important to carefully prepare for the arbitration hearing. Accordingly, you may be asked as a paralegal to assist the lawyer with the following preparations:

PREPARATION FOR ARBITRATION

☐ Gather all documentation and papers that support your side's position.

You will need to make sufficient copies of the documents and papers so that the attorney can give one copy to the arbitrator and one copy to each opposing party, and retain one copy for the attorney's own use during the arbitration.

☐ Subpoena documents from other parties if your client does not have access to all the documentation needed for the arbitration.

Many states have rules permitting the arbitrator to issue a subpoena to compel other parties or even nonparties to bring the documents to the arbitration hearing.

☐ Determine who will be called as witnesses at the arbitration.

If possible, interview all the witnesses in advance and make a written summary of what each witness' testimony will be.

☐ Assist the attorney in preparing questions for direct and cross-examination of each witness.
☐ Assist the attorney in preparing a written arbitration brief.

The arbitration brief is similar to a trial brief. It will outline your client's version of the facts and cite appropriate legal authorities that will help the arbitrator decide the law to be applied to the facts in the case.

Although arbitrations are simple to initiate, the preparation for the arbitration hearing demands work similar to the preparation for a trial. Keep in mind that nonjudicial arbitrations are binding and, except under very limited circumstances (such as fraud or bias by the arbitrator), the award of the arbitrator cannot be appealed if your side is the losing party. Accordingly, it is necessary for both sides to do their best in presenting the case.

E. THE ARBITRATION HEARING

In general, the arbitration will proceed very much like a trial, with both sides presenting their witnesses and evidence. The arbitrator, however, is not bound by the rules of evidence. Accordingly, arbitrators usually listen to all the evidence, and make their own determination about the relevancy or admissibility of the evidence.

CCP §1141.10 specifically declares that it is the intent of the legislature that arbitration "hearings shall be as informal as possible and shall provide the parties themselves maximum opportunity to participate directly in the resolution of their disputes, and shall be held during nonjudicial hours whenever possible."

Unlike a trial, a court reporter will not be present at the arbitration to make a written transcript of the proceedings unless requested by the parties. The hearing will take place in the offices of the arbitration. This usually makes for a much more relaxed atmosphere for both the parties and their attorneys.

After both sides have presented their cases, the arbitrator will declare the hearings to be closed. The arbitrator then has 30 days in which to render the arbitration award. The prevailing party may then petition the appropriate court to confirm the award. The arbitration award will be confirmed unless there are special circumstances, such as proof of bias on the part of the arbitrator or some fraud in the proceedings on the part of the prevailing party or arbitrator. Once the award is confirmed, it becomes an enforceable judgment.

CHAPTER SUMMARY

With rising legal costs, arbitration and mediation are popular alternatives to litigation. Mediation may help the parties resolve their dispute by reaching an acceptable settlement. If mediation is not possible, arbitration can provide a faster and less expensive alternative to proceeding in court.

Arbitration is available whenever the parties have a contract that specifically provides for arbitration. In addition, even if no such contract provision exists, the parties can voluntarily agree to submit their dispute to arbitration. The agency most frequently used to arbitrate disputes the American Arbitration Association.

Once a demand for arbitration is filed with the AAA, the case administrator will take care of the procedural details, such as setting a hearing and arranging for the appointment of an arbitrator. However, thorough preparation is still needed for the arbitration hearing since there are limited circumstances in which a party can have a court trial after resolution of a dispute through arbitration.

KEY TERMS

American Arbitration Association	Judicial arbitration
Arbitration	Mediation
Arbitration award	Mediator
Case administrator	Neutral
Claimant	Respondent
Demand for arbitration	Trial de novo

REVIEW QUESTIONS

1. What are the differences between judicial and nonjudicial arbitration?

2. What are the advantages and disadvantages between arbitration and litigation?

3. How is an arbitration commenced?

4. Describe the mediation process.

INTERNET RESOURCES

Information on alternative dispute resolutions may be found at the following websites:

www.adr.org
www.hg.org/adr.html
www.law.cornell.edu/wex/index.php/ADR
www.findlaw.com

Litigation File: *Jones v. Smith*

This appendix is part of the litigation file in *Jones v. Smith*, an automobile collision case. It illustrates each basic step in the pleadings, discovery, motions, and settlement stages of the litigation process.

FACTS

John Jones, a 23-year-old delivery truck driver, was involved in a collision with Susan Smith. The collision occurred on September 2, 2007, at the intersection of First Street and Adams Blvd. in Los Angeles, California. Jones injured his stomach, neck, back, a shoulder, and an ankle and was out of work for a month. His car was also damaged.

Jones brings suit in Superior Court in Los Angeles, California. He claims that Smith negligently ran a red light at the intersection and crashed into his car (he was not operating a delivery truck at the time). Jones is a resident of Orange County, California; Smith is a resident of Los Angeles County, California. The lawsuit was filed on January 10, 2008.

SUPERIOR COURT OF THE STATE OF CALIFORNIA
FOR THE COUNTY OF LOS ANGELES

John Jones,
      Plaintiff
    v.
Susan Smith, and
Does 1 through 10,
      Defendants

No. _____

<u>COMPLAINT FOR
NEGLIGENCE</u>

The "Caption" includes the court, the parties, and the case number.

Plaintiff John Jones ("Jones") complains of defendant Susan Smith ("Smith") as follows:

<u>FIRST CAUSE OF ACTION FOR NEGLIGENCE</u>
(Against All Defendants)

1. Jones is, and at all times relevant herein was, a resident of the County of Orange, California.

2. Smith is, and at all times relevant herein was, a resident of the County of Los Angeles, California.

It is standard to include the residence of the parties so that it can be ascertained whether venue is proper.

3. The true names and capacities of Does 1 through 10 herein are unknown to Jones at this time, and Jones therefore sues such defendants by these fictitious names. At the time that the true names and capacities of Does 1 through 10 are ascertained, Jones will amend this Complaint to identify the true names.

A fictitious Doe defendant paragraph needs to be included in the state court complaints.

4. On September 2, 2007, at approximately 2:00 P.M., Jones was driving a vehicle northbound on First Street toward the intersection of First Street and Adams Blvd. in Los Angeles, California. Smith was driving a vehicle eastbound on Adams Blvd. toward the same intersection.

The factual allegations should be clear and simple. This makes it more likely that they will be either admitted or denied outright, making the pleadings easier to understand.

5. Jones is informed and believes, and therefore alleges that Smith failed to stop for the red light at the intersection of First Street and Adams Blvd., and negligently drove her vehicle into Jones' vehicle.

The negligence and causation claims are kept separate.

6. As a direct and proximate result of Smith's negligence, Jones injured his stomach, neck, back, a shoulder, an ankle, and other bodily parts, received other physical injuries, suffered physical and mental pain and suffering, incurred medical expenses, lost income, and will incur further medical expenses and lost income in the future.

The injury allegations are usually spelled out in some detail.

In personal injury complaints the dollar amount is not stated. Accordingly, it is proper to just state that the injuries are greater than the jurisdictional limit of the court.

WHEREFORE, plaintiff Jones demands judgment against defendant Smith in an amount in excess of the jurisdictional limit of this court, plus interests and costs of suit.

Dated: <u>January 10, 2008</u>

Anne Johnson

Anne Johnson
Attorney for Plaintiff
100 Congress Street
Los Angeles, CA 90039
882-1000

Exhibit L-1.

SUMMONS
(CITACION JUDICIAL)

NOTICE TO DEFENDANT: *(Aviso a Acusado)*

FOR COURT USE ONLY
(SOLO PARA USO DE LA CORTE)

SUSAN SMITH AND DOES 1 through 10

YOU ARE BEING SUED BY PLAINTIFF:
(A Ud. le está demandando)

JOHN JONES

You have **30 CALENDAR DAYS** after this summons is served on you to file a typewritten response at this court.

A letter or phone call will not protect you; your typewritten response must be in proper legal form if you want the court to hear your case.

If you do not file your response on time, you may lose the case, and your wages, money and property may be taken without further warning from the court.

There are other legal requirements. You may want to call an attorney right away. If you do not know an attorney, you may call an attorney referral service or a legal aid office (listed in the phone book).

Después de que le entreguen esta citación judicial usted tiene un plazo de 30 DIAS CALENDARIOS para presentar una respuesta escrita a máquina en esta corte.

Una carta o una llamada telefónica no le ofrecerá protección; su respuesta escrita a máquina tiene que cumplir con las formalidades legales apropiadas si usted quiere que la corte escuche su caso.

Si usted no presenta su respuesta a tiempo, puede perder el caso, y le pueden quitar su salario, su dinero y otras cosasde su propiedad sin aviso adicional por parte de la corte.

Existen otros requisitos legales. Puede que usted quiera llamar a un abogado inmediatamente. Si no conoce a un abogado, puede llamar a un servicio de referencia de abogados o a una oficina de ayuda legal (vea el directorio telefónico).

CASE NUMBER: *(Número del Caso)*

The name and address of the court is: *(El nombre y dirección de la corte es)*

SUPERIOR COURT
111 N. HILL STREET
LOS ANGELES, CA

The name, address, and telephone number of plaintiff's attorney, or plaintiff without an attorney, is:
(El nombre, la dirección y el número de teléfono del abogado del demandante, o del demandante que no tiene abogado, es)

Anne Johnson   100 Congress St. Los Angeles, CA 90039
882-1000

DATE:
(Fecha) January 10, 2008

Clerk, by _____, Deputy
(Actuario) _____ *(Delegado)*

[SEAL]

NOTICE TO THE PERSON SERVED: You are served

1. [X] as an individual defendant.
2. [ ] as the person sued under the fictitious name of *(specify):*

3. [ ] on behalf of *(specify):*

under: [ ] CCP 416.10 (corporation)
[ ] CCP 416.20 (defunct corporation)
[ ] CCP 416.40 (association or partnership)
[ ] other:

[ ] CCP 416.60 (minor)
[ ] CCP 416.70 (conservatee)
[ ] CCP 416.90 (individual)

4. [X] by personal delivery on *(date):* January 11, 2008

Form Adopted by Rule 982
Judicial Council of California
982(a)(9) [Rev. January 1, 1984]

(See reverse for Proof of Service)
SUMMONS

CCP 4*2.20

Exhibit L-1. Continued

PROOF OF SERVICE — SUMMONS
(Use separate proof of service for each person served)

1. I served the
   a. [x] summons [x] complaint [ ] amended summons [ ] amended complaint
      [ ] completed and blank Case Questionnaires [ ] Other *(specify)*:
   b. on defendant *(name)*:

      Susan Smith
   c. by serving [x] defendant [ ] other *(name and title or relationship to person served)*:

   d. [x] by delivery [x] at home [ ] at business
      (1) date: 01-11-08
      (2) time: 3:00 p.m.
      (3) address: 200 Palmer Way Los Angeles, CA

   e. [ ] by mailing
      (1) date:
      (2) place:

2. Manner of service *(check proper box)*:
   a. [x] **Personal service.** By personally delivering copies. (CCP 415.10)
   b. [ ] **Substituted service on corporation, unincorporated association (including partnership), or public entity.** By leaving, during usual office hours copies in the office of the person served with the person who apparently was in charge and thereafter mailing (by first-class mail, postage prepaid) copies to the person served at the place where the copies were left. (CCP 415.20(a))
   c. [ ] **Substituted service on natural person, minor, conservatee, or candidate.** By leaving copies at the dwelling house, usual place of abode, or usual place of business of the person served in the presence of a competent member of the household or a person apparently in charge of the office or place of business, at least 18 years of age, who was informed of the general nature of the papers, and thereafter mailing (by first-class mail, postage prepaid) copies to the person served at the place where the copies were left. (CCP 415.20(b)) *(Attach separate declaration or affidavit stating acts relied on to establish reasonable diligence in first attempting personal service.)*
   d. [ ] **Mail and acknowledgment service.** By mailing (by first-class mail or airmail, postage prepaid) copies to the person served, together with two copies of the form of notice and acknowledgment and a return envelope, postage prepaid, addressed to the sender. (CCP 415.30) *(Attach completed acknowledgment of receipt.)*
   e. [ ] **Certified or registered mail serivce.** By mailing to an address outside California (by first-class mail postage prepaid, requiring a return receipt) copies to the person served. (CCP 415.40) *(Attach signed return receipt or other evidence of actual delivery to the person served.)*

   f. [ ] Other *(specify code section)*:
      [ ] additional page is attached.

3. The "Notice to the Person Served" (on the summons) was completed as follows (CCP 412.30, 415.10, and 474):
   a. [x] as an individual defendant.
   b. [ ] as the person sued under the fictitious name of *(specify)*:
   c. [ ] on behalf of *(specify)*:
      under: [ ] CCP 416.10 (corporation) [ ] CCP 416.60 (minor) [ ] other:
             [ ] CCP 416.20 (defunct corporation) [ ] CCP 416.70 (conservatee)
             [ ] CCP 416.40 (association or partnership) [ ] CCP 416.90 (individual)
   d. [x] by personal delivery on *(date)*: January 11, 2008
4. At the time of service I was at least 18 years of age and not a party to this action.
5. Fee for service: $ 25.00
6. Person serving:
   a. [ ] California sheriff, marshal, or constable.
   b. [x] Registered California process server.
   c. [ ] Employee or independent contractor of a registered California process server.
   d. [ ] Not a registered California process server.
   e. [ ] Exempt from registration under Bus. & Prof. Code 22350(b).

   f. Name, address and telephone number and, if applicable, county of registration and number:

   Kelly Warner
   7544 Elliot St.
   Burbank, CA
   545-9824

I declare under penalty of perjury under the laws of the State of California that the foregoing is true and correct.

(For California sheriff, marshal, or constable use only)
I certify that the foregoing is true and correct.

Date: 01-11-08

▶ _____
(SIGNATURE)

Date:

▶ _____
(SIGNATURE)

982(a)(5) (Rev. January 1, 1984)

SUPERIOR COURT OF THE STATE OF CALIFORNIA
FOR THE COUNTY OF LOS ANGELES

John Jones,
    Plaintiff
    v.
Susan Smith, et al.
    Defendants
	No. _____
	
	DEFENDANT'S
	ANSWER TO
	COMPLAINT

After the initial complaint, "et al." can be used in the caption to identify all other parties after the first named defendant.

For herself and herself alone, defendant Susan Smith ("Smith") answers the plaintiff's complaint dated January 10, 2008 (the "Complaint") as follows:

1. Smith admits the allegations contained in paragraphs 1, 2, and 4 of the Complaint.

2. Smith is without sufficient information or knowledge to either admit or deny the allegations contained in paragraph 3 of the Complaint and on that ground denies each and every allegation contained therein.

3. Smith denies each and every allegation contained in paragraph 5 of the Complaint.

4. Answering paragraph 6 of the complaint, Smith is without sufficient information or knowledge to either admit or deny the allegations with respect to the injuries suffered by the plaintiff and on that ground denies each and every allegation contained therein, and further denies each and every remaining allegation contained in paragraph 6.

If a paragraph in the complaint has allegations to which you do not have sufficient information to respond, and other allegations which you want to deny, specifically indicate which allegations you do not have sufficient information to respond to, and deny all remaining allegations.

FIRST AFFIRMATIVE DEFENSE

5. Plaintiff's complaint fails to state facts sufficient to state a cause of action.

Each defense should be set out separately.

SECOND AFFIRMATIVE DEFENSE

6. Plaintiff's claimed injuries and damages were caused by plaintiff's own negligence, which was the sole and proximate cause of any injuries and damages plaintiff may have received.

WHEREFORE, Smith prays that the plaintiff takes nothing by the Complaint, that the Complaint be dismissed and that Smith be awarded her costs of suit herein.

Dated: <u>February 10, 2008</u>

William Sharp
_____

William Sharp
Attorney for Defendant
100 Broadway Ave.
Los Angeles, CA 90054
881-1000

A proof of service should always be attached to the back of every court paper showing how proper service was made.

<u>PROOF OF SERVICE</u>

I, Helen Thompson, declare that my business address is 100 Broadway Avenue, Los Angeles, CA 90054, and that I am not a party to this action. On February 10, 2008, I served "Defendant's Answer to Complaint" on the Plaintiff John Jones by depositing in the U.S. mail, postage prepaid, a copy in a sealed envelope addressed to Plaintiff's attorney of record as follows:

Anne Johnson
100 Congress Street
Los Angeles, CA 90039

I declare under penalty of perjury under the laws of the State of California that the foregoing is true and correct.

Dated this 10th day of February, 2008

Helen Thompson
_____

Helen Thompson

SUPERIOR COURT OF THE STATE OF CALIFORNIA
FOR THE COUNTY OF LOS ANGELES

John Jones,
         Plaintiff
         v.
Susan Smith, et al.
         Defendants
	No. _____
	
	DEFENDANT'S
	<u>INTERROGATORIES</u>
	<u>TO PLAINTIFF</u>

Interrogatories will usually be the first discovery device the parties serve on each other.

Pursuant to Code of Civil Procedure Section 2030, defendant Smith requests that plaintiff Jones answer the following interrogatories under oath, and serve them on the defendant within 30 days:

1. Describe the personal injuries you received as a result of the occurrence described in the complaint (hereafter "THIS OCCURRENCE").

2. State the full names and present addresses of any physicians, osteopaths, chiropractors, and other medical personnel who treated you as a result of THIS OCCURRENCE, each such person's areas of specialty, the dates of each examination, consultation, or appointment, the amount of each such person's bill, and whether each bill has been paid.

3. Were you confined to a hospital or clinic as a result of THIS OCCURRENCE? If so, state the name and address of each such hospital or clinic, the dates of your confinement at each facility, the amount of each such facility's bills, and whether each bill has been paid.

4. Have you incurred other medical expenses, other than those requested in Interrogatory Nos. 2 and 3, as a result of THIS OCCURRENCE? If so, state each expense incurred, the nature of each expense, when the expense was incurred, to whom it was incurred, and whether each expense has been paid.

5. Have you incurred any expenses as a result of THIS OCCURRENCE other than medical expenses? If so, state the nature of each expense, the date incurred, the amount of each expense, the reason for incurring each expense, and whether each expense has been paid.

6. Were you unable to work as a result of THIS OCCURRENCE? If so, state the dates during which you were unable to work, each employer during these dates, the type of work you were unable to do, and the amount of lost wages or income from each employer.

Note how each interrogatory deals with a separate, defined category and asks for all relevant data for the category. This will usually generate more complete answers. It also gives the answering party the opportunity of answering the interrogatory by producing the relevant records that contain the answers.

The plaintiff's current condition and medical history are important areas that should be explored thoroughly. This can then be verified during the plaintiff's deposition.

7. Have you recovered from the claimed injuries that resulted from THIS OCCURRENCE? If not, state the claimed injuries from which you have not recovered and any present disability.

8. During the ten years preceding September 2, 2007, have you suffered any other personal injuries? If so, state when, where, and how you were injured and the name and address of each medical facility where, and physicians by whom, you were treated for these injuries.

9. During the ten years preceding September 2, 2007, have you been hospitalized, treated, examined, or tested at any hospital, clinic, physician's office, or other medical facility for any conditions other than those requested in Interrogatory No. 8? If so, state the name and address of each such medical facility and physician, the dates of such services, and the medical conditions involved.

Occurrence witnesses are obviously important in this kind of case. It's a good practice to break them up by category in appropriate cases.

10. State the full name and address of each person who witnessed, or claims to have witnessed, the collision between the vehicles involved in THIS OCCURRENCE.

11. State the full name and address of each person who has any knowledge of the facts of the collision other than those persons already identified in Interrogatory No. 10.

12. Describe your vehicle that was involved in THIS OCCURRENCE, any damage to your vehicle as a result of THIS OCCURRENCE, the name and address of any firm repairing your vehicle, the amount billed for repairs, when such repairs took place, and whether the repair bills have been paid. If your vehicle has not been repaired, state where it is presently located and its condition.

Dated: <u>March 1, 2008</u>

William Sharp
_____
William Sharp
Attorney for Defendant
100 Broadway
Los Angeles, CA 90054
881-1000

A proof of service must be attached.

SUPERIOR COURT OF THE STATE OF CALIFORNIA
FOR THE COUNTY OF LOS ANGELES

John Jones, 　　　　Plaintiff 　　v. Susan Smith, et al. 　　　　Defendants	No. _____ PLAINTIFF'S ANSWERS TO INTERROGATORIES

Plaintiff John Jones answers Defendant's interrogatories as follows:

Interrogatory No. 1: Describe the personal injuries you received as a result of the occurrence described in the complaint (hereafter "THIS OCCURRENCE").

The usual way of answering interrogatories is to set out the questions and the answers, making it easy to correlate the two.

Answer: Cervical, dorsal, and lumbar sprain and strain; cerebral concussion; multiple contraction headaches and concussion headaches; left hemi paresis with ataxia; ankle sprain; numbness; multiple contusions and abrasions.

Interrogatory No. 2: State the full names and present addresses of any physicians, osteopaths, chiropractors, and other medical personnel who treated you as a result of THIS OCCURRENCE, each such person's areas of specialty, the dates of each examination, consultation, or appointment, the amount of each such person's bill, and whether each bill has been paid.

Answer:

Doctors Hospital
1947 East Thomas Road
Los Angeles, CA 90638

Leo L. Lang, M.D.
333 East Campbell Avenue
Los Angeles, CA 90638

Frank Hoffman, M.D.
222 West Thomas
Suite 100
Los Angeles, CA 90754

J. Franks, D.C.
55 North 27th Avenue
Los Angeles, CA 90614

Interrogatory No. 3: Were you confined to a hospital or clinic as a result of THIS OCCURRENCE? If so, state the name and address of each such hospital or clinic, the dates of your confinement at each facility, the amount of each facility's bills, and whether each bill has been paid.

Answer: No; treated, but not confined, at Doctors Hospital.

Interrogatory No. 4: Have you incurred other medical expenses, other than those requested in Interrogatory Nos. 2 and 3, as a result of THIS OCCURRENCE? If so, state each expense incurred, the nature of each expense, when the expense was incurred, to whom it was incurred, and whether each expense has been paid.

Answer:

Doctors Hospital	$257.18
Leo Lang, M.D.	39.70
Frank Hoffman, M.D.	140.00
J. Franks, D.C.	697.80
Walgreen Pharmacy	23.13

Those bills have been paid.

Interrogatory No. 5: Have you incurred any expenses as a result of THIS OCCURRENCE other than medical expenses? If so, state the nature of each expense, the date incurred, the amount of each expense, the reason for incurring each expense, and whether each expense has been paid.

Answer:

Broken wristwatch	$75.00
College tuition and books (tuition $110/books $52)	162.00

Wristwatch repair bill has been paid.

Interrogatory No. 6: Were you unable to work as a result of THIS OCCURRENCE? If so, state the dates during which you were unable to work, each employer during these dates, the type of work you were unable to do, and the amount of lost wages or income from each employer.

Answer: Yes. September 2, 2007, to October 1, 2007. Devo Wholesale Florist. Delivery truck driver. $1,700—one month's salary.

This is a typical interrogatory answer. It provides all the facts requested, does so efficiently, and does not volunteer anything not asked for.

Interrogatory No. 7: Have you recovered from the claimed injuries that resulted from THIS OCCURRENCE? If not, state the claimed injuries from which you have not recovered and any present disability.

Answer: Plaintiff still experiences headaches, neck pain, and lower back pain.

Interrogatory No. 8: During the ten years preceding September 2, 2007, have you suffered any other personal injuries? If so, state when, where, and how you were injured and the name and address of each medical facility where, and physicians by whom, you were treated for these injuries.

Answer: No.

Interrogatory No. 9: During the ten years preceding September 2, 2007, have you been hospitalized, treated, examined, or tested at any hospital, clinic, physician's office, or other medical facility for any conditions other than those requested in Interrogatory No. 8? If so, state the name and address of each such medical facility and physician, the dates of such services, and the medical conditions involved.

Answer: No.

Interrogatory No. 10: State the full name and address of each person who witnessed, or claims to have witnessed, the collision between the vehicles involved in THIS OCCURRENCE.

Answer:

John Jones, plaintiff
Susan Smith, defendant
Carol Brown, 42 E. Cambridge, Tarzana, CA
Mary Porter, 42 E. Cambridge, Tarzana, CA
Officer Steven Pitcher, Los Angeles, Police Department

Witness lists must frequently be supplemented over time, since the ongoing investigation will often uncover additional witnesses.

Interrogatory No. 11: State the full name and address of each person who has any knowledge of the facts of the collision other than those persons already identified in Interrogatory No. 10.

Answer: See persons listed in answer to Interrogatory No. 4; John Jones, Sr., and Mary Jones, plaintiff's parents; James Devo, plaintiff's employer.

<u>Interrogatory No. 12:</u> Describe your vehicle that was involved in THIS OCCURRENCE, any damage to your vehicle as a result of THIS OCCURRENCE, the name and address of any firm repairing your vehicle, the amount billed for repairs, when such repairs took place, and whether the repair bills have been paid. If your vehicle has not been repaired, state where it is presently located and its condition.

This is another typical answer. It provides the facts called for, yet does not volunteer anything.

<u>Answer:</u> 2003 Toyota Corolla four-door sedan. Extensive damage to left and front side of car. Jack's Auto Repair, 2000 E. Valley Road, Buena Park, $2,213. Repairs completed about September 30, 2007. Repair bill has been paid.

Dated: <u>March 25, 2008</u>

John Jones
——————————————
John Jones, Plaintiff

Interrogatory answers must be signed under oath by the party making them.

Like any court papers, the answers must be served on every party. A proof of service, showing how service was made, must be attached to the answer.

I, John Jones, state that:

I am the plaintiff in this case. I have made the foregoing Answers to Interrogatories and know the answers to be true to the best of my knowledge, information, and belief.

I declare under penalty of perjury that the foregoing is true and correct.

John Jones
——————————————
John Jones, Plaintiff

SUPERIOR COURT OF THE STATE OF CALIFORNIA
FOR THE COUNTY OF LOS ANGELES

John Jones, 　　　　Plaintiff 　　v. Susan Smith, et al. 　　　　Defendants	No. _____ DEFENDANT'S DEMAND TO INSPECT DOCUMENTS

Pursuant to Code of Civil Procedure Section 2031, defendant requests that plaintiff produce within 30 days, in the law offices of William Sharp, 100 Broadway, Los Angeles, CA 90054, the following documents for inspection and copying:

　1. All medical reports, records, charts, X-ray reports, and all other records regarding any medical examinations and treatment received by plaintiff for the injuries claimed in the complaint.

　2. All United States Income Tax returns filed by plaintiff for the years 2003, 2004, 2005, 2006, and 2007.

　3. All exhibits plaintiff will offer at the trial of this case.

Document requests are often served at the same time as interrogatories.

Document requests usually depend on interrogatory answers to identify the relevant documents. Here, however, what the defendant wants is both simple and obvious, so the defendant decides to serve the requests with interrogatories.

These kinds of records should already be in the plaintiff's possession.

Dated: <u>March 1, 2008</u>

William Sharp
_____

William Sharp
Attorney for Defendant
100 Broadway
Los Angeles, CA 90054
881-1000

A proof of service must be attached.

SUPERIOR COURT OF THE STATE OF CALIFORNIA
FOR THE COUNTY OF LOS ANGELES

John Jones, 　　　　Plaintiff 　　　v. Susan Smith, et al. 　　　　Defendants	No. _____ PLAINTIFF'S RESPONSE TO DEMAND FOR INSPECTION

In addition to producing the documents on the date and place designated by the demanding party, the responding party should also serve a timely response to each document request indicating whether the documents will be produced, or identifying, if appropriate, any objections to the items requested.

Plaintiff responds to defendant's Demand for Inspection of Documents as follows:

1. Plaintiff will produce copies of all reports in plaintiff's possession regarding medical examinations and treatment of plaintiff for his injuries. These copies will be delivered to defendant's attorney on or before April 1, 2008.

2. Plaintiff herewith produces his U.S. Income Tax Returns for the years 2003 through 2007.

3. Plaintiff to the extent known at present will produce copies of all exhibits he will offer at trial of this case. These copies will be delivered to defendant's attorney on or before April 1, 2008.

Dated: March 25, 2008

Anne Johnson

Anne Johnson
Attorney for Plaintiff
100 Congress Street
Los Angeles, CA 90039
882-1000

Exhibit L-2.

982(a)(15.4)

ATTORNEY OR PARTY WITHOUT ATTORNEY *(Name, state bar number, and address)*	FOR COURT USE ONLY
William Sharp 100 Broadway Los Angeles, CA 90054 TELEPHONE NO 881-1000　FAX NO 881-1002 ATTORNEY FOR *(Name)* Susan Smith	

NAME OF COURT Superior Court STREET ADDRESS 111 N. Hill St. MAILING ADDRESS CITY AND ZIP CODE Los Angeles, CA 90017 BRANCH NAME	

PLAINTIFF/PETITIONER　John Jones

DEFENDANT/RESPONDENT　Susan Smith et. al.

DEPOSITION SUBPOENA For Personal Appearance and Production of Documents and Things	CASE NUMBER

THE PEOPLE OF THE STATE OF CALIFORNIA, TO *(name, address, and telephone number of deponent, if known)*:

James Devo, 3731 First St. Los Angeles, CA

1. YOU ARE ORDERED TO APPEAR IN PERSON TO TESTIFY AS A WITNESS in this action at the following date, time, and place:

Date: March 15, 2008　Time: 10:00 am　Address: 100 Broadway, Los Angeles, CA

　a. ☐ As a deponent who is not a natural person, you are ordered to designate one or more persons to testify on your behalf as to the matters described in item 4. (Code Civ. Proc., § 2025, subd. (d)(6).)

　b. You are ordered to produce the documents and things described in item 3.

　c. ☒ This deposition will be recorded stenographically ☐ through the instant visual display of testimony, and by ☐ audiotape ☐ videotape.

　d. ☐ The videotape deposition is intended for possible use at trial under Code of Civil Procedure section 2025(u)(4)

2. The personal attendance of the custodian or other qualified witness and the production of the original records are required by this subpoena. The procedure authorized by Evidence Code sections 1560(b), 1561, and 1562 will not be deemed sufficient compliance with this subpoena.

3. The documents and things to be produced and any testing or sampling being sought are described as follows:

　All records of employment for John Jones

　☐ Continued on Attachment 3.

4. If the witness is a representative of a business or other entity, the matters upon which the witness is to be examined are described as follows:

　☐ Continued on Attachment 4.

5. IF YOU HAVE BEEN SERVED WITH THIS SUBPOENA AS A CUSTODIAN OF CONSUMER OR EMPLOYEE RECORDS UNDER CODE OF CIVIL PROCEDURE SECTION 1985.3 OR 1985.6 AND A MOTION TO QUASH OR AN OBJECTION HAS BEEN SERVED ON YOU, A COURT ORDER OR AGREEMENT OF THE PARTIES, WITNESSES, AND CONSUMER OR EMPLOYEE AFFECTED MUST BE OBTAINED BEFORE YOU ARE REQUIRED TO PRODUCE CONSUMER OR EMPLOYEE RECORDS.

6. At the deposition, you will be asked questions under oath. Questions and answers are recorded stenographically at the deposition, later they are transcribed for possible use at trial. You may read the written record and change any incorrect answers before you sign the deposition. You are entitled to receive witness fees and mileage actually traveled both ways. The money must be paid, at the option of the party giving notice of the deposition, either with service of this subpoena or at the time of the deposition.

DISOBEDIENCE OF THIS SUBPOENA MAY BE PUNISHED AS CONTEMPT BY THIS COURT. YOU WILL ALSO BE LIABLE FOR THE SUM OF FIVE HUNDRED DOLLARS AND ALL DAMAGES RESULTING FROM YOUR FAILURE TO OBEY.

Date issued:

03-01-08

(TYPE OR PRINT NAME)

▶ _____

(SIGNATURE OF PERSON ISSUING SUBPOENA)

Attorney for Defendant

(TITLE)

(Proof of service on reverse)

Form Adopted for Mandatory Use Judicial Council of California 982(a)(15.4) [Rev. January 1, 2000]	DEPOSITION SUBPOENA FOR PERSONAL APPEARANCE AND PRODUCTION OF DOCUMENTS AND THINGS	Code of Civil Procedure §§ 2020, 2025 Government Code § 68097

SUPERIOR COURT OF THE STATE OF CALIFORNIA
FOR THE COUNTY OF LOS ANGELES

John Jones,
            Plaintiff
v.
Susan Smith, et al.
            Defendants
	No. _____
	
	NOTICE OF
	DEPOSITION OF
	JOHN JONES

A subpoena is not necessary since the deponent is a party.

TO JOHN JONES AND HIS ATTORNEY OF RECORD:

PLEASE TAKE NOTICE THAT the undersigned will take the deposition of John Jones, Plaintiff, on April 15, 2008, at 2:00 P.M. at 100 Broadway, Los Angeles, CA. You are hereby notified that the plaintiff is to appear at that time and place and submit to a deposition under oath.

Dated: March 25, 2008

William Sharp
_____
William Sharp
Attorney for Defendant
100 Broadway
Los Angeles, CA 90054
881-1000

A proof of service must be attached.

SUPERIOR COURT OF THE STATE OF CALIFORNIA
FOR THE COUNTY OF LOS ANGELES

John Jones,	
Plaintiff	No. _____
v.	
Susan Smith, et al.	DEPOSITION OF
Defendants	JOHN JONES

DEPOSITION of John Jones, taken at 2:13 P.M. on April 15, 2008, at the law offices of William Sharp, at 100 Broadway, Los Angeles, CA, before Nancy Post, a Notary Public in Los Angeles, CA.

Appearance for the plaintiff:

Anne Johnson
100 Congress St
Los Angeles, CA 90039

Appearance for the defendant:

William Sharp
100 Broadway
Los Angeles, CA 90054

JOHN JONES

Called as a witness, having been first duly sworn, was examined and testified as follows:

EXAMINATION BY MR. SHARP:

Q. This is the deposition of the plaintiff, John Jones, being taken in the case of John Jones v. Susan Smith. It is being held at the law office of William Sharp, 100 Broadway, Los Angeles, CA. Today's date is April 15, 2008. Present in addition to Mr. Jones are myself, William Sharp, attorney for defendant Smith, Anne Johnson, attorney for plaintiff Jones, and Nancy Post, a certified court reporter and notary public. Mr. Jones, you were just sworn to tell the truth by the court reporter, correct?

This is a standard introductory statement.

a. Personal background.

Note the form of the questions and the tone of the examination. If the questioner has decided that the principal purposes of the deposition are to acquire information and assess the plaintiff as a trial witness, then, accordingly, the questions are usually open-ended, designed to elicit information and have the plaintiff do the talking. The questions are asked in a pleasant and friendly way.

b. Work experience.

c. Accident and health history must be explored, since preexisting injuries would affect the damages picture.

A. That's right.

Q. It's important that you understand the questions and give accurate answers. If there's anything you don't understand, or anything you don't know or aren't sure of, you let us know, all right?

A. Yes.

Q. Please tell us your name.

A. John J. Jones.

Q. How old are you?

A. I'm 23.

Q. Are you married or single?

A. Single.

Q. Where do you live?

A. 1020 North 50th Street, Buena Park, CA.

Q. How far did you go in school?

A. I graduated from high school—Central High, 2003.

Q. What did you do after high school?

A. I joined the army.

Q. Tell us about your army experience.

A. After basic training, I was sent to an infantry division, and did most of my three years in Afghanistan. I was a corporal when I received my honorable discharge. That was in August 2006.

Q. What did you do after that?

A. I came back to Buena Park, California, moved into my parents' house, and started working for Devo Wholesale Florist.

Q. Where is that located?

A. It's at 3731 First Street, La Mirada.

Q. What kind of work do you do there?

A. I started as a sales clerk, then I became a driver on one of their trucks.

Q. What do you do as a driver?

A. I deliver flowers from the store to customers in the Los Angeles area.

Q. What were your hours in August and September 2007?

A. It varied, but it was usually 6:00 A.M. to 2:00 P.M.

Q. Were those your hours the day of the accident?

A. Yes.

Q. Other than your job for Devo Florist, did you have any other jobs or activities in September 2007?

A. I didn't have any other job. I was a part-time student at Glendale Community College.

Q. Mr. Jones, were you ever involved in an automobile accident before September 2, 2007?

A. No.

Q. Did you ever receive personal injuries of any kind before September 2, 2007?

A. No.

Q. During the past ten years, other than for this accident, did you ever see a physician for any reason?

A. Well, our family doctor is Dr. Hoffman. I would see him from time to time for checkups, shots, and things like that. But I never had any serious injury or illness that I went to Dr. Hoffman for.

Q. Mr. Jones, tell me each injury you feel you've received as a result of the accident on September 2.

A. Okay. I hurt the left side of my neck, my lower back, my left ankle, my left shoulder, and my stomach.

Q. Let's start out with the left side of your neck. What injuries did you receive there?

A. I think I whipped my head to the side when the car crashed into me and I strained my neck. I had these shooting pains in my neck whenever I tried to move it.

Q. How long did that pain continue?

A. Well it was pretty severe for about a week, and then it started getting better. I still get pains there from time to time.

Q. Tell me about the injuries to your lower back.

A. Well, that was sort of the same thing. I must have wrenched my back from the force of the collision. Just like my neck, it was stiff and hurt for a while. After about a week it started getting better, and today I only get the pain from time to time, especially toward the end of the work day.

Q. Tell me about your left ankle.

A. I sprained my ankle during the accident. That was probably the worst injury. I had to stay off my feet for about two weeks, and I really couldn't start walking on it for three or four weeks. That's the injury that kept me out of work for a month.

Q. When did your ankle start getting better?

A. About a month after this happened it was well enough so I could start working, although I was still limping for quite a while. It probably took about four months before the ankle healed up completely.

Q. Tell me about the injury to your left shoulder.

A. I got some cuts and scratches and bruises on my left shoulder when I crashed into the dashboard of the car. That hurt for maybe two weeks, and then went away.

Q. Finally, tell me about the injuries to your stomach.

A. I guess I injured my stomach when I smashed against the steering wheel. It was just painful inside of my stomach. That went away after a few days.

d. Each claimed injury should be explored in detail.

The "tell me" form of questions is used to get the witness to disclose everything.

If the plaintiff at trial tries to claim additional injuries, he can hardly say he didn't mention all his injuries during the deposition because the lawyer didn't give him a chance to do so. Since pain and suffering will probably be the largest single element of damages, these questions are important to "pin down" the witness and prevent later exaggeration at trial.

The "any other injuries" question is always useful. Again, it prevents later exaggeration.

e. Medical treatment.

Note how this deposition is organized chronologically (with the exception of the accident itself). If you are drafting a deposition outline, this is usually the best way to organize the questions, unless you have a specific reason for doing it another way.

f. Recovery period.

Since the defendant's purpose is to minimize the extent and length of the

Q. Other than these injuries to your neck, lower back, ankle, shoulder, and stomach, did you receive any other injuries?

A. Oh yeah. I received a concussion on the left side of my head. That's what the doctor told me.

Q. Mr. Jones, let's talk about the medical treatment you received for these injuries following the accident. First, how did you get to Doctors Hospital?

A. An ambulance came to the intersection and they put me on a stretcher and drove me to the hospital.

Q. What happened when you arrived at Doctors Hospital?

A. The ambulance attendants took me into the emergency room, and some nurses checked me over, took my pulse and blood pressure, and stuff like that. After a while one of their doctors examined me. I think his name was Dr. Lang. I told Dr. Lang where I hurt and about the accident.

Q. What kind of treatment did you receive at the hospital?

A. Well, they examined me, X-rayed, cleaned up some of the cuts on my shoulder and chest, and put my ankle in a cast. It wasn't one of those big plaster casts; it was a cast that went around the back of my ankle and foot and was surrounded with an elastic bandage. I must have been there a couple of hours, and by that time my parents had come to the hospital, and they took me home.

Q. Did you receive any medication prescription?

A. The doctor gave a prescription for Tylenol with codeine, which my mother picked up at the drug store. The doctor told me to follow instructions on the bottle and take the medication if I needed it for the pain.

Q. Mr. Jones, tell us about the month you spent before you went back to work.

A. Well, the first week I pretty much spent in bed. Sometimes I got up and lay on the couch and watched TV. At that time everything was aching—my neck hurt, my head hurt, my stomach hurt, my ankle was swollen up. I spent all my time with my foot up to keep the swelling down, and I was taking the medicine to keep the pain down.

Q. How long was it before you were able to move around the house?

A. I'd say the first week or ten days I pretty much spent on my back. After that period of time the pain in my head, shoulder, and stomach started going away, and the swelling in my ankle was starting to go down. I got a pair of crutches and started moving around the house a little bit. I couldn't stay on my feet very long before the foot would swell up if I stood up for any length of time.

Q. At the end of September 2007, what was your physical condition like?

A. The scratches and bruises had gone away. The pains in my neck, shoulder, stomach, leg, and back had started to get better. The only places that really kept on hurting was my lower back and my ankle.

Q. Tell me about those.

A. Well, my back would have these stabbing pains from time to time. It felt real stiff. My ankle was stiff. My ankle was still swollen, and I couldn't walk on it yet. Dr. Hoffman, my family doctor, had removed the cast about three weeks after the accident and I could start walking without crutches, but I was still limping and the ankle would get sore if I walked on it for any length of time.

Q. When did you see Dr. Hoffman?

A. My mom took me to Dr. Hoffman about three weeks after the accident. He checked me out, removed the soft cast from my ankle, and told me it was okay to start walking around without the crutches if I could stand it.

Q. When did you stop using the crutches?

A. I stopped using them when I went back to work at the beginning of October.

Q. What did you see Dr. Franks, the chiropractor, for?

A. Well, my mom thought that going to a chiropractor might help my back and ankle. My back still hurt, and my ankle was still sore. She thought that it might be a good idea to get some physical therapy to see if that might help. That's why I went to Dr. Franks.

Q. How many times did you see Dr. Franks?

A. I went to him for the first time around October 1st. I went to see him maybe twice a week for the next couple of months.

Q. What kind of treatment did Dr. Franks perform?

A. He would give me physical therapy. That involved bending my back, stretching it, applying heat treatments, things like that. The same thing was true for the ankle.

Q. Did it help?

A. Yes. About two months later, maybe by Christmas, most of the stiffness and pain had gone away.

Q. From December 2007 to the present day, describe your physical condition.

A. It's better. I still have pain from time to time in my back and ankle.

Q. When do you get the pain there?

A. Well, it depends on how much or how hard I work. The more I work the more likely I am to get those pains.

Q. How often do you get those pains?

A. It's maybe once a week for an hour or two, usually at the end of the work day.

---

pain, these questions are important. Again, they prevent later exaggeration.

The history of the plaintiff's treatments is, of course, available from the medical records, which the defendant will have before the deposition. Nonetheless, these questions test the witness' recall and propensity to exaggerate.

These questions effectively limit the damages.

Q. When was the last time you took Tylenol with codeine?

A. I took that stuff for maybe six weeks.

Q. Did you ever take any painkillers other than Tylenol with codeine?

A. I sometimes take aspirin when I get these pains.

Q. Other than what you've told me about, do you have any other injuries or problems that you feel were caused by this accident?

A. No, you pretty much covered it.

g. Expenses and lost income.

Q. Mr. Jones, let's talk about some of the bills involved here. First, the medical bills. Your interrogatory answers show that the bills from Doctors Hospital, Dr. Lang, Dr. Hoffman, and Dr. Franks have all been paid. Who paid those bills?

While the fact that most of the bills have been paid by insurance is not admissible at trial, it will have some effect on the settlement picture.

A. I'm not sure. I know they were paid by my health insurance. I think my mother paid the Walgreen Pharmacy bill.

Q. Who paid for the wristwatch repair?

A. My mom paid that. I'm supposed to pay her back.

Q. You claim college tuition and book expenses in the amount of $162. Tell us about that.

A. Well, I was a part-time student at Glendale Community College. I had already paid the tuition and bought the books for the two courses I was taking. When I got injured, I couldn't take the courses I signed up for.

Q. How much income did you lose as a result of this accident?

A. I get paid $1700 a month salary from Devo Florists. I went back to work October 1, 2007. The way I figure it, I lost one month's salary, or $1700.

Q. The $1700 is your gross income, isn't it?

A. Yes.

Q. What's your take-home pay?

A. We get paid on the first and fifteenth of the month. My take-home for half a month is about $570.

h. The accident.

Q. Mr. Jones, let's talk about how this accident happened. Describe the vehicle you were driving.

Note that here the questioner has saved the accident as the last topic. Some lawyers save the most important part of a deposition for the end, on the theory that the lawyer then has a better "feel" for the witness and the witness' guard will be down by that time.

A. It's a 2003 Toyota Corolla four-door. I bought it when I got out of the service. It was in really good shape, because I took good care of it.

Q. Is the title to that car in your name?

A. Yes.

Q. The accident happened around 2:00 P.M.?

A. Yes.

Q. At the time of the accident, where were you coming from?

These scene description questions are useful to see how effectively the plaintiff can describe the scene, and are good questions to see how effective a trial witness he will make.

A. I was coming from work at the flower shop.

Q. Where is that flower shop located?

A. On First Street and Adams Blvd.

Q. First Street is the north-south street, correct?

A. Yes.

Q. Where is the flower shop in relation to the intersection?

A. It's not right at the corner. It's on First Street, maybe 300 feet south of Adams.

Q. Which side of First Street is the flower shop on?

A. It's on the east side.

Q. Tell me how you went from the flower shop north on First Street.

A. My car was parked in the lot next to the flower shop. When I got out of work, I pulled out of the lot and started going north on First Street.

Q. Describe what First Street looks like.

A. It's a pretty wide street. It has three lanes of traffic in each direction. In addition, it has left-turn lanes at the major intersections.

Q. There are traffic lights at the corner of First Street and Adams, right?

A. Yes.

Q. Where are they located?

A. I think there's one at each corner and on the median strips.

Q. How many lights face the northbound traffic on First Street?

A. Probably around three.

Q. When you pulled onto First Street, which lane did you pull into?

A. I got into the inside lane, right next to the median strip.

Q. Mr. Jones, when was the first time you looked at the traffic lights at the corner of First Street and Adams?

A. When I first pulled onto First Street and got in the inside lane.

This is a useful answer since he was only about three seconds from the intersection before he looked at the lights.

Q. How far were you from the intersection at that time?

A. I guess around 100 feet.

Q. How fast were you going at that time?

A. Maybe 20 or 25 miles per hour.

Q. What was the color of the traffic lights at that point?

A. Green.

Q. What happened as you went northbound on First Street?

A. Well, it all happened really quickly. As I went north, the light turned yellow just before I got into the intersection. I was going through the intersection on the yellow light when suddenly I got smashed by another car from the driver's side.

This answer is also useful since it suggests that the plaintiff was not paying much attention as he entered the intersection.

Q. How long had the light been yellow at the time the other car collided with you?

A. It couldn't have been more than two or three seconds.

Q. How fast were you going when you were hit?

A. Maybe 25 or 30 miles per hour.

Note how the questions become more specific. The questioner's purpose now is to "pin down" the witness to specific facts.

Q. Did you ever see the car that hit you before the impact?

A. Not really. I first saw it just before it was about to smash into me. It couldn't have been more than 10 or 15 feet from me. Before I could even put on my brakes, the car hit me.

Q. Tell us what happened from the moment the two cars hit.

A. Well, I remember putting on my brakes, I kind of skidded in the intersection, and the other car seemed to be stuck against the side of my car. I can remember getting bounced around inside the car and smashing my head and chest against the inside of the car and the steering wheel.

Q. Were you wearing a seat belt at that time?

A. No.

Q. Did your car have seat belts?

A. Yes.

Q. What happened when your car came to a stop?

A. I was pretty much numb. I can remember people coming up to me when I was in the car telling me not to move. I wasn't going to move anyway. I just hurt all over. I don't know how long it was, but after a while an ambulance came and they got me out of the car and put me on a stretcher.

Q. Mr. Jones, just before the impact, describe exactly what you were doing.

A. Well, I remember starting into the intersection. Since the light was yellow, I remember looking to the right to make sure that there weren't any cars taking a turn that might get in my way. I just looked to my right and then looked back up the road, then I saw the other car coming from my left just before it crashed into me.

Q. Did you ever put on your brakes before the impact?

A. No, I don't think so, there wasn't time to react.

Q. Mr. Jones, is there anything you remember about how this accident happened that you haven't told me about this afternoon?

A. No, nothing that comes to mind. I think I've pretty much told you everything.

Q. That's all the questions I have at this time. Do you have any questions, Ms. Johnson?

Ms. Johnson: No.

Mr. Sharp: Will you waive signature?

Ms. Johnson: No, we'd like to see the transcript.

Margin notes:

This is important, since this fact may be admissible to show plaintiff's own negligence or failure to prevent damages.

Some lawyers always ask this kind of question, since it's potential impeachment if the plaintiff "remembers" more at trial.

The party deponent should not waive signature, since he should review the transcript for accuracy.

(The deposition was concluded at 3:06 P.M.)

John Jones
_____
John Jones

Note that the plaintiff's lawyer asked no questions. This is the usual practice, unless the party gave incorrect or confusing answers that need to be corrected or clarified.

Note also that the plaintiff's lawyer made no objections during the deposition. The questions were proper so objections were unnecessary.

State of California | SS.
County of Los Angeles |

The foregoing deposition was taken before me, Nancy Post, a Notary Public in the County of Los Angeles, State of California. The witness was duly sworn by me to testify to the truth. The questions asked of the witness were taken down by me in shorthand and reduced to typewriting under my direction. The deposition was submitted to the witness and read and signed. The foregoing pages are a true and accurate transcript of the entire proceedings taken during this deposition.

The court reporter must arrange a meeting with the deponent so he can review the transcript, note any claimed inaccuracies, and sign the transcript. Any claimed inaccuracies are usually put on a separate sheet and attached to the transcript.

Dated: <u>May 1, 2008</u>

Nancy Post
_____
Notary Public

My commission expires on December 31, 2008.

SUPERIOR COURT OF THE STATE OF CALIFORNIA
FOR THE COUNTY OF LOS ANGELES

John Jones, 　　　　Plaintiff 　　v. Susan Smith, et al. 　　　　Defendants	No. _____ REQUEST FOR ADMISSION OF FACTS AND GENUINENESS OF DOCUMENTS

If this case goes to trial, the plaintiff will need to establish basic facts. These requests cover facts that the defendant will probably not contest, and that will streamline the plaintiff's case during trial.

Plaintiff requests defendant, pursuant to Code of Civil Procedure Section 2033, to admit within 30 days the following facts and genuineness of documents:

1. Defendant was the owner of a 2001 Buick Skylark sedan on September 2, 2007.

2. Defendant was driving the 2001 Buick Skylark sedan when the collision occurred on September 2, 2007.

3. Defendant was a driver licensed by the State of California at the time of the collision.

4. Each of the following documents, attached as exhibits to this request, is authentic:

Exhibit No.	Description
1.	Los Angeles Police Dept. accident report.
2.	Title and registration documents from the California Dept. of Motor Vehicles showing defendant to be the owner of a 2001 Buick Skylark sedan.
3.	Driver's license issued to defendant by the California Dept. of Motor Vehicles.

Dated: June 1, 2008

Anne Johnson
_____
Anne Johnson
Attorney for Plaintiff
100 Congress Street
Los Angeles, CA 90039
882-1000

A proof of service must be attached.

SUPERIOR COURT OF THE STATE OF CALIFORNIA
FOR THE COUNTY OF LOS ANGELES

	No. _____

John Jones,
         Plaintiff
    v.
Susan Smith, et al.
         Defendants
	<u>DEFENDANT'S</u>
	<u>ANSWER</u>
	<u>TO PLAINTIFF'S</u>
	<u>REQUEST FOR</u>
	<u>ADMISSION OF</u>
	<u>FACTS AND</u>
	<u>GENUINENESS OF</u>
	<u>DOCUMENTS</u>

   Defendant answers plaintiff's Requests for Admission of Facts and Genuineness of Documents as follows:

<u>Request No. 1:</u> Defendant was the owner of a 2001 Buick Skylark sedan on September 2, 2007.

<u>Answer:</u> Admits.

<u>Request No. 2:</u> Defendant was driving the 2001 Buick Skylark sedan when the collision occurred on September 2, 2007.

<u>Answer:</u> Admits.

<u>Request No. 3:</u> Defendant was a driver licensed by the State of California at the time of the collision.

<u>Answer:</u> Admits.

<u>Request No. 4:</u> Each of the following documents, attached as exhibits to this request, is authentic:

<u>Exhibit No.</u>	<u>Description</u>
1.	Los Angeles Police Dept. accident report.
2.	Title and registration documents from the California Dept. of Motor Vehicles showing defendant to be the owner of a 2001 Buick Skylark sedan.

Like interrogatories, the usual practice in answering is to set out both the request and the answer. This avoids confusion.

3.   Driver's license issued to defendant by the California
        Dept. of Motor Vehicles.
        <u>Answer:</u> Admits.

Dated: <u>June 20, 2008</u>

William Sharp
_____
William Sharp
Attorney for Defendant
100 Broadway
Los Angeles, CA 90054
881-1000

A proof of service must be attached.

SUPERIOR COURT OF THE STATE OF CALIFORNIA
FOR THE COUNTY OF LOS ANGELES

John Jones,
        Plaintiff | No. _____

    v.

Susan Smith, et al.
        Defendants | OFFER OF
                            JUDGMENT

    Pursuant to Code of Civil Procedure Section 998, defendant offers to allow judgment to be taken against her in the amount of SEVENTEEN THOUSAND FIVE HUNDRED and 00/100 DOLLARS ($17,500.00), and costs of suit incurred to the date of this offer.

    This offer is being made under Section 992 of the Code of Civil Procedure. If this offer is not accepted within 30 days, the offer will be deemed withdrawn.

By this time defendant has sufficient facts to assess the case's settlement value. The offer of judgment will put additional pressure on the plaintiff to consider a realistic settlement.

Dated: <u>August 1, 2008</u>

William Sharp
_____

William Sharp
Attorney for Defendant
100 Broadway
Los Angeles, CA 90054
881-1000

A proof of service must be attached.

SUPERIOR COURT OF THE STATE OF CALIFORNIA
FOR THE COUNTY OF LOS ANGELES

No. _____

John Jones,
        Plaintiff
    v.
Susan Smith, et al.
        Defendants

NOTICE OF
MOTION AND
MOTION FOR
ORDER TO
COMPEL
PLAINTIFF'S
PHYSICAL
EXAMINATION

Since plaintiff has not accepted the offer of judgment, defendant must continue her trial preparations. Getting a current evaluation of the plaintiff's medical condition and prognosis from a physician who has not previously seen the plaintiff is vital.

Keep in mind that local rules may have other requirements that must be followed.

PLEASE TAKE NOTICE THAT on October 5, 2008, at 9:00 A.M. in courtroom number 4 of the above-entitled court, Defendant will move under Code of Civil Procedure Section 2032 for an order compelling plaintiff to submit to a physical examination. In support of her motion defendant states:

1. Plaintiff's physical condition is genuinely in controversy since the complaint alleges a variety of physical injuries.

2. Plaintiff during his deposition stated that he still suffers from the consequences of the accident that is the basis for his complaint. These include periodic pain in his back and ankle.

3. There exists good cause, in light of the above, for a physical examination of the plaintiff to evaluate the plaintiff's current physical condition and prognosis.

4. Rudolf B. Anton, M.D., a board-certified neurologist, has agreed to examine and evaluate the plaintiff at his medical office located at 4401 N. Ventura Blvd., Suite 301, Burbank, California, on October 15, 2008, at 5:00 P.M., or at another time, as directed by this court. This motion is based upon this Notice of Motion and Motion, the accompanying Memorandum of points and authorities, the Declaration of William Sharp, and such other oral and other documentary evidence as may be presented at the hearing on the motion.

Dated: <u>September 1, 2008</u>

William Sharp
_____
William Sharp
Attorney for Defendant
100 Broadway
Los Angeles, CA 90054
881-1000

A proof of service must be attached.

SUPERIOR COURT OF THE STATE OF CALIFORNIA
FOR THE COUNTY OF LOS ANGELES

| John Jones,
    Plaintiff
        v.
Susan Smith, et al.
    Defendants | No. _____

JOINT PRETRIAL
MEMORANDUM |

Not all courts require a joint pretrial memorandum. If they do, judges frequently have instructions on what the memorandum should contain and how it should be organized. This is a sample of one type of joint pretrial memorandum.

Pursuant to Local Rule, plaintiff and defendant submit the following joint pretrial memorandum:

I

Uncontested Facts

These facts have all been admitted in the pleadings or during discovery.

Plaintiff Jones and Defendant Smith were involved in a vehicle collision on September 2, 2007. The collision occurred at the intersection of First Street and Adams Blvd. in Los Angeles, California, at approximately 2:00 P.M. At the time of the collision Jones was driving his car, a 2003 Toyota Corolla four-door sedan, north-bound on First Street; Smith was driving her car, a 2001 Buick Skylark sedan, eastbound on Adams Blvd. The intersection is controlled by traffic lights.

On September 2, 2007, Jones was employed as a delivery driver by Devo Wholesale Florist and was being paid gross wages of $1700 per month.

II

Contested Issues of Fact and Law

1. Did Smith run a red light?
2. Did Jones run a red light?
3. Was Smith negligent?
4. Was Jones negligent?

III

Exhibits

A. Plaintiff Jones' Exhibits   Objections, if any
   1. Doctors Hospital records
   2. Dr. Lang's office records
   3. Dr. Hoffman's office records
   4. Dr. Franks' office records
   5. All bills for above
   6. X-rays taken by above
   7. Devo Wholesale Florist employment records
   8. Los Angeles Police Dept. reports — Objection, for reasons stated in attached memorandum.

   If any evidence is objected to, the judge may rule on the objections, if possible to do so, during the pretrial conference.

   If objections are made, the objecting party should state the basis for the objection, with supporting citations.

   9. Accident scene photographs
   10. Jack's Auto Repair records and bill
   11. Watch repair bill
   12. Glendale Community College bills
   13. Walgreen Pharmacy bill
   14. Accident scene diagrams

   Defendant Smith's
B. Exhibits   Objections, if any
   1. Plaintiff's hospital and medical records
   2. Rudolf Anton, M.D., medical records
   3. Accident scene photographs
   4. Accident scene diagrams
   5. Los Angeles Police Dept. reports to extent admissible

IV

Witnesses

A. Plaintiff Jones' Witnesses
   1. Plaintiff
   2. Carol Brown, 42 E. Cambridge, Tarzana, CA
   3. Mary Porter, 42 E. Cambridge, Tarzana, CA
   4. Dr. Lang
   5. Dr. Hoffman
   6. Dr. Franks
   7. James Devo, Devo Wholesale Florist
   8. John Jones, Sr., and Mary Jones, plaintiff's parents
   9. Officer Steven Pitcher, Los Angeles Police Dept.
   10. Defendant
   11. Personnel from Jack's Auto Repair, to qualify exhibits
   12. Personnel from above hospitals and physicians, to qualify exhibits

B. Defendant Smith's Witnesses
   1. All of plaintiff's witnesses
   2. Dr. Rudolf Anton

V

Jury Instructions

Plaintiff's and defendant's proposed jury instructions are attached.

1. Plaintiff objects to defendant instruction nos. 6, 7, and 9, for the reasons stated in plaintiff's attached memorandum.

2. Defendant objects to plaintiff instruction nos. 2, 3, 4, and 6, for the reasons stated in defendant's attached memorandum.

RESPECTFULLY SUBMITTED,

Date: <u>November 1, 2008</u>

Anne Johnson
_____
Anne Johnson
Attorney for Plaintiff

William Sharp
_____
William Sharp
Attorney for Defendant

Pretrial memoranda frequently also contain a memorandum of law from each party that discusses any legal issues that the judge will need to resolve before or during trial.

The judge's final pretrial order will usually track the language and organization of the memorandum and contain all rulings on admissibility issues that were made at the conference.

RELEASE

A release would be the standard way of settling this case, since it is a complete settlement by all the parties.

The parties would usually execute a separate settlement agreement detailing the terms of the settlement.

In consideration of the sum of thirty thousand dollars ($30,000), which plaintiff acknowledges receiving, Plaintiff John Jones agrees to release Defendant Susan Smith and her heirs, survivors, agents, and personal representatives from all claims, suits, or actions in any form or on any basis, because of anything that was done or not done at any time, on account of the following:

All claims for personal injuries, property damage, physical disabilities, medical expenses, lost income, loss of consortium, and all other claims that have been or could be brought, including all claims now known or that in the future might be known, which arise out of an occurrence on or about September 2, 2007, at First Street and Adams Blvd., in Los Angeles, California, when plaintiff claims to have sustained injuries as a result of a collision between an automobile driven by plaintiff and an automobile driven by defendant.

As a result of this collision plaintiff has brought suit against defendant for damages. Defendant has denied both liability and the claimed extent of damages. This release is a compromise settlement between Plaintiff John Jones and Defendant Susan Smith.

The parties expressly waive any and all rights under Section 1542 of the California Civil Code.

This agreement is a release and shall operate as a total discharge of any claims plaintiff has or may have, arising out of the above occurrence, against this defendant and any other persons.

Plaintiff John Jones and Defendant Susan Smith also agree to terminate any actions that have been filed, particularly a claim by this plaintiff against this defendant currently filed as civil action No. 470912 in the Superior Court of California, for the County of Los Angeles. Plaintiff and defendant agree to execute a Stipulation of Dismissal, with prejudice, and file it with the Clerk of the above Court, thereby terminating that action in its entirety, within five days of the execution of this agreement.

Date: <u>December 1, 2008</u>

<u>*John Jones*</u>   The parties must sign the release.
John Jones, Plaintiff

<u>*Susan Smith*</u>
Susan Smith, Defendant

SUPERIOR COURT OF THE STATE OF CALIFORNIA
FOR THE COUNTY OF LOS ANGELES

John Jones, 　　　　　Plaintiff 　　v. Susan Smith, et al. 　　　　　Defendants	No. _____ STIPULATION OF DISMISSAL

The stipulation of dismissal terminates the lawsuit. No court order is necessary.

　　Plaintiff John Jones and Defendant Susan Smith agree to dismiss this action with prejudice, and each party will bear its costs.

Dated: December 2, 2008

Anne Johnson
_____
Anne Johnson
Attorney for Plaintiff

William Sharp
_____
William Sharp
Attorney for Defendant

Glossary

Abstract of judgment. A lien on all real property owned by the debtor.

Administrative litigation. The process by which administrative agencies resolve disputes that concern their administrative rules and regulations.

Admission of a party opponent. Any statement made by an adverse party in the lawsuit.

Affidavit. A written statement by a witness made under oath and acknowledged by a notary public.

Affidavit of service. A notice at the end of a pleading stating that service of the pleading has been made upon a particular party and including the notarized signature of the individual signing the notice.

Affirm. The appellate court rules that the decision of the court below should remain the same.

Affirm with modification. The appellate court rules that the decision of the court below should remain the same with the exception that a particular element of the decision be modified.

Affirmative defense. Defense pled by the defendant in the answer that, if proven, denies recovery to the plaintiff.

Amended pleadings. The changing or correcting of a pleading after the pleading already has been filed and served.

American Arbitration Association. A private tribunal that administers arbitration that does not go through the court system.

Answer. A response by the defendant to the plaintiff's complaint, which response admits or denies the various allegations and usually asserts a number of affirmative defenses.

Appellant. The party bringing an appeal in either federal or California state court.

Appellee. The party defending against an appeal in federal court.

Arbitration. The submission by the parties of their dispute to an impartial tribunal for resolution.

Assignee. The person or entity that has received a claim through an assignment.

Assignment. A claim that has been transferred to another person or entity. In such a case, the assignee has a right to sue in the assignee's own name.

Assignor. The person or entity that transfers the claim in an assignment.

Attachment. Pretrial order of the court seizing property of the defendant for later satisfaction of any judgment received by the plaintiff.

Attorney-client privilege. Protection that allows communications between an attorney and client to remain confidential; also extends to communications between a client and a paralegal.

Attorney's lien. A claim by the lawyer on any judgment or recovery obtained by the client to ensure payment of the lawyer's fee.

Authenticated. Establishing through witness testimony a foundation for the evidence presented before the trier of fact.

Authorization forms. Forms signed by the client that permit the lawyer to obtain personal records of the client such as medical records, employment records, and police reports.

Bank levy. A seizure of funds held in a debtor's bank account.

Bates Stamp. A stamp used to automatically number documents.

Bench. Where the judge sits during a hearing or trial.

Best evidence rule. Under the common law, a requirement that an original writing had to be produced if the writing was going to be used as evidence. Duplicates are generally admissible as evidence in both federal and state court.

Breach of contract. A cause of action that requires the plaintiff to allege a contract that was breached by the defendant, causing damages to the plaintiff. Plaintiff must also allege that plaintiff has either performed under the contract or is excused from performing on the contract.

Business records. Records made by employees in the course of their employment and made on behalf of the business in which they are employed; admissible as evidence.

California Rules of Court. Rules adopted by the courts on a statewide basis.

Caption. Identification in a pleading of the parties, court, and case number. This information must be included in every pleading.

Case-in-chief. The evidence supporting the particular party's position.

Case or controversy. A case that is ripe for adjudication. An actual case that is not moot or merely advisory.

Cases. Court decisions interpreting the law.

Cause of action. Theory of recovery that entitles the plaintiff to recover against the defendant.

Certificate of compliance. A written statement by the lawyer certifying that the lawyer has attempted to meet in good faith with the opposing party to resolve their discovery dispute before bringing a motion to compel discovery.

Certificate of service. A notice at the end of a pleading indicating that service of the pleading has been made upon a particular party.

Chain of custody. Establishing location of a piece of physical evidence at all times prior to its possible use at trial.

Character traits. A person's distinctive qualities; admissible as evidence only if character is an essential element of a claim or defense.

Chronological summary. A deposition summary organized sequentially; it starts at the beginning of the deposition and continues through to the end of the deposition.

Citizenship. The place where a natural person or legal entity resides. For a natural person, the citizenship is the person's domicile. For a corporation, the citizenship is the place of incorporation and the corporation's principal place of business.

Civil litigation. Resolution of disputes between private parties through the court system.

Claim for relief. Another name for a cause of action.

Class action. A lawsuit brought by individuals representing a large group of identifiable members.

Closing arguments. The statements made by the lawyers at the close of all the evidence. The statements generally include a summary of the important evidence that was presented during the trial.

Code of Civil Procedure. The procedural rules governing litigation filed in California state court.

Codes. Laws enacted by state or federal legislatures, such as the California Code of Civil Procedure.

Commercial litigation. Civil litigation involving businesses.

Common law. Body of law brought to America by colonists; developed in England from custom and usage and affirmed by the English judges and courts. Term sometimes used to refer to case law.

Compensatory damages. Money damages that compensate the injured party, including damages that flow directly from the injury or breach. Compensatory damages may be general, such as compensation for pain and suffering, or specific, such as payment for medical expenses and lost time from work.

Competent witness. A witness who is qualified to testify because such witness has the ability to communicate either orally or by gestures and is capable of relating facts truthfully.

Complaint. The document filed by the aggrieved party to commence litigation.

Compulsory cross-complaint. A cross-complaint that must be brought against the plaintiff by the defendant or else the defendant will lose the right to assert the claim.

Concurrent. When used in reference to jurisdiction, the term means that a lawsuit may be brought in either federal or state court because each court has jurisdiction over the dispute.

Conflict of interest. Occurs when two or more parties with adverse interests are represented by the same counsel.

Consent order. An order drafted and agreed to by both parties that disposes of a pending motion.

Consolidation. The combining of two trials or hearings into one.

Constitution. The highest law of federal and state governments. In addition to the United States Constitution, each of the fifty states has its own constitution. No state constitution or state or federal law may violate the federal Constitution.

Consulting expert. Expert who has been retained or employed to assist during the litigation process, but who is not expected to be a witness at trial.

Contention interrogatories. Can accompany a request to admit facts, ask the opposing side for the basis of any denial of a request. The answering party may decide to admit the request rather than attempt to justify the denial in the interrogatory answer.

Contingency fee. An agreement between the lawyer and client whereby the lawyer will receive as compensation for the lawyer's fee a certain percentage in the recovery ultimately obtained by the client. If the client receives no recovery, the lawyer will not receive any fee. This type of fee arrangement is common in personal injury actions.

Contingent claim. A claim that may arise, but has not yet arisen.

Contradiction. Method of impeachment that shows that the true facts are different from those stated by the witness.

Contribution. A theory of apportioning payment for a liability. When one party to a joint and several obligation pays more than that party's share of the obligation, the paying party may be entitled to receive a proportionate sum from the other jointly liable parties.

Corporation. A legal entity composed of shareholders who own the entity but whose existence is separate and distinct from the entity. Shareholders generally cannot be held liable for the obligations of the corporation.

Costs. The out-of-pocket expenses incurred by the lawyer during the course of representation of the client and that are reimbursed by the client. These costs are distinguished from the fee charged by the lawyer. Costs include such items as filing fees, court reporter fees, travel expenses, postage, and long-distance telephone charges.

Courts of Appeal. The intermediate appellate courts under the state court system.

Covenant not to sue. A contract between two or more parties in which the plaintiff agrees not to sue or pursue an existing claim against one or more defendants.

Criminal litigation. Litigation commenced by a governmental body against individuals who have committed crimes against society.

Cross-claim. A complaint brought by defendant against the plaintiff, or one codefendant against another codefendant, or one party to the lawsuit against a third party.

Cross-complaint. The title of the pleading filed to assert a cross-claim.

Damages. Monetary compensation requested by the plaintiff from the defendant.

Declarant. The person making either a written or oral statement.

Declaration. A written statement by a witness that is signed by the witness under penalty of perjury.

Declaratory relief. Equitable remedy used by the plaintiff when a controversy arises over the rights and obligations of the parties and neither party is yet in breach of these obligations.

Default judgment. Judgment entered against a defendant who fails to appear and defend against the lawsuit after having been given proper notice of the lawsuit.

Defaults. A failure of a party to respond to the pleading of the opposing party. Usually occurs in the case of a defendant who does not respond to the plaintiff's complaint.

Defendant. The party who defends an action brought by the plaintiff.

Demand for arbitration. The form that a party files to commence arbitration through the American Arbitration Association.

Demonstrative evidence. Exhibits such as photographs, diagrams, models, and maps that represent real things.

Demurrer. A type of motion that asks the court to dismiss the other side's pleading because the pleading is not legally sufficient.

Deponent. Witness who gives testimony at a deposition. The deponent's testimony is given under oath, and the deponent can be cross-examined by the attorney for the opposing side.

Deposition transcript. A written record of everything communicated orally during the course of a deposition.

Depositions. Oral questions asked by one party to another during the discovery stage. The answers are stated under oath before a court reporter who usually is also a notary public.

Directed verdict. Verdict returned by the jury in favor of a party as directed by the trial judge.

Discovery. The formal method by which a party receives information from the other parties in the lawsuit.

Dispositive motions. Motions heard by the court any time before trial that have the effect of deciding and terminating the lawsuit without the necessity of a trial.

Diversity jurisdiction. The power of the federal court to hear controversies between citizens of different states. In order for the federal district courts to have jurisdiction, "complete diversity" must exist: Each plaintiff must have a different state citizenship from each defendant.

Divider method. A way to organize trial materials. Trial materials are organized by putting all papers pertinent to each phase of the trial in a separate folder.

Doe defendants. Fictitious defendant names in a complaint until the true names and capacity can be ascertained.

Domicile. The permanent residence of a natural person. No person can have more than one domicile at one time.

Due process. A constitutional doctrine requiring fairness in judicial proceedings.

Elements. Items that must be proven for each claim, relief, and defense.

Equitable remedy. Relief requested by the plaintiff from the defendant that is usually designed to prevent some future harm. An equitable remedy is distinguished from money damages, which is a legal remedy.

Evidence. Facts presented to the judge or jury.

Ex parte. Without notice to the other side, or very limited notice to the other side.

Exemption. An amount of money that may not be used to satisfy a judgment.

Exhibits. Tangible items of evidence presented at trial.

Expert witness. A witness who has been qualified in a particular area and is used to assist the trier of fact with understanding or determining a fact in issue.

Extrinsic evidence. Evidence outside of the evidence that is being presented at a particular time. Thus, if a witness gives evidence, other evidence (i.e., the extrinsic evidence) may be used to impeach the evidence given by the witness.

Fact pleading. Requirement in California that all pleadings state sufficient facts to apprise the opposing party of the nature of the claim or defense.

Federal question jurisdiction. An issue brought before the federal court arising under the Constitution, laws, or treaties of the United States.

Federal Rules of Civil Procedure. The procedural rules governing litigation filed in federal court.

Fixed flat fee. An agreement between the lawyer and client whereby the lawyer receives a predetermined sum as the amount of the fee regardless of how much work is expended on the client's behalf.

For cause. When a juror is stricken from the jury panel for a particular reason. For example, the juror may be biased or prejudiced toward one party, may have an interest in the litigation, or may know any of the parties, or attorneys to the litigation.

Former testimony. Testimony given under oath in another action or at a former hearing or trial in the same action.

Forum state. The state where a lawsuit is being brought.

Foundation. Establishment of a basis for admission of evidence.

Good cause. What a party must have before a party can obtain a protective order. Good cause for a protective order includes reasons such as discovery is unduly oppressive and expensive. Good cause also refers to what a party must have to compel discovery responses by another party. Good cause for compelling discovery includes reasons such as the information is not available from any other source, the information sought is necessary, and the information is relevant to a particular issue in the litigation.

Guardian ad litem. A person appointed by the court to represent another, usually a minor or incompetent, in a lawsuit. The guardian ad litem can sue or be sued on behalf of the person represented.

Habit. The routine conduct of a person; may be admissible as evidence at trial.

Hague Service Convention. An international treaty that governs service of process in countries that are parties to the treaty.

Hearsay. An out-of-court statement used to prove the truth of the matter asserted in the statement.

Hourly rate. When the lawyer charges the client at a specific rate per hour multiplied by the number of hours spent on the client's behalf.

Impeachment. The discrediting of a witness' testimony so that statements made by the witness will not be believed by the trier of fact.

Impleader. The method for bringing into an action new parties who may be liable to a defendant for some or all of the judgment that the plaintiff may obtain against the defendant. Also sometimes referred to as a third-party complaint.

In personam jurisdiction. A court's power to personally bind the parties to the court's judgment.

In rem jurisdiction. The court's power to adjudicate rights in property located within the state in which the court sits.

Indemnification. A claim allowing one party who has paid for a liability to recover completely from another party.

Informally consulted expert. Expert who has not been retained to assist with the litigation, but has provided information during the litigation process.

Injunction. Equitable remedy used by the plaintiff to stop certain conduct or actions of the defendant.

Interpleader. Procedure under which a party may deposit into court a fund or property when the party is or may be subjected to double liability because two or more claimants are making a claim on a fund or property. The claimants are then forced to litigate their claim in order to determine who is entitled to the fund or property.

Interrogatories. Written questions submitted by one party to another during the discovery stage.

Intervention. The ability of a person, not a party to the lawsuit, to become a party to the lawsuit when such person has an interest in the outcome of the lawsuit.

Involuntary dismissal. Method of terminating a claim when the plaintiff or other claimant has been guilty of misconduct or inaction.

Irreparable injury. Injury to the party that cannot be repaired and that can be avoided by the granting of injunctive relief.

Joinder of claims. The bringing together in one lawsuit of the different claims that a party may have against another party.

Joinder of parties. The bringing together of different parties in one lawsuit.

Joint tortfeasors. Two or more persons who are liable to plaintiff for the same injury.

Judgment. The decision in the lawsuit.

Judgment debtor. The party who has lost a judgment and owes money to the other party. The other party is called the judgment creditor.

Judgment on the pleadings. A judgment entered after the pleadings have been filed, but before trial, when the undisputed facts as pled show that the movant is entitled to judgment. Similar to a demurrer.

Judicial arbitration. Refers to arbitration handled through the court system. Unless otherwise agreed to by the parties, such arbitration is nonbinding.

Judicial Council. The entity in California that has developed forms for use in litigation. Forms that have been approved by the Judicial Council are optional and may be used by parties. Forms that are adopted by the Judicial Council are mandatory.

Judicial notice. Evidentiary procedure in which the trial judge is asked to rule that certain facts are true.

Juror. A person who sits as part of the jury panel during trial and decides questions of fact.

Jury. A panel of individuals who decide questions of fact during a trial.

Jury chart. A diagram to be used during voir dire examination of the jury. Information obtained from each prospective juror is recorded on the chart.

Jury demand. A notice by a party that the party requests a trial by jury as opposed to a trial heard only by the judge.

Jury instructions. Instructions that itemize the elements for various claims, reliefs, and defenses.

Keeper. A law enforcement agent who stays on the premises of a business and collects cash or checks sufficient to satisfy a judgment. If insufficient funds exist, the keeper may also take possession of personal property and sell the property in order to satisfy the judgment.

Lawyer's fee. The amount charged by the lawyer for professional services rendered to the client. Also referred to as attorney's fee. A fee for professional services is distinguished from out-of-pocket costs incurred, which are generally not considered part of the fee.

Lay witness. Witness who has not been qualified as an expert in a particular area. Often referred to as a percipient witness, a lay witness is one who will testify to the facts as he or she has observed them.

Leave of court. Permission from the court to file a pleading.

Legal remedy. Generally a request by the plaintiff for money damages from the defendant.

LEXIS. A computer service that provides access to legal research materials.

Levy. The procedure by which assets of the debtor are seized for satisfaction of a judgment.

Lien. A claim by the creditor against property of the debtor as security for the debt.

Limited jurisdiction. A reference to courts that cannot hear all controversies, but rather only those controversies that fall under their specific powers. A municipal court is a court of limited jurisdiction because it can only hear matters that are $25,000 or less.

Lis pendens. A notice that is recorded against particular real property alerting potential purchasers of the property that there is a pending dispute that affects title to or possession of the property.

Litigation. Resolution of disputes through the court system.

Local rules of court. Rules of procedure that are adopted by each individual court and apply to all litigation commenced in that particular court.

Long-arm statute. The ability of a court to exercise jurisdiction over a defendant who is outside the geographical boundaries of the court.

Mediation. A formal conference between the parties and a neutral person with the intent to arrive at a settlement of the parties' dispute.

Memorandum of points and authorities. Legal document submitted with a motion setting forth background facts and legal authorities to support a position.

Minimum contacts. Sufficient contact by a defendant with the state attempting to exercise jurisdiction over the defendant.

Minute order. Form on which the clerk makes an entry reflecting the ruling by the judge.

Moot issue. When an issue no longer exists between the parties in a pending lawsuit. Courts will not decide moot issues.

Motion. Either a written or oral request made by a party to the court for some order or ruling by the court.

Motion calendar. The cases scheduled for hearing in court on any particular day.

Motion for judgment n.o.v. A motion to have judgment entered in a party's favor notwithstanding the jury's verdict against the party.

Motion for new trial after a judgment n.o.v. A motion by a party for a new trial after that party's verdict has been set aside because the judge has granted a motion for judgment n.o.v.

Motion to amend findings and judgment. A motion made after trial and entry of judgment to have the court amend the findings and to amend the judgment in conformity with the amended findings.

Motion to dismiss. A motion by the defendant, or on the court's own motion, that the complaint filed by the plaintiff be dismissed because of some specified defect such as a failure to proceed with the case in a timely fashion.

Motion to set aside judgment. Motion by a party to set aside the judgment entered by the court. The motion may be based on a number of grounds such as mistake, fraud, or newly discovered evidence.

Motion to strike. A motion to eliminate certain allegations from a complaint.

Movant. The party making a motion. Sometimes referred to as the moving party.

Narrative summary. A type of deposition summary that is in memorandum form with no reference to particular page and line numbers.

Negligence. Type of cause of action. To state a claim for negligence, the plaintiff must allege a duty of care by one party to another that was breached and that was the cause of plaintiff's damages.

Notice and claims provisions. Contract provisions usually requiring notice of intent to sue or presentation of claims before filing suit, and requiring that notice be given within a short period of time, usually much shorter than the applicable statute of limitations period.

Notice of appeal. Documents filed by the losing party in a trial court decision, which must contain the name of the party or parties taking the appeal and the name of the court to which the appeal is taken; it must also state the judgment, or part of the judgment, that the party is appealing from.

Notice pleading. A short and plain statement in the complaint of the claim that the plaintiff seeks to enforce and the relief that the plaintiff is requesting.

Objection. Statement made by the responding party in an interrogatory that indicates a reason for not answering the question asked.

Offer of judgment. An offer by a party defending a claim to have judgment entered in a specific amount. If the plaintiff refuses the offer and a judgment after trial is entered in favor of the plaintiff that is less favorable than the offer, the plaintiff becomes liable to the defendant for the defendant's costs that were incurred since the time of the offer.

On-call witnesses. Witnesses who are going to be called to testify at trial but who do not attend the trial until they are advised of the particular date and time they are needed.

Opening arguments. Statements made by the lawyers at the beginning of trial that explain their respective clients' versions of the facts and what they expect the evidence to prove.

Opponent. The party opposing a motion. Sometimes referred to as the responding party.

Oral argument. Opportunity for lawyers to answer any questions an appellate court may have and to more fully explain their respective clients' positions. Oral argument takes place after the submission by the parties of written briefs.

Original jurisdiction. The first court that has authority to decide the legal dispute.

Partnership. Legal entity created by two or more individuals who carry on a business and divide any profit or loss of the business.

Party statement. A written statement made by a party to the litigation.

Pattern interrogatories. Have been approved for some cases such as automobile personal injury suits. Usually taking the form of pre-printed questions, pattern interrogatories seek information commonly requested in all cases relating to a specific area of the law. For example, recurring interrogatory questions in a personal injury suit include identification of past injuries, the treating physicians, and the amount of damages sustained.

Pecuniary. Refers to monetary or economic affairs.

Penal. Refers to legal punishment.

Pendent jurisdiction. Jurisdiction by the federal court over nonfederal claims when both the federal and nonfederal claims derive from a common set of facts.

Percipient witness. A witness who testifies to facts as he or she has observed or perceived them. Same as lay witness.

Peremptory challenge. A method used to strike a juror from the jury panel; the term refers to an absolute right of the lawyer to strike a juror even if no cause for challenging that juror exists. However, the lawyer will be allowed only a limited number of peremptory challenges.

Permanent injunction. An injunction granted only after trial and that will exist for all time until the injunction is dissolved by court order.

Permissive counterclaim. A counterclaim that may be brought by the defendant against the plaintiff but that does not have to be brought in the same action.

Permissive joinder. A joinder of parties that is allowed—but not required—by the court.

Personal jurisdiction. The power of a court to bring a party before it and to make a decision binding on such a person.

Petition for writ of certiorari. Is directed to the Supreme Court and requests that it grant an appeal of a decision made by a court of appeals.

Physical and mental examinations. Medical examination of a party usually done by a doctor selected by the opposing party. May be done only if a court order is obtained or if the party agrees to submit voluntarily to the examination. The party's physical or mental condition must be in issue.

Physical evidence. Tangible personal property such as vehicles, machinery, and consumer products that may be used as trial exhibits.

Plaintiff. The party who brings an action.

Pleadings. Formal written documents by the parties to the litigation to either start or respond to the litigation. For example, the initial pleading is usually the complaint.

Prayer for relief. A section at the end of a complaint specifying the relief requested by the plaintiff.

Prejudicial errors. Errors that occur in the trial that, if such errors had not occurred, might have changed the outcome of the trial.

Preliminary injunction. An injunction granted after a hearing. The preliminary injunction maintains the status quo until trial.

Pretrial conference. A meeting between the parties before the court after litigation has commenced, but before trial begins. At the meeting the parties will attempt to agree on all undisputed facts and narrow the issues for trial.

Pretrial memorandum. A written statement provided to the court in advance of trial generally setting forth the uncontested facts, contested issues of fact and law, exhibits, witnesses, and jury instructions.

Pretrial motions. Motions made after litigation has commenced but before the trial begins.

Pretrial order. Order that identifies the issues, witnesses, exhibits, and order of proof for trial, and acts as a guide for the trial. The order is prepared after the pretrial conference.

Prima facie case. Case in which each element in the plaintiff's claim can be proven.

Principal place of business. The state where a corporation conducts a majority of its business, or, if this is not certain, the state where corporate headquarters is located.

Prior statements. Statements made under oath by a witness at a previous hearing or deposition.

Privileges. Rules providing that certain communications are inadmissible because the communications are deemed to be confidential.

Probative. Having a tendency to prove or disprove a fact in issue.

Proof of service. A notice that usually appears at the end of a pleading or motion stating that the pleading or motion was served on the other parties to the lawsuit, the date service was made, and the manner of service.

Propounding. The act of sending discovery requests to another party.

Proprietary. Refers to ownership of property.

Prosecute. To vigorously pursue a claim.

Protective order. An order from the court restricting or limiting discovery by one party to another.

Prove up. Demonstration by a plaintiff at a motion for default hearing that service on the defaulting party was proper and that the allegations of the complaint are true. Plaintiff also must be prepared to show what the proper damages are.

Provisional remedies. Include temporary restraining orders, preliminary injunctions, writs of attachment and possession, and lis pendens. Under proper circumstances these remedies allow a plaintiff to essentially obtain the relief requested from the defendant before going to trial.

Public bodies. Governmental agencies operated for the benefit of the general public.

Public records. Business records generated by governmental entities; admissible as evidence at trial.

Punitive damages. Damages given to the plaintiff when the defendant's conduct is willful or malicious. Such damages are meant to punish the wrongdoers for their conduct and may be awarded in addition to compensatory damages. Punitive damages are sometimes called exemplary damages.

Qualified privilege. Privilege that is not absolute. The privilege will not exist if the other party can show a substantial need for the information.

Quash. To vacate by court order.

Quasi in rem jurisdiction. Reference to actions in which the court does not have in personam jurisdiction over the defendant, but the court does have jurisdiction over particular property of the defendant that allows the court to subject that property to claims asserted by the plaintiff.

Questions of law. Issues that raise a legal question and not a fact question.

Real evidence. Information that is what it purports to be; can also refer to physical objects.

Real party in interest. The party who, under applicable substantive law, has the right that the lawsuit seeks to enforce.

Rebuttal evidence. Evidence refuting the evidence presented by the defendant as part of the defendant's case-in-chief.

Record on appeal. Includes the transcript, original documents, exhibits, and a copy of the docket sheet listing all documents filed in the trial court.

Recorded recollections. A record made of events at about the time the events occurred.

Recording. An action that places notice of some action, lien, or judgment on the title of real property. Thus, any potential buyers of real property are put on constructive notice that an action, lien, or judgment exists.

Recoupment. A right by the defendant to have any damages awarded to the plaintiff reduced because of some entitlement by the defendant to damages from the plaintiff.

Redact. To cover up a portion of a document that should not be produced to the opposing side.

Relation back. A doctrine that permits a pleading to be deemed to have been filed at an earlier time. For example, an amended complaint will be deemed to have been filed at the time of the initial complaint for purposes of determining if the statute of limitations has run.

Release. A discharge of all claims against the parties as well as against any persons against whom the same claims are or could have been asserted.

Relevant evidence. Evidence that proves or disproves something in issue in a lawsuit.

Reliable evidence. Evidence that is based on firsthand knowledge or otherwise trustworthy information.

Remedies. The relief sought by the plaintiff from the defendant.

Removal. The procedure in which a defendant may transfer a case already filed in a state court to the federal district court for the same district in which the state action is pending.

Representative. Any individual representing a party such as a lawyer or other agents.

Requests for admission. Written statements by one party to another requesting admission of certain facts or the genuineness of particular documents.

Requests to produce. Written requests by one party to another seeking formal permission to obtain copies of records, documents, and other tangible things for inspection, copying, and testing.

Res. A Latin word referring to either real or personal property, usually in the context of in rem actions.

Res judicata. A doctrine that provides that any judgment is binding on the parties forever. Literally means "a thing decided."

Respondent. Name of party responding to an appeal in state court.

Retainer fee. The amount the client pays to the lawyer at the commencement of the representation. This fee is credited against the fees and costs incurred by the client.

Reverse. The appellate court rules that the decision of the court below should be changed.

Reverse and remand. The appellate court rules that the decision of the court below should be changed and that the case should be sent back to the court below for further proceedings.

Sanctions. A penalty a court may impose for certain violations of court rules and orders. The penalty often includes reasonable expenses such as attorney's fees.

Senior lienholder. Someone who has a claim that is before another's claim. The senior lienholder has priority, and the senior lienholder's claim must be satisfied before any other claims are paid.

Separate trials. Where parts of the same case are tried separately. For example, the court may order separate trials on the complaint and counterclaim.

Service of process. The delivery of a legal document to the opposing party. Usually refers to the actual delivery of the initial pleading to the defendant.

Settlement. A resolution by the parties of their dispute without the necessity of a trial.

Settlement brochure. A brochure that sets out the background of the plaintiff and plaintiff's family along with the evidence showing liability and damages.

Shareholders. The owners of a corporation. The percentage of ownership is determined by the number of shares the owner holds in the corporation.

Sole proprietorship. Business owned by one person and usually operated under a fictitious business name.

Sovereign immunity. The insulation of the government from being sued when functioning in an official government capacity, unless the government consents to being sued.

Special appearance. An appearance by the defendant for the sole purpose of contesting personal jurisdiction.

Stakeholder. The party who holds funds or property for another and has no interest in the funds or property.

Standard of review. Determines how an appellate court should look at the issues in deciding an appeal. For example, was there substantial evidence to support the judgment of the trial court? The appropriate standard of review should be addressed within the argument in an appellate brief.

Standing. The right of a person to challenge in court the conduct of another.

Status quo. The conditions that presently exist.

Statute of limitations. Statute that limits the time period in which an action may be brought.

Statutes. Laws enacted by state or federal legislatures; sometimes referred to as "codes."

Strike system. A method for jury selection. Each prospective juror will be questioned and then the lawyers will exercise their challenges to the jurors by striking certain jurors from the panel.

Structured settlement. A settlement under which the plaintiff receives periodic payments rather than one lump sum.

Subject matter jurisdiction. The power of the court to hear particular matters.

Subject matter summary. A deposition summary that categorizes each topic by subject matter regardless of where the subject appears in the deposition transcript.

Subpoena. Court order compelling a nonparty to appear or produce documents or other tangible items.

Subpoena ad testificandum. An order of the court requiring a witness to appear and give testimony. Same as subpoena.

Subpoena duces tecum. An order of the court requiring a witness to appear and produce documents.

Subrogation. When one party becomes obligated to pay for the loss sustained by another, that party may be substituted as a proper party to collect against the wrongdoer for such loss.

Substitution of parties. When a different party replaces one of the original parties, such as in the case of the death of a party.

Summary adjudication of issues. Judgment granted as to fewer than all causes of action within a complaint.

Summary judgment. A judgment rendered by the court before a trial. A summary judgment is a motion brought by one party to the litigation against another in order to obtain a judgment without the necessity of a trial. Summary judgment may be granted only if there are no triable issues of fact. The court's judgment must be based solely on issues of law.

Summons. Notice accompanying the complaint that commands that the defendant appear and defend against the action within a certain period of time or else judgment may be entered against the defendant.

Superior Court. The trial court in Court with general jurisdiction, meaning that it can hear all types of cases and all cases involving money in excess of $25,000.

Supplemental pleading. A change or correction in a pleading that already has been filed when transactions, occurrences, and events have occurred since the time of the filing of the original pleading.

Surrebuttal. Evidence presented by the defendant that explains or denies the rebuttal evidence.

Temporary restraining order. An order from the court temporarily prohibiting a party from doing some act until such time as a hearing for an injunction can be heard. A temporary restraining order usually stays in effect for no longer than 10 to 15 days.

Tentative ruling. A ruling by the judge based on the written briefs submitted by the parties and before oral argument is heard. The ruling is subject to change after oral argument.

Testifying expert. An expert who will be called as a witness at trial.

Testimony. Evidence given by a witness under oath.

Theory of the case. The lawyer's position on, and approach to, all the undisputed and disputed evidence that will be presented at trial. Another name for your side's version of the facts.

Third party. Someone who is not a party to the lawsuit but who is in possession of evidence necessary for the lawsuit.

Till tap. Collection of cash and checks on hand at a business in order to satisfy a judgment.

Tolls. Refers to the stopping of the time limitations.

Topic index. A type of deposition summary that is an outline of the general topic areas.

Tort. A civil wrong or injury not based upon contract.

Trial court. The court where the complaint is filed and litigation commences.

Trial notebook. Method for organizing trial materials. All necessary materials for each part of the trial are placed in a three-ring notebook in appropriately tabbed sections.

Trial preparation materials. Documents and other tangible things prepared by a party or the party's representative in anticipation of litigation.

Trier of fact. Either the judge or jury who decides questions of fact during a trial.

UCC. An abbreviation for the Uniform Commercial Code, which is a code that regulates commercial transactions. It has been adopted in at least some form by most states.

Uncontested. Refers to when a party fails to oppose a motion filed by another party.

Under submission. Refers to the judge delaying decision on a motion until the judge has an opportunity to further research or consider the issues presented by the parties during the course of oral argument.

Unincorporated associations. Social organizations, churches, homeowner groups, etc., that operate under a common name for the common benefit of all members.

United States Code. Laws enacted by Congress.

United States District Court. The name of the trial court under the federal court system.

Value. In a litigation case the term refers to the monetary worth of the case should the plaintiff prevail.

Venue. The geographic area where a lawsuit may properly be heard.

Verdict. A decision of the judge or jury on a question of fact.

Verified. Refers to a pleading signed by a party declaring that all the statements in the pleadings are true and correct to the best of the party's information and belief.

Voir dire. Occurs when the judge and, in some courts, the lawyers ask specific questions of the prospective jurors to ascertain any bias, prejudice, or other information that would affect the decision of the prospective juror in the case.

Voluntary dismissal. A withdrawal of a claim by the party originally asserting the claim.

Wage garnishment. A direction to an employer of a debtor to withhold a certain amount of money from each paycheck of the debtor for a limited period of time.

WESTLAW. A computer service that provides access to legal research materials.

With prejudice. Once dismissed, the claim may not be refiled.

Without prejudice. Once dismissed, the claim may be filed again.

Witness statements. A written statement made by a nonparty witness.

Work product. Work performed by an attorney during the course of representing a client in anticipation or preparation of litigation, such as notes, internal memoranda, and reports of consulting experts. Also includes work performed by a paralegal. Generally not subject to discovery.

Writ of execution. An order from the court empowering the sheriff, marshal, or other appropriate law enforcement agent to levy upon the assets of the judgment debtor.

Writ of possession. Is issued in a case where the defendant has given a plaintiff a security interest in some tangible personal property for repayment of a debt. If a debt is in default, the plaintiff may then sue for repayment of the debt and delivery of the personal property to the plaintiff.

Index